The Future of Multi-Pillar Pensions

Pension systems are under serious pressure worldwide. This pressure stems not only from the well-known trend of population aging, but also from those of increasing heterogeneity of the population and increasing labor mobility. The current economic crisis has aggravated these problems, thereby exposing the vulnerability of many pension schemes to macroeconomic shocks. This book reconsiders the multi-pillar pension scheme against the background of these pressures. It adopts an integral perspective and asks how the pension system as a whole contributes to the three basic functions of pension schemes: facilitating life-cycle financial planning, insuring idiosyncratic risks and sharing macroeconomic risks across generations. It focuses on the optimal balance between the various pension pillars and on the optimal design of each of the schemes. It sketches a number of economic trade-offs, showing that countries may opt for different pension schemes depending on how they react to these trade-offs.

LANS BOVENBERG is Professor of Economics at Tilburg University. He founded the research network Netspar (Network for Studies on Pensions, Aging and Retirement).

CASPER VAN EWIJK is Professor of Economics at the University of Amsterdam and Deputy Director of CPB Netherlands Bureau for Economic Policy Analysis.

ED WESTERHOUT is project leader of the Netspar theme "Multi-pillar Pension Schemes and Macroeconomic Performance" at CPB Netherlands Bureau for Economic Policy Analysis.

The Future of
Multi-Pillar Pensions

Edited by

LANS BOVENBERG, CASPER VAN EWIJK AND
ED WESTERHOUT

CAMBRIDGE
UNIVERSITY PRESS

University Printing House, Cambridge CB2 8BS, United Kingdom

Published in the United States of America by Cambridge University Press, New York

Cambridge University Press is part of the University of Cambridge.

It furthers the University's mission by disseminating knowledge in the pursuit of education, learning and research at the highest international levels of excellence.

www.cambridge.org
Information on this title: www.cambridge.org/9781107022263

© Lans Bovenberg, Casper van Ewijk and Ed Westerhout 2012

First published 2012

A catalogue record for this publication is available from the British Library

Library of Congress Cataloguing in Publication data
    The future of multi-pillar pensions / [edited by] Lans Bovenberg, Casper
    van Ewijk, Ed Westerhout.
        pages cm
    Includes bibliographical references and index.
    ISBN 978-1-107-02226-3
    1. Pensions–Finance.   2. Pension trusts–Investments.   3. Pension
    trusts–Netherlands–Case studies.   4. Global Financial Crisis, 2008–2009.
    I. Bovenberg, Ary Lans, editor of compilation.   II. Ewijk, Casper van,
    editor of compilation.   III. Westerhout, E. W. M. T., editor of compilation.
    HD7091.F88 2012
    331.25′2–dc23
    2012011692

ISBN 978-1-107-02226-3 Hardback

Contents

Figures

Tables

Boxes

Contributors

Nicholas Barr	London School of Economics and Political Science
Roel Beetsma	University of Amsterdam
Leon Bettendorf	CPB Netherlands Bureau for Economic Policy Analysis
Zvi Bodie	Boston University
Henning Bohn	University of California, Santa Barbara
Lans Bovenberg	Tilburg University
Jeffrey Brown	University of Illinois, Urbana-Champaign
Alessandro Bucciol	University of Verona
Richard Hinz	The World Bank
Thijs Knaap	APG Asset Management
Theo Nijman	Tilburg University
Henriëtte Prast	Tilburg University
Casper van Ewijk	CPB Netherlands Bureau for Economic Policy Analysis
Ed Westerhout	CPB Netherlands Bureau for Economic Policy Analysis
Asghar Zaidi	European Centre for Advanced Research in Economics and Statistics (ECARES), Brussels

1 | Introduction

ED WESTERHOUT

Pension systems are under serious pressure worldwide. The pervasive trend of population aging will dramatically affect the functioning of pension systems in almost any country in the world. In addition, trends like individualization, increasing heterogeneity of the population, financial innovation and increasing (international) labor mobility impact pension systems as well. All these trends call for rethinking the optimal pension design.

The recent worldwide financial crisis, which has become a global economic and public debt crisis, provides another challenge. This crisis has affected pension systems in the world very differently. Countries featuring a strong second pillar of funded pensions have suffered severe losses of pension wealth following the fall in stock market prices. Pay-as-you-go (PAYG) pension schemes cannot be regarded as a safe haven, either; the dramatic deterioration of government finances has only aggravated the pressure on first-pillar pension schemes. Indeed, the financial crisis represents a serious test of pension systems, which have been under reform in the past decades in most countries.

Rethinking the design of pension systems can best be done by starting from the 1994 World Bank Report *Averting the Old Age Crisis*. Intriguing questions emerge. Does the three-pillar system, as sketched by the World Bank in its report, still provide a proper model? Is this three-pillar system sufficiently geared to its tasks of providing robust pensions to the old and redistributing and smoothing shocks between and within generations – given that demographic and economic trends change the economic environment and the international financial crisis has put the world economy on a lower growth path? Can the modifications made by the World Bank in its 2005 report be regarded a step in the right direction? What is the optimal size of the pension pillars and what are optimal investment policies, now that the crisis has made clear how vulnerable pension schemes can be with respect to worldwide adverse shocks?

This book reconsiders the multi-pillar pension scheme against the background of demographic and other trends and a severe financial and debt crisis. It adopts an integral perspective and asks how the total of pension pillars contributes to the three basic functions of pension schemes: (1) facilitating life-cycle financial planning; (2) insuring idiosyncratic risks; and (3) sharing macroeconomic risks across generations. It also discusses the relation between functions and pillars. Here, it argues that the relationship between functions and pillars is not one-to-one; functions can be organized in different pillars.

The subject gives the book an international flavor. The demographic and other trends have international applicability and the financial and debt crisis has indisputably also an international character. Countries differ in the pension schemes they have set up and the book will stress the role of the various elements of pension schemes. As an application, the book focuses primarily upon the Netherlands. The lessons that will be drawn have wider applicability, though. Indeed, the case of the Dutch pension system is particularly interesting, as this system is generally thought to resemble the "ideal" three-pillar pension system as sketched by the World Bank in 1994, featuring a Beveridge-type first pillar providing a flat-rate pension to every citizen, a similarly large funded Bismarck-type second pillar providing pensions to workers that are related to their individual labor market history and a third pillar providing funding on a voluntary basis. Yet, the Dutch pension is under serious discussion: public finances are unsustainable due to, among other things, the first-pillar pension system with an as yet unchanged retirement date. Many pension funds face serious underfunding after the dramatic fall in stock market prices and the increase of pension liabilities on account of declining interest rates.

The book consists of four parts. The first part, "The multi-pillar pension scheme," puts central the functioning of multi-pillar pension systems. It assesses the likely impact of pervasive trends in the world economy and that of the economic crisis. It also discusses the appropriateness of a multi-pillar approach, both on a conceptual and a more practical level. The second part of the book, "Intergenerational risk sharing and distribution," puts central one of the basic functions of any pension scheme, which is risk sharing between generations. It discusses the allocation of this function between pension funds and the government, assesses the role of various types of indexed bonds and explores the redistributive impact of pension funds and the government for a number of aggregate shocks. The third part of the book, "Pensions and financial planning over the life cycle," focuses on two additional issues: that of a lack of both willpower and financial knowledge on the part of individual pension plan participants and that of optimal pension policies in the decumulation phase. The final part of the book, "The future of multi-pillar pension systems," explores the impact of trends and crisis upon optimal pension policies and the relation between functions and pillars of pension schemes. It discusses both the issue of convergence between countries and the non-unique character of optimal pension policies.

The multi-pillar pension scheme

Zaidi

The first part of the book, "The multi-pillar pension scheme," focuses on the idea of a pension scheme that consists of several pillars, each playing their own role. It takes off with the chapter "Population aging and financial and social sustainability challenges of pension systems in Europe: a cross-national perspective," written by Asghar Zaidi. This chapter discusses demographic trends that can be observed worldwide and that can in fact be viewed as one of the reasons for reconsidering multi-pillar pension schemes. In particular, it sketches how low fertility rates and decreasing mortality rates combine to produce aging populations throughout the industrialized world. The dependency ratio (number of 65+-year-olds in terms of the number of people aged 15–64) in the EU-27 is expected to about double from 25 percent in 2010 to 53 percent in 2060. The chapter stresses also that although the demographic trends are international, there are large cross-country differences. On one side of the spectrum, Poland is expected to face a more than tripling of its dependency ratio. On the other side, the expected change in the dependency ratio in the UK is only about 75 percent.

The chapter also discusses the budgetary implications of population aging. Using European Commission estimates, Zaidi shows that if current fiscal and social security institutions are left unchanged, the aging of the population will produce ever-increasing public deficit and public debt levels. Ultimately, fiscal policies will become unsustainable. Again, cross-country differences are huge. However, observing that about three out of four EU-27 countries are considered to be at medium or high risk, one can characterize fiscal sustainability as a truly European issue.

Zaidi shows how policymakers in the EU have responded to the challenge of fiscal sustainability. Many EU countries have taken steps to enhance the employment rate of the working-age population, with a focus on groups that feature low employment rates (e.g., mothers with young children and older workers). Pension policy reforms have also contributed to this goal: for example, by creating greater incentives for longer working careers. Regarding pension policies, Zaidi distinguishes three groups in the EU area. Countries in the first group have implemented reforms that improved pension adequacy by protecting low-wage earners. The UK and Belgium are part of this first group. Countries in the second group reformed their pension systems in order to strengthen the link between pension contributions and benefits. This will improve the functioning of the labor market, but may reduce pension adequacy. Poland and Slovakia belong to this second group. In the third group of countries, which includes Portugal and Italy, reforms have been implemented that have a similar impact on benefits for low, average and above-average earners. Summing up, in terms of pension adequacy, no single trend can be observed.

Hinz

The whole idea of a multi-pillar pension scheme got a strong impetus from the World Bank Report *Averting the Old Age Crisis*. As explained by Richard Hinz in "The World Bank's pension policy framework and the Dutch pension system: a paradigm for the multi-pillar design?" this idea was derived from the principle that the primary functions of pension systems (namely, poverty alleviation, consumption smoothing and insurance) should be organized in separate pillars. The World Bank's multi-pillar approach, which was published in 1994, incorporated three pillars: a first pillar that is mandatory and publicly managed, a second pillar that is also mandatory but privately managed and a third one that is voluntary. The second pillar could be made up of personal savings plans or occupational plans – although the World Bank pointed out the drawbacks of earnings-based defined benefit (DB) systems.

Since 1994, the world has changed drastically. A large number of countries have implemented pension reforms and have accumulated experience on account of both these reforms and developments in other countries. This led the World Bank to refine and adapt its design of a multi-pillar pension scheme. In particular, in its 2005 Report *Old Age Income Support in the 21st Century: An International Perspective on Pension Systems and Reform*, the World Bank developed a scheme consisting of five pillars: (1) a zero pillar that is non-contributory; (2) a first pillar that is mandatory and has DB elements; (3) a second pillar that is also mandatory, but – different from the first pillar – is of the defined contribution (DC) type; (4) a third pillar that is essentially voluntary; and (5) a fourth pillar that includes access to informal support, such as from families or housing.

As regards the Dutch pension system, Hinz notes that its structure is quite consistent with the principles of the World Bank's multi-pillar model. The Dutch system features separate elements that perform well-defined functions, and includes all three components of the 1994 World Bank model. Hinz argues that the Dutch system deviates from the World Bank model in two important aspects, however. First, the scope of the AOW (*Algemene Ouderdoms Wet*) is relatively large, from the perspective of the zero pillar in the 2005 World Bank model, and also when compared with other countries that are quite similar to the Netherlands. The high replacement rates that follow from the Dutch first-pillar pension scheme AOW and occupational schemes create distortions on labor markets and leave little room for voluntary savings that can better accommodate individual preferences. Second, occupational schemes incorporate redistribution that is non-transparent, rather unpredictable and probably large. Indeed, transparency and equity would be better guaranteed by individual savings schemes.

Barr

In his chapter "Credit crisis and pensions: international scope," Nick Barr provides an overview of the various pension systems that can be observed in the world of today. He argues that any pension system faces multiple risks, has multiple objectives and can be set up in multiple ways, ranging from pure DC to pure DB or notional defined contribution (NDC). The systems vary in several dimensions, including who bears what part of a shock, how much room they leave for flexibility or how vulnerable they are to political pressure. Different pension systems do not differ in terms of the amount of macroeconomic risk. Indeed, the total amount of this risk is given, and it can only be allocated differently over the various shareholders. In terms of risk sharing, one pension system may be more efficient than another.

Barr indicates that the financial crisis did not reveal any new risks. Instead, it made many aware of the risks that had always been there. Initially, many countries responded to the crisis by increasing spending on pensions. Subsequently, many countries started to reduce pension benefits, by cutting them, by reducing the degree of their indexation or by increasing the retirement eligibility age. In all cases, the effect of the reforms was to make the pension systems less vulnerable to shocks. In addition, Barr observes that pensioners and older workers suffered much larger losses under DC plans than under DB systems. This is due to, among other things, less intergenerational risk sharing in DC plans, which tended to be invested heavily in equity.

As to pension design, Barr stresses the virtue of automatic adjustment to demographic change and the range of instruments used to absorb shocks. As regards the latter, he argues that adjustments should embrace both benefits and contributions. He considers as strong points of the Dutch pension system that it has many elements of adjustment to systemic risk. In this regard, he welcomes the use of a formula that links the pension eligibility age to life expectancy, as included in the recent pension agreements between social partners in the Netherlands. Further improvement could be achieved by differentiating between cohorts of different ages – for example, by introducing an age-related indexation rule.

Bovenberg and Van Ewijk

In "Designing the pension system: conceptual framework," Lans Bovenberg and Casper van Ewijk develop an analytical framework for the design of pension systems, thereby taking the functions of the pension system as the guiding principle. The chapter distinguishes three basic functions of pension schemes: (1) facilitating life-cycle financial planning; (2) insuring idiosyncratic risks and (3) sharing macroeconomic risks across generations. Life-cycle financial planning concerns consumption smoothing over the individual life cycle and takes into account individual circumstances and preferences. The second basic function of pension schemes concerns pooling of intra-generational risks in the face of imperfect insurance markets.

The third function concerns intergenerational risk sharing of aggregate shocks in the face of incomplete markets. Bovenberg and van Ewijk translate this issue into two questions. The first is what optimal risk sharing implies for savings and the risk exposures of various cohorts. They derive formally that optimal policies imply that generally all cohorts share risks, and that in reaction to an unexpected shock the consumption of different cohorts moves in the same direction. In addition, under some assumptions, all age cohorts optimally exhibit the same risk exposure, if risk exposure is defined in terms of total wealth (i.e., including human wealth).

The second question is how this optimal risk sharing can be achieved: through capital markets, through the government or through mandatory occupational pensions. The authors observe that capital markets can accomplish only a limited part of the desired intergenerational risk sharing. One reason is the limited liability of human capital. This constrains the exposure to capital risk that young agents can take on through leverage. Another one is the impossibility of committing future generations to an intergenerational risk-sharing contract. Hence, other institutions than capital markets, such as the government or pension funds, are needed to help generations share risk optimally. Risk sharing through the government is costly too, however. Taxes have distortionary effects and governments investing in equity may give rise to political risks. Moreover, risk sharing through the public accounts is hampered by the difficulties that governments have in setting up complete contracts. Indeed, contracts that involve the government are generally incomplete, reflecting the political economy of a democracy in which voters can always undo earlier commitments. Risk sharing through mandatory collective pension funds avoids political risks, but is hampered by more discontinuity risk: it is easier to avoid high pension contributions that are levied by one pension fund than it is to avoid taxes that apply to the national level.

Intergenerational risk sharing and distribution

Bohn

The second part of the book, "Intergenerational risk sharing and distribution," starts with the chapter by Henning Bohn, "Private versus public risk sharing: should governments provide reinsurance?" This chapter examines alternative arrangements for intergenerational risk sharing in a small open economy that is subject to various types of macroeconomic shocks, including shocks in labor productivity, the return to capital and longevity. Bohn observes that whereas markets dealing with financial risks are well developed, markets for dealing with risks in labor productivity and longevity are generally not. This is an argument for pension funds: DB and hybrid DB/DC type occupational pensions can be regarded as insurance mechanisms that deal with these types of risk.

However, efficient risk sharing seems to call for a greater role of the government. One reason is that the ability of traditional corporate pension plans to reallocate risks has declined as mobility and financial engineering erodes firms' and workers' ability to enter long-term contracts. Mobility refers to the ability of workers to exit firms when large negative shocks to their plan require excessively high future contributions. Industry funds mitigate this problem because exiting from an industry is more difficult than leaving a firm. Insurance provided by the government could mitigate the problem further. It would take the form of wage- and longevity-indexed contracts or bonds.

Another reason is incomplete markets. Pension promises must be backed by assets or by a plan sponsor – a firm or an industry. However, rapid technological change, industrial restructuring and advances in financial engineering have eroded the ability of firms to offer their equity capital as collateral. Wage- and longevity-indexed bonds issued by governments would help, as reducing the mismatch between pension assets and liabilities would reduce the pension fund's dependence on corporate sponsors. A third reason originates in imperfections in risk sharing abroad. In particular, most foreign countries fail to integrate young and unborn generations into risk-sharing arrangements – through pension funds or governments. Hence, wage risk is not priced; governments could therefore provide insurance that is welfare-improving.

Bettendorf and Knaap

In "The redistribution of macroeconomic risks by Dutch institutions," Leon Bettendorf and Thijs Knaap also analyze the insurance provided by pension funds and governments. Indeed, they focus upon the insurance actually provided by occupational pension funds and the government in the case of the Netherlands. They do so by examining how a large variety of aggregate shocks impact upon the macro economy and the position of different generations, including the unborn. To mimic the Dutch institutions and economy, they adopt a computable general-equilibrium model that incorporates most of the relevant institutional rules of the pension fund sector and the government sector.

The range of shocks that is studied is broad. First, it includes what the authors call simple shocks: two shocks to labor productivity (a temporary and a permanent one), a shock in asset prices, two shocks in the interest rate (one that is short-lived and another that is long-lived) and, finally, a shock in mortality rates. The analysis accounts for the autocorrelation of these shocks found in empirical data. Second, it includes mixed shocks. Unlike simple shocks, these shocks combine shocks in different variables, reflecting the fact that some of the simple shock processes are correlated in the data. The most relevant type of mixed shock, they argue, is a rare disaster (Barro, 2006): a combination of a large drop in labor productivity, a falling interest rate and a large drop in asset prices that occurs with a frequency of about once every 70 years.

Both pension funds and the government act to redistribute shocks. A drop in labor productivity, for example, is redistributed by pension funds; these funds provide wage-linked benefits to the retired, so that workers lose part of their increase in wage income through an increase in pension contributions. The government also redistributes towards the old because it uses the additional tax revenues to increase benefits to all cohorts. Another example is a drop in mortality rates. In this case, pension funds redistribute towards the elderly because they provide benefits as long as the retired are alive. The government does the same through first-pillar pensions. A major result from the numerical simulations in this chapter is that the redistribution through the government sector is quantitatively more important than the redistribution through the pension fund sector.

Beetsma and Bucciol

In "The consequences of indexed debt for welfare and funding ratios in the Dutch pension system," Roel Beetsma and Alessandro Bucciol explore the economic and welfare effects of different types of nominal debt. Most occupational pension schemes in the Netherlands provide pension benefits that are (conditionally) indexed to prices or wages. If price-indexed debt, wage-indexed debt or longevity-indexed debt were available, this would therefore help pension funds in reducing the mismatch risk between their assets and liabilities. Hence, a case can be made for the Dutch government to issue these types of public debt.

Beetsma and Bucciol adopt a model of a two-pillar pension system, designed after and calibrated to the Dutch situation. They use this model to explore the implications for the funding ratio of pension funds and the welfare of individuals of replacing nominal debt in the pension funds' portfolio with indexed debt. They do so for a variety of shocks: shocks in fertility, mortality, labor productivity, inflation, equity and bond returns and the term structure are included. The model distinguishes between not only different generations, but also different skill groups within each generation. The model includes the institutional details of the first and second pillar of the Dutch pension scheme that provide public basic pensions and occupational supplementary pensions, respectively.

Beetsma and Bucciol find that, as expected, including price-indexed debt or longevity-indexed debt in the pension funds' portfolios reduces the volatility of the funding ratio. It also reduces the variability of the consumption of participants of pension plans, which is welfare-increasing. Quantitatively, the effects of the policy reforms on the funding ratio and welfare are quite modest. The reasons are that the types of debt investigated give protection against only one type of risk, whereas pension funds face a number of other aggregate risks. Furthermore, pension funds invest only part of their financial wealth in these debt instruments.

Pensions and financial planning over the life cycle

Bodie and Prast

In "Rational pensions for irrational people: behavioral science lessons for the Netherlands," Zvi Bodie and Henriëtte Prast examine the implications of behavioral economics for Dutch supplementary pensions. They argue that the second pillar of the Dutch pension scheme faces two major challenges. First, the global economic crisis has made clear that the current system is unsustainable. Second, a large part of the expanding group of self-employed people lacks pension coverage.

The question then arises how can lessons from behavioral economics help to take up these challenges?

According to Bodie and Prast, the five most important aspects of behavioral economics are the following. First, preferences are time-inconsistent, and people lack willpower to implement optimal pension plans. Second, more choice may not improve decision making and, instead, may even worsen it. Third, passive choice is so common that it is crucial to design carefully the (explicit or implicit) default option of any saving and investment decision. Fourth, people do not learn from their mistakes, either because there is no possibility to repeat a decision (as with the pension saving decision) or because people are overconfident. Finally, marketing strategies by profit-maximizing firms tend to exploit the inconsistencies and biases of their customers.

As regards the pension scheme in the Netherlands, Bodie and Prast argue that the mandatory participation of employees in occupational schemes avoids that they procrastinate in saving for retirement. Within the mandatory system, they propose to introduce limited, meaningful choice for the employee as regards his retirement age, his aspiration income and his risk tolerance. To assist in the decision-making process, employees should be offered a carefully designed default (for example a safe portfolio that offers a guaranteed real pension). As regards the self-employed, Bodie and Prast propose to change the current system of voluntary participation in third-pillar products. Either the self-employed should automatically enroll in a pension plan unless they choose not to participate or the self-employed should be required to make an active choice whether or not to participate in a pension plan.

Brown and Nijman

In "Opportunities for improving pension wealth decumulation in the Netherlands," Jeffrey Brown and Theo Nijman focus on the pension pay-out phase. In deciding on how fast to decumulate pension wealth in the retirement phase, an individual faces the problem of lifetime uncertainty. Life annuities eliminate longevity risk by allowing an individual to exchange a lump sum of wealth for a stream of payments that continue so long as the individual (and possibly a spouse) is alive. Under a set of assumptions, annuities are welfare-increasing, and full annuitization (i.e., the annuitization of all pension wealth) would be optimal. However, not all of these assumptions hold in reality, and a number of reasons (such as bequests, the illiquidity of annuity products and imperfections in annuity markets) make incomplete annuitization optimal.

The Dutch pension system features mandatory full annuitization of pension wealth, both in the first and second pillar. The Dutch thus attach high priority to ensuring that individuals are provided with sustainable levels of lifelong income. This strong emphasis on annuitization stands in stark contrast to many other countries – such as the US – in which the retirement system is more focused on wealth accumulation than on retirement income security. Brown and Nijman argue that the Dutch system may be overannuitized, and that subjecting only part of pension wealth to mandatory annuitization could be welfare-improving.

In particular, the authors propose replacing full annuitization with a system that mandates annuitization of only a part of it, namely the part of pension wealth needed to cover the retirees' basic needs. In addition, they propose that this part should be protected against inflation. This is in contrast with the current Dutch system in the second pillar (in which pension funds index pensions to inflation only if their financial reserves allow them to) and also in the third pillar (which features nominal pay-outs). Furthermore, above the minimum floor of inflation-indexed annuitization, additional annuitization should be encouraged. Default annuitization may be an effective way to achieve this goal, while preserving individual choice. Finally, the choice of annuity products could be enhanced: ideally, individuals would have access to fixed, inflation-indexed, variable and deferred annuity products, reflecting the preference heterogeneity in the population.

The future of multi-pillar pension systems

Bovenberg and Van Ewijk

In the final chapter of the book, "The future of multi-pillar pension systems," Lans Bovenberg and Casper van Ewijk describe the evolution in pension systems and utilize the results of the other chapters in the book to explore the challenges that remain for the future. For the three basic functions of pension schemes as elaborated in Chapter 5 (i.e., life-cycle planning, intra-generational risk sharing and intergenerational risk sharing), they discuss the most important trade-offs. They also describe how various trends affect these trade-offs, how institutions have responded to these trends and which challenges remain.

Bovenberg and Van Ewijk show that different pension systems have responded in similar ways to the same trends. Therefore, they argue, one could speak of convergence of pension systems. Yet, they do not expect different pension systems to fully converge to a unique system. One reason is that underlying the design of pension systems are fundamental trade-offs – on which different countries want to take different positions. Second, there appears not to be a one-to-one relation between a position on a trade-off and the institutional design of the pension system: different types of institutions can achieve the same outcome. Pension design is therefore path-dependent, with an important role for history.

This chapter presents also a typology of pension systems, based on two dimensions. The first dimension involves the governance of pensions, where pension systems can be classified from state oriented to private oriented. The second dimension concerns the scope for individual choice in pension insurance. Here, pension systems can be classified from choice oriented to mandatory oriented. Combining these two dimensions leads to four prototype models: the state model, the market model, the liberal model and the corporatist model. Although each of these four prototype models can in principle perform all functions of the pension system, they feature strengths and weaknesses. To illustrate, the state model and corporatist model are better geared to solving problems of adverse selection and to organizing intergenerational risk sharing. The market model and liberal model are better able to deal with heterogeneity across individuals and also with financial risks.

References

Barro, R.J., 2006, Rare disasters and asset markets in the twentieth century, *Quarterly Journal of Economics*, vol. **121**(3): 823–66.

World Bank, 1994, *Averting the Old Age Crisis: Policies to Protect the Old and Promote Growth*, Oxford University Press.

2005, *Old Age Income Support in the 21st Century: An International Perspective on Pension Systems and Reform*, World Bank, Washington DC.

PART I

The multi-pillar pension scheme

2 | *Population aging and financial and social sustainability challenges of pension systems in Europe: a cross-national perspective*

ASGHAR ZAIDI

2.1 Introduction

Unexpected events cause shock and uncertainty, which then bring a wave of introspection and questions about past practices and likely future developments. The shock to economic systems caused by the financial near-meltdowns in 2008/2009 has begun to recede now, but the question remains how the effects are likely to linger with us in the decades to come. Such a shock, combined with other long-term challenges such as population aging, is likely to affect the fabric of the welfare state that we, the Europeans, had got used to.

The current state of affairs is nothing to brag about. Many European economies are now saddled with structural debts, partly as a result of spending choices during the boom years and partly in implementing the unavoidable and for the most part effective stimulus packages during 2009/2010. Although signs of economic recovery are visible, as most European economies are returning to positive economic growth (during 2010 and 2011), it is not clear how steady this development is. The effects on employment are lagging behind, as unemployment is

The author is grateful for the work of Katrin Gasior of European Centre Vienna in preparing the graphs included in this chapter. Comments from Ed Westerhout of the Netherlands Bureau for Economic Policy Analysis as well as from Sean Terry of Oxford Brookes University (UK) are also gratefully acknowledged. This chapter was first presented at the conference of the Belgian Presidency of the Council of the European Union, "Assuring Adequate Pensions and Social Benefits for All European Citizens," held at Liège, September 6–8, 2010. Many thanks to the Belgian Federal Public Service Social Security, particularly Koen Vleminckx, and the Cypriot Department of Social Welfare Services at the Ministry of Labour and Social Security, particularly Toula Kouloumou for the support in carrying out this work. The views expressed here are the author's own and are not necessarily shared by the Cypriot and Belgian governments or by the European Commission.

17

persisting at around the 10 percent mark for the EU on average (during 2011). Moreover, most EU countries have also now embarked on various budgetary consolidation measures (starting during late 2010, and taking on a momentum of their own during 2011 and 2012) and the impact of cutbacks required for fiscal consolidations on the vulnerable groups of society, particularly children and pensioners, could run deep.

Furthermore, population aging remains a key long-term challenge for many European countries, and its magnitude, speed and timing vary across European countries (Lanzieri, 2011). The implications on the size and shape of government budgets and also on future growth and living standards, not just for the current elderly but also for the rest of the society, can be considerable. All of this has serious implications for the financial and social sustainability of public welfare systems across the European countries.

In the 50 years following the end of World War II, population aging (be it longevity gains or in terms of fertility level decline due to a higher emancipation of women) has been posited in the context of a societal development showing consistent upward economic progress – an outlook that can no longer be automatically taken for granted. In an area where the welfare of elderly people has been broadly defined relative to the well-being of the working-age population, it cannot now be assumed that the well-being of the comparator, working-age population is on a continued upward track. To the extent that structural damage of the crisis has holed the economies of the European countries, the sustainability of the pension systems and the expectations of the pensioners will be conversely – and, for the most part, adversely – affected.

So, what constitutes "sustainability"? A unanimously approved definition will remain elusive, especially as the term "sustainability" can be expected to refer to different things in different contexts. In the context of analyses included in this chapter, the definition needs to be factual and scientific, a clear statement of a quantifiable destination while – most important in the current context – serving as a call to action towards the achievement of common goals and values. The most widely quoted definition of sustainability is from the Brundtland Commission of the United Nations (on March 20, 1987): "sustainable development is development that meets the needs of the present without compromising the ability of future generations to meet their own needs" (United Nations, 1987).

As for *financial sustainability* aspects, the European Commission position (in its *Sustainability Report 2009*) is that there is no clear-cut definition of a sustainable financial position. They say that, as a first instance, the definition "involves a (public) debt level that does not entail – either now or in the foreseeable future – interest payments so large that they cannot be paid." Thus, the financial sustainability is the ability of a government to service its own obligations (including welfare payments as well as the costs of its current and future debts) through future revenues (Economic Policy Committee, 2009b). An uncomfortable fact, according to this definition, is that there are currently five countries in Europe (at least) which are probably bankrupt and face serious insolvency issues, and whose situation has become increasingly contagious to other Eurozone countries.

A less discussed and also less clearly defined goal is that of *social sustainability*, which encompasses the ideas of adequacy of pension incomes and a solidarity and cohesion across generations. The notion of social sustainability requires that a balance is achieved between the distribution of resources across different generations at a single point in time (such as between young and old), and ensuring that future generations of old and young have the same or greater access to social resources as their counterparts in the current generation (for a discussion, see Zaidi *et al.*, 2010). Social sustainability also captures a wider conception that goes beyond incomes and provision of public services (such as access to affordable and good quality health and social services). In fact, what has become obvious is that the societies experiencing population aging will have to embrace the need for mutually beneficial and satisfying relationships between generations. Without the awareness of importance of socially cohesive intergenerational relationship and public policies, a strong risk of perverse "competition" for limited resources across young and old will develop – to the detriment of both generations and society in general. Social sustainability requires developing effective solutions which are cooperative and mutually beneficial to current and future generations. Fiscal stresses arising out of austerity measures are putting additional strains on the solidarity between young and old generations.

It is crucial to highlight here that without success in solving the financial sustainability issues, the idea of social sustainability becomes more and more simply that – an idea. In the short to medium term, government actions to deal with financial sustainability issues will

result in cuts all around, which will affect present and future generations of pensioners. The choice elements resolve around choosing the
lesser of the evils.

Also, in a world in which each individual saves for his or her own
retirement, aging of the population would be fairly unproblematic. The
problem lies in the fact that the public pay-as-you-go (PAYG) pension
schemes, and also funded pension schemes, provide retirement income
insurance to the elderly by promising benefits that are unrelated to
labor and capital market developments (for example, in defined benefit pension schemes). On account of this (implicit) insurance, shocks
have to be borne by the working cohorts, who are projected to shrink
in size because of lower fertility. Thus, it is the institutional setting of
the pension provision, combined with the population aging phenomenon, which together give rise to sustainability problems.

At all events, the questions Paul Gauguin asked at the turn of the
nineteenth century in moments of personal turbulence comparable to
the public contexts we live in now – D'où Venons Nous / Que Sommes
Nous / Où Allons Nous[1] (Where Do We Come From? What Are We?
Where Are We Going?) – have become particularly pertinent for policymakers of current times. It is now the time to frame the answers to
his third question, i.e., our future direction, in identifying challenges
linked with the financial and social sustainability of the European welfare states. This chapter addresses specifically the financial sustainability of European public pension systems and, correspondingly, the
welfare of our pensioners in the 2040s, 2050s and onwards. While
recognizing that each country has its own approaches, and varying
extent of challenges linked with the crisis and population aging, there
will be a need to ensure that the pension elements of any policy package are executed with lessons learned from the crisis as well as from
mutual experiences of challenges faced and policy reforms adopted.
A review of fundamentals is essential in making a fresh assessment of
the social objectives of pension policy, and to re-examine whether, and
how, recent policy reforms compromise the goals of pension income
adequacy, and what policy measures can improve the intertwined
financial sustainability of pension systems while maintaining some
level of pension income adequacy.

---

[1] This is the title of Gauguin's 1897 painting, displayed at the Boston Museum of
Fine Arts, Boston, USA.

The shape and design of future pension policies, and how they – in response to the current crisis and impending population aging challenges – will affect the welfare of future pensioners will be discussed in this chapter. The analysis undertaken comes in five parts. Section 2.2 sets the context by highlighting sustainability challenges arising from population aging, and the financial, fiscal and economic crises. Section 2.3 analyzes the aggregate impact of pension reforms, using the indicator "benefit ratio," as calculated by the Working Group on Ageing of the EU's Economic Policy Committee.[2] Section 2.4 extends the discussion on pension income adequacy by examining how pension reforms have reshaped the structure of pension systems across (selected) EU countries. These results are derived from the simulations of pension income entitlements for future retirees, undertaken by OECD (2009 and 2011).

The next part (Section 2.5) presents data on changes in the entitlement of public pension income during the period 2006–2046. The indicator in use is the net "Theoretical Replacement Rate," as provided by the Indicators Sub-Group of the EU's Social Protection Committee. Like OECD calculations, it is calculated for stylized workers, approximating impact of pension reforms for the income entitlement of future retirees. Section 2.6 discusses policy challenges that EU countries face going forward, with a dual focus on pension policy challenges as well as the fiscal and labor market policy.

2.2 The financial sustainability concerns

2.2.1 *The population aging phenomenon and its challenges*

No challenge is said to be "as certain as global aging, and none is as likely to have as large and enduring an effect – on the size and shape of government budgets, on the future growth in living standards, and on the stability of the global economy and even the world order."[3] Many areas of the world are facing an unstoppable and often rapid aging of

---

[2] Note here that this chapter discusses various ways to assess the impact of pension reforms. Hinz and Bovenberg and van Ewijk in their chapters included in this volume provide discussions on functions of pension schemes.

[3] Quote from Richard Jackson, Center for Strategic and International Studies Global Ageing Initiative, at National Press Foundation presentation, May 22, 2011, and also from White House Conference on Ageing: July 20, 2005.

their populations, largely as a consequence of falling fertility levels and birth rates and rising life expectancy levels. An essential starting point for this chapter is therefore to assess the varying extent of population aging challenges faced by the European countries.

Since the study of population aging is often driven by concerns over the burdening of the retirement income system, the old-age demographic dependency ratio is used as a related measure of population aging.[4] Figure 2.1 shows the ratio of over 65s to working-age (15–64) population in the 27 EU countries, with the trend between 1960 and 2010 (actual, black) and between 2010 and 2060 (projected, light gray)[5] – 2010 is taken as the central year from which we can look half a century backwards as well as forwards. For convenience of analysis, the evidence is presented by clustering countries into four groups: Central and Eastern European countries; Southern-Mediterranean European countries; Central-Western European countries; and the North-Western European countries of Scandinavia (Denmark, Finland and Sweden).

It is instructive to look at the changes in the dependency ratio over the 100-year span from 1960. During 1960, the dependency ratio was about 19 percent for Ireland and France, implying 19 older persons for every 100 working-age persons. Belgium, Austria, Sweden and the UK were only marginally lower, at 18 percent, but most other countries, in particular those belonging to the Central and Eastern European bloc, have lower values. The most notable rise during the period 1960–2010 is observed for Italy and Germany, where the dependency ratio almost doubled to about 31 percent.

---

[4] Another indicator commonly used is the "System Dependency Ratio" (SDR) in public pension schemes, as given by the ratio of the number of pensioners to the number of insured workers. It is not included here for reasons of brevity, and because the projection of the SDR also relies on additional assumptions about the evolution of labor market participation of future workers (in particular labor force participation rates of workers aged 55–64).

[5] These projected figures are taken from the Eurostat Population Projections 2010-based (Europop2010). They should not be considered as forecasts but as one of the possible future demographic developments, which could occur if certain assumptions about future trends in fertility, life expectancy and net migration will hold. One of the main assumptions is that the values of these three main drivers of population change are set to converge across countries in the very long run (for details, see European Commission 2011).

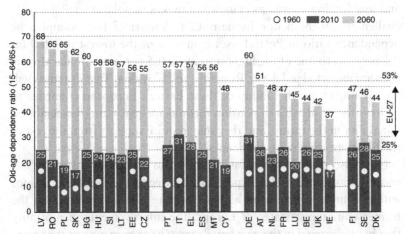

Figure 2.1 The demographic old-age dependency ratio (Number of 65+/ Number of 15–64) across 27 EU countries, 1960, 2010 and 2060
See Appendix 2.A.2 for the country abbreviations.
Source: Results reported here are taken from the latest Eurostat publication (Lanzieri, 2011). The projected results for 2060 are drawn from the Eurostat Population Projections 2010-based (Europop2010), on the basis of the assumptions of the convergence scenario.

The projected average for the EU-27 in 2060 is 53 percent, and this is a staggering increase from the average 25 percent recorded in 2010. This implies that, on average, the EU is projected to move from having four working-age people for every person aged 65+ to a ratio of two to one.[6] This steep rise will exert not just significant, and fairly unsustainable, additional demands on future public finances in the form of rising expenditures on pensions, health and long-term care (all other things being equal), but also they will have an adverse impact on growth potential at national levels.

Note also the list of countries on the left-hand side of the graph – a bloc of countries from the former communist states of Central and Eastern Europe (CEE). The unique conjunction of rising longevity

---

[6] These baseline projections are carried out on the basis of commonly agreed assumptions, and they ensure clarity and comparability across countries. However, given the uncertainty surrounding these assumptions, sensitivity tests have also been carried out with respect to assumptions about the life expectancy, fertility rate and net migration. For a discussion on sensitivity to alternative assumptions, see Eurostat (2010).

and low fertility as well as emigration makes population aging a truly challenging phenomenon in many CEE countries.[7] For example, the dependency ratio in Poland rises from one of the lowest in 1960 (at 9.5 percent) to one of the highest in 2060 (65 percent). Similar drastic rises are expected in Latvia, Romania and Slovakia. This situation will greatly impact on the ability of these Eastern European countries to address the challenges of pension income adequacy and financial sustainability in the future, and they may require support from the rest of the EU in meeting these challenges.

Note also that these national trends also do not reveal the differences in mortality and life expectancy between socio-economic groups within countries. From the best-performing Nordic countries to the former communist states of Europe, the improvements in mortality that have occurred in the past few decades have been among the socio-economically advantaged groups, and least or non-existent among the disadvantaged (Leon, 2011; Andreev *et al.*, 2009; Leinsalu *et al.*, 2009; Shkolnikov *et al.*, 2009). These differences have important implications for the analysis of pension systems and also for the design of future pension policies (for a discussion on the pension implications of socio-economic differences in life expectancy, see Whitehouse and Zaidi, 2008).

Some argue that the world has yet to reach a limit of human life expectancy (Oeppen and Vaupel, 2002), while others – referring to the global increase in obesity – raise the concern that the increase in life expectancy in Europe and other high-income countries may come to an end (Olshansky *et al.*, 2005). However, as yet, there is no conclusive evidence about the changing trends in life expectancy, and it is unclear what consequences there will be for an uninterrupted demographic transition in European countries.

Population aging challenges can also be viewed in terms of rising age-related government expenditure, pertaining mainly to pensions, health care and long-term care (see Figure 2.2 below). This rise in the public provision of age-related transfers and services is observed despite the

[7] See Leon (2011) for possible reasons underlying the current low life expectancy in CEE countries in comparison with Western Europe. The discussion there, and also in Velkova *et al.* (1997), implies that the improvements in conditions amenable to medical intervention, in particular dealing with non-communicable diseases, will see a faster rise in life expectancy in CEE countries and thus close the gap with the Western European countries.

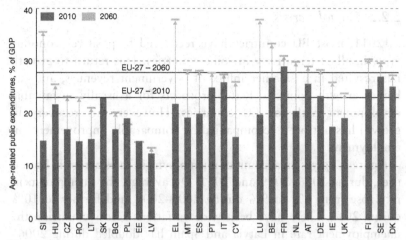

Figure 2.2 Projected changes in the age-related public expenditures (on pensions, health care, long-term care, education and unemployment), as percentage of GDP, during 2010–2060

See Appendix 2.A.2 for the country abbreviations.
Source: Economic Policy Committee (2009b), Table II.1.2, p. 29.

fact that many EU countries had enacted pension reforms during the 1990s and 2000s, largely to motivate workers to extend their working careers but also involving a partial switch to private funded pension schemes (e.g., in Bulgaria, Estonia, Latvia, Poland and Sweden).

On average, age-related government expenditures are projected to increase by 4.6 percentage points of GDP by 2060 in the EU. There are however notable differences across EU countries. The increase in public age-related spending is likely to be considerable in Luxembourg and Greece (18.2 and 16.0 percentage points of GDP by 2060, respectively), but also in Slovenia, Cyprus, Malta, the Netherlands, Romania, Spain and Ireland (on average, 10 percentage points of GDP or more in these nine countries). The second group of countries consists of Belgium, Finland, Czech Republic, Lithuania, Slovakia, the UK, Germany and Hungary and here the cost of aging is more restricted but still high: between 4 and 7 percentage points of GDP. The changes in Bulgaria, Sweden, Portugal, Austria, France, Denmark, Italy and Latvia are expected to be more moderate: 3 percentage points of GDP or less; for Estonia and Poland there is even a decrease (for more details, see Economic Policy Committee (2009b).

2.2.2 *The jobs crisis*

In 2011, most EU countries have recovered to positive economic growth, albeit tentatively in some countries. This return to growth has resulted in a steadier influx of government revenues, and the higher growth points to better prospects for a fiscally sustainable development path for EU countries. However, this recovery in growth has not been accompanied by comparable improvements in employment.

Figure 2.3 gives an account of unemployment rates across EU countries, during 2006, 2009 and 2011. On average, the unemployment rate rose from 8% to 9% during 2006–2009, and further to 10% during 2011. There have been wide variations across countries: the unemployment rate in Latvia and Spain has doubled during 2006–2009, and reached in excess of 20% in 2011 for Spain. The unemployment rate in the Netherlands and Austria, by contrast, remained steady, closer to 5% during the whole of this period.

Once again, the CEE countries, with five out of the seven countries with the highest unemployment rate during 2011, stand out as a grouping. For example, in Latvia and Lithuania, the unemployment rate is in excess of 15 percent during 2011. Thus, it is obvious that workers in CEE countries face the much greater likelihood of a disrupted working career, which will adversely affect their accumulation of pension rights, in public schemes as well as privately. The future challenges in sustaining economic growth and competitiveness in CEE countries can be expected to be disproportionate in comparison with other Central-Western EU countries. The worker position is compounded by the young market economy status that CEE countries have, as we shall refer to later, and also by the fact that the youth's employment prospects suffered disproportionately more than the other age groups during the recent crisis.

2.2.3 *The fiscal crisis*

During 2009, the key policy challenge across the world has undoubtedly been to counteract the recession. Consequently unprecedented fiscal (and monetary) policy measures were put in place (quite rightly), so as to stimulate economies and stabilize financial markets. Heavy public spending either in the form of large fiscal stimulus packages

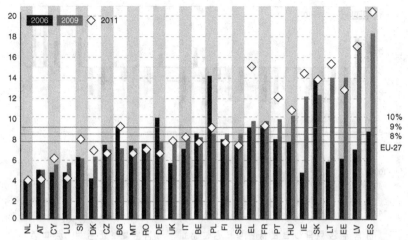

Figure 2.3 Unemployment rate in percent, during 2006, 2009 and 2011
See Appendix 2.A.2 for the country abbreviations.
Source: Various European Commission publications from Directorate Economic and Financial Affairs (ECFIN). The latest data are drawn from Statistical Annex of European Economy, SPRING 2011.

or in automatic stabilizers put enormous additional strain on public finances during 2009, and almost all European governments faced a significant deterioration in their public finances. Government deficits among EU states rose substantially, from an average of –1.4 percent of GDP in 2006 to about –6 percent in 2009 and 2010 (see Figure 2.4 below), leading to an accumulation of large government debts. This fiscal situation raises fresh concerns regarding the sustainability of public finances in many EU states, which remains a live and ongoing challenge in many EU countries, not least due to the population aging phenomenon.

As discussed in detail in Zaidi and Rejniak (2010), CEE countries face serious sustainability challenges, attributed largely to their young market economy status. Having made the transition to the market economy during the 1990s, these countries have not had the benefit of prolonged periods of economic growth and also have gone through the political transition towards democratic institutions relatively recently. While EU accession and increased opportunities of trade cooperation and foreign direct investment strengthened their transition to the market economy, it is nonetheless somewhat ironic that the same greater

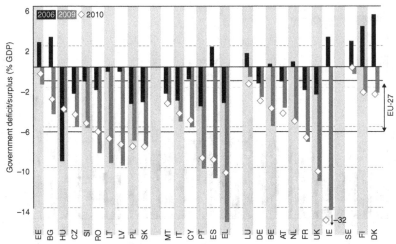

Figure 2.4 Government deficit (−) / surplus (+) in EU countries, in terms of percentage of GDP, 2006, 2009 and 2010
See Appendix 2.A.2 for the country abbreviations.
Source: Eurostat (2011).

links with the global economy that followed EU membership were a big factor in making these countries particularly vulnerable to economic shocks.

Note also that the EU countries have sided with the "austerity now" arguments and have therefore already embarked on various budgetary consolidation measures (during 2010/2011). Such a choice is in some cases driven by the IMF and the EU conditionalities, so as to raise market confidence on public governance in these countries, and also due to these countries' own ambitions to deal with their structural problems. The CEE countries may have been driven additionally by a desire to join the Eurozone countries (Zaidi and Rejniak, 2010, p. 8).

2.2.4 Aging as a contributory factor for financial sustainability challenges

A pertinent question is how the combination of aging populations and fiscal crisis will affect EU countries' financial sustainability in the future. The gains in longevity have indeed been a positive trend, particularly in CEE countries where until now life expectancy has been lower than that in other EU countries. But, rising longevity combined with falling fertility has led to a shrinking proportion of working-age populations in many EU countries. An additional challenge for the CEE countries is the emigration of a large number of workers to other EU countries.

Another clear lesson from the public finance crisis is the need to further refine the quality, consistency and independence of the evidence base from which policy decisions are made: the more high-quality evidence is admitted to this debate as the accepted starting point for discussion on what to do next, the easier it becomes to formulate policy responses and persuade the public about the need for and the consequences of change. The EU's Economic Policy Committee's Working Group on Ageing has made important progress in this respect, by collating results on the indicator of financial sustainability gap (namely: S2), which can be analyzed here to highlight the varying extent of sustainability challenges faced by EU countries (Economic Policy Committee, 2009b). The analysis of the S2 indicator presented below draws from those included in Zaidi (2010b), but with a focus on how population aging contributes to the financial sustainability challenges.

The S2 indicator approximates the gap (as percent of GDP) that must be closed off permanently in order to ensure that the government will be able to finance all future public budget obligations. The indicator provides a compact measure to approximate the size of risks to public finance sustainability when a long-term perspective is taken. The S2 indicator can be deconstructed into two components, so as to also point to the sources of the risks and appropriate policy responses required.

- First, there is the gap arising due to the adverse fiscal position in the base year. The component is referred to as the Initial Budgetary Position (IBP). The IBP exerts a negative pressure in many countries because of the budget deficit during 2009, largely due to the economic downturn experienced during 2008–2009.
- Second, there are the additional costs related to population aging and expenditures on pensions, health care and long-term care. This component is referred to as the Long Term Changes (LTC).

The S2 sustainability indicator is derived from the intertemporal budget constraint that a government faces. It imposes that current total liabilities of the government, i.e., the current public debt and the discounted value of all future expenditure, should be covered by the discounted value of all future government revenue over an infinite horizon.

The advantage of this measure (over the traditional public pension liability measures) is the information contained in the decomposition, where we can disentangle the long-term impact of population aging from that of the current fiscal imbalances faced by European countries.

It needs to be emphasized here that the picture that emerges in Figure 2.5 errs on the "optimistic" side, because the bulk of the raw data used in the calculation of the S2 indicator was collected prior to the onset of the current public finance crisis. Arguably, the revised projections will, when adjusted in line with the current economic realities of large government deficit and debt and also (un)employment, present a less comfortable picture, and a darker prognosis.

Results in Figure 2.5 show that, at the EU-27 level, the total S2 gap is 6.5% of the GDP. On average, the contribution of two components is almost the same: 3.2% for the IBP and 3.3% for the LTC. Wide variations across EU countries are also observed, and countries are divided into categories of high, medium and low risk of financial sustainability. As many as 13 EU countries are being considered high-risk countries. Among them, Ireland, Greece, the UK, Slovenia and Spain have a sustainability gap in excess of 10% of GDP. Latvia, Romania and Cyprus also do not fare well, at just below 10%.

Countries also differ remarkably in terms of sources of risks, i.e., the contribution of the IBP and the LTC. Within the high-risk countries, the contribution of the LTC is particularly high in Greece, Slovenia, Cyprus, Malta and the Netherlands, whereas the relative contribution of the IBP is large in the UK and Latvia. Within the group of medium- and low-risk countries, Luxembourg and Finland and also Belgium and Germany stand out for a larger contribution of the LTC. As for the high IBP contribution, Poland is most notable, but also France and Portugal.

How have policymakers been responding to these sustainability challenges? In many EU countries, the policy responses within the remit of labor market policies has been to enhance the employment rate of the working-age population, especially for those within traditional low employment groups (e.g., mothers with young children, older workers and disabled persons with reduced work capabilities). Pension policy has sought to complement labor market policy, with greater incentives towards longer working careers, improvements in the coverage of public pension schemes, the provision of suitable mechanisms to encourage private personal savings and, where possible, a scaling-down of pension benefit provisions to improve affordability

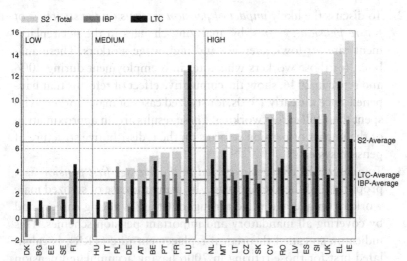

Figure 2.5 Sustainability gap (S2 indicator) across EU countries and the contribution of the IBP and the LTC, 2009
See Appendix 2.A.2 for the country abbreviations.
Source: Economic Policy Committee (2009b), Table III.1.1, p. 35.

of public pension schemes (for further details on pension reforms in EU countries, see Zaidi and Grech, 2007; OECD 2009, 2011). These reforms have contributed towards improvements in the financial sustainability as well as ensuring a better fairness between and within generations and between men and women. Some pension reforms have also addressed the issue of pension income adequacy, especially those that improved the coverage and the indexation of minimum pensions.

Nonetheless, it can be argued that until recently the issue of adequacy has not been a priority in many of these reforms, and this paper provides a glimpse into how the current generations of workers are expected to fare with respect to their incomes when they will be retiring. On the basis of the information available, three possible ways can be adopted to examine the evolution of pension incomes of future retirees in EU countries:

1. To examine changes in the *benefit ratio* that measures the evolution of pension expenditures per pensioner in relation to the wages per worker. The period under consideration for these analyses is between 2007 and 2060, and these results provide the macro impact of the pension reforms across EU countries.

2. To discuss the likely *impact of pension reforms on the structure of future pension systems*, by analyzing changes in the net replacement rate for low-, average- and high-wage workers. These analyses, for those workers who enter into employment during 2006 and retire in 2046, show the cumulative effect of reforms that happened since the early 1990s, for stylized cases of male workers who spent their full career working. These results are an approximation of the impact of pension reforms on the redistributive structure of pension systems.

3. To analyze the *changes expected in the average first pension* as a proportion of the average wage, by using the case of stylized male workers on average wage throughout their working careers and by covering all mandatory and important pension schemes. This indicator, so-called theoretical replacement rate (TRR), is calculated first for those retiring in 2006 having accumulated pension rights under the current pension policies. Then, the base TRR is compared with the prospective TRR of those retiring in 2046 accumulating rights under the new reformed pension system, so as to measure how pension reforms will affect future pension entitlements.

These three streams of analysis provide insights into how pension incomes for future retirees are likely to be affected, and the next three sections of this chapter address them one by one.

2.3 The macro impact of pension reforms: progression of the benefit ratio

Evolution of benefit ratio over time charts the likely development of two measures: the relative value of the average pension (total public pension spending divided by number of pensioners) and the average wage (approximated by the GDP per hours worked). All other things being constant, a decline in the benefit ratio over time points to a fall in the generosity of public pensions, relative to wages.

The projected reduction in the benefit ratio can also be a sign of improving public finances. However, it can also lead to greater expenses in the form of social assistance from the government if the falling benefit ratio resulted in an increase in the poverty among older people in the future. Moreover, falls in the benefit ratio may occur because the

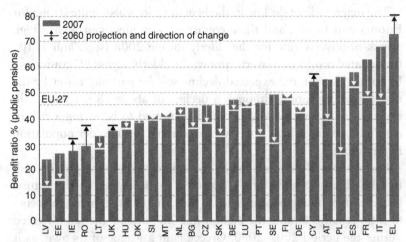

Figure 2.6 Changes in the benefit ratio percent (average public pensions/average economy-wide wage) across 27 EU countries, for the period 2007–2060
Note: EU-27 – unweighted average.
See Appendix 2.A.2 for the country abbreviations.
Source: Economic Policy Committee (2009a), p. 97.

pension system has moved partly towards private schemes, and thus revenues and expenditures from public pension schemes will be lower in the future. Such observations should be kept in mind when interpreting results for the changes in the benefit ratio presented below.

The results presented here are derived from the recently completed assessment of aging-related public expenditures by the European Commission. Figure 2.6 shows that the projected benefit ratio will be declining in the majority of EU countries, over the period 2007–2060 (Economic Policy Committee, 2009a, p. 97). There are also important variations across EU states. The main findings with respect to the development of the benefit ratio can be summarized as follows.

The decline in the benefit ratio is quite strong for Poland (–54%), Sweden (–39%), Austria (–30%), Slovakia (–27%) and France (–25%). With the exception of Slovakia, this decline in public pension generosity will not be offset by other mandatory private pension schemes because the fall in the benefit ratio will still be more than 20 percent. Thus, in the absence of any counteracting policy changes to improve adequacy, future retirees in Poland, Sweden, Austria and France run the risk of being more often poor than is the case now.

The magnitude of decline in the benefit ratio is also quite strong for Estonia and Latvia, and these countries were identified with a high at-risk-of-poverty rate for the elderly during 2008 (see Zaidi 2010a for updated results on poverty among the elderly across EU countries). In both countries, the expected decline will be partially offset by the new private pensions, although a decline of about 18 percent is still expected in Estonia. Thus, Estonia is expected to be facing a risk of continuing to be a high poverty risk country for its older population in the future.

Portugal could be identified as the country where the poverty risk for the elderly population is expected to be higher in the future, because of its falling benefit ratio. In Italy, on the other hand, the benefit ratio remains among the highest in 2060, despite the fall observed during the period 2007–2060. Greece is in a league of its own, as it remains the country with by far the highest benefit ratio, despite a fall during the period in question. However, these results do not show the probable impact of the most recent reforms in the public pension system in that country which involves cuts in pension payments and raising of the retirement age for both men and women. Spain and Cyprus are also countries that will continue to have a high benefit ratio in the future.

2.4 Simulating the impact of reforms on the structure of future pension systems

An informative way to analyze future changes in pension systems is to compare the Net Replacement Ratio (NRR) for stylized workers before and after pension reforms on low-, average- and above-average wage workers. These results are provided in *Pensions at a Glance* (OECD, 2009, Chapter 2). Results for 12 EU countries are included in Table 2.A.1 (Appendix 2.A.1) and they simulate the impact of reforms for those workers who entered the labor market in 2006. They compare the pension entitlement of a person who spent a full career under the reformed pension system with the pension entitlement that would have been received had the system not been changed. The results for six countries are shown in Figure 2.7, and they are reported in terms of the NRR: that is, the value of the pension in retirement, after taxes, compared with the level of earnings when working.

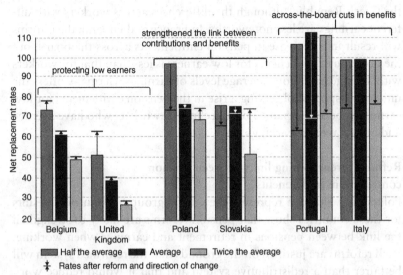

Figure 2.7 Changes in the benefit ratio percent (average public pensions/average economy-wide wage) across 27 EU countries, for the period 2007–2046
Source: OECD (2009), p. 80.

For each country, the first bar shows the position of stylized low earners: workers earning 50 percent of the economy-wide average each year of their entire working life. The middle bar shows the NRR for average earners and the third bar for above-average earners (workers earning 150 percent of the average). By comparing the impact of reforms across these three earnings groups, results provide an indication of changes in redistributive aspects of pension systems, arising from the cumulative reforms that have taken place during the past 10–15 years.

Depending on the effect of the pension reforms on the retirement incomes of workers at different earnings levels, countries can be divided into three groups, and they are analyzed below.

Reforms protecting low-wage earners
Results for the UK and Belgium are presented first and they stand for the group of countries where pension reforms have protected low earners. In these two countries, pension reforms are likely to leave the pension entitlements of average and above-average earners unchanged, but they will increase the benefits for low earners (by nearly 23 percent for the UK, and 6 percent for Belgium). Similar results are observed for

the Czech Republic, although the differences across workers with different earnings are less noteworthy. In France and Finland, the reforms
will result in a decrease in pension entitlements across the board, but
the decrease in the benefits for low earners is less than that for workers
with average and above-average levels of earnings. Germany offers the
unique prospect of observing a rise in the pension entitlements for low
earners to be accompanied by a decline for workers who have average
and above-average earnings.

Reforms strengthening links between pension contributions and benefits

Poland and Slovakia represent the second group of countries. Results
for these countries show that pension reforms are likely to strengthen
the link between pensions in retirement and earnings when working.
Such reforms are justified on the grounds that the reformed system will
be fairer than a redistributive system and that it would reduce work
disincentive distortions in the labor market. However, these reforms
have also raised concerns regarding the adequacy of pension benefits
for future retirees. In Poland, there is a strong decline in the public pension entitlement of those who are low earners: −23%. In contrast, the
pension entitlement is expected to fall only slightly for average earners
and there will be a rise for high earners (8%). The reform impact in
Slovakia is along the same lines as observed for Poland, but the decline
in the pension entitlements for low earners is smaller (−13%) and the
rise observed for high earners is considerably higher (43%).

Across-the-board cuts in pension benefits

The third group of countries falls in the category in which reforms
will result in a similar impact on benefits for low, average and above-
average earners. Portugal and Italy are likely to experience across-the-
board cuts in pension benefits. Portugal is set to observe the highest
decline in the NRR, followed by Italy. Despite these across-the-board
cuts, these countries will continue to offer an impressively high net
replacement rate (around 70 percent).

In summary, no single trend exists and more information of this sort
is required for other EU countries, especially for CEE countries. The
adequacy concerns will be arising for Poland and Slovakia as well as
for Portugal and Italy. In contrast, the pension systems have become
more redistributive than before in Belgium and the UK (and also in

Germany and Ireland), and these countries are addressing issues of elderly poverty. Other trends observed are that Hungary had been moving in the other direction to the neighboring Poland and Slovakia: higher replacement rate and rising (thus, raising further concerns regarding the financial sustainability in Hungary).

2.5 Changes in the average first pension to reflect impact of pension reforms

Another indicator pertinent in the analysis of the adequacy of pension incomes of future retirees is to examine the changes expected in the average first pension as a proportion of the average wage. The indicator in use is the net "Theoretical Replacement Rate" (TRR), and it is the change in the TRR that is adopted by EU member states to reflect the impact of pension reforms in their countries (see Social Protection Committee, 2009).

In the base case scenario, the prospective TRR is calculated for a male worker entering into the labor market in 2006, staying in employment for a full career (40 contribution years), earning average wage, retiring at 65 and accumulating pension rights under the reformed pension system. The first pension income entitlement for this hypothetical worker is divided by the projected average wage in the immediate previous time period to calculate the TRR. This prospective TRR is then compared with the base TRR for someone who would have accumulated pension rights under the current pension policies and would have retired in 2006. The change will then approximate how pension reforms will affect future pension entitlements.

The calculations for the base TRR for 2006 are carried out by respective countries and provided to the Indicators' Sub-Group of the Social Protection Committee. The calculations for prospective TRR are carried out using the OECD model for all EU countries except Belgium, France, Italy, Cyprus and Austria which used their own national models. The calculations cover pension entitlements from public pensions and mandatory private schemes as well as other private schemes with a significant role in the pension incomes of future retirees.

Figure 2.8 displays the change in the TRR from the current situation to the prospective situation in 2046. There are wide variations across EU states. The TRR (net) is projected to decline in 13 countries, and the most notable falls are observed for the Czech Republic

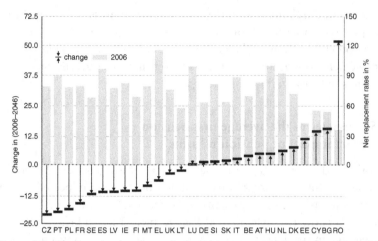

Figure 2.8 Changes in the theoretical replacement rate (net), for the period 2006–2046, for a stylized full career male worker on average wages retiring at 65

See Appendix 2.A.2 for the country abbreviations.

Source: Social Protection Committee (2009) (Annex Country fiches), 2009.

(–21%-points), Portugal (–20%-points) and Poland (–19%-points). Closely behind them are Sweden, Spain and Latvia (–12%-points) and Ireland and Finland (–11%-points). This decline in the TRR is a reflection of reforms that have taken place in these countries over the recent past, which has lowered future benefits. An increase in the TRR is expected for fourteen EU states, and the most notable of them is Romania (52%-points). Other significant increases are observed for Bulgaria (15%-points) and Cyprus (14%-points). For the last-mentioned three countries, the base TRR was relatively low in 2006.

2.6 Policy implications

The cross-national perspective presented in this chapter substantiates the wide variations that exist in the challenges faced by EU countries in ensuring both the financial sustainability of pension systems as well as maintaining adequacy of pension incomes. In reality, no single solution fits all these varying circumstances, especially in view of the differential impact of the recent financial, economic and fiscal crises, as well as the varying extent of population aging challenges. Most EU national governments nonetheless face a common challenge in the near future as they look for a mix of economic and social policies which will not only strengthen a sustainable recovery from the crisis and help them stay clear of dangers of a return to recession but also ensure a permanent financial sustainability in public finances in view of population aging. Achieving this delicate balance between current and future economic and social policy issues requires not only the political will to make tough policy decisions, but also political dexterity in persuading the public that its own interest lies in making sacrifices to ensure sustainability of future welfare systems in Europe.

As for the fiscal policy challenges, an obvious conclusion is that budgetary consolidations are required in many EU countries so as to achieve a permanent sustainability in public finance systems. The question is not whether to consolidate or not, but its timing and also how to limit the size of the welfare state without compromising its overarching social objectives. There has appeared a consensus across EU countries towards "austerity now," and it is important that countries also prepare themselves for corrective expansionary measures if this strategy puts economic recovery at risk.

The salient challenges for labor market policies involve activation and an improved re-integration of groups with typically low employment prospects, particularly mothers, older workers and people with disabilities. Undoubtedly, a longer and less disruptive working career will promote both financial and social sustainability of public pension systems. Not so obvious is how best to encourage behaviors towards extending working life, so as to devote the gains in the life expectancy to working lives. Not so obvious is to determine how to compensate mothers for childcare responsibilities but without affecting incentives for them to return to work. How to improve financial education and change behaviors towards greater work and savings towards retirement? What policies to be aimed at improving employers' attitude towards hiring and retaining older workers? What improvements in the health and safety environment of work places are absolutely essential for a greater employment of older workers? Each country will have to find the most appropriate labor market policy package to deal with these challenges.

As for pension policy implications, the EU countries will have to continue closing off early retirement pathways and raise pension eligibility age in accordance with development of life expectancy. This is despite the fact of low youth employment rates and low labor demand in general in the European economy now, so as to ward off any chances of returning to and staying with the culture of early retirement. In light of the financial market volatility, it is not so obvious anymore whether a move towards the private funded second pillar still remains the right course. Or, are parametric adjustments to the public PAYG system suffi-cient? What regulations are required, at the national and the European level, especially in view of lessons learned from the financial crisis? What simpler, more direct, policies to address poverty in old age are avail-able, especially those that do not stigmatize poor older people? Is raising social minimum pension levels to the level of national poverty line the way forward and is it politically feasible? What balance between incen-tives to work and save is required, but without compromising provision of a social safety net in the form of a social pension? Certainly, there are more questions than answers, and these issues are best resolved in the national policymaking, and surely lessons can be drawn from differen-tial experiences of EU countries as presented in this book.

While recognizing that each country will have its own approaches, there is a need to ensure that its processes are based on sound eco-nomic, financial and fiscal fundamentals – approaches that would avoid a repeat of the 2008–2009 crashes and the subsequent after-shocks. And also, that the pension elements of any packages are properly planned and executed, having learned useful lessons from the crisis. Thus, in the process, each country is looking for a solution fitting to its own economic circumstances, in alignment with its exist-ing and past pension policies, appropriate to the pace in the aging of its population and also in line with its citizens' aspirations towards the type and size of the welfare state. A review of fundamentals is essential for all concerned, particularly in re-examining whether, and how, policy reforms towards stimulating economies out of the recession and introducing cuts in fiscal consolidation measures com-promise the pension income adequacy of future retirees, and what policies can potentially improve both the sustainability and the pen-sion income adequacy.

Despite the difference between countries, with respect to the speed and the impact of population aging and with respect to the policy reforms implemented and their likely long-term effects, population aging is a common trend and thus many countries face similar prob-lems, although obviously the extent and details of these problems differ between countries. As a result, as stressed above, each country should take measures that fit best in this country's tradition. Nonetheless, the similarity of the problems faced by different countries would imply that they can learn from each other, which does not mean that they should strive for uniform measures that neglect country-specific circumstances.

The crisis in the sustainability of public finance and concerns about adequacy of future pension incomes also highlight the need to further refine the quality and the independence of the evidence base from which challenges for each nation can be identified and appropriate policy decisions made. The more high-quality comparative evidence that can be admitted to this debate as the accepted starting point for discussion on what to do next, the easier it becomes to formulate policy responses and persuade the public about the need for and the consequences of a policy change. The results presented in this chapter, while far from the *best possible* evidence, certainly represent the *best evidence possible*, given uncertainties about the future. One can argue that these quantitative results offer a critical departure from having no such information available, as was the case until recently, in Europe, and they give pertinent information about what the future holds for pension income sustainability in Europe.

References

Andreev, E.M., R. Hoffmann, E. Carlson, V.M. Shkolnikov and T.L. Kharkova, 2009, Concentration of working-age male mortality among manual workers in urban Latvia and Russia, 1970–1989, *European Societies*, vol. 11(1): 161–85.

Economic Policy Committee, 2009a, The 2009 Ageing Report: Economic and Budgetary Projections for the EU-27 Member States (2008–2060), Joint Report prepared by the European Commission (DG ECFIN) and the Economic Policy Committee (AWG), European Economy 2|2009.

2009b, *Sustainability Report 2009*, European Economy 9|2009.

European Commission, 2011, Demography Report 2010, Commission Staff Working Document, Luxembourg: Publications Office of the European Union.

Eurostat, 2010, Work session on demographic projections, Lisbon, April 28–30, 2010, edition Methodologies and Working papers, Luxembourg: Publications Office of the European Union.

2011, Provision of deficit and debt data for 2010 – first notification, Eurostat News Release: Euro Indicators, 60/2011–26 April 2011, Luxembourg: Publications Office of the European Union.

Lanzieri, G., 2011, The greying of the baby boomers, a century-long view of ageing in European populations, Population and social conditions, *Statistics in focus*, 23/2011.

Leinsalu, M., I. Stirbu, D. Vagero, R. Kalediene, K. Kovács, B. Wojtyniak, W. Wróblewska, J.P. Mackenbach and A.E. Kunst, Educational inequalities in mortality in four Eastern European countries: Divergence in trends during the post-communist transition from 1990 to 2000, *International Journal of Epidemiology*, vol. 38: 512–525.

Leon, D., 2011, Editorial: Trends in European life expectancy: A salutary view, *International Journal of Epidemiology*, vol. 40: 271–77.

OECD, 2009, *Pensions at a Glance 2009: Retirement-Income Systems in OECD Countries*, Paris.

   2011, *Pensions at a Glance 2011: Retirement-Income Systems in OECD and G20 Countries*, Paris.

Oeppen J., and J.W. Vaupel, 2002, Demography. Broken limits to life expectancy, *Science*, vol. 296(5570): 1029–31.

Olshansky, S.J., D.J. Passaro, R.C. Hershow, J. Layden, B.A. Carnes, J. Brody, L. Hayflick, R.N. Butler, D.B. Allison and D.S. Ludwig, A potential decline in life expectancy in the United States in the 21st century, *N Engl J Med*, vol. 352: 1138–45.

Shkolnikov, V.M., E.M. Andreev, D.A. Jdanov, D. Jasilionis and T. Valkonen, 2009, To what extent do rising mortality inequalities by education and marital status attenuate the general mortality decline? The case of Finland in 1971–2030, MPIDR Working Paper WP-2009–018.

Social Protection Committee, 2009, Updates of Current and Prospective Theoretical Pension Replacement Rates 2006–2046, available at: http://ec.europa.eu/social/main.jsp?langId=en&catId=752&newsId=551&furtherNews=yes (accessed July 3, 2011).

United Nations, 1987, "Report of the World Commission on Environment and Development: Our Common Future," Report transmitted to the General Assembly as an Annex to document A/42/427 – Development and International Co-operation: Environment, New York.

Velkova, A., J.H. Wolleswinkel-van den Bosch and J.P. Mackenbach, 1997, The East-West life expectancy gap: Differences in mortality from conditions amenable to medical intervention, *International Journal of Epidemiology*, vol. 26(1): 75–84.

Whitehouse, E., and A. Zaidi, 2008, Socio-economic Differences in Mortality: Implications for Pensions Policy, Social, Employment and Migration Working Papers 71, OECD, Paris.

Zaidi, A., 2010a, Poverty Risks for Older People in EU Countries – An Update, Policy Brief Series, the European Centre Vienna, January 2010.

2010b, Fiscal and Pension Sustainability: Present and Future Issues in EU Countries, Policy Brief Series, the European Centre Vienna, February 2010.

Zaidi, A., and A. Grech, 2007, Pension policy in EU25 and its impact on pension benefits, *The Journal of Poverty and Social Justice*, vol. 15(3): 229–311.

Zaidi, A., and M. Rejniak, 2010, Fiscal Policy and Sustainability in View of Crisis and Population Ageing in Central and Eastern European Countries, Policy Brief Series, the European Centre Vienna, August 2010.

Zaidi, A., K. Gasior and A. Sidorenko, 2010, Intergenerational Solidarity: Policy Challenges and Societal Responses, Policy Brief Series, the European Centre Vienna, July 2010.

Appendix 2.A.1

Table 2.A.1 *Impact of pension reforms on net replacement rates by earnings level, stylized estimates from OECD for full career workers, 2009*

Countries	Earnings level	Before (%)	After (%)	Change (% points)	Change (%)
Reforms that protected low earners					
Germany	Half the average	56.4	59.2	2.8	5
	Average	66.6	61.3	5.3	−8
	Twice the average	66.4	60.3	−6.1	−9
France	Half the average	79.7	76.2	−3.5	−4
	Average	78.2	65.7	−12.5	−16
	Twice the average	70.8	60.2	−10.6	−15
Finland	Half the average	75.9	73.2	−2.7	−4
	Average	71.4	62.4	−9.0	−13
	Twice the average	72.4	63.8	−8.6	−12
UK	Half the average	51.9	63.8	11.9	23
	Average	39.8	40.9	1.1	3
	Twice the average	28.3	29.2	0.9	3
Belgium	Half the average	74.2	78.7	4.5	6
	Average	62.1	63.7	1.6	3
	Twice the average	50.6	51.7	1.1	2
Czech Repub.	Half the average	86.7	95.3	8.6	10
	Average	58.1	64.1	6.0	10
	Twice the average	44.6	49.4	4.8	11

Table 2.A.1 (*cont.*)

Countries	Earnings level	Before (%)	After (%)	Change (% points)	Change (%)
Reforms that strengthened the link between contributions and earnings					
Poland	Half the average	97.1	74.4	−22.7	−23
	Average	76.9	74.9	−2.0	−3
	Twice the average	69.7	75.0	5.3	8
Slovakia	Half the average	76.4	66.3	−10.1	−13
	Average	75.9	72.7	−3.2	−4
	Twice the average	52.2	74.9	22.7	43
Hungary	Half the average	85.9	94.3	8.4	10
	Average	83.2	105.5	22.3	27
	Twice the average	79.1	99.2	20.1	25
Across-the-board cuts in benefits					
Austria	Half the average	98.4	90.5	−7.9	−8
	Average	99.2	90.3	−8.9	−9
	Twice the average	95.1	86.3	−8.8	−9
Italy	Half the average	99.1	74.8	−24.3	−25
	Average	99.1	74.8	−24.3	−25
	Twice the average	99.2	77.1	−22.1	−22
Portugal	Half the average	106.1	63.7	−42.4	−40
	Average	112.0	69.6	−42.4	−38
	Twice the average	110.8	72.0	−38.8	−35

Source: OECD (2009), p. 80.

Appendix 2.A.2 Country abbreviations

AT	Austria
BE	Belgium
BG	Bulgaria
CY	Cyprus
CZ	Czech Republic
DE	Germany
DK	Denmark
EE	Estonia

EL   Greece
ES   Spain
FI   Finland
FR   France
HU   Hungary
IE   Ireland
IT   Italy
LT   Lithuania
LU   Luxembourg
LV   Latvia
MT   Malta
NL   The Netherlands
PL   Poland
PT   Portugal
RO   Romania
SE   Sweden
SI   Slovenia
SK   Slovak Republic
UK   United Kingdom

3 | The World Bank's pension policy framework and the Dutch pension system: a paradigm for the multi-pillar design?

RICHARD HINZ

3.1 Introduction

During the past two decades the World Bank has emerged as a central player in the development and reform of pension systems. In part this has been a consequence of its traditional role in providing loans to middle- and low-income countries. World Bank lending that was directly related to the establishment or reform of pension systems grew from very minimal levels to more than $1.5 billion when it reached its peak in the years from 1997 through 2000. Overall the World Bank lending that was in some manner associated with pension systems totaled more than $7.5 billion between 1984 and 2007, representing about 1.0–1.5 percent of the total lending by the Bank during this period (Hinz *et al.*, 2009).

However, the influence of the World Bank extends beyond the direct impact of its lending. As the Bank has evolved from the primary role for which it was originally envisioned (a source of financial intermediation for reconstruction and development to fill the gap in private markets following World War II) to a broader mandate under which it has become a source of knowledge, policy analysis and technical assistance, it has increasingly sought to develop and disseminate policy and implementation guidance that provides theoretical and practical foundations to guide its work.

The Bank's policy and research efforts on pension systems and reform is one of the more notable examples of this evolution in its role. Beginning in the early 1990s the Bank undertook an extensive program of research to support the development of a policy framework to address the impending demographic transition brought on by rapid increases in longevity, the aging of the post war "baby boom" generation and the precipitous decline in fertility experienced by countries at all levels of development. This effort was initially motivated by the need to cope with the fiscal challenges imposed by pension systems that had been implemented in Latin America and Central and Eastern Europe in the early and middle parts of the twentieth century. The challenges faced by these systems, many of which sought to emulate the social insurance arrangements introduced in Western Europe during the previous century, were brought to the fore by the financial crisis in Latin America in the late 1980s and the collapse of the formerly socialist governments in Central and Eastern Europe. The necessity to resolve the fiscal challenges in Latin America and facilitate the transition to a market economy in Central and Eastern Europe thrust pensions to the forefront of fiscal and policy debates in the early 1990s, making the reform of pension systems a central element in the structural reforms of the period and a critical determinant of the ability of the fledgling market economies and nascent democracies in Europe to survive.

This Bank's research and policy formulation effort led to the publication in 1994 of a World Bank Policy Research Report entitled *Averting the Old Age Crisis* (World Bank, 1994). In addition to the underlying analytical work on demographic trends and patterns of old-age income provision, this report provided the initial formulation of what was to become the central theme in the World Bank's policy framework, the multi-pillar concept of pension system design. The influence of this conceptual approach to system design and the various interpretations applied in its implementation have likely exerted a far greater influence in the thinking about pension systems and reform than any of the Bank's lending operations. It has also become one of the more controversial elements of World Bank policy and a lightning rod for the ongoing debate between the proponents of the traditional "Bismarckian" approach to the design and financing of social insurance that is based on earnings related benefits and pay-as-you-go (PAYG) financing and the advocates of mandatory funded individual account systems pioneered by the Chilean reforms of the early 1980s.

In the intervening years the World Bank's pension policy framework has been the source of considerable controversy and debate within as well as outside of the institution. In response to the emergence of new evidence and experience, the original framework has been adapted and refined. This has resulted in a somewhat more complex formulation although the underlying analysis and essential principles remain remarkably consistent with those set forth nearly 20 years ago. This chapter begins by briefly outlining the analysis of pension systems underlying the initial policy framework and discusses how this provided the rationale for the original multi-pillar policy framework. It then briefly traces the motivation for the subsequent refinement and extension of these principles leading to the current articulation in the 2005 publication *Old Age Income Support in the 21st Century*. The chapter concludes by considering the pension system of the Netherlands in relation to the World Bank's multipillar policy framework and the extent that the Dutch system can be perceived to achieve the outcomes and objectives envisioned by this approach to pension system design.

3.2 "Averting the old age crisis" and the origins of the multi-pillar policy framework

3.2.1 *Defining criteria: the three functions of a pension system*

Underlying the World Bank's diagnosis of existing systems that led to the formulation of the multi-pillar design framework articulated in 1994 is the view that all pension systems should be considered in the context of their capacity to effectively perform three sets of functions. These functions are not intended to be the exclusive functions that pensions should perform. There is also considerable overlap among them with some of the functions of a pension system falling within more than one of the groups. Rather than a rigorous analytical paradigm these were envisioned as a more general conceptual basis for the critical analysis of existing pension systems that comprises the main focus of the Bank's early work. The three functions are articulated in the overview section of *Averting the Old Age Crisis* as:

Consumption smoothing – The capacity to organize and facilitate savings instruments and individual behavior to smooth consumption over a life cycle that is likely to have considerable variability in earnings and consumption requirements. For pension systems this specifically focuses on the ability to efficiently transfer consumption from periods of economic activity that are likely to reach a peak considerably in advance of withdrawal from active labor followed by a gradual decline in earnings culminating in pure consumption in old age. This function implicitly includes establishing institutions and instruments that enable and facilitate life-cycle planning. It overlaps considerably with redistribution functions as well in addressing poverty alleviation objectives at the individual level.

Redistribution – The ability to efficiently, effectively and equitably transfer income and resources among various income groups to achieve a defined set of policy objectives. This is most specifically focused on the capacity to achieve poverty alleviation and ensure that low-income workers achieve a minimal level of retirement income. It includes both intra-generation redistribution associated with poverty alleviation or broader social or economic policy objectives and also intergenerational redistribution associated with an implicit "social compact" to enable earlier generations to share in subsequent economic growth. The evaluation of redistributive outcomes of pension systems and the extent to which they represent the implementation of explicit policy objectives in a transparent manner, or conversely, are outcomes that are unintended and non-transparent is perhaps the central theme in critique of existing pension systems in the initial research.

Insurance – The capacity to provide effective risk management and fairly spread the costs across the full range of relevant individuals. This includes managing volatility in earnings and financial markets, and most importantly for pension systems, the capacity to manage mortality risks by spreading coverage widely across the population. This function is overlapping and often difficult to distinguish from consumption smoothing. It includes both the management of idiosyncratic risks among individuals through participation in large or national level risk pools as well as the management of macroeconomic risks through investment requirements, public guarantees and the establishment of requirements and mechanisms for the receipt of benefits as lifetime annuities.

Pension systems are evaluated in consideration of the extent that they perform these functions in an efficient and transparent manner. Pensions are considered as an element of a broader system of social insurance as well as private saving and insurance instruments. At the core of the analysis is consideration of what combination of design, operation and outcomes of these institutions can be expected to achieve equitable results in the most cost-effective manner. A related focus is assessing how the outcomes of various approaches to the design of pension systems have varied in relation to the level of economic development in which they are implemented.

3.2.2 Diagnosis of existing systems

The 1994 report examined the evidence on existing pension systems and concluded that most were unable to effectively achieve these goals, both because the underlying designs were flawed but also because the environment in which they have been implemented could not be expected to support designs imported from other settings. This was based on several main conclusions derived from the review of existing systems. The central tenets of the analysis were:

The immutable demographic transition that will occur in countries at all levels of development will impose challenges that require rethinking the designs that were viable under the very different conditions under which many pension systems were established.

One of the most readily apparent relationships in economic development is the strong link between the level of development (per capita GDP), the proportion of the population that is elderly, coverage under public pension systems and most critically the level of public expenditures for pensions. Improvements in basic necessities such as nutrition and sanitation in conjunction with better working conditions and access to health care services significantly extend life expectancy during the transition to the industrial and post-industrial economies. This extends life expectancy well beyond the usual age of economic activity for an increasingly larger proportion of individuals. Reductions in fertility associated with this process dramatically change the share of the population that is elderly from the less than 5 percent characteristic of the early twentieth century to the more than 20 percent now observed in many OECD countries, a level that is projected to increase to nearly 40 percent within the next 50 years.

This rapidly growing old-age dependency ratio dramatically increases the burden imposed on successive generations to support the elderly. These changes in fertility and longevity occurred over a period of more than a century within the OECD countries enabling them to establish and maintain public social insurance systems based on direct transfers between generations. The post-World War II "baby boom" – the leading edge of which is now approaching old age – and the collapse of fertility levels in recent decades has now moved the ratio of elderly to working age from 1 to every 6–8 workers to levels approaching

1 to 3. However, the more rapid pace of industrialization in the modern global economy in conjunction with the associated transmission of medical technology, contraception and other factors has accelerated this demographic transition. This has resulted in today's developing countries "becoming old before they become rich," precluding their capacity to engage in the transitional stage in which PAYG systems could provide adequate benefits without imposing tax rates in excess of one third of workers' earnings that would distort behavior and hinder economic development.

Informal systems and individuals cannot be expected to fully address this challenge

Concurrent with industrialization has been a collapse of the informal intergenerational systems that support the elderly in traditional societies. Movement of workers to urban areas and the erosion of traditional family structures make multi-generational households the exception in industrial societies. Individuals are limited by their high discount rates, myopia and the inability to access and process relevant information to be able to compensate for the dissolution of traditional means of caring for the elderly. There is scant evidence of any systematic capacity of individuals in any society, on their own, to be able to effectively plan and manage savings and consumption decisions over the full life cycle. This should come as no surprise given the vagaries of human nature and the fact that even among the most skilled economists there is no consensus about how to effectively forecast earnings, manage individual risks and achieve an optimal pattern of savings and consumption over the lifetime. The rapidly emerging field of behavioral finance seems to confirm the perspective that even when provided with the appropriate information few individuals are capable of making rational decisions in this area.

Markets are unlikely to deliver the products required to support solely private or individual solutions

Similar (and undoubtedly closely related) to the experience with individual behavior there is scant evidence of markets' ability to deliver products that respond to the need for effective management of life-cycle savings and consumption without substantial public intervention. In addition to the limitations from the demand side, the provision of pension and annuity products face formidable structural challenges in the form of "moral hazard" and "free riding" in which individuals perceive that their failure to save will ultimately be addressed by a societal norm that finds poverty in old age to be unacceptable. In addition, "information asymmetries" and "adverse selection" problems, in which the buyers of products whose value is linked with mortality possess far more knowledge about their individual circumstances than the seller, limit the viability of market solutions. These lead to private annuity markets with prohibitive risk premiums.

Pension systems that seek to combine all three required elements in a dominant single component that is earnings based and publicly managed nearly always face insurmountable efficiency and distributional problems.

The earliest pension systems that emerged in European countries and quickly spread to the Americas sought to address these challenges by creating social insurance systems that provided income support in old age through earnings-based systems that transfer resources directly from current workers to the elderly, the "Bismarckian" PAYG model. While this has proven to be an effective approach during periods when the number of workers grew or remained relatively stable in proportion to the elderly, the reliance on this design faces an array of formidable challenges when faced with the degree of demographic transition nearly all countries will experience in the forthcoming decades.

These systems are able to deliver relatively high benefits to the early generations because they produce high cash flows in the initial periods. However, when they become mature, unless substantial reserves have been accumulated, the required tax rates will have to be rapidly increased imposing successively greater burdens on the following generations. This, however, becomes increasingly difficult in no small part because of the secondary consequences of high tax rates that distort labor markets by creating incentives for early withdrawals and informal labor to evade contributions. The more rapid pace of demographic change in today's developing countries that will increase the share of the elderly at four to five times the rate experienced in Western Europe makes this design even more problematic.

The analysis also finds distributional and equity issues arising from the design of many earnings-based systems. Benefits that are derived from reported earnings and linked to payroll taxes, while in principle seeming to provide direct linkages between earnings levels and benefits, often result in outcomes that redistribute in favor of higher income groups. This is due to the greater likelihood of higher income individuals to be engaged in the formal wage and salary sector and therefore to be covered by these systems and their lesser propensity to evade contributions when they are covered. Equally importantly it is because high earners tend to have a much greater probability of patterns of lifetime earnings (in contrast to the relatively flat patterns of lower income individuals) or to show significant spikes in reported earnings in the years just before retirement. Most earnings-based systems utilize relatively short reference wage periods in their benefit formulas (typically the highest three to five years or the years just before retirement) which provide significantly greater benefits in proportion to lifetime contributions for higher income individuals.

A central corollary to the economic critique is derived from observations about the political economy of a dominant earnings-based design. In this regard the 1994 report notes that:

Given their separation of benefits from contributions, their low initial costs that rise thereafter, and their complexity and non transparency, large earnings related pay-as-you-go public pillars are prone to pressure from influential groups. These groups want provisions that will benefit them, they want others to finance these benefits, and pay-as-you-go defined benefit schemes make it easy for them to introduce poor design features that accomplish this goal in the early years of the plan. In this political sense, the design features may be inherent – not incidental – and they come back to haunt the country in later years.[1]

3.2.3 The multi-pillar policy framework

To address these shortcomings *Averting the Old Age Crisis* proceeds from the diagnosis to propose the initial formulation of the multi-pillar design. A primary impetus for this approach was the perceived need to clearly distinguish the savings and consumption-smoothing objectives from the poverty and redistributive functions by separating

[1] World Bank, 1994, p. 237.

Table 3.1 *The pillars of old-age income security*

	Mandatory publicly managed	Mandatory privately managed	Voluntary
Objectives	Redistribution plus coinsurance	Savings plus coinsurance	Savings plus coinsurance
Form	Means tested, minimum pension guarantee, or flat pension	Personal savings plan or occupational plan	Personal savings plan or occupational plan
Financing	Tax financed	Regulated fully funded	Fully funded

these into two distinct mandatory "pillars" of the pension system. It was envisioned that these would fulfill the core social insurance functions and could then be supplemented by additional components to enable groups or individuals that had a particular need or willingness to accrue higher benefits levels to do this on a voluntary basis. This delineation of the two primary functions into separate institutions was also intended to provide transparency that would facilitate adjustments to their parameters so that they could be more easily constrained so as not to impose undue costs or distortions in behavior through their financing requirements. The expectation was that risk management and coinsurance functions (especially the pooling of management costs and mortality risk) would be distributed among all three of the elements.

This theoretical framework is summarized in the diagram from the report that delineates the objectives, form and financing of what were termed the "The Pillars of Old Age Income Security" shown in Table 3.1 above.[2]

This proposes to isolate the poverty alleviation and associated redistributive elements of the system into a publicly managed component that could be constructed in a variety of ways depending on objectives and prevailing conditions. One form this could take is an age-based flat pension available to all persons. Alternatively

[2] World Bank, 1994, p. 15.

it could be coordinated with the central pillar by establishing it as a means-tested minimum benefit that is offset in proportion to the value of benefits accrued in the individual savings or occupational pillars or as a minimum guaranteed level of pension income that would supplement the value of benefits accrued within the other components. The essential point of this approach is that by organizing this element of the system separately and clearly distinguishing it from the others any redistributive or minimum income objectives would be made explicit and transparent. This is intended to have the advantage of making the costs more predictable and constraining the potential for unintended or hidden redistribution in favor of higher income groups. Making this pillar the only element of the system with direct tax financing would limit the future fiscal exposure as well.

The most important innovation (at least in regard to prevailing practice) of this formulation, and certainly that which achieved the greatest notoriety, is the suggestion that, when the basic redistribution and poverty alleviation functions had been achieved through a tax-financed publicly managed program, the broader consumption smoothing and insurance functions are likely to be best achieved through individual savings or occupational arrangements that are privately managed. This perspective was largely derived from the critique of existing public earnings-based systems and the view that funded individual accounts would improve incentives and efficiency and achieve positive synergies with the development of capital markets that was assumed to create a "virtuous circle" that would support economic development. It is important of note that the report does not categorically reject the ability of other types of designs (including the traditional public PAYG approach) to achieve this function. It does, however, very strongly suggest that reliance in individual account design will result in fewer of the identified shortcomings of existing systems, especially in developing and middle-income settings.

3.2.4 The design of the middle pillar

The most controversial aspect of this policy framework was the suggestion that the choice of design of the middle pillar was likely to be between "personal savings plans and occupational pension plans set

up and run by employers"[3] a formulation that, in the perception of
many readers, implicitly excluded any role for earnings-based defined
benefit (DB) systems. The conflation of this presentation with the
statement that "earnings based benefits are a poor choice for the public pillar" (which was in fact a reference to the design of the first rather
than second pillar) led many to perceive the main policy message of
the report to be advising all countries to replace earnings-based public
systems with private individual savings accounts in the manner that
Chile had sought to do in the early 1980s.

Despite the prevalence of this perception among its critics, the
view that the central tenet of the World Bank's pension policy was to
replace all earnings-based benefit formulas and PAYG financing with
privately managed individual savings accounts represents an oversim-
plification that became almost a caricature. Despite the perception
of many, the 1994 report does not categorically reject the idea that
a well-designed and effectively managed PAYG or partially funded
earnings-based system could effectively fulfill the mix of consumption
smoothing and insurance functions of the middle pillar in the framework.[4] It does however point out in very strong terms how many of
these earning-based arrangements have, in practice, resulted in non-
transparent redistribution among income groups and between generations. It also argues in quite strong language that the result is that
most will be unable to remain fiscally sustainable over the long term.
Unfortunately, the simplified diagram shown above has contributed to
this perception because it does not include earnings-based PAYG systems in the examples for the second pillar. However, a full reading of
the text indicates that while this is not recommended for most settings
it is not fully excluded either.

The report contrasts the experience and what are deemed to be
inescapable characteristics of earnings-based systems with the perceived advantages of individual savings accounts. Primary among
these are the inherently tighter linkage between contributions and
benefits that limit the incentives for the manipulation of earnings
records or evasion and that remove many of the incentives for early
exit from the labor force which are also perceived to eliminate the

---

[3] World Bank, 1994, p. 18.
[4] For a discussion of misperceptions of the policy position espoused in the 1994
publication see the essay by its lead author (James, 2008).

potential for redistribution in favor of higher earners. The report argues that the perception of increased security of DB arrangements is illusory due to their vulnerability to prospective changes in benefit formulas that may subject participants to the vicissitudes of future political decisions. It is important to note that a considerable part of the skepticism about PAYG financing is not with the inherent nature of the design but instead with the assessment of the political risks associated with any government's capacity to deliver promised benefits when faced with the fiscal challenges of aging societies.

3.2.5 Occupational plans

Although the framework presents the design choices for the second pillar as including personal savings arrangements and occupational plans, based on the evidence reviewed on occupational plans, it articulates concerns about their ability to achieve the broader objectives of a pension system. Several advantages of occupational schemes are noted including the capacity to utilize payroll deductions that are potentially less distorting than social insurance contributions because they are not perceived as taxes and the capability to achieve low operating costs and access financial and managerial expertise in the private sector. It notes however that these advantages are largely offset by the inability of occupational plans to achieve broad coverage (especially in developing countries) and the perverse redistribution associated with the tax preferences afforded to these systems when they are voluntary and tend to cover only the upper segments of the income distribution. It also notes that the incentives for employers in these arrangements are to impose vesting restrictions and preclude portability of benefits thereby introducing limitations on labor mobility. It notes that occupational funds expose workers to the risks of underfunding and employer defaults concluding that "personal savings plans are probably preferable except for countries that already have substantial coverage under well functioning occupational schemes."[5]

Despite these reservations, a mandatory occupational plan paired with a flat benefit or means-tested tax-financed public scheme is

[5] World Bank, 1994, pp. 18, 248.

recommended as one possible combination for a multi-pillar system.[6] This however is coupled with the observation such a design would not offer the economies of scale of mandatory savings systems in which pension funds tend to be highly concentrated. Advocacy of occupational schemes is conditioned on the presence of a regulatory regime to address the prudential and insolvency risks and a design that makes benefits portable to avoid possible labor market distortions. The challenges of achieving these conditions in even the most developed economies, however, are noted as well, which contributes to the perceived bias in favor of individual savings accounts. A careful reading of the report however reveals that this is carefully couched in the observation that "personal savings plans would seem to have the edge" rather than an explicit recommendation.

On balance, what has come to be perceived by many as the main message of the early policy framework, an unambiguous endorsement of mandatory individual savings accounts, is in fact far more a critique of the manner in which public earnings-based DB systems have been operated rather than a complete repudiation of them. This is based primarily on skepticism about the capacity of governments to adhere to responsible policies and maintain these systems in a manner that does not impede economic efficiency through distortions in retirement behavior, excessive tax rates that distort labor markets and the risk of future default on benefit promises. When combined with what are perceived to be inherent advantages in all of these areas of the alternative design, *Averting the Old Age Crisis* presents very strong arguments in favor of mandatory individual savings accounts and (to a lesser degree) mandatory occupational plans, provided that either is linked to a mandatory first pillar designed to ensure that minimum poverty alleviation, insurance and consumption-smoothing functions are fulfilled. It does not however, as it is often characterized, promote individual savings arrangements to the exclusion of other designs.

3.2.6 Management of assets

The other major aspect of the policy framework is the view that decentralized private management of the assets of any saving (or partially funded DB) system offers a superior alternative to public management.

[6] World Bank, 1994, p. 248.

This position is derived from the evaluation of the record of the investment performance of provident funds and the reserves of partially funded arrangements. A review of these is shown to indicate that they have historically achieved low or negative real returns. This evidence is buttressed with the more theoretical view that private management would be less vulnerable to the direction of assets into government debt or low yielding instruments with potentially conflicting social or developmental objectives. It is also argued that private management creates positive synergies by developing "new financial institutions and deepening capital markets by mobilizing long-term savings and allocating it to the most productive uses, including uses in the private sector."[7] It also posits that privately managed funded systems will have some ability to increase overall rates of savings.

This conclusion leads to one of the strongest recommendations in the report (in addition to the need for the first two pillars to be mandatory) which concludes that as a general proposition, any funded pillar is best organized on the basis of decentralized private management. A very important qualification however is attached to this position, which is that there be both sufficient development and depth in the capital markets and that effective regulation of both the markets and any prospective pension system is required before private management should be considered. The report presents these largely as principles and does not go into depth to define the relevant enabling conditions or suggest any specific threshold to be reached before funding and private management becomes feasible.

3.2.7 Applying the principles

After setting out the diagnosis and suggested elements of the multi-pillar framework the report proceeds to address some key decisions in implementation. This section of the report notes that the relationship between the pillars and the key design choices within each pillar will vary considerably depending on the context in which a system is to operate. The primary distinction is in relation to the level of development of the country. This is illustrated by applying the principles to three settings: (1) young low-income economies; (2) young but rapidly aging economies; and (3) older economies with large public pillars.

[7] World Bank, 1994, p. 18.

For the first group of countries a greater initial emphasis on establishing the environment and regulatory infrastructure to support a mandatory savings pillar is suggested in conjunction with an effort to achieve poverty alleviation among the elderly through the development of social assistance programs that will reach the elderly poor. It is suggested that in these environments any contributory public system be operated on the basis of flat benefits and be introduced in conjunction with the phasing-out of centrally managed provident funds that are susceptible to poor investment performance and other types of abuse.

In the young but rapidly aging settings the recommendations are similar in regard to an immediate focus on developing the supporting institutional and regulatory framework for privately managed savings and seeking to implement this as rapidly as possible to preclude pressure from an emerging middle class to establish a dominant public earnings-related pillar with its attendant shortcomings. In the case of countries with already established public pension programs (which include OECD countries as well as others in Latin America and Central and Eastern Europe) the suggested path of reform is parametric adjustments to retirement age and benefit formulas to downsize the system concurrent with establishment of privately managed individual savings. A gradual process of reallocation of contributions in favor of the second pillar is proposed as the means of making this transition.

The overview of the report concludes with the often overlooked observation:

The right mix of pillars is not the same at all times and places. It depends on a country's objectives, history and current circumstances, particularly its emphasis on redistribution versus savings, its financial markets and its taxing and regulatory capability.[8]

3.3 Experience and refinement of the multi-pillar theme

3.3.1 New policy direction and experience with pension reforms

In the 16 years since the publication of *Averting the Old Age Crisis* and the considerable reaction that it engendered from both its supporters

---

[8] World Bank, 1994, p. 22.

as well as critics, the World Bank became involved in pension reforms in a wide range of settings. This experience (as well as the reaction to the earlier report) and continued research has motivated an ongoing reassessment, refinement and extension of the policy framework. A number of key issues and experiences have informed the evolution of thinking in this area. Some of the most important of these are described in this subsection:

The Social Risk Management (SRM) framework

The SRM was articulated as the conceptual foundation for the World Bank's first Social Protection Strategy in 2001 (World Bank, 2003) to guide its work on labor markets, social funds and social safety nets as well as pensions. The SRM posited that throughout their lives individuals face a range of risks and shocks, some of which are individualized or idiosyncratic and others that are systemic in nature. It proposed that social protection systems should be explicitly constructed in consideration of the nature of these risks and how they may vary for different groups and countries. This theoretical approach importantly notes that poor people and those in developing countries may face very different risks than others and emphasizes the importance of tailoring the various elements of any system to the particular characteristics and requirements of the relevant populations. It also sought to delineate between several types of risk management instruments and strategies, distinguishing between prevention, mitigation and coping strategies.

This conceptual paradigm moved the Bank's thinking on pension systems from the initial perspective that was largely oriented to considering the experience and expected overall outcomes associated with the various types of pension institutions toward an approach that introduced a risk assessment and management point of view into the policy framework. The practical result of this was to direct the thinking on pension systems towards a greater emphasis on evaluating differences in individual country circumstances and toward providing institutions and instruments that address the particular risk characteristics of the lifetime poor and those working in the informal sectors. The SRM approach was also used to sharpen consideration of the aggregate capacity of the pension system to reduce the risks in conjunction with other social protection instruments, the various combinations of individual characteristic and systemic risk that contribute to elderly poverty and how these differ in settings and among groups, the kinds of risk faced by earnings-based and funded pillars and the degree to which less than perfect correlation between these can improve benefit outcomes at equivalent costs. These concepts of diversification and risk management were interpreted to strengthen the argument in favor of the multi-pillar design but to move it towards a more complex formulation beyond the original three-pillar model.

The challenges of achieving positive synergies with capital market development and saving

An important premise supporting arguments in favor of a greater role for funded privately managed saving arrangements was that these would facilitate depth in the capital markets and create the demand for new types of financial instruments that would have positive development and growth effects (Holzmann, 1997; Davis and Hu, 2008). Although the advocacy of funded second pillars was conditioned on the presence of some minimal "pre-conditions" including banking and payment systems, there was an assumption that the demand for long-term and higher yielding investment instruments would be conducive to economic growth (Musalem and Tressel, 2003). The reality proved to be far more complex and challenging. In order to provide the perceived level of security necessary to support the reform of pension systems through the substitution of funded individual savings accounts for future benefits of unsustainable earnings-based systems, most of the new systems sought to manage investment risks in under-developed capital markets by requiring funds to invest in presumed safe government debt. This was an approach that, not coincidently, converged with the financing needs of many governments. In most cases the process of market development proved to be much more difficult and slower than the expectations that had been derived more from theory than experience. Although evidence of positive growth effects from a move to funded accounts has been asserted to have resulted in Chile and posited for other Latin American settings conclusive evidence in other environments proved to be elusive.[9] The funded systems proved to be far more vulnerable to the political exploitation and instability

---

[9] For a discussion of the positive effects in capital markets see Walker and Lefort (2002). For a more recent discussion of the issues and evidence that funded pensions do not have discernable growth effects see Zandberg and Spierdijk (2010).

that had formed the basis for some of the critique of the PAYG earnings pillars. Empirical evidence of improved national savings levels from funded systems proved to be difficult to confirm as well.

The difficulties in achieving the behavioral outcomes from expected incentives

A considerable impetus for the initial multi-pillar framework that included the strong endorsement of an individual savings account design was the view that the more direct linkage between contributions and benefits would diminish evasion of contributions, especially among younger workers, and limit distortions in labor markets. This was predicated on the idea that individuals would not perceive and respond to mandatory contributions to these accounts as a tax but rather treat them as personal savings. For a variety of reasons, however, the expected outcomes did not occur as anticipated. The Latin American countries that reformed their pension systems to incorporate individual accounts as a supplement or substitute to earnings-based systems experienced stagnant or in some cases diminished rates of coverage (Rofman and Luchetti, 2008). Although rates of switching some portion of contributions to individual accounts exceeded expectations in the Central and Eastern European countries that established funded second pillars (Whitehouse, 2006), overall participation and contributions continued to decline as many workers transitioned to the informal economy or found other means of evasion. The challenge of coverage became especially apparent in relation to the lifetime poor, many of whom did not participate in the formal economy at all, remaining fully outside of formal pension systems.

The simple structural change apparently did not alter the perception of many that any form of mandatory contributions constituted taxation. Strong skepticism remained regarding the security and ownership of funded system assets, a perception that was reinforced in many settings by requirements that the majority of assets be invested in government debt and the highly visible appropriation of pension fund assets in Argentina. The emerging field of behavioral economics research confirmed the seemingly irrational and short-term orientation of many individuals, especially in relation to life-cycle savings and consumption decisions. This challenged the assumptions about behavior change on which the endorsement of funded individual accounts was based.

The challenges of transition costs and administrative costs
Making the transition from a PAYG scheme to funded accounts without defaulting on the substantial (and unfunded) commitments of existing systems required countries to find a mechanism to fund transition costs without requiring the transition generations to pay twice, once to continue the benefits of the retired generation and again to fund their savings accounts. The approach utilized in Chile, issuing recognition bonds that delayed cash flows for accrued benefits to the future, proved to be far more difficult to achieve in countries without a similar strong fiscal position at the time of the reform. Countries seeking to fulfill stringent fiscal criteria for potential entry into the EU or to be able to continue to issue and service high levels of existing public debt found this to be an infeasible proposition that stymied efforts to design reforms making large transitions to the mandatory funded pillars. One solution that emerged was the Notional (or Non-Financial) Defined Contribution (NDC) design pioneered in the Swedish pension reform of the late 1990s which effectively created a PAYG individual account framework that linked outcomes to wage growth rather than capital market returns, effectively mimicking some key attributes of earnings-based systems with inherent controls on future spending.[10]

Early experience with mandatory funded accounts also indicated that keeping administrative expenses to a level that could achieve the efficiencies in outcomes that were expected proved to be a formidable challenge. Administrative (especially marketing) costs proved to be high in most settings and establishing regulatory ceilings seemed to result in most companies setting fees at the maximum level and competing for market share on non-financial factors. The hoped-for competition on price and investment performance did not materialize and most markets were characterized by high and increasing concentration (Impavido *et al.*, 2010).

Greater understanding of the importance of the political economy of reform
The initial policy framework was largely predicated on economic analysis and principles. However, pension reforms are inevitably implemented through a political process. This became especially important

---

[10] For a discussion of the emergence of NDC arrangements see World Bank (2006).

in the nascent democracies of Central and Eastern Europe that (in addition to Latin America) became the focus of pension reform efforts in the 1990s and early years of the new millennium. Experience with this process illuminated the path dependency of any reform process especially in regard to starting points and the capacity of interest groups in the pluralistic process to marshal political resources. This led to a greater consideration of the political economy of reform and the degree to which feasible system designs are equally a function of the unique political dynamics of a country as derived from economic theory, regardless of its elegance or correctness.[11]

3.3.2 *Extension of the multi-pillar framework* – Old Age Income Support in the 21st Century

Based on this experience and the lessons derived from it, an updated multi-pillar policy framework is articulated in the 2005 World Bank publication *Old Age Income Support in the 21st Century: An International Perspective on Pension Systems and Reform* that was produced by a team from the various units of the Bank that had been involved in the development of the earlier framework and the subsequent pension reform work.

This new report incorporates an extension and some refinements of the original multi-pillar framework. Most fundamentally it extends it from three to five pillars. The original first pillar, that is broadly construed to include a range of systems including a non-contributory pension that might go to all persons above a certain age as well as means-tested benefits for the elderly or is somewhat more narrowly specified to have a greater focus on poverty alleviation. It is suggested that this basic pillar be directed to meeting the needs of the lifetime poor or groups with very low likelihood of participation in the earnings-based or individual savings components. This narrower version of the original first pillar was designated as a "zero pillar."

Most importantly, the new framework splits the original second-pillar concept into two parts that are now relabeled as the first and second pillar. This is intended to address the widespread perception that the original formulation excluded the possibility of an earnings-based

---

[11] For a discussion of political economy issues and experience informing the World Bank's perspective see Holzmann *et al.* (2003).

PAYG or partially funded arrangement. This potential for a traditional earnings-based DB element is now explicitly formulated as the new first pillar rather than left as an implicit (though discouraged in most settings) possibility for the earlier second pillar.

More significantly, the revised framework seeks to better differentiate the functions of the pension system among the various pillars by separating what had been overlapping objectives of poverty alleviation and consumption smoothing spread across the first two original pillars by more specifically differentiating these among the first three components of the new framework. This was an effort to both separate the functions and emphasize the importance of evaluating how each of the elements of the multi-pillar system would manage distinctive risks and perform the more clearly distinguished functions. It was also motivated by an effort to move away from the perception that the earlier approach was focused on the structure of the system (proposing individual private accounts to the exclusion of publicly managed earnings-based systems) rather than consideration of the outcomes in terms of risk management and benefit delivery.

This policy formulation also incorporates an increased emphasis on individual country conditions to address the perception that the earlier framework was prescribing a similar design for most countries. It emphasizes the importance of inherited systems in establishing both the motivation for reform and the constraints on feasible reform options and the importance of the enabling environment in determining feasible options. The new framework focuses on identifying the core objectives of country pension systems and considering broader questions of social protection and social policy towards the poor in designing an effective pension system. It is focused on the capacity of systems to align their components with the relevant risks associated with various elements of the population and manage these risks more efficiently through diversification among the various pillars. It suggests that choices and combinations among the pillars will differ widely among countries with optimal combinations derived from the evaluation of the starting point and varying priorities. It is less oriented to the critique of the limitations of dominant earnings-based pillars or the inherent advantages of funding and private management while maintaining the position that in most cases the goals of a pension system are likely best met through some elements of pre-funding. It suggests that funded privately managed systems should be a "benchmark not a blueprint" in considering reforms, suggesting that options can be evaluated in relation to a fully pre-funded individual account to illustrate choices in dynamics and outcomes.

The 2005 report also seeks to incorporate new experience and designs into the possibilities for the design of the various pillars. Most important among these is the endorsement of the NDC systems originating in the Swedish pension reforms of the 1990s that rapidly spread to countries in Central and Eastern Europe. The new framework specifically includes these as a possible design for a mandatory first pillar. The NDC design is presented as an approach that embodies the effort to move beyond existing structures to designs that achieve the desired functions and fiscal sustainability. The NDC design is included because it is able to incorporate automatic adjustment mechanisms (such as cohort-specific annuity conversions) that facilitate sustainability without requiring political interventions, more directly links financing and benefit through the DC design and choice of crediting factors yet operates primarily on a PAYG basis that manages a large part of the challenges of transition costs.

The five element multi-pillar framework is presented in the overview published in 2008 (Holzmann *et al.*, 2008) as:

(1) A *non-contributory "zero pillar"* that extends some level of old-age income security to all of the elderly where social conditions warrant and fiscal circumstances can sustain such a system.
(2) An *appropriately sized mandatory "first pillar"* with the objective of replacing some portion of lifetime pre-retirement income through contributions linked to earnings, and which is either partially funded or financed on a PAYG basis.
(3) A *funded mandatory defined-contribution "second pillar"* that typically provides privately managed individual savings accounts establishing a clear linkage between contributions, investment performance and benefits, supported by enforceable property rights and which may be supportive of financial market development.
(4) A *funded voluntary "third pillar"* taking many forms.
(5) A *non-financial "fourth pillar"* that includes access to informal support such as from families, other formal social programs such as health and housing, and individual assets.

This approach to evaluating a pension system design seeks to focus on the overall outcomes that result from the pension system rather than the characteristics of any of the individual elements. To do this it establishes an analytical framework for the evaluation of the system that distinguishes between a few primary and some additional secondary criteria.

The primary criteria are:

(1) *Adequacy*, ability of the system to provide benefits sufficient to prevent old-age poverty (at a country-specific absolute level) to the full breadth of the population in addition to providing a reliable means to smooth lifetime consumption for the vast majority of the population.
(2) *Affordability*, the ability to remain within the financing capacity of individuals and the society without unduly displacing other social or displacing economic imperatives or having untenable fiscal consequences.
(3) *Sustainability*, the feasibility for the system to remain financially sound and be maintained over a foreseeable horizon under a broad set of reasonable assumptions.
(4) *Robustness*, the capacity to withstand major shocks, including those coming from economic, demographic and political volatility.

In addition to the primary criteria some secondary evaluation criteria related to the ability of the pension system to contribute to output and growth are incorporated into the framework. These include the capacity to: (1) minimize labor market distortions; (2) contribute to savings mobilization; and (3) to support financial market development. A central tenet of the approach is the view that because pension benefits are claims against future economic output, it is essential that, over time, pension systems contribute to growth and output to support the promised benefits.

The updated policy framework is summarized in Table 3.2 below.

3.4 The pension system of the Netherlands in the context of the World Bank's multi-pillar model

Originating in 1832 with the establishment of a pension fund for civil servants (now one of the largest pension funds in existence) and later expanded to include some of the first occupational schemes in the early twentieth century, the pension system in the Netherlands is one of the oldest and most well established. The current form of the system

Table 3.2 *Summary of the updated policy framework*

Initial conditions	*I. Inherited system* • Elderly vulnerability and poverty prevalence in absolute terms and relative to other age groups • Existing mandatory and voluntary pension systems • Existing social security schemes • Existing levels of family and community support *II. Reform needs* – such as modifying existing schemes in the face of fiscal unsustainability, coverage gaps, aging and socio-economic changes assessed against the primary and secondary evaluation criteria below *III. Enabling environment* • Demographic profile • Macroeconomic environment • Institutional capacity • Financial market status
Core objectives of pension systems	• Protection against the risk of poverty in old age • Consumption smoothing from work to retirement
Modalities for achieving objectives	• *Zero pillar* – non-contributory social assistance financed by the state, fiscal conditions permitting • *First pillar* – mandatory with contributions linked to earnings and objective of replacing some portion of lifetime pre-retirement income • *Second pillar* – mandatory DC plan with independent investment management • *Third pillar* – voluntary taking many forms (e.g., individual savings; employer sponsored; DB or DC) • *Fourth pillar* – informal support (such as family), other formal social programs (such as health care or housing) and other individual assets (such as home ownership and reverse mortgages)
Primary evaluation criteria	• Adequacy • Affordability • Sustainability • Robustness
Secondary evaluation criteria	• Contribution to output and growth through: • Lowering labor market distortions • Contributing to savings • Contribution to financial market development

largely takes its shape from legislation enacted in the 1950s, nearly two generations before the initial articulation of the multi-pillar policy framework by the World Bank. The Dutch system, however, has many attributes that bear close resemblance to the organization and operating characteristics that are set out in both versions of the World Bank's multi-pillar model and, as noted in the early publications, it provided an example that motivated the concept. The following section provides a brief analysis of the extent to which the current system in the Netherlands may be perceived as fulfilling the objectives of this design and policy framework.

3.4.1 *The organization of the Dutch pension system*

Although, as discussed previously, it is largely a misconception to view even the earliest presentations of the multi-pillar approach as primarily structural in their approach, it is nevertheless useful to consider the Dutch system initially from the perspective of its overall organization in relation to the multi-pillar model.

The foundation of the system is a mandatory first pillar established in 1957, the *Algemene Ouderdomswet* that is more commonly known by the acronym AOW. This provides a basic pension to all citizens reaching the age of 65 that is designed to deliver a minimum flat benefit equivalent to 70 percent of the minimum wage to all persons who have been residents of the country for 50 years before the age of eligibility. The value of the benefit is reduced by 2 percent for each year of non-residency below this minimum threshold. Persons with insufficient residence history are eligible for other sources of social assistance on a means-tested basis. No distinctions are made for eligibility or benefit levels on the basis of gender, occupation or work history; there are no means tests for eligibility or any offsets for other sources of income. This basic pension is financed through an earnings-based contribution. However, persons with no earnings do not pay the contribution but remain eligible for benefits. The AOW is administered through a public agency, the *Sociale Verzekeringsbank* (SVB), the Social Insurance Bank.

The second pillar of the Dutch system is an extensive program of occupational funds that has achieved one of the highest coverage rates of any supplementary pension system in the world at a level that exceeds 90 percent of the working population. This is comprised of three types of funds, company-specific pension funds, industry-wide funds and pension funds operated by professional organizations for the self-employed. In addition, insurance providers manage group insurance products for some individual employers. While the vast majority of the funds are individual company funds the industry-wide funds cover about 85 percent of members with a proportional share of the assets. The pension funds take the legal form of foundations that are governed by independent boards with representatives of employers and employees through the trade unions. Nearly all of the funds are organized as DB arrangements that target income replacement rates of 70–80 percent with the benefits fully integrated with the basic pension through an offset to the value of the occupational funds target benefit equal to the value of the so-called *AOW franchise*. Over the past decade the majority of the funds have evolved to what has been termed a "hybrid" DB form, in which post-retirement benefit indexation has become conditioned on the value of funding levels making it effectively a function of investment performance. Benefits are required to be pre-funded based on specific standards that are linked to accruals and investment performance. No specific floors on asset classes are imposed and considerable latitude is afforded in investment strategies that are regulated through a comprehensive set of risk-based standards finalized in 2007.[12] The system is supervised by a public agency, the De Nederlandsche Bank (DNB), pursuant to a comprehensive legal framework.

This form of a second pillar is well aligned with the initial formulation of the multi-pillar framework. The earnings-based benefit formulas are explicitly designed to achieve consumption smoothing and function through a collective model that pools risks and supplements the basic pension. The DB structure, annuity form of pay-outs and the organization primarily on an industry-wide basis provide the envisioned insurance and risk pooling functions by spreading mortality and investment risks across broad populations. The funds are organized as decentralized and privately managed entities that are subject to a well-developed regulatory and supervisory regime. The assets of the funds are held in well-diversified portfolios on a large scale that operate at low costs relative to what is observed in many other countries (Bikker and de Dreu, 2006). These are constituted as separate

---

[12] For an overview of the risk-based supervision see Hinz and van Dam (2008).

entities and assets are fully segregated from the sponsoring employers, a form that inherently separates insolvency risk from other labor-related risks.

Benefit promises are pre-funded and fully permitted to be invested in private markets thereby facilitating market development and depth and potentially enhancing national savings levels. Although the system is ostensibly voluntary, Dutch labor law can impose a requirement for all employers in an industry to provide coverage if more than 60 percent of the workers in an industrial branch participate in an industry-wide fund, a requirement that effectively makes the system mandatory for a large share of the workforce. The high coverage in industry-wide funds which by design create the portability of benefits at least within industries and the sharing of contributions between individual workers and employers address the concerns about labor market distortions.

The third pillar is a variety of individual products sold at the retail level on a voluntary basis. These may be either annuity or savings products that are supervised also by the DNB. This part of the system has been relatively small historically although it began to grow rapidly in the late 1990s and is now taking on greater significance, although the assets backing these products have been estimated to be less than one tenth of those of the occupational funds. These pension savings are afforded a consumption tax treatment in which taxes are deferred on contributions and investment earnings and benefit payments are taxed as income. The amount of income that can be shielded from taxes in this manner is subject to some limitations to ensure that these do not become a means of tax avoidance by higher income persons.

3.4.2 The structure of the Dutch system in relation to the World Bank multi-pillar framework

Overall the structure of the Dutch pension system is very consistent with the principles of the multi-pillar model. It is a system with several distinctive separate elements that perform well-defined functions and includes all three of the components of the original three pillars. There is far greater room for interpretation of the form in relation to the later five-pillar formulation. In general, the AOW can be construed to fulfill the role of the "zero" pillar. The quasi-mandatory occupational funds are consistent with the role of the main middle pillar (second in the three-pillar model or first in the five-pillar construct. The fourth and fifth pillars are provided in the form of voluntary pension-specific savings products and residual informal family and community-based support for the elderly.

The first pillar is closely aligned with recommendations of the World Bank's framework for the basic pillar. It is a publicly managed program that provides a guaranteed minimum level of income through a flat benefit to all persons reaching a specified age. In contrast to the suggestion that this pillar be tax financed, the AOW is funded through an earmarked earnings-based contribution rather than general taxation. This somewhat limits redistribution although to a significant degree this is muted by the absence of linkages between contributions and benefit levels giving it far more the character of tax financing in outcomes if not form. The financing potentially has a mixed character that may emerge in the near future as the contribution is limited to a fixed levy on earnings with any deficits payable from general revenues. It operates primarily on a PAYG basis and therefore does not seek to accumulate large reserves. The limited reserves that are accumulated are invested solely in government debt. This avoids the challenges of public management of assets that is identified as one of the key shortcomings of public systems.

It is managed separately from the other pillars and as the occupational system matures it increasingly distinguishes the objectives of poverty protection and minimum income support from a more general goal of consumption smoothing. It is more consistent with the mixed consumption smoothing and poverty alleviation role of the original three-part formulation because benefits are paid to all who meet the qualifying conditions without regard to need and is typically integrated with benefits from the occupational DB systems to achieve income replacement targets.

Participation is mandatory and it is designed to perform redistribution and reinsurance functions that are explicit and relatively transparent. The accrual of rights and payment of benefits are clearly defined and (through the formula derived from the minimum wage) indirectly but likely to be closely linked to the minimum income and poverty alleviation objectives. It largely functions in a manner that does not require political interventions in the pension system provided that the minimum wage level is adjusted periodically in a consistent manner. It clearly fulfills the overall objective of limiting fiscal exposure through a clearly defined and universally available benefit with earmarked financing and is not readily vulnerable to manipulation for political purposes.

The AOW, however, deviates somewhat from the principles of the envisaged or zero pillar in several respects. The scope is relatively large, currently on the order of 30 percent of the income of the elderly. This is more in line with what is envisioned in the earlier formulation that anticipates a mix of consumption smoothing and poverty alleviation functions rather than the later concept that is oriented towards separating these functions. The scope of the AOW is more in line with what would be anticipated in a developing or middle-income setting during a transitional phase in which formal wage-based employment is becoming more widespread and the capacity for an earnings-based system is just emerging rather than a country with a well-established occupational system. Although the relative role of this basic pillar continues to diminish (declining to half the share of retirement income than in earlier decades as the occupational system reaches full maturity) until it is means tested or otherwise more targeted to poverty alleviation it maintains somewhat of a different character than the envisioned "zero pillar."

The linkage of the benefit formula to the minimum wage rather than to a consumption price or poverty index also raises some issues of potential redistribution and transparency. If the benefit is manipulated through ad hoc supplements and adjustments (as has occurred since 2005) the nature and objectives of this pillar become less distinct and transparent. Moreover, if the minimum wage moves in a manner that no longer makes it a consistent proxy for poverty prevention, for example if overall wage levels change in response to a decline in the size of the future labor force (a distinct possibility given current demographic trends) or the demand for low-wage labor declines through structural changes, a variety of relatively non-transparent types of redistribution can result. Rather than being fully consistent with the delineations of the Bank's model, the AOW and the occupational system together (because they are explicitly integrated and have nearly full coverage) have the character of a very robust version of an earnings-based first pillar that is universal and therefore obviates the necessity for a zero pillar. This is not inconsistent with the objectives but differs in form. Most importantly it does not achieve the same degree of transparency in redistribution that is a key objective of the World Bank framework.

Consideration of the system of occupational funds within the five-pillar model is more complex. This element of the system includes some characteristics of the earnings-based pillar through the DB formulas that are linked to earnings records and the fact that it is effectively mandatory. It also incorporates elements of the suggested second pillar through relatively strictly controlled pre-funding, private management and the conditional nature of benefits that partially links benefit obligations to investment outcomes. In this regard it can perhaps best be interpreted as a combination of the first and second pillars falling somewhere in between without meeting the full specifications of either, a sort of pillar one and one half.

An alternative perspective might perceive the combination of the AOW and occupational funds as jointly encompassing the functions of pillars one through three in the five-part model. The integration of the benefit formula with the AOW to provide a relatively high share of income replacement for the lower half of the income distribution achieves essentially the same outcome as a basic pension in combination with a publicly managed DB arrangement that is supplemented by widespread occupational plans that produce similar rates of income replacement for higher earnings groups. The conditional indexation of benefits that has become the norm mimics some of the results of savings arrangements by linking benefits to some degree with portfolio performance although this remains indirect and entails highly variable outcomes for different groups as discussed below. The main difference from this perspective is the degree of collectivization of risks. The current Dutch system only partially imposes the more individualized exposure to investment risks of personal savings accounts. While this is certainly a design that is reflective of inherited conditions and societal norms, whether it results in more effective risk management or the imposition of common outcomes on individuals who may have highly diverse preferences and utility is a matter of perspective as well.[13]

Overall the structure of the system can be perceived to be very consistent with fulfilling the basic functions of poverty alleviation, redistribution and consumption smoothing with instruments that separate these functions and operate in a relatively (at least compared to most other systems) transparent manner. It includes a universal basic

---

[13] For a discussion of the limitations on individual utility imposed by collective pension funds see Bovenberg *et al.* (2007).

pension and effectively mandates participation. The system cleanly distinguishes between public and private management, avoiding the pitfalls of public control over assets. It facilitates market development with relatively unconstrained parameters in regards to asset types and assigns investment management to the private sector where it is efficiently performed. The organization of the pension funds as independent foundations with required representation by workers and employers provides a governance structure that is representative of the interests and residual claims of the various stakeholders, although one that leaves retirees potentially unrepresented. The large scale in which the funds are organized achieves the scale efficiencies and risk management capacity that are envisaged in the model.

Where the structure of the system may be seen to fall short of the ideals espoused in the multi-pillar approach is in the relative balance among the three pillars. The high income replacement rates in the middle pillars leave little space for voluntary components. The mandatory pillars consequently require high contributions by employers who are estimated to pay 70–80 percent of the contributions. This creates some distortions within labor markets as there is likely not a full incidence of costs especially for older workers. These contributions fall evenly across the life cycle of workers so effectively mandating a very high replacement rate imposes homogeneous savings rates at all ages which is certainly suboptimal in theory and does not easily accommodate variation in individual preferences.

The two areas of greatest divergence from the theoretical framework are in the structure of the benefits and the potential for redistribution. The system is nearly entirely directed to the payment of benefits in the form of lifetime annuities. The overall scope of the system aspires to provide essentially full consumption replacement requiring high contribution levels thereby crowding out other forms of retirement saving for most participants. This leads to undiversified portfolios that are inefficient on an individual level (see Chapter 10) and leads to a large portion of wealth invested in the relatively homogeneous portfolios of the large collective pension funds. This is inconsistent with the principle behind the multi-pillar model and the preference for a significant reliance on individual savings accounts to accommodate variations in utility preferences among individuals. It also, due to the very strict solvency standards and absence of a residual risk-bearing sponsor of occupational funds, limits portfolio composition that may constrain diversity and innovation in financial markets. The greatest divergence from the model, as discussed below, is related to the level and transparency of redistribution that results from the design.

3.4.3 The Dutch system in relation to the evaluation criteria

The multi-pillar framework is derived from concerns about fiscal sustainability, equity and transparency of redistribution. The reformulation of the model presented in 2005 further develops these principles by suggesting that systems should be evaluated through analysis of the degree the overall pension system is aligned with country-specific conditions in relation to the (a) enabling environment, (b) inherited programs and institutions and (c) the prevailing political economy and societal values.

It proposes primary evaluation criteria of (a) adequacy, (b) affordability, (c) sustainability, (d) robustness and secondary consideration of how well the system contributes to output and growth through (a) lowering labor market distortions, (b) contributing to savings and (c) contributing to financial market development. The Dutch system is considered in relation to these standards and criteria in the section that follows.

Enabling environment
The heavy reliance on pre-funding through private asset management and the flexible functionally oriented (as opposed to the more prevalent rules based) nature of the regulatory and supervisory approach is reflective of deep and sophisticated financial markets. The innovative risk-based regulatory system that enables individual funds to tailor investment strategies to their particular circumstances effectively exploits the depth of financial markets and products and the high capacity of Dutch financial institutions, a strong rule of law and a high level of supervisory capability. The solvency standards and risk buffer requirements (the *Financieel Toetsings Kader*, usually referred to as FTK, that had its origin in actuarial standards imposed in 1997 and later developed in much greater depth becoming fully effective in 2007) utilize market valuations, market-derived discount rates and sophisticated assumptions about patterns of asset performance and correlation matrices to establish funding standards that allow full flexibility and innovation in investments. This flexibility and the

potential to achieve highly efficient results are reflective of the analytical capacity of the industry and take advantage of the sophistication
and depth of the capital markets. There is however some evidence that
pension funds do not take full advantage of the potential of the capital
markets found in a recent study indicating that the small and medium-
sized funds exhibit a variety of potentially suboptimal choices in asset
allocation and diversification leading to low-risk lower return strategies (de Dreu and Bikker, 2009).

Inherited institutions, political economy and social norms

The system is the result of an extension of existing programs and legal
foundations, gradually emerging over more than a century from coverage of civil servants and voluntary occupation programs to include
a universal basic pension and nearly universal occupational-based
coverage. The effectively mandatory coverage of the occupational system has its origins more than 50 years ago and has developed over
the ensuing decades consistent with a policy framework reflective of
the political and social context (Omtzigt, 2007). The level of benefits
that are guaranteed, while potentially imposing some efficiency constraints as discussed above, seems to be reflective of societal norms
that emphasize security, consistency and solidarity over efficiency and
wealth optimization. The governance of the pension funds is well
aligned with the Dutch political environment reflecting the tradition
of governing through consensus and participation of the "social partners" in cooperation with industry representatives.

Adequacy

Certainly one of the strongest attributes of the system has been its
ability to deliver very high income rates. The targeted benefit levels of
70–80 percent replacement of final pay for a full career worker from
what is effectively a mandatory system for wage and salary workers
are among the highest mandated benefit levels of any country and are
consistent with what analysts generally assume is required to maintain individual consumption levels in retirement. Assuming that the
Netherlands maintains the hump-shaped age earnings patterns characteristic of developed countries this should support consumption in old
age at a level that would remain near or above the lifetime average. The
nearly full transition from final pay to career average benefit formulas
over the last decade will likely bring initial income replacement rates

down somewhat in the future. However, the pension funds have compensated for the longer (and therefore lower) reference wage periods by targeting 80 percent of indexed lifetime average rather than the previous 70 percent of final pay. The presence of the AOW that guarantees a benefit of 70 percent of the minimum wage and the accessibility of other forms of social assistance provides a social safety net for the elderly that provides effective poverty alleviation.

Where the system potentially faces challenges in the future in regard to adequacy of benefits is in the impact of the new conditional indexation design which may reduce the real value of retirees' benefits to achieve short-term solvency of funds when returns in the capital markets are low. Under certain conditions, for example a return to the "stagflation" of the 1970s and early 1980s, the formulas that limit indexation to stay within the solvency framework of the FTK could, over an extended period, have a serious effect on the capacity of the system to sustain consumption at the targeted levels. The vulnerability to adequacy concerns in the future arises from the dual "steering" mechanism in the current regulatory structure that permits a choice between contribution increases and reductions in benefit indexation to revert pensions to the quite strict (by international standards) solvency requirement. The organization of the pensions funds as independent bodies with few having specific obligations by sponsoring employers to increase contribution levels creates a significant degree of vulnerability to future benefit reductions. Thus far sponsors have been willing to raise contributions to compensate for much of the adverse experience in the markets which has precluded the need for dramatic benefit cuts. Required contributions to fulfill the solvency standards have increased by approximately 50 percent over the last decade and there is no assurance that this will be feasible over the long run when the pressures from population aging become more acute.

Another area of concern is the crowding out of voluntary retirement savings by the high benefit levels. The market for voluntary products is relatively small in the Netherlands which will make it more difficult to achieve low management costs and diminish the pool of lives over which mortality risk is spread resulting in costs in the private insurance sector that are far higher than those of the collective pension funds (Bikker and de Dreu, 2007). This potentially threatens the ability of the system to provide effective venues for pension savings to the

self-employed or other informal sector workers who fall outside of the
occupational plans.

Affordability/sustainability

The generous benefits impose some challenges in regard to long-term
affordability. From a narrow public fiscal perspective the Netherlands
receives relatively high marks in regard to affordability. The publicly
financed benefits now represent about one third of overall benefit payments which is relatively high for comparable countries. The financing
of public benefits is income based so has some, albeit indirect, linkage
to the benefit formula that is self-adjusting. The basic pension (AOW)
however is beginning to show some signs of strain as expenditures
are likely to soon exceed income because of the statutory cap on the
contribution level. The accelerating demographic transition will no
doubt exacerbate the problems with the solvency of public benefits
(van Ewijk *et al.*, 2006).

Sustainability of the current benefit promises in the occupational
funds however has emerged as perhaps the most significant concern
for the Dutch pension system as the impact of the two financial crises
of the past decade have worked their way through the system. On the
positive side of the ledger, unlike nearly all other mandatory pension
systems the occupational funds in the Netherlands have virtually no
unfunded pension debt on a current basis and now hold assets that
are among the highest proportions of GDP in the world. The buffers
required under the FTK target surplus funding levels that should be
on the order of 25 percent of the present value of the liabilities with
funding deficiencies required to be made up over the very short period
of three years and funding buffers restored in 15 years.

However, the FTK framework requires the funding of future benefit obligations on a nominal basis which significantly understates the
level of their obligations. The funding level on an indexed basis is
estimated to be only about 70 percent at present. The Goudswaard
Committee report notes that pension contribution rates would have to
rise from the current 13 percent of the wage bill to 17 percent in the
next 15 years to fulfill the current "ambitions" of the system, raising
serious concerns regarding the long-term financial sustainability of a
system that is reliant on negotiated level rates of contributions by the
sponsors. It is important to note that while daunting to a system that
aspires to full funding these projected deficiencies are likely well below

those of other large occupational DB systems in countries like the US and UK.

The main problems of affordability and adequacy for the system is identified in the reports of the two recent government committees (known by the names of the Chairs as the Goudswaard and Frijns Committees) is the absence of a comprehensive approach to addressing increases in life expectancy that have consistently proven to be above the anticipated levels. Currently neither the AOW nor occupational funds incorporate adjustments in their benefit levels to reflect the longer period in retirement of current and future cohorts. Resolving this will require either significantly increasing contributions, which is inherently difficult given the way in which the system is structured, or significant reductions in benefit levels for future retirees.

The Social Partners "Pension Accord" issued in the spring of 2010 recognizes this challenge and proposes increasing retirement ages or reducing benefits to align lifetime contributions with aggregate benefits received when life expectancy increases in order to stabilize future contribution requirements.[14] This would move the system that is already conditioning post-retirement indexation to asset performance a step closer to the NDC model that translates account "balances" into annuity payment on the basis of cohort-specific longevity projections. The 2010 Accord proposes that similar changes to periodically adjust the AOW in line with life expectancy gains be made. While enhancing future affordability and intergenerational equity these changes would achieve this through diminished benefit levels. Given the already high level of benefits promised by the two parts of the system such changes are unlikely to severely threaten overall benefit adequacy in the near term and might actually induce a better balance of voluntary savings.

Robustness

The capacity of the Dutch system to remain robust in the face of economic volatility remains one of the principal challenges for the future. The development of the "risk based" approach to supervision by the DNB in which oversight and remedial interventions are aligned with a comprehensive assessment of management capabilities and financial risk is a leading example of innovation in this area that promises to

---

[14] Stichting van de Arbeid "Pension Accord Spring 2010," June 4, 2010.

contribute to the long-term stability of the system. The related requirements that every fund have a fully developed risk management process
and the very specific standards related to the governance of the funds
that are further strengthened in the new legislation effective in 2007
will likely make the funds more responsive and resilient to stress in the
future. Basing the FTK standards on nominal benefits and the manner
in which they are calculated which does not fully address the risks are
also noted as challenges to the capacity of the system to retain solvency when faced with the kinds of volatility in financial markets of the
past decade.

The recently imposed solvency standards contained in the FTK
are likely to be more complex in their impact. These will surely
impose rapid responses to market volatility in quickly imposing
requirements to restore funding to nominal levels when markets are
disrupted. The longer-term impact however is likely to be more complex. Imposing high funding buffers that are based on current market
valuations and discount rates in conjunction with the requirement
for quick recovery periods when these fall below minimum thresholds may direct portfolios into more conservative allocations that
are unable to support the high benefit promises. Sponsors' willingness to absorb losses in asset values through higher contributions
to the extent that has occurred in the past decade may not continue in the future which will limit the resiliency of the system to
future volatility in the financial markets. Most consequential however is that the finding standards are based on nominal benefits and
therefore do not recognize the aspirations or "soft benefit claims" of
post-retirement inflation indexation. This severely compromises the
robustness of the system from the perspective of expectations.

3.4.4 Transparency and redistribution

Perhaps the strongest divergence of the Dutch system from the World
Bank's model is in the transparency and scope of redistribution that
occurs within the occupational funds. As discussed earlier, in addition
to enhancing fiscal probity, the primary motivation behind the multi-
pillar model is to make redistribution explicit and transparent through
separate instruments that have readily distinguishable characteristics.
The emphasis on the use of a DC individual account second pillar to

perform consumption smoothing is based on the fact that there is only minimal potential for redistribution of any sort.

The occupational funds in the Netherlands, however, have evolved to create the potential for considerable redistribution that is likely to be hidden from participants and to a significant degree inadvertent. Redistribution is always a challenge in any earnings-based DB system which is one of the main reasons that the initial presentation of the policy framework expressed such strong skepticism about the ability of DB systems to achieve equitable outcomes. There are two primary aspects of the system that particularly contribute to this problem, the "level" contribution and accrual rates that do not distinguish by age, gender or other characteristics and the recent movement to hybrid arrangements (motivated by the tight solvency standards of the FTK) that either adjust contribution levels or reduce indexation of benefits to rapidly bring funds within the stringent solvency corridors. Secondary sources of redistribution originate in the tax treatment of pension funds and the investment portfolios that the risk-based regulatory structure may direct the pension funds to adopt.

The level premium structure of the funds charges each member the same annual rate regardless of characteristics that lead to meaningful differences in the value of annual benefit accruals. This uniform pricing structure redistributes value from persons with short life expectancy to those with longer life expectancy and from those with more rapid rates of income growth over their lifetime to those who exhibit flat or declining earnings patterns. The practical result is that, like any similar DB schemes, the Dutch occupational funds transfer value from men to women and from less educated lower income workers to more educated higher income workers (Bonenkamp, 2007). Similarly the equal premiums for all covered members results in a transfer from those with short working careers who may depart from coverage early in their lives and later receive benefits based on salary levels that are low compared with even average lifetime earnings (Aarssen and Kuipers, 2007).

The earnings-linked DB structure of the systems inevitably results in the "back loading" of the accruals in which later years of participation become credited in relation to many preceding years of service and have a much higher present value through the closer proximity to the receipt of the payment at retirement (Bovenberg and Nijman, 2009). This results in a potentially large and non-transparent transfer of value from younger to older workers, an outcome that is facilitated by the industry-wide organization of the funds. In a single employer DB arrangement the cost differential might be adjusted through wage offsets for older employees who value the benefit and have incentives to remain with an employer. The employer contributing to the collectively managed fund has no similar means or incentive to make this adjustment simply by paying a per capita rate. None of this redistribution is readily apparent or can be easily calculated by members and is not likely to be understood by most even if they are made aware. The scope of the redistribution for any member is contingent on a variety of individualized factors and cannot, even in the aggregate, be reliably estimated by pension experts. The nominal liabilities of retirees, that are settled first, are required to be fully funded. The younger workers therefore are bearing considerable risks on behalf of the retirees. This however is obscured by the complex and difficult to quantify nature of this relationship and the conditional nature of indexation for retirees. This complex array of structural redistribution under the rubric of "solidarity" has been diminished somewhat by the transition from final pay to career average benefit formulas as a cost-saving measure over the past decade but nevertheless remains substantial, representing a material departure from a central objective of the multi-pillar design.

Somewhat more transparent and perhaps better intuitively understood by individuals is the redistribution resulting from the introduction of conditional indexation of benefits that has accompanied the concurrent imposition of the FTK funding standards, tight recovery periods and the dual financial crises in the first decade of the new century. The change to conditional indexation creates a complex pattern of gainers and losers depending on the age of members (Ponds and van Riel, 2007). The significant "buffer" funding requirements and short recovery periods may lead funds to increase contributions resulting in a transfer in favor of retirees or to reduce current indexation in favor of restoring funding levels without altering contributions, potentially preserving the capacity for future indexation and creating transfers in the other direction. Therefore decisions made by the pension fund can create complex reallocation of value depending on the response to a shock to the value of assets or movement of interest rates that will trigger a similar result from revaluing liabilities (Bonenkamp *et al.*, 2007).

Similar forms of nearly invisible redistribution result from the secondary consequences of the funding standards and contemplation of governing bodies of facing difficult decisions regarding choices between "catch-up contributions" or reneging on aspirations for benefit indexation. To diminish the likelihood of facing such unpleasant outcomes the managers of pension funds may skew portfolio composition away from otherwise optimal long-term asset allocation, reducing equity exposure to manage the risk. Lowering the risk and returns of the funds to increase the probability of remaining within funding corridors transfers value from the young to the older members and retirees in ways that are unlikely to be apparent to either group (Hoevenaars and Ponds, 2007; Bikker *et al.*, 2009). The unpredictable and contingent nature of these sources of redistribution within and among generations are antithetical to the principles of transparency and equity that motivate the strong preference for a significant individual savings element to all of the World Bank's formulations of a multi-pillar system.

3.4.5 Limiting distortions in labor markets

The impact of the pension system on labor markets needs to be considered in the context of the underlying DB design and the "backloading" of benefits which reduces incentives for labor mobility and raises related equity issues for those who may move to employment outside of the industry funds yet cannot take the market value of the premium with them. While this surely imposes greater limitations on mobility than a pure individual account system, the predominance of industry-wide plans limits these effects relative to what is experienced in other kinds of occupational DB systems. It nevertheless impedes mobility across sectors. The high benefit levels and fixed retirement age likely have the greatest impact by creating sharp break points in the value of pension benefits that surely impacts the labor supply decisions of older workers. Although it has been mitigated considerably by the adoption of conditional indexation the high cost exposure to employers is also likely to be a problem.

3.4.6 Contribution to savings and capital market development

Decentralized private management and the absence of categorical requirements or restrictions in investment requirements make the system highly conducive to supporting capital market innovation. The strong funding requirements that should result in overfunding of nominal benefit obligations through the buffer requirements direct a high level of assets into the capital markets as reflected in levels that are among the highest in the world, exceeding 125 percent of GDP in recent years. In this regard the system can be perceived to be among the most successful in supporting market depth and development. Mandating high levels of what are essentially forced savings through the dominance of occupational plans and their high funding requirements, although it surely crowds out other forms of savings, given the evidence of myopia among individuals in other settings without this strong mandate, can likely be assumed to increase aggregate savings levels. The strong influence of behavioral issues combined with nearly universal coverage and self-selection of individuals into various part of the pension system make constructing a counterfactual to test whether it actually increases overall savings extremely difficult. In both of these areas, however, the Dutch system surely rates among the strongest in the world today.

3.5 Concluding observations

A review of the World Bank's multi-pillar pension policy framework in relation to the design and recent developments in the pension system of the Netherlands indicates that the structure of the Dutch system includes many of the intended characteristics of the multi-pillar policy framework. The effectively mandatory nature of the system that achieves nearly universal coverage and clear separation of public and private functions achieves many of the fundamental objectives. The system has a relatively high degree of separation of its functions among three main components each of which is primarily designed to achieve a distinctive purpose. The three elements are effectively coordinated and most of the redistribution occurs within a publicly managed pillar that is simple and relatively transparent in design.

The system operates on a large scale to achieve efficiencies and constrain costs and is subject to rigorous oversight under a comprehensive legal framework administered by a well-financed and organized supervisor. It has a relatively high degree of pre-funding with privately managed assets subject to a flexible and risk-based regulatory regime that facilitates economic and capital market development.

The predominance of the central occupational pillar mandating a heavy reliance on DB differs significantly from the more balanced approach and greater reliance in individual accounts to achieve optimal incentives and sustainability that are implied in the Bank's description of an ideal system. The perceived negative consequences of these deviations are to some degree offset by the adjustments that have been made to more traditional forms of occupational DB through stringent funding rules, the independent governance structure of the funds and their hybrid nature resulting from the relatively recent adoption of conditional indexation.

There are however significant concerns about the sustainability of the benefits promised by the system as the funding requirements are not fully consistent with the promised benefits. Hence, either benefits will need to be reduced or a significant rise in contributions will need to be accepted by workers and employers. Increases in life expectancy and financial volatility are not yet well managed by the system. Perhaps most significantly, the high reliance on DB results in non-transparent redistribution.

The Dutch system therefore does not yet completely fulfill the ideals toward which the multi-pillar design is directed. Although it faces challenges to maintain the generous benefits that Dutch citizens have come to expect imposed by a demographic transition and the recent turbulence in financial markets, the system remains one of the very few today that comes close to embodying the principles that motivated the development of the policy framework and a model that others could do well to emulate. Despite some evident shortcomings the system remains far better than most of the current alternatives.

References

Aarssen, K., and B.J. Kuipers, 2007, Everyone Gains, But Some More Than Others, in: O.W. Steenbeek and S.G. van der Lecq (eds.), *Costs and Benefits of Collective Pension Systems*, Springer, Berlin, 137–56.

Bikker, J.A., and J. de Dreu, 2006, Pension Fund Efficiency and the Impact of Scale, Governance and Plan Design, DNB Working Paper 109, De Nederlandsche Bank.

2007, Operating Costs of Pension Schemes, in: O.W. Steenbeek and S.G. van der Lecq (eds.), *Costs and Benefits of Collective Pension Systems*, Springer, Berlin, 51–74.

Bikker, J.A., D.W.G.A. Broeders, D. Hollanders and E.H.M. Ponds, 2009, Pension Fund Asset Allocation: A Test of the Life Cycle Model, DNB Working Paper 223, De Nederlandsche Bank.

Bonenkamp, J.P.M., 2007, Measuring Lifetime Redistribution in Dutch Occupational Funds, Netspar Discussion Paper 2007–036.

Bonenkamp, J.P.M., M.E.A.J. van de Ven and E.W.M.T. Westerhout, 2007, Macroeconomic Aspects of Intergenerational Solidarity in: O.W. Steenbeek and S.G. van der Lecq (eds.), *Costs and Benefits of Collective Pension Systems*, Springer, Berlin, 205–226.

Bovenberg, A.L., and T. Nijman, 2009, Developments in pension reform: the case of Dutch stand-alone collective pension schemes, *International Tax and Public Finance*, vol. 16(4): 443–67.

Bovenberg, A.L., R. Koijen, T. Nijman and C. Teulings, 2007, Saving and investing over the life cycle and the role of collective pension funds, *De Economist*, vol. 155(4): 347–415.

Davis, E., and Y.-W. Hu, 2008, Does funding of pensions stimulate economic growth?, *Journal of Pension Economics and Finance*, vol. 7(2): 221–49.

De Dreu, J., and J.A. Bikker, 2009, Pension Fund Sophistication and Investment Policy, Netspar Working Paper 05/2009–016.

Ewijk, C. van, N. Draper, H. ter Rele and E. Westerhout, 2006, Ageing and the Sustainability of Dutch Public Finances, CPB Netherlands Special Publication 61.

Hinz, R., and R. van Dam, 2008, Risk Based Supervision of Dutch Pension Funds, in: *Risk Based Supervision of Pension Funds: Emerging Practices and Challenges*, World Bank, Washington DC.

Hinz, R., S. Biletsky and M. Egilmezler, 2009, Pensions in World Bank Lending and Analytical Work, 1984–2007 in: *Social Protection and Labor at the World Bank, 2000–2008*, World Bank, Washington DC.

Hoevenaars, R.P.M.M. and E.H.M. Ponds, 2007, Intergenerational Value Transfers Within an Industry Wide Pension Fund – a Value Based ALM Analysis, in: O.W. Steenbeek and S.G. van der Lecq (eds.), *Costs and Benefits of Collective Pension Systems*, Springer, Berlin, 95–117.

Holzmann, R., 1997, Pension Reform, Financial Market Development, and Economic Growth: Preliminary Evidence from Chile, *Staff Papers International Monetary Fund*, vol. 44(2), 149–178.

Holzmann, R., L. MacKellar and M. Rutkowski, 2003, Accelerating the European Pension Reform Agenda: Need, Progress, and Conceptual Underpinnings, in: R. Holzmann, M. Orenstein and M. Rutkowski (eds.), *Pension Reform in Europe: Process and Progress*, World Bank, Washington DC, 1–46.

Holzmann, R., R. Hinz and M. Dorfman, 2008, Pension Systems and Reform Conceptual Framework, Social Protection Discussion Paper 0824, World Bank, Washington DC.

Impavido, G., E. Lasagabaster and M. Garcia-Huitron, 2010, New Policies for Mandatory Defined Contribution Pensions, The International Bank for Reconstruction and Development/World Bank, Washington DC.

James., E., T. Packaerd and R. Holzmann, 2008, Reflections on Pension Reform in the Americas, in: S. Kay and T. Sinha (eds.), *Lessons from Pension Reform in the Americas*, Oxford University Press, 164–184.

Musalem, A., and T. Tressel, 2003, Institutional Savings and Financial Markets, in: *The Future of Financial Markets: The Role of Contractual Savings Institutions*, Brooking Institution Press, Washington DC.

Omtzigt, P.H., 2007, Mandatory Participation for Companies, in: O.W. Steenbeek and S.G. van der Lecq (eds.), *Costs and Benefits of Collective Pension Systems*, Springer, Berlin, 187–201.

Ponds, E.H.M., and B. van Riel, 2007, The Recent Evolution of Pension Funds in the Netherlands: The Trend to Hybrid DB-DC Plans and Beyond, Center for Retirement Research at Boston College Working Paper 2007–9.

Rofman, R., and L. Luchetti, 2008, Pension Systems in Latin America: Concepts and Measurements of Coverage, Social Protection Discussion Paper 0616, World Bank, Washington DC.

Walker, E., and F. Lefort, 2002, Pension Reform and Capital Markets: Are There Any (Hard) Links?, Social Protection Discussion Paper 0201; World Bank, Washington DC.

Whitehouse, E., 2006, Individual Decisions To Switch Between Public and Private Pension Schemes, DELSA/ELSA/WP1(2005)13, The Organization for Economic Cooperation and Development, Paris.

World Bank, 1994, *Averting the Old Age Crisis: Policies to Protect the Old and Promote Growth*, Oxford University Press.

2003, *Social Risk Management: The World Bank's Approach to Social Protection in a Globalizing World*, World Bank, Washington DC.

2005, *Old Age Income Support in the 21st Century: An International Perspective on Pension Systems and Reform*, World Bank, Washington DC.

2006, *Pension Reform: Issues and Prospects for Non-Financial Defined Contribution Schemes*, World Bank, Washington DC.

Zandberg, E., and L. Spierdijk, 2010, Funding of Pensions and Economic Growth: Are They Really Related?, Netspar Discussion Paper 12/2010–082.

4 | Credit crisis and pensions: international scope

NICHOLAS BARR

4.1 Introduction

All pension systems face risks. That has always been known, but is sometimes forgotten.

> The headline figures are frightening. The financial crisis has meant that private pension funds lost 23% of their investment's value, or some USD 5.4 trillion on aggregate in the OECD, in 2008 ... Across the OECD, economic output is expected to fall by 4.3% in 2009 and growth is not expected to return until 2011. (OECD, 2009, p. 9)

The financial crisis provided a stress test of pension systems. It did not reveal any new risks, but makes appallingly clear the magnitude of the risks we already knew about, and thus provides a firm reminder to policymakers of two lessons:

- Any discussion of pension design should pay considerable attention to risk sharing;
- Sharing risks more broadly can reduce the risk that each individual faces.

One of the effects of the crisis is to force policymakers to accelerate adjustments to longer-term pressures. Pension systems with contributions, benefits and retirement ages established in earlier decades are incompatible with the longer retirements implied by the long-run trends of increasing life expectancy, earlier average retirement and the additional rise in dependency rates arising from declining fertility.

This chapter builds on joint work with Peter Diamond (Barr and Diamond, 2008, 2009, 2010a, 2010b, in press), and on comments on an earlier version of this chapter. I am grateful to Axel Börsch-Supan for help in disentangling the intricacies of the German pension system, and to the editors for very helpful comments on earlier versions.

These trends would not cause problems for the finance of the system if benefits adjusted fully actuarially to longer retirements; the problem arises because (a) people are living longer *and* (b) the design of pension systems contains insufficient automatic adjustment. Thus some adjustment is necessary, and would be necessary even without the baby boom, as illustrated by strikingly similar age pyramids projected for 2050 for China (which has a one-child policy), the United States, which had a baby boom, and India, which had neither (Barr and Diamond, 2008, Figure 1.5).

Thus a chapter written in 2006 would attribute financing problems to long-term sources connected with demographic change, medium-term sources such as the baby boom and the post-war expansion of pension systems, and the failure of governments in most countries to come to grips with those issues. To these pressures are now added the effects of the economic crisis.

This chapter discusses systemic risk. The opening section sets out the multi-dimensional nature of the issues. Section 4.3 discusses pension design to address systemic risk in a first-best context. Section 4.4 extends the discussion to a second-best context. Section 4.5 considers some of the main responses to the economic crisis. Section 4.6 outlines some policy directions. The concluding section draws out some key lessons.

4.2 A multi-dimensional set of problems

Pension systems show multiplicity of risks that they face, of objectives, of types of organization and of ways of adjusting.

4.2.1 *Multiple risks*

It is helpful to distinguish different elements.

- Individual (or idiosyncratic) risk concerns the distribution of a given average risk across individuals, for example the risk that an airline will lose a person's luggage.
- Systemic risk (or common shocks) arise when the average risk changes; such risks affect all or many individuals. Inflation, for example, affects everyone.[1]

---

[1] There are no ill effects from fully anticipated inflation in a world with complete markets. As a practical matter, neither condition holds.

Some risks have both elements: someone aged 65 faces a probability distribution of remaining life expectancy (individual risk); but the average remaining life expectancy of successive cohorts can rise over time (systemic risk).

Box 4.1 summarizes the range of risks – individual and systemic – which pension systems may face. This chapter focuses on the systemic risks and the ways that different pension designs can share them. It is important to remember that though systemic reform may be able to reduce aggregate risk (e.g., making the use of seat belts mandatory reduces the risk of serious injury from an automobile accident) it is generally not possible to make aggregate risk disappear, merely to share it in different ways.

- Within a generation, protecting one group (e.g., retirees) more fully from shocks implies that other current and/or future participants, such as workers, consumers and taxpayers, have to bear more shock.
- Or it is possible to offer current workers and retirees some protection by sharing risk with future cohorts. That option, however, depends on the ability of the pension system (or government more generally) to draw on accumulated assets or to borrow.

Box 4.1 Multiple risks and uncertainties facing individuals

An individual may experience poor pension outcomes for reasons that can loosely be divided into systemic risks, market risks and risks connected with individual behavior.

Systemic risks

- Macroeconomic risk affects output, prices (including asset prices) or both.
- Demographic risk arises mainly through longer life expectancy and lower fertility.
- Political risk.

Market risks arise from systemic shocks, but also have idiosyncratic elements:

- Earnings risk: a worker's earnings profile has both deterministic elements (e.g., the decision to invest in human capital) and stochastic elements, relating to labor markets and health risks.

- Investment risk: accumulations held in the stock market are vulnerable to market fluctuations. Accumulations in nominal bonds face inflation risk. At its extreme, if a person with a fully funded individual account is obliged to retire on her 65th birthday, there is a lottery element in the value of her pension accumulation.
- Annuities market risk: an individual faces the risk of outliving his or her savings and for that reason many systems make it compulsory to convert pension savings at least partly into an annuity. For a given accumulation, a person's annuity at a given age will be affected by the life expectancy of his birth cohort and by the discount rate used by the annuity provider. And annuity providers can fail.

Risks connected with individual behavior

- Principal risk arises through bad decisions by participants, for example about when to retire. Poor choices can arise from imperfect information, e.g., investing too heavily in equities too close to retirement, or failing to understand the importance of administrative charges. Poor choices can arise also for reasons which behavioral economics explains. For fuller discussion, see Barr and Diamond (2009, Boxes 4.2 and 4.3).
- Agency risk can arise through incompetent or fraudulent fund management. More importantly, as the financial crisis has shown with stark clarity, managers in private systems may have different incentives from plan participants (see, for example, Woolley, 2010).

Many of these elements face policymakers not only with risk (where the probability distribution of outcomes is known or can be estimated with a small variance), but also with uncertainty, where the probability distribution of outcomes is not well known. Actuarial insurance can in principle deal with risk, but faces problems with uncertainty.[a]

---

[a] This distinction goes back to Frank Knight (1921). See also Bronk (2009, pp. 214–16). It can be argued that no economic risks represent the type of risk present in games of chance or physics so to that extent all important risks are uncertain. If one takes that view, the question becomes that of the degree of confidence one draws around a projection.

4.2.2 *Multiple objectives*

Pension systems have multiple objectives and have to address multiple risks. It is helpful to start by considering a rational individual in a world of certainty, where nobody is poor on a lifetime basis.

Consumption smoothing: in a world of certainty, a rational individual will borrow and save so as to maximize her lifetime utility, for example, saving during productive middle years to finance consumption in retirement. In this simple case, the purpose of pensions is to transfer consumption from one's younger to one's older self. If nobody is poor on a lifetime basis, no additional action by the state is necessary.

Poverty relief: relaxing the assumption that nobody is lifetime poor opens a role for the state in supporting consumption in old age of people who are lifetime poor. In practice action is needed to address also transient poverty.

Insurance: relaxing the assumption of certainty means that we have to consider at a minimum the longevity risk – people generally do not know how long they will live after retirement. Actuarial insurance, for example, annuities, can address this type of risk. But, as just discussed, the problem is much more widespread, embracing uncertainty as well as risk, and systemic as well as idiosyncratic risk.

The choice of boundaries between the main objectives is to some extent terminological. In this chapter, consumption smoothing refers to intertemporal redistribution by an individual over his or her life cycle. However, insurance can be thought of as consumption smoothing across different contingencies (e.g., the risks and uncertainties in Box 4.1). Thus some writers take a broader view of consumption smoothing. Similarly, formulae that subsidize the pensions of lower-paid workers can be thought of as part of poverty relief, or as insurance against contingencies like adverse labor-market outcomes.

More broadly, social policy has well-known equity objectives and less widely known efficiency purposes (Barr, 2001). Risk, which in important respects lies at the heart of social policy, has elements of both. Providing the least well-off with some protection in the face of risk has a clear equity dimension. But optimal risk sharing across the contingencies in Box 4.1 also has important efficiency aspects. If individuals face too little risk, as in the communist economic system, growth stagnates; but if they face too much risk, as in countries with limited social safety nets, they are less likely to take risks like starting a business, again to the detriment of growth. In the other direction, they might take the very big risk of illegal migration, e.g., from Mexico to the US.

4.2.3 Different types of pension arrangement

Pensions can be pay-as-you-go (PAYG), partially funded or fully funded. Separately they can be defined contribution (DC) or defined benefit (DB). Once more, it is necessary to define terms. It assists discussion to start with the two polar cases.

DC plans

In the simplest DC plan, each worker saves a fixed percentage of his or her earnings to purchase assets, which are accumulated in the worker's account, as are the returns earned by those assets. The size of the worker's pension is determined by the value of assets accumulated in his account over his career. The benefit may take the form of a lump sum, or a series of payments, or an annuity, but in all cases is determined only by the size of the worker's lifetime pension accumulation. Thus in the polar case, the individual bears the full risk. The simple arrangement can be modified: the contribution rate can be allowed to vary; and there can be redistribution across workers' accounts or between general revenues and the accounts.

For some purposes it is useful to distinguish two cases, with separate terminology (used where relevant throughout the chapter) to describe them.

- In a DC scheme (a) the individual bears the full risk and (b) the contribution rate is fixed. Thus risk manifests itself through its effects on the individual's consumption in retirement.
- With an individual account, the individual in principle bears the full risk but can vary the contribution rate.[2] Thus the individual can at least partly offset low asset returns by saving more. In this case, preserving the individual character of a person's lifetime budget

---

[2] With complete capital markets the individual can in principle transfer all risk. In practice, capital markets are incomplete, so the individual can protect himself only partially, for example, through the capital market (for example, by life-cycle investing) or insurance (e.g., buying an annuity).

constraint, risk manifests itself on lifetime consumption, but gives the individual some choice over how any fall in consumption is divided between consumption in working years and in retirement.[3]

DB plans

In the simplest DB plan, the size of a worker's pension is determined as a function of his history of pensionable earnings. The formula may be based on the worker's final wage and length of service or on wages over a longer period, for example, his full career. The sponsor's contribution is conceptually the endogenous variable ensuring that the system remains in financial balance; thus risk falls on the employer, or on the insurance company if the employer buys annuities for retiring workers on a rolling basis. A DB scheme can be fully funded, but in principle need not be.

Again, the simple arrangement can be modified.

- Some risk can be transferred from contributions to benefits, by adjusting the rules for accrual or the indexation rules for benefits in payment.
- Some risk can be transferred to future participants if the plan is less than fully funded.
- There can be government guarantees, government bailouts or mandatory insurance of pension funds.

In sum, in the polar cases, in a DC plan, benefits adjust to available finances; in a DB arrangement, finances adjust to maintain benefits.

Notional defined-contribution (NDC) plans

These are conceptually similar to DC plans in that contributions are notionally accumulated to determine a balance which is converted into an annuity at retirement, but NDC plans are different in that they are not fully funded and may be PAYG. Thus the accumulation in each participant's account follows a rule rather than necessarily equaling the actual returns on the assets held.

---

[3] The choice of terminology is purely for convenience. It is equally possible to share risks between consumption during working years and in retirement through DC plans with fixed contributions combined with supplementary voluntary accounts.

4.2.4 *Multiple ways of adjusting pensions*

Box 4.2 summarizes multiple ways of adjusting pensions. In some ways the task of this chapter is to map these multiple forms of adjustment onto the risks – particularly the systemic risks – in Box 4.1.

Box 4.2 Mechanisms for adjusting pensions

At a strategic level pension systems can adjust on the contributions side, on the benefit side, or both. Thus the elements discussed below are not mutually exclusive.

Increasing the income of the pension system – pensions can adjust through:

- Higher savings by today's plan participants (fully funded individual accounts) or higher contributions by today's workers (a less than fully funded defined-benefit social insurance system). Thus the extra revenue comes from today's working participants.
- Higher contributions by the plan sponsor (a defined-benefit plan). As discussed below, depending on elasticities in labor, capital and product markets, the extra revenue comes from some or all workers and shareholders in the firm or industry concerned, from taxpayers, from customers, and/or perhaps tomorrow's workers.
- Higher contributions by insurance companies where retirees or plan sponsors have bought annuities. In that case, again depending on the relevant elasticities, the extra revenue comes from the insurance company's workers or shareholders or future customers.
- Higher contributions by today's taxpayers (a public pension). Thus the extra income comes from today's taxpayers and hence also, if desired, tomorrow's taxpayers, thus allowing intergenerational risk sharing.

Reducing pension spending

Total pension spending is the product of (a) the level of the average pension and (b) the number of pensioners. The main determinant of the latter is earliest eligibility age. Policies to reduce pension spending can operate on either or both.

Box 4.2 (*cont.*)

- Policies to reduce the monthly pension at a given eligibility age.
  - During accumulation: a lower rate of accrual during working life through (a) a lower return to financial assets (a fully funded defined-contribution pension), or (b) a less generous legislated accrual rule (an NDC system or occupational pensions in the Netherlands).
  - Pensions in payment: less generous indexation of pensions in payment, or a reduction in pension, either by legislation or in the case of variable annuities.
- An increase in earliest eligibility age, hence shorter duration of retirement: this approach affects workers but not retirees.
  - With less than actuarial adjustment: total spending on pensions declines, e.g., a defined-benefit plan.
  - With actuarial adjustment: in this case there is no saving in total pension spending, but a given volume of spending can maintain a desired replacement rate (fully funded defined-contribution pensions or an NDC system). In this case the purpose of an increase in eligibility by age is to address adequacy rather than sustainability.

4.3 Setting the scene: pension design and systemic risk in a first-best context

This section starts with a brief summary of where risk falls under different pension arrangements, initially considering only the simple cases. Subsection 4.3.2 discusses how these cases can adjust to demographic and economic shocks in a first-best setting. Section 4.4 broadens the discussion of adjustment by modifying the simple cases in a second-best context.

Before taking discussion further, however, Box 4.3 establishes a fault line that divides approaches to pension design.

4.3.1 *Pension design: the simple cases*

DC pensions

In a fully funded DC plan, a person's pension, other things equal, is determined by the size of his or her lifetime pension accumulation.

Box 4.3 How much discretion is optimal in the design of a pension system?

Consider the following statements:

- A major advantage of fully funded defined-contribution pensions or individual accounts is that they are transparent *ex ante* about how risks are shared between the different stakeholders and, partly for that reason, less prone to interference.
- Partial funding in an NDC system or a public or occupational defined-benefit plan plays two important roles. One is to buffer shocks to the system so that short-run perturbations can be accommodated through long-run adjustments rather than large immediate changes. Second is to spread the costs and benefits of the pension system across cohorts. The combination of a sufficiently large fund, together with automatic adjustments to projected long-run imbalances, makes it possible for policy to focus on long-run sustainability rather than requiring sharp changes in the short term.

The first statement argues against discretion; the price is that all risk falls on current participants. The second argues that less than full funding makes it possible to share risks more widely. In principle, that is possible without discretion if the system incorporates automatic adjustments but, as the discussion in Sections 4.3 and 4.4 makes clear, it has not thus far proved practical to design a wholly automatic system that works in a satisfactory way in all circumstances. Thus at some stage discretionary legislative action is likely.

The second statement is true if the process is one of long-run optimization. The empirical question is whether that model is a good description of the actual behavior of government or other plan sponsors. If government is prone to government failure, policy may be driven more by short-term political considerations than by long-run optimization. If so, the potential benefits of wider risk sharing may be offset by the costs arising from suboptimal behavior. Such costs could include excessive postponement of necessary adjustment; or growing deficits could lead to the sponsor reneging on past promises. In that case, the potential benefits of wider risk sharing could be illusory.

Box 4.3 (*cont.*)

The choice between (a) a more stringent defence against government failure but less risk sharing and (b) wider risk sharing, necessitating somewhat less defence against government failure, is fundamental. The right answer depends, inter alia, on the weight policymakers give wider risk sharing and an empirical view of the quality of government in the country in question. However, the answer is far from clear-cut. Fully funded individual accounts are not immune from government interference such as changing their tax privileges, interfering with their investment decisions or outright nationalization (e.g., Argentina). Barr and Diamond (in press) explore the potential gains in terms of wider risk sharing from allowing some discretion.

Thus individuals face many of the risks in Box 4.1, including systemic risk and market risks. They can, of course, shift some of those risks: they could buy indexed government bonds rather than equities, but at a cost of a lower, albeit safer, rate of return; or they could buy an annuity, or a deferred annuity, but again at a cost.

If the system allows individual choice, principal risk and agency risks are also relevant. If the contribution rate is fixed, these risks emerge through adjustments in the level of the individual's monthly pension; if it is not fixed, the risks can affect consumption both during working years (if the individual saves more) and in retirement.

DB pensions – private plans

Assume initially that the plan sponsor provides the pension (i.e., does not buy annuities from insurance companies), and that the sponsor survives. In that case, the risk of varying rates of return on pension assets falls on the sponsor. In a private plan, the risk falling on the employer can be spread over several groups – current workers (through effects on wage rates), the firm's shareholders and the taxpayer (through effects on profits), its customers (through effects on prices) and/or its future workers.

If the sponsor buys annuities for workers when they retire, the risk of poor asset performance falls on the sponsor during accumulation and on the firm providing the annuity, once benefits are in payment. If the sponsor goes bankrupt or defaults on its pensions promise in other ways, the risk falls both on current contributors and (in the absence of annuitization) on retirees. If the firm providing the annuity goes bankrupt, the cost falls on retirees. All these risks can be modified, for example if the government provides or mandates insurance for occupational plans.

Where the sponsor of a DB plan can spread risk over future participants, it is in principle possible to share risks more widely than in a fully funded DC plan, which can spread risks only among current participants. That argument, however, needs to be qualified, as discussed in Box 4.3. If DB occupational plans are required at all times to be fully funded, risks are borne by current participants, hence not shared more widely than in a DC plan.

The flexibility of less than full funding is double-edged. On the one hand, it allows risks to be spread across generations. On the other, as noted, sponsors may go bankrupt or renege on pension promises (a cynical view is that in corporate plans the firm creams the surplus in good times and reneges on pension promises in bad times). At its worst, it can be argued that DB plans give participants a promise of security that is illusory, for example if a DB plan is converted to DC. To that extent, a DC arrangement, where it is clear who bears the risk, is more transparent. The question for policy design is whether flexibility is more realistically regarded as a threat or a promise.

DB pensions – public plans

In a public DB system, adjustment comes from changes in the contribution rate (generally a dedicated payroll tax), so that risk is shared with current workers. If there is a trust fund which can accumulate assets or borrow, risk can be shared also with future workers. If benefits are financed partly from general revenues, risk is shared with taxpayers, including pensioners and, through government borrowing, also with future taxpayers.

In a PAYG system, current benefits are financed from current contributions, precluding intergenerational risk sharing. The same is true of fully funded systems. If a system is partially but not fully funded, it can be financed from past trust fund surpluses or trust fund borrowing, or from tax revenues, thus sharing risks with future cohorts. The conclusion, once more, depends on one's view of government. If government is regarded as responsible (or can be constrained by rules to act responsibly), the ability to share risks across generations is a major benefit, suggesting that it is generally optimal to have a PAYG element in a pension system. A view of government as prone to failure suggests that flexibility invites agency risk. Thus, as with private plans, the question is whether flexibility is regarded as beneficial.

NDC

In an NDC system that is PAYG, the individual faces only some of the risks in Box 4.1, notably the systemic risks, the earnings risk and the longevity risk. In an NDC system that is partially funded, the individual also faces investment risk. Note that a partially funded NDC system can in principle share risks widely, including across generations. Once more, there is the potential for agency risk. The purpose of well-designed rules and explicit procedures for legislative action offer at least partial protection. Yet again, the issue arises of whether flexibility is more likely to be used well or badly.

4.3.2 The effects of systemic risk in the simple cases in a first-best world

This section discusses adjustment to demographic risk (changes in mortality and in fertility) and economic risk for the simple cases discussed above, assuming a first-best world.

Responses to increasing life expectancy
There has been a long-run trend increase in life expectancy in many countries, with widespread agreement about the expected direction of change, though less about its speed.

The view of rising life expectancy as a problem is profoundly mistaken: people are living not only longer lives, but longer healthy lives, in important respects one of the greatest triumphs of the twentieth century.[4] The fact that longer lives increase the cost of a given pension at a given age should not obscure that fact. Much of this chapter is about how pension systems should adjust.

---

[4] I tell my students that they have as much academic freedom as I do, with one exception: the term "aging problem" is ideologically unsound, and terrible things will happen to anyone who uses it.

A DC system – whether funded or notional – adjusts automatically to rising life expectancy by reducing benefits at a given retirement age. Individuals may choose to offset that reduction, at least in part, by retiring later (i.e., extending working years) or by saving more (i.e., consuming less during working years), or both. In a first-best world such decisions are voluntary. Later discussion considers why reliance on voluntarism on its own might be suboptimal.

In a DB system, without automatic adjustments the plan's income is adjusted so that it matches the cost of the plan's promises. Increased life expectancy raises the cost of the system. In a private plan, as noted, the extra resources come from the plan sponsor, hence from workers, shareholders, taxpayers, and/or customers, and/or future workers, or a mix. In a public pension in which contributions are required to cover benefits and where the system is not allowed to accumulate a surplus or to borrow, the extra resources come from workers through higher contributions. If the system is allowed to borrow, some or all of the extra resources can come from current or future taxpayers.

Responses to declining fertility

A declining trend in fertility has been widespread and long term. Initially, in many countries, declining child mortality more than offset the decline in fertility, leading to rapid growth of the population of working age. But in many countries child mortality rates have declined to the point where the scope for further decline is limited, and consequently growth of the labor force has slowed.

A slowdown in the rate of growth of the labor force has a direct impact on the financing of the pension system. If such a slowdown were the only change, it would be expected to lead to higher wages and lower rates of return on assets.

In a fully funded DC system, if interest rates fall, other things being equal, a person's pension accumulation will grow more slowly and hence his total accumulation at a given age will be smaller. Individuals can offset that reduction, at least in part, by saving more or by retiring later. In a first-best world, these changes occur voluntarily. Behavioral economics explains why that is unlikely to happen, a topic discussed further below.

In an NDC system matters are more complex. If the notional interest rate is the rate of real wage growth, w, the notional accumulation of a given worker will grow faster; if the notional interest rate is the rate of growth of the total wage bill, wL, where L is the size of the workforce, the effect on a worker's accumulation will depend on whether the increase in w does or does not offset the decline in L.

In a DB system with partial funding, a decline in interest rates creates problems for the plan sponsor. If benefits promises are kept, contributions to the plan have to increase. In a private plan, those increases, once more, can come from some or all of workers, shareholders, taxpayers and future workers. In a public pension, the extra resources come from workers through higher contributions, taxpayers and/or future taxpayers. In practice, as noted, benefits may also be adjusted.

Responses to economic turbulence

In an economic downturn, the return on assets declines, reducing the growth of pension accumulations; interest rates decline as savers shift from equities to safer assets, raising the cost of annuities; and the wage base grows more slowly, or declines, hence so do contribution revenues. The effects of these changes emerge in different ways in different pension arrangements. As noted earlier, it is not possible to make aggregate risk disappear, but it is possible to share it in different ways.

In a fully funded DC system, a decline in the value of assets reduces a worker's pension accumulation and also the rate of return on which his or her annuity is based. Younger workers can respond by doing relatively little, relying on later growth to rectify the situation; or they can choose to save more. Workers close to retirement cannot rely on later growth and have only limited scope to increase their saving sufficiently to offset any decline in asset values. If they have hedged risk earlier, e.g., by moving from equities into bonds as they age, the effect of economic turbulence is less acute. Otherwise, the main response for such workers is either to postpone retirement or to accept lower consumption in retirement.

Many commentators have advocated mandatory individual funded accounts,[5] not least because of the intuitive power of the argument that building up a pile of savings makes a person more independent of government. However, many of those arguments are incomplete or mistaken, as discussed in Box 4.4 as far as systemic risk is concerned.

[5] One of the major historical examples is World Bank (1994); for a more nuanced restatement, see Holzmann and Hinz (2005).

Box 4.4 Analytical errors in the advocacy of mandatory individual funded accounts

The assertion that individual funded accounts are a dominant policy design is widespread and persistent, so that it is worth setting out the analytical errors that such arguments frequently make (for fuller discussion, see Barr and Diamond, 2008, 2009, and for a retreat from its former position, World Bank, 2006).

- Tunnel vision: good policy design needs to take account of all the objectives of pension systems. The greater the focus on individual accounts, the greater the emphasis on consumption smoothing. Good analysis needs to take account also of poverty relief (which may be dealt with by another element in the pension system). Poverty relief becomes particularly salient during an economic crisis.
- Improper use of first-best analysis: much of the adjustment to shocks assumes a first-best world in which people's voluntary decisions accord with simple economic theory, for example, responding to a decline in the value of pension assets by voluntarily saving more and/or delaying retirement. Such theory ignores information problems, behavioral issues and transaction costs; second-best analysis (Section 4.3) takes account of such factors.
- Improper use of steady-state analysis: steady-state analysis is the correct approach if we compare states of the world A and B – for example comparing the USA today with a mainly PAYG system with the USA that would have resulted had it always had a funded system. Mostly, however, the issue is a different one, that of the move from steady state A (PAYG) to steady state B (funded). Such a move has transition costs, which are particularly problematical in the face of economic turbulence, Argentina being a sad example.
- Incomplete analysis of the effects of funding: it is frequently argued that funding is an appropriate response to demographic change. That is true where funding makes an independent contribution to output growth; funding may do that, but not necessarily or everywhere. If, for example, an increase in mandatory saving is offset by an equal decline in voluntary saving, the total

---

Box 4.4 (*cont.*)

volume of saving is unchanged. The error lies not in discussing the link, but in assuming that it always and necessarily holds.

- Ignoring distributional effects: a move towards funding that increases saving reduces the consumption of today's workers to the benefit of future workers and/or pensioners. Such redistribution is an inescapable companion of a decision to increase the extent of funding. Such a move may or may not be good policy; but it is mistaken analysis to ignore its intergenerational redistributive effects.

These errors are not arguments against individual funded accounts as part of a pension system, but against assertions that such accounts are necessarily superior.

In an NDC system, a decline in w or wL will reduce the notional interest rate attributed to notional accumulations but, in contrast with the previous case, the decline does not affect the value of notional accumulations made before the macroeconomic turbulence started, so that the effect on accumulations is less acute than in the fully funded case. To the extent that accumulations made before the start of turbulence are protected, it follows that adjustment has to fall on the future value of the accumulations of current workers and hence on their future benefits, and on benefits being paid to current retirees. As the discussion of the Swedish "brake" mechanism in Subsection 4.5.2 illustrates, the effect can be large. To the extent that the pension of a worker close to retirement is adversely affected, the main response is to postpone retirement.

In a DB system which fulfills past promises a decline in the wage base will reduce contribution revenues. In a private plan, the sponsor will have to make up any shortfall; once more, the cost of doing so can fall on any or all of current workers, shareholders and taxpayers, or future workers. In a public plan, the cost of making up any shortfall will fall on workers, through higher contributions, taxpayers and/or future taxpayers.

If economic turbulence is severe, however, plan sponsors and taxpayers may be unwilling or unable to meet the full costs of past promises. Thus many private DB plans are closing to new members, and

being replaced by DC arrangements. State systems in the short run
have generally maintained their promises in OECD countries, but as
the solvency of the public finances is threatened, governments in many
countries are taking action in the medium term to increase retirement
ages, or adjusting indexation to make it more parsimonious. On the
face of it, as already discussed, DB plans share risk more widely than
DC plans, thus offering participants greater protection. The empirical
question is whether in practice that protection is real or illusory – is
DB really DB, or under pressure does it become more like DC.

4.4 Pension design and systemic risk in a second-best context

A fully funded DC system adjusts benefits to match available funds;
the same is true of an NDC pension plan that is in financial balance;
thus adjustment is all on the benefit side. A DB system adjusts
funds to meet anticipated obligations; thus adjustment is all on the
contributions side.

Two aspects of the discussion in Section 4.3 require fuller analysis:

- None of the simple systems uses the full range of instruments for adjustment;
- A first-best approach relies mainly on voluntary adjustments.

This section discusses (a) how pension design should make use of
the full range of adjustments, (b) lessons from behavioral economics
about the limitations of relying on voluntarism, and (c) lessons about
the desirability, but also the limitations, of automatic adjustment. We
discuss in turn optimal risk sharing (Subsection 4.4.1), adjustment
mechanisms in practice (4.4.2), adjusting to demographic risk (4.4.3)
and adjusting to economic risk (4.4.4).

4.4.1 Optimal risk sharing

Gollier argues that "by using their reserves efficiently, pension funds
can smooth shocks in their asset returns, and can thus facilitate intergenerational risk sharing" (2008, Abstract). He sets out an optimal
path of benefit adjustments on a rolling basis for any realization of
random variables. As early work in risk sharing, his analysis does not
include adjustments in contributions, nor fluctuations in earnings. Like

optimal taxation, this approach offers a powerful framework for analysis rather than a blueprint for practical policy. The discussion below makes no pretence at such generality, but explores the characteristics of different approaches to risk sharing.

The analysis does, however, incorporate one strategic argument: that adjustment should respect differences in risk aversion. Even where there is no age-related difference in people's utility functions, retirees have more limited options for adjustment. Workers have their human capital and also have more time to cushion shocks, for example by increasing their voluntary pension savings, and hence are better able to accommodate large adjustments. Among current workers, those closer to retirement have more constrained options for adjustment than younger workers. Adjustment in the face of systemic risk should accommodate age-related differences in the ability to adjust.

4.4.2 Adjustment mechanisms in practice

The starting point is to observe that many plans deviate from the pure cases. In the case of DCs, corporate plans may allow workers to increase their contributions if returns on their pension savings are below expectations. The outcomes of individual accounts can be altered by government transfers (e.g., to protect the pension rights of unemployed workers), or by government guarantees. In addition, if there is a large drop in asset values or a pension fund fails, a government will face pressure to protect participants close to retirement.

When a DB plan faces financial difficulties, firms and governments adjust not only contributions but also benefits; as already noted, this type of flexibility is double-edged, and may be used well or badly. While governments typically have the power to change both benefits in payment and future benefits, legal restrictions usually limit the ability of private providers, provided the sponsor does not go bankrupt, to change accrued benefits (but not prospective benefits). In addition, some countries provide guarantees for employer pensions, shifting some of the risk to other firms through mandatory insurance contributions, as in the US and UK, and perhaps also to taxpayers if the insurance arrangement requires public subsidy. Insurance generally covers less than 100 percent of a worker's benefits, so that current and future beneficiaries also face some of the risk.

One element in adjustment is whether it affects contributions or benefits. In the latter case, adjustment can operate via changes in the accrual rate, via changes in the rule by which pensions in payment are indexed, or both. Reducing the accrual rate reduces a worker's entitlement to a pension in the future. Or the number of years necessary to qualify for a full pension in a DB system can be increased. Indexation of pensions in payment can also be made less generous, for example by indexing by less than the rate of price inflation if a pension plan is running a deficit. Gradual adjustment of this sort has two potential advantages: if habit formation is important (see Bovenberg *et al.*, 2007, especially Section 6.3), individuals find it easier to adjust consumption more gradually rather than instantaneously; and the approach also helps with macroeconomic stabilization.

Such deviations from the simple cases have been largely pragmatic. The rest of this section explores how such adjustments can be analyzed more systematically.

4.4.3 Adjusting to demographic risk

Reducing benefits
In a DC system, at a given retirement age and with a given pattern and duration of saving, rising life expectancy means that a person's accumulation on average has to be spread over more years, and declining fertility, if it reduces the return on savings, reduces the size of a person's accumulation. The result, in both cases, is to reduce benefits at a given retirement age.

An NDC system, similarly, reduces benefits at a given retirement age. If the system is still not in balance, there can be further automatic reduction in benefits in line with changes in contribution revenues; we discuss this further below in the context of the Swedish "brake" mechanism.

In Germany a person's pension is determined by the number of pension points he has accumulated (which depend, inter alia, on his earnings history and number of years of service) and the value of each point. Under a "sustainability factor" introduced in 2005, the system adjusts the value of each point based on a combination of changes in wages and the age dependency rate, the latter reflecting changes both in life expectancy and in fertility and other influences on the size of the labor force.[6] This arrangement automatically reduces pension benefits to keep the system in financial balance. A deterioration in the sustainability factor means that pensions in payment will not be fully indexed to earnings growth. Its application affects all current workers and pensioners equally, since accrued rights and future accruals are changed proportionately.

In all these cases individuals can at least partly offset a reduction in pension benefits (and hence a reduction in consumption in retirement) by retiring later, saving more, or both. In a first-best world such decisions would be voluntary.

Extension 1: Raising the earliest eligibility age

As the literature on behavioral economics seeks to explain, many people retire as soon as they are allowed even if that condemns them or their survivors to elderly poverty. In the limit, therefore, in the face of demographic pressures, progressively larger actuarial adjustments to the level of benefits at a given earliest eligibility age lead to a continuing decline in a person's monthly pension. If there is an adequate first-tier pension, the issue is less one of inadequate poverty relief than of inefficient consumption smoothing. This line of argument suggests that there should be adjustment both to the level of benefit at the earliest eligibility age and to the earliest eligibility age itself. The latter should bear some sensible relationship to rising life expectancy. Designing such adjustment, however, is not simple. There are theoretical issues, empirical issues and implementation issues.

Theoretical issues

The choice of earliest eligibility age needs to balance a series of factors.

- People are living longer healthy lives, so that it makes sense to work longer rather than to consume less in retirement. This factor points to a higher eligibility age.
- Rising incomes make leisure in later life more affordable, and leisure is a superior good. This factor points to a lower eligibility age.
- The productivity of older workers, which is influenced by the speed of technological change and the availability of retraining, affects both the demand and supply of labor. The effects of this factor go

---

[6] The dependency rate is measured as the ratio of "standardized" beneficiaries to the number of contributors. The dependency ratio is "equivalized," taking into account the fact that high-earning contributors pay more into the system than low earners.

in both directions: higher productivity raises the opportunity cost of leisure, but makes it more affordable.

- The operation of labor markets for older workers including, for example, EU legislation banning mandatory retirement influences the likelihood that older workers will be able to find a job.

Thus the factors that determine how many workers gain and how many lose from raising the earliest eligibility age vary not only with increases in average life expectancy and the average level of earnings, but also with individual circumstances and decisions. The theory of what is optimal in the face of these factors has yet to be developed, though the argument for somewhat later retirement is strong. A simple rule making the earliest eligibility age proportional to life expectancy has advantages in terms of transparency but may be suboptimal in theoretical terms given the factors outlined above, and also because improvements in life expectancy tend to vary across income classes. These considerations suggest that eligibility age should rise by less than the increase in life expectancy.

A number of rules are possible.

- The UK Pensions Commission (2005) adopted as a rule of thumb that the increase in the state pension age should broadly maintain the current ratio of one year of retirement for every two years of work, so that pension age should rise by eight months for every increase in life expectancy of one year. The problem with this approach is that it takes no account of the effect of rising incomes on desirable retirement age.
- A variant of this rule would relate to healthy life expectancy rather than total life expectancy.
- A different approach would raise eligibility age by enough to keep the contribution rate constant. This approach imposes all the adjustment on the benefits side.

Empirical issues

There are also empirical problems, notably the accuracy of projections of life expectancy. Even if such projections are on average accurate in the long run, history suggests that significant deviations from trend are likely in the short and medium term. In 1981, official UK projections suggested that male life expectancy at 65 in 2004 would be 14.8 years; the outcome was 19 years, a 28 percent error. Thus there is a widening funnel of doubt about future outcomes. If legislation includes adjustment factors, they will generally not match actual outcomes. It is, of course, always possible to change the adjustment factors. But legislating change may be difficult, especially during a crisis, so there are advantages if a system is able, at least up to a point, to respond to uncertain outcomes as they happen.

Once more, there is no perfect arrangement.

- One approach is a system that adjusts benefits on the basis of actual changes in mortality. In Sweden this is done by using historic mortality data in calculating pensions, with no adjustment for anticipated improvements after a cohort has retired. With rising life expectancy, this arrangement imposes the cost of adjustment on workers.
- Another approach is through year-by-year adjustments based on year-by-year changes in mortality. With rising life expectancy, this arrangement shifts the cost of adjustment onto retirees.
- A third approach is to base benefits on projections of life expectancy. This approach works best where projections are – and are widely perceived to be – analytically sound and politically unbiased. If life expectancy rises more rapidly than projected, this arrangement shifts the cost of adjustment onto taxpayers, workers and/or retirees depending on how the resulting deficit is made up.

Implementation issues

Should eligibility age be increased by an automatic mechanism or not? Given the theoretical and empirical issues just discussed, an automatic rule on its own will not be enough. Thus, for example, the system in Canada includes automatic changes, delayed for a period to allow a legislative alternative. Or variation from the default rule should be on the basis of recommendations from a non-partisan commission. The procedure of such a commission, including the process of choosing its members and the criteria against which it makes its decisions, should be set out in advance.

Once a government has decided to adjust pension benefits and eligibility rules regularly, the adjustment should be phased in carefully, as explained in Box 4.5.

Extension 2: Adjusting both benefits and contributions

Thus far adjustment to demographic risk reduces a worker's pension and hence his consumption in old age or, if he responds by saving more, his consumption during working life. In all these cases, the cost of

---

Box 4.5 Principles for adjusting pensionable age

If benefits and eligibility are to be adjusted for mortality changes, automatic adjustment should be based on three principles.

- The rules should relate to date of birth, not to the date of retirement; otherwise there will be a wave of retirements just before any reduction in the generosity of benefits goes into effect.
- Changes should be made annually, to avoid large changes in benefit levels across nearby cohorts. Large changes are inequitable and politically difficult, since benefits could differ significantly between people born in successive years, sometimes only days apart. The combination of large changes and rules determined by date of retirement would exacerbate the inefficient incentive to early retirement.
- As far as is sensible, rules for changing benefits should be explicit. Automatic adjustment with explicit rules leads to greater predictability and decreased political pressure. Automatic adjustments may function better if based on actual mortality outcomes rather than projections. Nevertheless, as with the indexation of income tax brackets, there always remains the option of legislation to change whatever the automatic rules produce.

The legislated increase in women's pensionable age in the United Kingdom, announced in 1991, illustrates all three of these principles. The key date is April 6, 1950. For women born before that date, the state pensionable age is 60. The pensionable age for a woman born on May 6, 1950 (one month after the key date) was 60 years and one month, which occurred in 2010, 19 years after the legislation, for a woman born on June 6, 1950, 60 years and two months, and so on. For women born on or after April 6, 1955, the pensionable age will be 65.

Source: Barr and Diamond (2010a, Box 5.4).

---

demographic change falls on the individual. A mechanism that shares the cost of increasing life expectancy more broadly (Diamond and Orszag, 2005, Chapter 5) is a life expectancy adjustment: in each year calculate the increase in the cost of pensions caused by the increase in life expectancy; decrease future initial benefits to cover part of the cost, and raise contributions (i.e., the tax rate) to cover the remainder. The cost sharing could be 50:50, or some other division, depending, inter alia, on the existing level of contributions which, for a given level of benefits, depends not only on mortality but also on fertility rates. The optimal division between changes in contributions and changes in benefits will be influenced by the cause of financial pressure. With shocks in the rate of return, adjustment will fall both on contributions and benefits; with financial pressures from increased healthy life expectancy it is reasonable to expect more of the changes to be absorbed on the benefits side, for example through later retirement.

Extension 3: Intergenerational risk sharing
The adjustments to fully funded systems share risks between current participants. A partially funded system, for example a partially funded DB system, can share risks more broadly, with potential welfare gains. This line of argument suggests that if a plan has a shortfall from its desired level of funding, the speed with which the shortfall is addressed should be optimized, not maximized. The dilemma in a private DC plan is that the gains from a slower return to full funding need to be set against the risk that the plan may fail, for example if the sponsor goes out of business. In a state scheme, the risk is that of government failure. The speed of adjustment is one of the central topics in Subsection 4.4.4.

4.4.4 Adjusting to economic risk

Increasing life expectancy and declining fertility are generally long-run trends, making it possible to adjust gradually. In contrast, macroeconomic turbulence tends to arrive at short notice and the effects can be large. For both reasons, additional adjustment mechanisms are necessary.

Adjusting NDC pensions
It is helpful to start with discussion of automatic adjustment in Sweden before turning to broader discussion of ways of adjusting NDC pensions.

The Swedish "brake" mechanism adjusts benefits in the Swedish NDC system when the system is not in financial balance. Box 4.6 describes the system.[7]

---

[7] For a summary, see Sundén (2009) and Swedish Pensions Agency (2009), and for more detailed discussion, Palmer (2002), Settergren (2001), Könberg *et al.* (2006) and Bovenberg (in press). On automatic balancing mechanisms more broadly, see Vidal-Melia *et al.* (2009).

Box 4.6 The balance mechanism and brake in the Swedish NDC system

In Sweden's NDC pension system, a worker's notional accumulation is scheduled to increase each year by an interest rate of w, the rate of growth of average earnings. Pensions in payment are indexed each year by w −1.6 percent, where 1.6 percent is intended to represent the long-run growth of real wage rates. So long as real wages grow as projected, accumulations rise in line with the real wage rate, and pensions in payment in line with long-run average price change.

Solvency is tested by comparing the assets and liabilities of the system. The Balance Ratio (BR) is defined as

$$\frac{\text{Contribution asset} + \text{buffer funds}}{\text{Pension liabilities}}$$

where: The contribution asset, calculated as a three-year moving average, is intended to capture the present value of projected contribution revenues, based on recent data; and pension liabilities, also calculated as a three-year moving average, are a measure of the present value of the flow of pensions due to current retirees and current workers, also based on recent data.

The system is designed to adjust the default arrangement automatically if sustainability is projected to be a problem. As the definition of the ratio makes clear, key drivers of sustainability are the growth of employment, which affects contributions, and the performance of financial markets, which directly affects the value of the buffer fund. The methods of measuring contribution assets and pension liabilities in the balance ratio have a critical bearing on the operation of automatic adjustment.

When the balance ratio is less than one, a "brake" is automatically applied, whereby the accrual rate of workers' accumulations and the indexation of pensions in payment are both reduced below the growth rate of earnings. Specifically, both accruals and the indexation of pensions in payment are based not on w, but on $(1+w)\text{BR}-1$, and these lower rates of indexation continue until financial balance is restored. If the balance ratio moves above one, there is catch-up for the period with a lower ratio. In contrast, the

> **Box 4.6** (*cont.*)
> discount rate used to calculate a person's annuity at retirement does
> not change.[a]
>
> [a] Annuities are calculated using an annuity divisor determined by life
>   expectancy and an interest rate of 1.6 percent, as an estimate of long-run
>   real wage growth.

Though this is not the place for detailed discussion of the Swedish
mechanism, some criticisms assist better design of automatic
adjustment.

• Adjustment is all on the benefits side: the brake reduces benefits
  if contributions fall or the return to the buffer fund declines. In
  addition, there is no upward adjustment for higher contribution
  revenues later. Though there is no long-run effect on the average
  level of benefits, for some periods benefits fall below their long-run
  trajectory.
• The adjustment can be large: the mechanism in Box 4.6 implies a reduction in real benefits in Sweden in 2010 of 4.6 percent (Sundén, 2009,
  Table 2), rather than adjusting gradually. Not least for this reason, as
  discussed in Subsection 4.5.2, the full adjustment was not applied.
• The reduction in benefit could last for a long time, although there is
  no long-term experience yet.
• The adjustment applies both to accruals and to benefits in payment.
  Thus the previous two factors are important, since a reduction of
  pension benefits occurs at a time when the individual has little or no
  time to adjust.

These problems suggest lessons for policy design, discussed further in
Section 4.7.

Ways of adjusting NDC pensions

There are in principle four sets of parameters which can be adjusted
to keep an NDC system in long-run balance: the notional interest rate,
which affects the accrual rate of current workers and hence their initial
benefit; the indexation rule for benefits in payment; earliest eligibility
age; and the contribution rate. The appropriate response depends on
whether there is an immediate need for an improvement in net cash
flows or whether the issue is one of long-run sustainability.

Adjusting the interest rate: automatic adjustment of the notional interest rate is a sensible response to projected problems of long-run sustainability. One way to make such adjustment is in terms of the balance ratio, as in Sweden, with both a reduction and a catch-up provision. The role of projections is important. The greater the independence of the actuarial office responsible for projections and the greater the public acceptance of those projections, the greater the space for discretionary policy. In contrast, the less the perceived independence and the less the public acceptance, the more important it is to have exact rules.

Adjusting benefits in payment: adjusting the interest rate addresses long-term sustainability in response both to demographic and economic outcomes. It is, however, not good policy to place sole reliance on this instrument. Benefits in payment require separate consideration since retirees have less time to adjust by working more or increasing other forms of pension saving and hence are less able to bear risk than younger workers. The fact that retirees have a more limited range of ways to adjust does not imply that they should necessarily always be fully protected, but does suggest that they should as far as possible be protected from sharp short-run shocks. One approach is to protect benefits in payment where the adjustment is to long-run trends, and to consider reducing benefits only where there is a severe short-run cash flow problem. The latter will happen only in the face of serious turbulence to a system with only a small buffer stock. In that case it might be necessary to cut benefits, but with a limit to the size of any real decrease.

Increasing earliest eligibility age: automatic adjustment of the earliest eligibility age in an NDC system does not help to contain pension spending given quasi-actuarial adjustment, but increases the replacement rate at a given age, and hence may be an appropriate way of offsetting the effects of a medium-term reduction in the interest rate, for example as life expectancy rises.

Adjusting contribution rates: it may be appropriate to adjust contribution rates as well as benefit levels when adapting the system. As life expectancy increases, there will be a quasi-actuarial reduction in benefits. In a first-best world, a worker could fully offset the decline in benefits by choosing to retire later, depending, inter alia, on his or her health and productivity and labor markets for older workers. In practice, as noted earlier, for reasons that behavioral economics addresses, many people retire as soon as they are allowed even if it leads to poverty in old age. Thus it is unlikely that the quasi-actuarial reduction in benefits will be fully offset by delayed retirement, so that the typical replacement rate will fall. In a system where contribution rates are not too large, a possible response is an automatic increase in contributions. For example, each year there could be a calculation of the increase in contribution rate needed to preserve the replacement rate of a new cohort of workers in the light of projected increased life expectancy, assuming that a fraction, say two thirds, of the decline in the replacement rate is offset by longer careers.[8] Recall that higher contributions automatically result in higher benefits for those facing higher contributions. Thus on a rolling basis, contributor rates would rise over a person's working life to avoid the complexity of different contribution rates for workers of different ages.

Adjusting private DB plans: the case of the Netherlands

Alongside the citizen's pension in the Netherlands is a system of occupational pensions, which are required to be funded.[9] The system has evolved over the years in the face of financial pressures.

- In 1998 about one quarter of workers were in career-average DB plans and about two thirds in final-salary plans.
- In the early 2000s there was a move from final pay to career average, which reached three quarters of the workforce by 2004, and a smaller move to DC plans.
- As a response to stricter funding requirements and declining financial returns, there was a restructuring of pension plans, with automatic reduction in the generosity of indexation of benefits – both the accrual rate for workers and of benefits in payment – if funding fell below a threshold, and with some increase in contributions, the extent of adjustment depending on the solvency of each fund.

At the end of 2008, the main characteristics of the system were as follows (Kortleve and Ponds, 2010).

- A uniform accrual rate across all workers in a plan.
- A uniform contribution rate for all workers in a plan.

---

[8] Diamond and Orszag (2005, Chapter 10) suggest a similar approach for adjusting the US social security system.
[9] For a summary, see Kortleve and Ponds (2010), and for fuller discussion, Kortleve and Ponds (2009) and Ponds and van Riel (2009).

- A uniform mix of assets.
- A uniform indexation rule for all participants in a plan: a typical plan indexes with the wage growth of the industry or company; some plans index pensions during build-up in this way but pensions in payment in line with price inflation. Crucially, the actual indexation rate depends on the solvency of the plan.

Since funding helps to smooth adjustments by providing a financial buffer, Dutch pensions fell less during the economic crisis than pensions under the Swedish "brake" mechanism. However, Kortleve and Ponds (2010) report that between September 2008 and February 2009 the fraction of plans with funding below 105 percent (the threshold at which underindexation began) rose from 12 percent of plans to 85 percent, calling into question the sufficiency of these adjustments. Because of the resulting doubts about the robustness of the system, the 2010 Spring Accord moved closer to a DC arrangement.

The Pension Accord of Spring 2010 identified two core problems: the absence of adjustment to rising life expectancy, and the fact that the system was insufficiently shockproof, and recommended a series of reforms to the citizen's pension and occupational plans.

- A ceiling on contributions.
- Strengthening the citizen's pension, at the same time increasing the eligibility age to 66 in 2020 and to about 67 in 2025, with actuarial adjustment for someone who starts benefit later than the eligibility age.
- Analogously, the earliest eligibility age of occupational pensions should rise in response to increasing life expectancy, together with flexible retirement and actuarial adjustment where a person delays taking benefit.
- A separate line of reform was to discuss how to change the indexation rules to reduce nominal guarantees, making pension rights more dependent on financial market outcomes, so as to make the system more resilient to macroeconomic shocks.

Thus there have been two waves of reform. In the middle of the decade, the Netherlands modified a DB system with all adjustment on the contributions side into one where adjustment takes place also on the benefits side. That arrangement shared risks among workers, employers and pensioners more broadly than in either a conventional DB system (where the risk in a simple plan falls on the employer) or a conventional DC plan (where the risk in a simple plan falls on the worker). In the second wave of reform proposals, almost all adjustment is on the benefits side. In that sense, the changes are starting to look like the move in other countries, for example, the UK, from DB to DC, with risks borne increasingly by current participants, and less by employers or future generations.

Adjusting public DB plans

In a DB system, for example, a system of social insurance which is not allowed to borrow, the effects of macroeconomic turbulence fall on workers, whose contributions have to rise to pay promised benefits. Depending on the pension formula (e.g., how pensions are indexed), some risk can fall also on pensioners. In either case, however, risk can be pooled only among current participants.

In contrast, if legislation permits the social insurance fund to accumulate a surplus or borrow to finance a deficit, it becomes possible to share risks more widely across cohorts. Where such activity is well done, there is a potential welfare gain from wider risk sharing, for example the Norwegian Government Petroleum Fund (Norway Central Bank, 2009) uses some of the revenue from oil taxation to build up an accumulation as a buffer against demographic change, thus providing some tax smoothing. On the other hand, the political risks might be larger than in a system where contributions are required to cover benefits. Legislation can change the rules of the game, which is an advantage with good government but courts the risk of government failure. Thus – the fault line discussed in Box 4.3 – the question recurs whether, as an empirical matter, political discretion is an additional risk or an insurance mechanism against unanticipated shocks. Since outcomes can be influenced by political choices the distribution of risks is not clear.

4.5 The financial and economic crisis

Space, time and expertise preclude a systematic comparative overview of how different systems performed. The aim of this section is more modest – to offer a selection of relevant examples, first describing the effect of the financial and economic crises on different types of pension system and then, in Subsections 4.5.2 and 4.5.3, setting out early responses and subsequent responses, respectively.[10]

4.5.1 What happened

OECD (2009; see also Pino and Yermo, 2010) makes the distinction between the financial crisis, whose major effect was on public and private pension funds, and the economic crisis, whose major effect was a decline in output and hence a shrinking contributions base for PAYG pensions.

Private pensions

Private pension funds across the OECD countries experienced a nominal loss of 21.4 percent in 2008 (in real terms a loss of 24.1 percent) (Pino and Yermo, 2010, p. 17), partly compensated by rising equity prices in 2009. The stock market crash of 2008, on top of that at the start of the decade, meant that equity performance over the decade as a whole was poor. DB plans faced a two-fold ill-effect: the decline in market valuations created or enlarged fund deficits; and the decline in interest rates, used as the risk-free discount rate, increased the measured size of those deficits.

Individual funded accounts

The most visible effect was on workers whose retirement income comes largely from individual accounts, as in the USA. Such pensions typically rely heavily on stocks, so that the large fall in stock values greatly reduced the retirement funds of many workers. For those near retirement the fall in asset values led to delays in planned retirement for many workers with the opportunity to continue working. Workers without such opportunities retired at a much lower income than anticipated. Some workers who had already retired returned to work, while others remained in retirement but with greatly reduced resources. See Sass *et al.* (2010).

The impact on workers and retirees also depended on the extent to which they had public and private DB pensions that were sustained.

---

[10] For detailed discussion of initial responses, see OECD (2009) or, more briefly, D'Addio *et al.* (2010).

Munnell and Muldoon (2008, p. 3), report that in the USA between October 9, 2007 and October 9, 2008,

the value of equities in retirement accounts declined by almost $4.0 trillion. Individuals were sheltered from the immediate impact of the $1.9 trillion of losses in defined benefit plans [from $4.4 trillion in October 2007]. But they did experience a direct hit on the $2.0 trillion in losses that occurred in 401(k)s and IRAs [from $4.7 trillion in October 2007]. In all likelihood, many panicked amid the turmoil and sold assets at depressed prices. And these people may be late in getting back into the market to enjoy gains as the market recovers. Equally important, holders of 401(k)s/IRAs were left feeling vulnerable and impotent as their savings evaporated. The question this crisis raises is whether pension participants need to be protected from this type of gut-wrenching volatility.

Funded occupational plans

There was also a major impact on the funding of DB pensions that were meant to be fully funded, particularly in the US and the Netherlands. As noted, Munnell and Muldoon report that DB plans in the US lost $1.9 trillion of their value of $4.4 trillion a year earlier, about half of the loss arising in private plans and half in state and local government plans. Kortleve and Ponds (2009, p. 2) report that in the Netherlands,

from 2007 onward, the funding ratio fell dramatically, from a high of 150 percent in mid-2007 to less than 90 percent in the first quarter of 2009. The drop resulted from the combined effect of the worldwide fall in stock prices and the fall in nominal interest rates, which drove up the (market) value of the plan's nominal liabilities.

This decline in funding has led to widespread revisions of DB plans, which have reduced anticipated benefits.

Public pensions

A major effect of the economic crisis for public pensions was to reduce contributions and increase the demand for income-tested benefits. In addition, public social security trust funds faced large losses in 2008. Among high-income countries with a diversified portfolio of assets in their trust fund, the largest loss was nearly 31 percent of fund value in Ireland, the smallest 16.4 percent in Finland. Pino and Yermo (2010, p. 12) point to the exposure to equity risk in those countries. Some of the loss was made up during 2009. In contrast, the US social security system, whose Trust Fund is wholly invested in US government bonds, made no loss.

Naturally the stock decline had less of an impact on partially funded systems, although the ensuing large recession affected such plans as well. For example, in Sweden,

The balance ratio was close to 1.0 through 2007. In 2008, the balance ratio fell – for the first time – below 1.0 [to 0.9672, i.e., a drop of 3.28 percent]. The main reason for the large deficit was the sharp decrease in equity prices during the fall of 2008. The buffer funds experienced a negative return of 21.3 percent.(Sundén, 2009, p. 2)

That is, a decline in the value of the buffer fund contributed to a 3.28 percent drop in projected assets relative to projected benefits. Someone claiming benefits one year after the application of the brake faced a 3.28 percent fall in benefits that year. In addition benefits in payment grow more slowly until the balance ratio is restored, after which benefit growth could speed up. In contrast, if a 21.3 percent decline in the value of assets experienced in the Swedish system were to occur in an individual DC account for someone on the verge of retirement, the result would be a 21.3 percent drop in benefits at retirement and in each later year.

Since US Social Security was fully invested in US Treasury bonds, the stock market decline had no effect on its financing, though the recession did. Comparing Trustee Reports, the actuarial deficit in the 75-year projection is 1.70 percent of taxable payroll in the 2008 report (relative to the 12.4 percent payroll tax) and 2.00 percent in 2009. This measure indicates the change that would be needed over the 75-year period as a whole if financed by an immediate increase in the rate of payroll tax.

Outcomes
Given earlier discussion, the strategic conclusions in an OECD assessment (2009, Table 1.1) of early outcomes should not be surprising.

• Deleterious effects were stronger for older workers and pensioners than for younger workers.
• Deleterious effects were stronger in DC plans, especially where exposure to risky assets was greater and where annuitization is

compulsory. At least initially, effects were more moderate in private DB plans and public PAYG systems, which have wider options for addressing deficits. Later responses are discussed shortly.

- Deleterious effects in the short run were stronger in countries which had (a) greater reliance on DC pensions, (b) poorer investment performance and (c) less well-developed safety nets. Thus pensions were hit hard in a country like Mexico, which scored badly on all three elements. There was more protection in the short run in countries like the Netherlands, with a fairly high citizen's pension, discussed further in Subsection 4.6.1, and a well-managed and substantial buffer fund, though precisely because the system could limit short-run shocks, the long-run effects are likely to be substantial.

It should be remembered, however, that systems that gave relatively more protection to older workers and pensioners gave relatively less protection to other groups, including current and future workers. In terms of the Netherlands, van Ewijk writes (2009, p. 349) that:

the distributional effects of ... policies are highly skewed. The older generations, in particular the cohorts born just after World War II, are hurt excessively by the shock of the crisis, losing up to almost 15% of consumption during their remaining life time. This contrasts with the younger generations who lose hardly any pension wealth. Even if one takes into account that younger generations are hit in their human capital – here taken at 3% on a life time basis – this does not balance with the losses of the older generations.

These findings illustrate the earlier argument that it is difficult to reduce aggregate risk; policy is mostly about choosing between different ways of sharing risk.

4.5.2 Early responses

In broad brush terms, public pensions responded in two phases.

- In the immediate aftermath of the crisis, there were three sets of responses: little change in the structure of state pensions; higher government spending on social protection; and higher government borrowing to finance the extra spending.

- A second phase saw more radical reform, given rising levels of government deficit and the resulting pressures from financial markets.

Early responses included:

Higher benefits
Some countries increased the level of benefits or announced future increases. Australia, Belgium, France, Spain and the UK increased the minimum retirement income. Finland introduce a new safety-net old-age income in 2011, 23 percent higher than the existing benefit.

Non-application of automatic adjustments
Some countries introduced discretionary modifications to the automatic adjustment mechanism in their systems. In Sweden, the balance ratio fell below one for the first time in 2008, calling for automatic adjustment in 2010, reflecting the lags in both calculation and implementation. The brake mechanism described in Box 4.6 implied a reduction of pensions in payment by 1.3 percent because of slow wage growth, amplified by application of the balancing mechanism, so that the full effect would have been a reduction of pensions in payment by 4.6 percent (Sundén, 2009, Table 2).

The policy response was rapid:

The balance ratio was published in March 2009 and, almost immediately, the five political parties that stand behind the pension reform – known as the Pension Group – started to discuss whether to propose smoothing the adjustment of pension benefits (+4.5 in 2009 and -4.6 in 2010). In particular, the group discussed if it was reasonable that the stock market crash should affect NDC benefits so much. The Pension Group suggested that, instead of using the market value of the buffer funds, a three-year average should be used to value the funds.(Sundén, 2009, p. 3)

After some debate, the government, supported by the Pension Group, went ahead with the proposal, passing legislation in October 2009.

As discussed earlier, the system in Germany has a sustainability factor which automatically adjusts the value of a pension point for changes in wages and the dependency rate. The optimistic economic outlook at the time that the sustainability factor was introduced in 2005 led the government to legislate increases 0.6–0.7 percentage points greater than specified in the rules in 2008 and 2009. And in mid-2009 legislation established a pension guarantee (*Rentengarantie*) which prevents reductions in nominal pensions in the face of declining wages (see Börsch-Supan *et al.*, 2010).

One-off payments as part of stimulus packages
Australia introduced a one-off payment of AUD 1,000. Greece, the UK and the USA had similar policies, which often extended beyond the elderly.

Reduced social insurance contributions
These were observed for example in the Czech Republic, Germany, Japan and Spain, and had two motives: to reduce employer costs in the hope of encouraging employment, and to increase the net earnings of workers.

Allowing early access to some retirement savings
Some countries (e.g., Denmark and Iceland) allowed individuals early access to their pension savings, an option already allowed in Australia in specific circumstances such as to prevent foreclosure of a family's mortgage. Though such a policy protects current family income and stimulates demand during recession, it increases the risk of future elderly poverty, particularly given the large losses in private pension funds.

Given the way that private pensions operate, most adjustment lagged the immediate impact of the crisis.

4.5.3 *Subsequent responses*

Public pensions
The initial response – no structural reform, but higher pension spending – was an understandable crisis response, but unsustainable given the effects of the recession on government revenues. In countries where doubts about government solvency were greatest, financial markets added pressure to accelerate reforms in public systems as a counterpoint to political reluctance to reduce spending sharply. Responses were various.

The OECD (2009, p. 79) supports the view that "one of the key motives for pension reform has been to improve the long-term financial sustainability of pension systems." Thus many countries, though not all, reduced benefits.

Lower benefits in payment have been implemented in different ways.

Across-the-board cuts
These took place in Austria, Finland, Germany, Italy, Japan, Korea, Portugal and Turkey.

Gross pension entitlements for people under the reformed rules will be an average of 22% lower for full-career workers than under the pre-reform rules in these countries. The largest cuts, of around 40%, will be in Korea and Portugal, with more modest changes of 10–25% in the rest of this group.

(OECD, 2009, p. 79)

Cuts that protect low earners
Cuts in France, Mexico and Sweden largely or wholly protected low earners from benefit cuts which affected others. In France and Sweden, the cuts are around 20 percent for workers with average earnings, but only about 5 percent for those with low earnings. This policy direction emphasizes the poverty relief function of pensions.

Strengthening the relation between contributions and benefits
This policy direction, in contrast, emphasizes the consumption-smoothing purpose of pensions. Reforms in Hungary, Poland and the Slovak Republic weaken the redistributive features of the system as well as reducing benefits. Low-earning workers in Poland and the Slovak Republic face benefit cuts of 25 percent and 13 percent, respectively; the comparable figures for workers on average earnings are less than 5 percent.

Alongside lower benefits in payment were cuts in future benefits.

Less generous indexation
Some countries made the rules about accrual rates more parsimonious, either explicitly or by increasing the number of years of contributions necessary for a full pension. Indexation of pensions in payment can also be made more parsimonious. For example, the UK is proposing to move indexation of the state pension from the retail price index (RPI) to the consumer price index (CPI), the effect being to reduce the rate of increase of pensions.[11]

---

[11] The CPI is based on the HCIP (Harmonised Consumer Index Prices), a measure which complies with standards throughout Europe. The RPI differs in a number of ways: (a) The RPI includes mortgage interest payments. Thus if interest rates are cut, the RPI will fall but not the CPI. (b) The RPI also includes council tax and some other housing costs not included in CPI. (c) The CPI includes some financial services not included in the RPI. (d) The CPI is based on a wider sample of the population for working out weights.

Higher eligibility age

In many countries, retirement ages are being increased. As discussed in Box 4.5, under 1991 legislation, the UK is in the process of raising women's retirement age from 60 to 65, to equalize that of men. Legislation in 2007 raised the state pension age from 65 to 66 in 2024, and to 67 in 2034. As a result of the crisis, the government has announced an accelerated timetable, whereby from December 2018 the state pension age for both men and women will start to increase, to reach 66 by April 2020. The government is also considering the timetable for future increases to the state pension age from 66 to 68.

In the Netherlands, an element in the Spring Accord of 2010 is to increase the earliest eligibility age for the citizen's pension to 66 in 2020 and to 67 in 2025, with a parallel increase for occupational pensions. Denmark and Germany have also passed legislation raising normal pension age gradually to 67 or 68, and the Czech Republic and Hungary are moving normal pension age to 65. Alongside increases in normal pension age, several countries, including Finland, are proposing to increase the age at which early retirement is allowed.

However, not all countries cut benefits. Higher pensions arise for a variety of different reasons. As discussed below, the state pension age is set to increase in the UK, which will allow people to build a larger entitlement. The same is true in the Czech Republic. In Australia and Norway benefits are set to increase because membership of private pensions has been made mandatory.

Private pensions

Under the Spring Accord of 2010 in the Netherlands, already discussed, the earliest eligibility age for occupational pensions would rise with that for the citizen's pension, together with flexible retirement and actuarial adjustment where a person takes benefits later. In addition, there will be consideration of adjusting the indexation rules so that pension rights are more dependent on financial markets, making the system more resilient in the face of shocks but exposing participants to more risk.

Private, funded DB plans in many countries, facing large deficits, have considered a range of responses. These include a move from DB to DC, for example by closing the DB arrangements to new entrants or, more stringently, preserving the acquired DB rights of current participants but with future contributions by current participants being put onto a DC basis. In most countries such moves have been a response to longer-term trends, notably greater life expectancy, rather than to the economic crisis. However, the crisis may accentuate the trend.

Another approach has been to make indexation less generous. The replacement of the RPI by the CPI as the basis of indexation for the UK state pension was noted earlier. It is proposed that occupational plans should also make that change.

It is interesting to speculate on how to interpret what is happening. The optimist's view is that pension systems adjusted initially as a Keynesian response to the crisis, with subsequent adjustment to restore sustainability. A less rosy view is that over the medium term the financial and economic shocks, coming on top of adjustment to demographic change that has been postponed for too long, will cause a long-term structural shift towards funded DC arrangements. This is exactly the fault line discussed in Box 4.3. The lessons from recent experience are taken up more fully in Subsection 4.7.1.

4.6 Policy directions

In considering lessons for pension design, a starting point is to note that there is no single best pension system (Barr and Diamond, 2009, Box 5). Thus the discussion that follows is not – because it cannot be – a single optimum recipe, but a series of ingredients on which reforms may draw.

4.6.1 Addressing elderly poverty

Over the past half century people's relationship with the labor market has become more diverse, an implication being less complete contributions records. In addition, family structures have become more fluid, so that basing a woman's entitlement to pension on her husband's contributions (whether or not it was ever desirable) is no longer feasible.

These economic and social changes underpin the argument for a non-contributory, citizen's pension paid on the basis of age and residence rather than of contributions, as in the Netherlands, New Zealand, Australia, Canada and Chile. A citizen's pension strengthens poverty relief in terms of coverage and adequacy, with advantages in terms of gender balance. Proposals to strengthen the citizen's pension in the Netherlands Spring Accord 2010 have already been noted.

The connection with systemic risk arises in several ways:

- Poor people have less of a cushion against downward shocks, particularly the elderly, who have fewer options and less time for adjustment than younger people. It is thus important to sustain the poverty relief element of pensions in the face of systemic risk.
- A larger first-tier pension reduces the relative importance of the second-tier pension.
- The citizen's pension can adjust to demographic change in parallel with changes to the second-tier pension, for example through a matching increase in the earliest age of eligibility, as proposed in the Netherlands.
- Being tax financed, the pension can share the risks of economic turbulence with future generations through government borrowing, though the ability to do so will depend on economic conditions.

4.6.2 Redefining retirement

We have already discussed why part of the response to demographic change is an increase in earliest eligibility age.

Alongside the argument for later retirement is the separate argument for more flexible retirement. Individuals have different tastes and face different constraints. Thus it is welfare enhancing to offer choice and flexibility over the move from full-time work to full retirement. Flexible retirement would be good policy even if there were no problems in paying for pensions. Separately, flexible retirement options, by giving workers another margin of adjustment, are another way of sharing risk.

4.6.3 Consumption smoothing: simple, low-cost savings plans

A third lesson, drawing on information economics and behavioral economics, is that reduced choice can be welfare enhancing.

Lessons from information economics

Choice and competition are beneficial when consumers are well informed. In the case of pensions, there is considerable evidence that consumers are extraordinarily badly informed. A survey found that 50 percent of Americans did not know the difference between a stock and a bond. Most people with a funded individual account do not understand the need to shift from equities to bonds as they age. Very few people realize the significance of administrative charges.

Lessons from behavioral economics

Simple economic theory predicts that people act rationally, and so will save voluntarily for their old age. What actually happens is very different.

- Procrastination: people delay saving, or do not save, or do not save enough.
- Inertia: with automatic enrolment many more people stay in the pension plan.
- Immobilization: if a person has to make a choice, particularly one that he does not understand, a likely result is to do nothing.

Thus there is considerable divergence between what simple economic theory predicts and what actually happens. Behavioral economics helps to explain why (Barr and Diamond, 2008, Box 9.6).

Implications

The conclusion from these literatures is that there is good reason to be skeptical about the gains from individual choice in mandatory accounts, suggesting a number of lessons.

- It is useful to make membership mandatory or to use automatic enrolment.
- Constrained choice is welfare enhancing.
- A good default option is necessary for people who make no choice.
- It is desirable to decouple account management from the investment decision, and to centralize all record keeping to keep administrative costs down.

The US Thrift Savings Plan (www.tsp.gov) for federal civil servants is an example of this approach. Workers are auto-enrolled and choose from about five funds, e.g., an equities fund, a government bonds fund, etc. There is centralized account administration to keep costs low, and wholesale management of funds in the private sector, where the firm concerned has to manage an identical portfolio for its private clients, thus providing some insulation against political interference. The arrangement simplifies the choice for workers, respecting information constraints, and keeps administrative costs low.

Box 4.7 The National Employment Savings Trust in the UK

A new pension arrangement, the National Employment Savings Trust (NEST), established under the UK Pensions Act 2008, will provide a low-costs savings vehicle, particularly for low-to-moderate earners (www.nestpensions.org.uk).

- From 2012 all eligible workers will be automatically enrolled either in NEST or another qualifying occupational scheme.
- The reforms will be introduced in stages, starting with the largest employers.
- When fully phased in, the minimum contribution will be 8 percent of earnings, comprising contributions of 4 percent from the worker, 3 percent from the employer and 1 percent in tax relief, with a maximum total contribution of £3,600 per year (indexed to earnings).
- A participant's savings pot is portable. Thus there is no continuing administration for employers when a member leaves their employment. Where a worker changes job, contributions in the new job can be added to their existing retirement savings pot. And more than one employer can contribute to a member's savings pot.

The UK is introducing a similar system, summarized in Box 4.7, from 2012, in essence a low-cost funded individual account similar to the Thrift Savings Plan.

KiwiSaver individual accounts in New Zealand, introduced in 2007, are a variant of this approach, and the first example of automatic enrolment on a national scale. Automatic enrolment is reinforced by a government match for contributions up to a ceiling plus a one-off payment when the account is first opened. The combined effect of these factors was considerable. In 2007, 13 percent of workers belonged to an occupational plan and 5.5 percent to a personal plan. KiwiSaver achieved coverage of 44 percent within its first year of operation, about three quarters of which were through occupational provision, the rest through personal plans. For further detail, see Rashbrooke (2009).

The lessons from the economics of information and behavioral economics apply also to the decumulation phase, suggesting that mandatory annuitization of at least part of a worker's accumulation becomes a relevant option. This is the case with the UK NEST pensions,[12] but not with the Thrift Savings Plan.

4.6.4 *Consumption smoothing: NDC*

The Thrift Savings Plan approach is one way to organize consumption smoothing. Another is through an NDC system that is partially funded to provide a buffer. Such plans can have a range of advantages. They are simple from the viewpoint of workers, and centrally administered, so with low administrative costs. With a sufficiently large buffer of partial funding, they can smooth the volatility of capital markets.[13] Indeed, Peter Diamond and I have argued that in the context of China, individual accounts make a lot of sense, but do not have to be funded; instead, we argue for notional accounts (see Barr and Diamond, 2010b).

NDC systems adjust to increasing life expectancy by actuarially reducing the pension at the earliest eligibility age. The brake mechanism in the Swedish system provides some automatic adjustment, but that adjustment (a) falls entirely on the benefits side, as in any DC system, (b) can be sharp and (c) of fairly long duration, (d) falls on benefits in payment as well as accruals, and (e) even so, may not bring the system back into financial balance. The next section discusses lessons for pension design.

4.7 Conclusions

4.7.1 *Main lessons*

Earlier discussion suggests lessons for designing pensions to respond to systemic shocks.

[12] Except for small accumulations, it used to be obligatory to annuitize at least 75 percent of the accumulation by age 75. Since 2011, the strict provisions have been somewhat liberalized.

[13] Note the requirement for a large buffer fund. Pensioners in the fully funded system in the Netherlands were more protected in the immediate aftermath of the crisis than those in the Swedish NDC system.

**Pension systems should contain a wide range of
automatic adjustment to demographic change**
Some such design is already in place. NDC pensions reduce pensions actuarially in respect of increased life expectancy. Demographic adjustment in the German system reduces pensions in respect of rising life expectancy and the size of the labor force, the latter addressing changes in fertility. All such adjustment, however, falls on monthly benefits. What is needed in addition is some automatic adjustment of the earliest eligibility age to rising life expectancy. Policymakers might regard one year of retirement for each two years of work as a feasible and desirable long-run average; thus eligibility age could rise by eight months for every one-year increase in life expectancy at that earliest eligibility age. Since the contributions base expands as people work longer, such an increase may be sufficient to keep contributions broadly constant.

Though such indexation may not be analytically optimal, it has several advantages: it is simple, hence transparent; it would transform political expectations, in particular so that retirement age is regarded as a variable rather than a parameter; and if anything, it errs on the side of parsimony – if economic conditions permit policymakers could apply a smaller increase in the eligibility age.

Adjustment should embrace both benefits and contributions
Where a plan is in deficit, reducing benefits imposes the risk on pensioners and higher contributions imposes it on workers. Unless there are good reasons for doing otherwise, adjustment to a current or prospective deficit should involve both benefits and contributions. In that sense, the system in the Netherlands during the economic crisis was like the Swedish brake, but with adjustment also on the contributions side;[14] as noted earlier, Diamond and Orszag (2005, Chapter 10) suggest this approach for adjusting the US social security system.

Where such adjustment takes place, there are gains if downward and upward adjustment are broadly symmetrical, so as to restore lost pension and/or reduce contributions when conditions allow.

---

[14] As noted earlier, the 2010 Spring Accord moved away from this arrangement, since the proposed ceiling on contribution rates places adjustment on the benefits side.

Default indexation should be designed carefully

As the default, contributions during working life should generally be indexed to the rate of growth of real wages. Benefits in retirement should be indexed to prices (many countries), wages (many plans in the Netherlands, at least until recently) or a weighted average of price and wage inflation (for example, Finland). There may need to be temporary movement away from these defaults in the face of adverse economic conditions. In some countries, the Netherlands being one, indexation is conditional on financial performance.

There are many examples of faulty indexation (see Barr and Diamond, 2008, Boxes 5.6 and 5.8 for problems in the US and UK, respectively); and the Swedish approach to indexing pensions in payment also has problems (Barr and Diamond, 2008, p. 76).

Adjustments should take account of the life cycle

Sharp downward adjustment in indexation may be appropriate for younger workers, but adjustment should avoid sudden large shocks, particularly for pensioners and workers close to retirement. This may imply a longer period before solvency is restored. This argument applies even if the underlying utility function of an older person is no more risk averse than that of a younger person; but with less time to adapt, the welfare loss from a given adjustment will be larger for an older person. The implication is not that pensioners should necessarily be protected from all risk, but that they should be exposed to less risk than younger participants. For example, if pensions in payment are indexed 20 percent to wages and 80 percent to prices, a fall in real wages will impact on pensions in payment, but with only 20 percent of the effect on the rate of accrual of benefits of younger workers.

Adjustments should reflect the time horizon of any shock

In considering adjustment mechanisms, it is useful to distinguish two circumstances. One is a temporary problem, for example caused by a sharp fall in asset values. Responding promptly is important because it is not clear how long the problem will last, but with a catch-up provision as the economy recovers. In contrast, where there are concerns about the long-run sustainability of a system, a less generous system may be needed permanently, which will generally require legislation.

A central question is whether adjustment that is appropriate for a temporary shock is also appropriate for a sustained period of stringency, perhaps because the growth of the labor force is slower than anticipated when the system was being designed. The experience with automatic adjustment in Germany, the Netherlands and Sweden suggests that even the most carefully designed automatic mechanisms face problems. This issue highlights one of the roles of periodic review, the last of the lessons discussed here.

An automatic mechanism will not suffice in all circumstances

The previous discussion suggests two reasons why automatic adjustment, though highly desirable, will not always be sufficient:

- Severe short-run turbulence may exceed the economically and politically acceptable tolerance of the automatic mechanism; or
- Long-run developments may cumulatively have the same effect, noting particularly that over the longer term pension systems have to adjust not only to changing economic and demographic circumstances, but also to changing social needs.

For either reason, it is likely that a country will at some time need some discretionary action to supplement a rules-based system. It is therefore desirable to include a mechanism for discretionary action as part of legislative design, not as later crisis response.

A minimalist approach would incorporate automatic adjustment, but implemented with a lag to allow a legislative alternative. The system in Canada has this feature. This approach, however, has the disadvantage of being party political.

An alternative approach is through a periodic independent review which would consider adjustment to either short- or long-run developments. Its remit should include:

- Contributions and benefits: The review could recommend potential adjustments to the rules for the accruals rate, to the discount rate used to calculate a worker's initial benefit, to the indexation of benefits in payment, and to the contribution rate.
- Eligibility age: The remit should also include the option of deviating from the automatic adjustment of the earliest eligibility age, an issue of sustainability as far as the citizen's pension is concerned, and of desirable replacement rates in a DC or NDC pension.
- Changing social needs: A recent example in many countries is the ability of unmarried partners to share pension accumulations in the same way as married couples.

The review is intended to guard as much as possible against government failure in the form of postponing necessary adjustment, or of phasing it in on a slow timetable determined by short-run politics rather than prudent long-term management of the pension system. To that end, two features are important. First, the review should meet at legislatively specified times, say every five years. Second, it should be non-party-political and independent, for example with the status of a Presidential Commission or Royal Commission.

In sum
The strategic questions about adjustment are (a) for whom, (b) how fast and (c) at which margins? Good design suggests that policy to accommodate demographic change and economic fluctuations should consider adjustments both of benefits and contributions, and should be phased to avoid abrupt changes, particularly for older workers and pensioners.

4.7.2 What implications for the Dutch pension system?

It is useful to discuss separately the implications of earlier discussion for the system in the Netherlands, and lessons from the Netherlands for other countries.

Implications for the Netherlands
It is clear that pension arrangements in the Netherlands already have many desirable elements of adjustment to systemic risk.

- The system is based on a citizen's pension which is high enough to provide effective poverty relief and for which eligibility is based on residence rather than contributions.
- The most recent agreement includes a formula for increasing the earliest eligibility age both for the citizen's pension and occupational pensions as life expectancy increases, with an actuarial increase for a delayed start to benefit.
- The system of occupational pensions used to be mainly DB, thus sharing risk more broadly than a system of individual accounts, though recent changes move the system more towards a collective DC system, and the 2010 Spring Accord almost completely.
- Therefore, the system has been able to protect pensioners and older workers from excessive sharp shocks.

- The system has adjusted to demographic change and macroeconomic turbulence, previously by adjusting both benefits and contributions, but in the latest agreement between social partners through adjustment on the benefits side. Policymakers have explicitly asked the right question – how should risk be shared?

Thus the system offers useful lessons in risk sharing. An additional desirable form of adjustment could easily be incorporated. Adjustment could (and should) be sensitive to the life cycle. As discussed, the cost of a given adjustment is more costly in welfare terms the less time there is to adjust. Thus, for example, there could be different funds for younger workers and older workers, the balance between equities and bonds shifting towards bonds for the older group. Or there could be an age-related indexation rule, with full, or almost full, price indexation of pensions in payment.[15]

Implications for other countries

The system in the Netherlands is highly sophisticated, both in a static context (e.g., the way that occupational pensions are the subject of agreement by the social partners), and in the way that it has adjusted to systemic risk, in particular the rather rapid evolution from final salary to career average DB, then to a hybrid in which adjustment falls not only on the contributions side but also on pensions in payment, and finally, through a ceiling on contributions, to a system that looks more like a collective DC arrangement, with retirement age linked to longevity.

Separately, DB plans create problems of labor mobility, at least across industries if not across firms. To the extent that the system moves closer to DC, the mobility problem becomes less acute, but at the price of less wide risk sharing.

But the fact that a system which uses "soft" rights to maintain solvency works well in the Netherlands does not mean that it can be replicated in other countries. There are path dependencies. The Netherlands is a relatively homogeneous country; and the political culture allows effective dialogue between social partners. Neither of those necessarily applies to other countries, for whom the main lesson of the Netherlands is that in the face of systemic risk pension design should make use of the full range of adjustment mechanisms.

[15] See, for example, Kortleve and Ponds (2009).

References

Barr, Nicholas, 2001, *The Welfare State as Piggy Bank: Information, Risk, Uncertainty, and the Role of the State*, London and New York: Oxford University Press.

Barr, Nicholas, and Peter Diamond, 2008, *Reforming Pensions: Principles and Policy Choices*, New York and Oxford: Oxford University Press.

2009, Reforming pensions: Principles, analytical errors and policy directions, *International Social Security Review*, vol. 62(2): 5–29 (also in French, German and Spanish).

2010a, *Pension Reform: A Short Guide*, New York and Oxford: Oxford University Press.

2010b, Pension Reform in China: Issues, Options and Recommendations, China Economic Research and Advisory Programme, http://econ.lse.ac.uk/staff/nb/Barr_Diamond_China_Pensions_2010.pdf (accessed January 18, 2012).

in press, *Pension Design: A Proposal*.

Börsch-Supan, Axel, Martin Gasche and Christina Benita Wilke, 2010, Konjunkturabhängigkeit der Gesetzlichen Rentenversicherung am Beispiel der aktuellen Finanz- und Wirtschaftskrise, *Zeitschrift für Wirtschaftspolitik*, vol. 59(3): 298–328.

Bovenberg, Lans, in press, Comment on E. Palmer, NDC Equilibrium, Valuation and Residual Risk Sharing through NDC Bonds, in: Robert Holzmann, Edward Palmer and David Robalino (eds.), *NDC Pension Schemes in a Changing Pension World, Vol. II: Gender, Politics, and Financial Stability*, Washington DC: World Bank and Swedish Social Insurance Agency.

Bovenberg, Lans, Ralph Koijen, Theo Nijman and Coen Teulings, 2007, Saving and investing over the life cycle and the role of collective pension funds, *De Economist*, vol. 155(4): 347–415.

Bronk, Richard, 2009, *The Romantic Economist*, Cambridge University Press.

D'Addio, Anna Cristina and Edward Whitehouse, 2010, Pension systems and the crisis: Weathering the storm, *Pensions: An International Journal*, vol. 15(2): 126–39.

Diamond, Peter A., and Peter R. Orszag, 2005, *Saving Social Security: A Balanced Approach*, rev. edn. Washington DC: Brookings Institution.

Ewijk, Casper van, 2009, Credit crisis and Dutch pension funds: Who bears the shock?, *De Economist*, vol. 157(3): 337–51.

Gollier, Christian, 2008, Intergenerational risk-sharing and risk-taking of a pension fund, *Journal of Public Economics*, vol. 92(5–6): 1463–85.

Holzmann, Robert, and Richard Hinz, 2005, *Old Age Income Support in the 21st Century: An International Perspective on Pension Systems and Reform*, Washington DC: World Bank.

Knight, Frank H., 1921, *Risk, Uncertainty, and Profit*, Boston, MA: Hart, Schaffner & Marx: Houghton Mifflin Co.

Könberg, Bo, Edward Palmer and Annika Sundén, 2006, The NDC Reform in Sweden: The 1994 Legislation to the Present, in: Robert Holzmann and Edward Palmer (eds.), *Pension Reform: Issues and Prospects for Non-Financial Defined Contribution (NDC) Schemes*, Washington DC: World Bank, 449–66.

Kortleve, Niels, and Eduard Ponds, 2009, Dutch Pension Funds in Underfunding: Solving Generational Dilemmas, Working Paper 2009–29, Chestnut Hill, MA: Center for Retirement at Boston College.

2010, How to Close the Funding Gap in Dutch Pension Plans? Impact on Generations, Issue Brief Number 10–7, April 2010, Chestnut Hill, MA: Center for Retirement at Boston College.

Munnell, Alicia H., and Dan Muldoon, 2008, Are Retirement Savings too Exposed to Market Risk?, Issue Brief Number 8–16, Chestnut Hill, MA: Center for Retirement at Boston College.

Norway Central Bank, 2009, The Government Pension Fund Global, Annual Report. Oslo. www.nbim.no/en/press-and-publications/Reports/ (accessed January 19, 2012).

OECD, 2009, *Pensions at a Glance 2009: Retirement-income Systems in OECD Countries*, Paris: OECD.

Palmer, Edward, 2002, Swedish Pension Reform: How Did It Evolve, and What Does It Mean for the Future?, in: M. Feldstein and H. Siebert (eds.), *Social Security Pension Reform in Europe*, NBER conference volume, The University of Chicago Press.

Pino, Ariel, and Yuan Yermo, 2010, The impact of the 2007–2009 crisis on social security and private pension funds: A threat to their financial soundness?, *International Social Security Review*, vol. 63(2): 5–30.

Ponds, Eduard, and Bart van Riel, 2009, Sharing risk: The Netherlands' new approach to pensions, *Journal of Pension Economics and Finance*, vol. 8(1): 91–105.

Rashbrooke, G., 2009, *Automatic Enrolment: KiwiSaver in New Zealand, The Changing Pensions Landscape in Asia and the Pacific*, OECD, Paris.

Sass, Steven A., Courtney Monk and Kelly Haverstick, 2010, Workers' Response to the Market Crash: Save More, Work More?, Issue Brief Number 10–3, Chestnut Hill, MA: Center for Retirement at Boston College.

Settergren, Ole, 2001, *The Automatic Balance Mechanism of the Swedish Pension System – A Non-technical Introduction*, Riksförsäkringsverket (The National Social Insurance Board).

Sundén, Annika, 2009, The Swedish Pension System and the Economic Crisis, Center for Retirement at Boston College, Issue Brief No. 9–25, December. http://crr.bc.edu/briefs/the_swedish_pension_system_and_ the_Economic_crisis.html (accessed January 18, 2012).

Swedish Pensions Agency, 2009, *Orange Report: Annual Report of the Swedish Pension System 2009*, www.pensionsmyndigheten.se/3051. html (accessed January 18, 2012).

UK Pensions Commission, 2005, *A new pension settlement for the twenty-first century: Second report of the Pensions Commission.* London: The Stationery Office.

Vidal-Melia, Carlos, Maria del Carmen Boado-Penas and Ole Settergren, 2009, Automatic balance mechanisms in pay-as-you-go pension systems, *The Geneva Papers*, vol. 34(2): 287–317(31).

Woolley, Paul, 2010, Why are financial markets so inefficient and exploitative – and a suggested remedy, in: *The Future of Finance: The LSE Report*, London School of Economics, 121–43.

World Bank, 1994, *Averting the Old Age Crisis*, Washington DC: The World Bank.

2006, *Pension reform and the development of pension systems: An evaluation of World Bank assistance.* Washington DC: Independent Evaluation Group, World Bank. lnweb18.worldbank.org:80/oed/ oeddoclib.nsf/DocUNIDViewForJavaSearch/43B436DFBB2723D085 257108005F6309/$file/pensions_evaluation.pdf (accessed January 18, 2012).

5 | Designing the pension system: conceptual framework

LANS BOVENBERG AND CASPER VAN EWIJK

5.1 Introduction

Countries exhibit considerable variety in the design of pension systems. Apparently, the pension system can be organized in many alternative ways, with alternative allocations of the functions of the pension system to different institutions or "pillars" in the system. Financial markets can provide for these functions to some extent, but market failures and "individual" failures call also for other institutions, including government intervention or mandatory occupational pension schemes. The pension system in fact involves a complex mapping of functions into alternative institutions, which exhibit strengths but also weaknesses. A single unique solution to the optimal design of a pension system thus does not exist. Each system is inevitably second best and involves important trade-offs.

This chapter develops an analytical framework for the design of pension systems taking the functions of the pension system as the guiding principle. It discusses the economic principles underlying these functions and their implementation in practice. In particular, it distinguishes the following three functions:

- facilitating life-cycle financial planning;
- insuring idiosyncratic risks;
- sharing macroeconomic risks across generations.

The first function concerns consumption smoothing over the life cycle (across both time and contingencies), in particular regarding the provision of adequate consumption at old age, taking into account individual circumstances and preferences. Pension institutions address failures in individual behavior ("internalities"). The second function concerns pooling of intra-generational risks in the face of imperfect insurance markets such as failing annuity markets. The third function concerns intergenerational risk sharing of systemic or "macroeconomic" shocks in the face of incomplete markets, such as the limited tradability of human capital and lack of markets to trade risks with future generations.

Poverty alleviation is not included as a separate function. In our set-up, poverty alleviation is an element of each of the three functions: It is included in the first function, as this function ensures a sufficient income in old age in various states of the world. It is part of the second function, as this function insures idiosyncratic risks at old age, e.g., costs for health care and long-term care. Finally, poverty alleviation may involve intergenerational transfers as well.

These three functions will be discussed in reverse order. Section 5.2 addresses the third function, starting from the underlying principles of optimal intergenerational risk sharing and life-cycle exposure to risks. Section 5.3 elaborates on the third function, discussing the roles of the following institutions in facilitating optimal intergenerational risk sharing: capital markets, government and pension funds. Financial markets can help to share risks between generations that are not far apart in time. If generations are too far apart in time to trade these risks in financial markets, the government can act as a representative of younger generations in taking on mismatch risk on its balance sheet and using public debt and generation-specific transfers (including the public pension system) as an instrument to reallocate risks across generations. Also private pension funds may play a role here.

Sections 5.4 and 5.5 turn to the first and second functions, which involve intra-generational heterogeneity. Section 5.4 discusses the principles underlying the pooling of idiosyncratic risks and optimal life-cycle planning in light of heterogeneous preferences and circumstances. Section 5.5 elaborates on the role of financial markets, government, pension funds and housing markets in implementing these functions.

5.2 Macroeconomic risks

5.2.1 Principles of optimal risk sharing

The optimal allocation of macroeconomic risks follows from the principle that risks should be borne in proportion to relative risk tolerance:

$$\tilde{W}^i = \left(\frac{1}{\theta^i} \middle/ \left(\sum_{j=1}^{N} \frac{\alpha^j}{\theta^j} \right) \right) \tilde{W} \quad i = 1, \ldots \ldots N \tag{5.1}$$

where W^i stands for total wealth (including human capital) of agent i, W, for aggregate wealth in the economy and $\alpha^i \equiv W^i/W$ is the share of agent i in aggregate wealth. θ^i denotes the coefficient of relative risk aversion of agent i, which is the reciprocal of relative risk tolerance. A tilde above a variable stands for a relative change in that variable as a result of an unexpected shock.

If all N agents feature the same relative risk aversion, then the relative changes in everybody's wealth $\tilde{W}^i$ correspond to the relative change in aggregate wealth $\tilde{W}$. This can be viewed as a case of perfect solidarity in sharing risk. Aggregate shocks are spread over all agents so that everybody's wealth is smoothed as much as possible over the various states of the world. Irrespective of the specific aggregate shock corresponding to a particular state of the world $\tilde{W}$, everybody shares in the same way in that shock so that $\tilde{W^i} / \tilde{W}$ is constant over the various aggregate shocks.

Expression (5.1) yields two important implications. First, everybody should be exposed to macroeconomic risk unless people are infinitely risk averse. Second, everyone's wealth should move in the same direction if an unexpected aggregate shock hits.

Intertemporal consumption smoothing

If preferences exhibit constant relative risk aversion (CRRA) during agents' lives and the shock does not change future expected returns or variances,[1] agents want to spread changes in wealth as broadly as possible over their lifetime. Hence, rather than concentrating them in a short period, the agents choose to absorb these changes in wealth in equal relative changes in consumption during the rest of their lives after the information about the shock becomes available at time t:

$$\tilde{C}^i_s = \tilde{W}^i_t \quad \text{for } s \geq t \tag{5.2}$$

where we have added a time subscript to indicate the time dimension. In the benchmark case of CRRA preferences, therefore, all future consumption of all individuals should absorb part of a pure wealth shock. If individuals feature the same risk tolerance, all future consumption

---

[1] This assumption implies that the shock is a pure wealth shock, which does not induce intertemporal substitution and leaves unaffected the propensity to consume from wealth and the tilt of the consumption path over time. Also

flows of all individuals should vary with the same percentage in response to such an aggregate shock.

Non-CRRA preferences

Expression (5.1) allows for differences in relative risk aversion across agents. These differences may have various origins. First of all, they can be due to differences in wealth levels; if preferences exhibit *decreasing* relative risk aversion instead of *constant* relative risk aversion, this relative risk aversion decreases with wealth W^i. Such preferences may emerge if agents require a positive amount of minimum consumption in any state of the world and exhibit constant relative risk aversion for consumption fluctuations above that minimum level. With these preferences, relative risk aversion is given by $\bar{\theta}^i \left/ \left(1 - \dfrac{X^i}{W^i}\right)\right.$, where $X^i > 0$ denotes the discounted value of the minimum consumption levels over the rest of the life cycle, W^i represents total wealth of individual i and $\bar{\theta}^i$ stands for the constant relative risk aversion above the minimum consumption level. The local curvature of the utility function thus depends on how far overall wealth is above wealth required for minimum consumption. People thus becomes less willing to tolerate risk if the wealth level drops and becomes closer to this minimum wealth level. This implies that richer people are less risk averse than poor people.

Habit formation

With habit formation, relative risk aversion typically declines over the planning horizon and increases with age. If relative risk aversion is not constant during life, the following relationship for intertemporal consumption smoothing replaces (5.2):

$$\widetilde{C^i}_s = \left(\frac{1}{\theta^i_s} \left/ \left(\sum_{k=t}^{D^i} \frac{\beta^i_k}{\theta^i_k}\right)\right.\right)\widetilde{W^i_t} \text{ for } s \geq t, \tag{5.3}$$

where θ^i_k denotes the coefficient of relative risk aversion of agent i at time k. β^i_k stands for the share of consumption at time k in total discounted

greater uncertainty may affect the time slope of expected consumption. In particular, more risk causes prudent consumers to reduce their consumption and increase their precautionary saving.

consumption[2] of agent i and D^i represents the planning horizon (i.e., the date at which the agent has passed away with certainty).

If relative risk aversion is not constant during life, the overall coefficient of relative risk aversion of agent i in (5.1) is defined by $\theta^i \equiv 1 / \left(\sum_{k=t}^{D^i} \frac{\beta_k^i}{\theta_k^i} \right)$. Substituting (5.1) into (5.3) to eliminate $\widetilde{W_t^i}$ and using the definition of θ^i, we can write

$$\tilde{C}_s^i = \left(1 / \left(\theta_t^i \sum_{j=1}^{N} \alpha^j \sum_{k=t}^{D^j} \frac{\beta_k^j}{\theta_k^j} \right) \right) \tilde{W}_t \qquad (5.4)$$

Compared to the case with preferences without habit formation, the immediate adjustment of consumption to a wealth shock is less, but adjustment is larger later on when habits have adjusted to the changed consumption level. Habit formation implies also that the willingness to absorb an unexpected shock increases if the time horizon lengthens over which the shock can be absorbed. This implies that younger agents with longer horizons can adjust more easily to shocks. Intuitively, they have more time to adjust their habits to new information.

Standard-of-living preferences

Another type of preference involves people measuring their consumption level compared with that in the rest of the economy. With these so-called standard-of-living or "keeping up with the Joneses" preferences, households want their consumption to evolve in the same way as that of others. In the extreme case in which people care only about their own relative standard of living, aggregate risks effectively become idiosyncratic risks in the sense that utility risks can be eliminated completely by sharing them.

Capital markets and risk premia

Capital markets allow agents to trade risks so as to achieve optimal risk sharing (5.1). Trade originates in differences in preferences (i.e.,

[2] The discounted value of consumption is computed with the shadow prices that are implied by the optimal allocation of risk. The optimal allocation of risk can be decentralized through capital markets in which these shadow prices would in fact be observed as market prices.

risk tolerance) and in endowment risks (i.e., the risks that agents face in the absence of trade in risks). Indeed, no trade would be necessary if agents would feature the same preferences and would experience the same risks.

In a complete capital market, all sources of risk – the so-called risk factors – are costlessly traded. In addition, a risk-free asset can be traded. In that case, rational agents can obtain their optimal exposure to the various risk factors on the capital market. The optimal exposure of agent i to risk factor k is given by[3]

$$f_k^i \sigma_k = \frac{\lambda_k}{\theta^i}, \tag{5.5}$$

where f_k^i represents the share of total wealth of the individual i that is invested in the risk factor k. σ_k stands for the (annual) standard deviation of the risk factor.

$\lambda_k \equiv \dfrac{\mu_k}{\sigma_k}$ denotes the Sharpe ratio of risk factor k. This ratio is the reward to risk taking, namely the expected excess return (over the risk-free return) μ_k per standard deviation of that excess return σ_k. Risk taking (i.e., volatility of wealth across various contingencies) as measured by the volatility of wealth, $f_k^i \sigma_k$, increases with the reward to risk taking, λ_k, and decreases with relative risk aversion, θ^i. For each individual, the various wealth shares of all the risk factors typically do not add up to unity; the risk-free asset makes up the balance.

General equilibrium

Optimal diversification of risks is important for welfare and economic growth. People are more willing to invest in risky technologies if they can share the associated risks with others. Since along the efficient frontier higher expected returns go together with more risk, trade in risks stimulates economic growth by allowing investors to share the risks of their investments.

---

[3] This expression assumes that the probability distributions of the independent risk factors are known and log normal. We have repressed time arguments but the expected returns and standard deviations may depend on time. In principle, they may also depend on the horizon of agent i. To illustrate, with mean reversion in equity returns, younger agents with a longer horizon feature a higher Sharpe ratio.

With linear production technologies, the supply of the various independent risk factors is infinitely elastic with respect to the price of risk λ_k. In that case, the risk premia are exogenous, while the exposure of the economy to risk depends on the demand for risk implicit in the attitude of households towards risk (as measured by risk aversion):

$$f_k = \sum_{j=1}^{N} \alpha^j f_j^k = \left(\sum_{j=1}^{N} \frac{\alpha^j}{\theta^j} \right) \frac{\lambda_k}{\sigma_k} \qquad (5.6)$$

where the second equality follows from expression (5.5). The more risk tolerant households are, the more risk the economy takes in equilibrium and the larger becomes the exposure of the economy to the risk factors. Agents who are more risk averse reduce not only macroeconomic risk but also expected economic growth. Indeed, risk taking is an important precondition for economic growth. At a macroeconomic level, society thus faces a trade-off between reducing risk and raising expected growth (see Obstfeld, 1994).

In reality, supply curves of alternative technologies are less than infinitely elastic. The higher the risk premium becomes, the lower the value of risky investments and the less attractive these investments are. Accordingly, preferences determine endogenous risk premia. The intuition for this case can be obtained from the extreme case in which the supply of technologies is completely fixed so that the supply of risk is completely inelastic with respect to the risk premia. In particular, if a standard deviation of risk factor k changes aggregate wealth by $100f_k\sigma_k\%$, then the equilibrium risk premium (in terms of the Sharpe ratio) is given by[4]

$$\lambda_k = \left(1 \Big/ \left(\sum_{j=1}^{N} \frac{\alpha^j}{\theta^j} \right) \right) f_k \sigma_k. \qquad (5.7)$$

In the general case with finitely elastic supply of risky technologies, both the risk premia λ_k and the exposure of the economy to the risk factors f_k are endogenous.

---

[4] Here we assume that expected (annual) return and (annual) standard deviation do not depend on the horizon of the agent.

5.2.2 Main macroeconomic risks in retirement planning

This subsection explores the most important macroeconomic shocks resulting in changes in aggregate wealth W in (5.1) and (5.4). These macroeconomic shocks originate in productivity shocks, demographic changes and shocks in discount rates, and affect returns on physical non-human assets and human capital.

Returns on non-human assets

The returns on (claims on) physical capital (including the housing stock and other real estate) and intangible capital (including the reputation of firms) are uncertain. Such long-lived assets are particularly sensitive to valuation risks, as their value reflects discounted dividend streams over rather long periods. Both discount rates (which reflect among other things risk aversion) and expectations about future earnings tend to vary over time. To illustrate, in downturns, expected dividends tend to be low while risk aversion and thus required returns are typically high. The combination of low expected dividends and high discount rates results in low valuations. In booms, in contrast, the opposite happens: low required returns and good dividend prospects give rise to high asset values.

Human-capital risks

Human capital represents the discounted value of future wages and is uncertain as well. In the short run, wages are typically less volatile than dividends and profits on non-human assets. Indeed, short-term fluctuations in productivity are reflected more in profits and dividends rather than wages, which are stickier in the short run. In the long run, however, wages, dividends and returns on non-human assets are more strongly correlated.[5]

Even though values of human capital are not observed in capital markets as claims on physical and intangible capital tend to be, also the values of human capital reflect fluctuations in discount rates due to changing attitudes towards risk. Nevertheless, the value of an

---

[5] See Benzoni *et al.* (2007). These correlations depend also on the nature of the human capital. In some professions, wage earnings are more strongly correlated with financial markets than is the case in other professions.

individual's human capital can be expected to be less volatile for two reasons. First, the time horizon of human capital of current generations is shorter due to the finiteness of life. Second, human capital may be less susceptible to erratic pricing and bubbles as it is not traded in financial markets. The values of claims on physical and intangible non-human capital, in contrast, involve the price risk at which younger generations are willing to buy these assets. These risks may give rise to bubbles in the pricing of these assets, which makes these assets rather risky. How fundamental these differences are remains open for debate, however. If human capital encompasses also the wages of future generations, then the argument of the shorter time horizon no longer holds. Similarly, if wage-indexed bonds allow human-capital risks to be traded, then bubbles may also be present in the markets for human-capital risks.

Demographic and health risks
Another macroeconomic risk is the demographic risk of aggregate longevity.[6] If agents live longer than expected, their consumption requirements expand. In this case, wealth does not fall but wealth per capita does if people cannot produce additional resources during their additional lifetime so that human capital does not increase. We thus must interpret aggregate wealth W as aggregate wealth per capita. Aggregate morbidity and the aggregate cost of health care are other, related macroeconomic risks. If people live on average longer in a sick rather than healthy state, resources that are available for non-health uses decline. Longevity risk would then be less relevant for per capita consumption, however, if shocks in life expectancy closely correlate with the number of healthy years so that a longer life goes together with more human capital.

Another important demographic risk is fertility risk. Fertility risk can be viewed as risk about the size of future human capital, which is affected by not only future labor productivity but also fertility. Whether a lower fertility rate is a burden or a benefit depends on the sign of the initial net transfer from current generations to future generations: that is, whether future generations are net debtors or net creditors. If this transfer is positive, higher fertility reduces per capita

---

[6] Demographic risk may also be one of the underlying determinants of risk on financial capital and human capital. Here we focus on the direct impact of demographic risk on aggregate consumption.

consumption because this transfer has to be distributed over a larger number of people. The opposite applies in the case of a negative transfer from current to future generations. In that case, future generations are net debtors and a higher level of fertility helps to share this burden over more people, thereby raising per capita consumption.

5.2.3 Optimal life-cycle exposure to risks

Households typically hold mainly human capital early in the life cycle. To provide for income after retirement, they build up financial wealth during their active years. This financial wealth is subsequently depleted to finance consumption during retirement. In the absence of risk sharing, households would thus be exposed to human-capital risks early in life, and to financial risks later in life. Hence, there is scope for trading risks across cohorts where younger generations buy financial risks and sell human-capital risks with the older generations as the counterparties.

The benchmark model
We first explore this trade in the context of a standard Merton–Samuelson model with uniform time-separable CRRA preferences, perfect markets for risk sharing, and two risk factors, namely the value of human capital and the value of financial claims on non-human physical and intangible capital (i.e., financial capital).[7] For simplicity, we assume that both these risk factors are random walks (possibly with drift) and are distributed identically and independently over time according to a lognormal distribution. With standard CRRA preferences and permanent wage shocks determining the shocks in the value of human capital,[8] equation (5.5) can be solved as

$$\frac{H^i + \bar{H}^i}{W^i}\sigma_w = \frac{\lambda_w}{\theta^i}, \tag{5.8}$$

[7] These claims comprise owner-occupied housing, closely held firms and an aggregate of equity and debt claims on the capital earnings of firms.

[8] We thus capture macroeconomic human capital risk as being determined by one risk factor, namely a random walk in wages. This allows us to treat human capital as a homogeneous asset. In practice, systematic human capital risk may involve several risk factors, for example not only current permanent but also anticipated future wage shocks (e.g., demographic shocks, climate

where $\overline{H^i}$ represents the demand for additional exposure to human-capital risk in addition to the individual's biological human capital, λ_w stands for the risk premium on the human-capital risk factor and σ_w is the standard deviation of permanent macroeconomic wage shocks. This additional human-capital risk exposure may be interpreted as an aggregate of wage-linked bonds of different durations. Thus, in case of constant risk tolerance over the life cycle, people would ideally maintain a constant wealth share of human capital in their portfolio during their life.

In general equilibrium, total human-capital exposure should match aggregate human capital. With homogeneous CRRA preferences, equation (5.5) implies

$$\lambda_w = \theta \frac{H}{W} \sigma_w, \tag{5.9}$$

where θ is the uniform coefficient of relative risk aversion and H and W represent aggregate human and overall wealth in the economy.

Substituting (5.9) into (5.8), we find the demand for additional wage exposure of individual i, $\overline{H^i}$, as

$$\overline{H^i} = \frac{H}{W} F^i - \frac{F}{W} H^i, \tag{5.10}$$

where $F = W - H$ stands for aggregate financial capital in the economy, and H^i and $F^i = W^i - H^i$ for human and financial wealth of individual i. In an analogous way, we can find the demand for additional financial exposure of an individual as[9]

$$\overline{F^i} = \frac{F}{W} H^i - \frac{H}{W} F^i. \tag{5.11}$$

so that $\overline{H^i} = - \overline{F^i}$.

change) and temporary shocks with different durations and different speeds of mean reversion. Moreover, human capital may be subject to various types of macroeconomic risks with different occupations featuring distinct exposures to these various risks. With more underlying risk factors, shocks in human capital will no longer be similar for all generations, and more assets (e.g., of various durations) are needed to trade these risks.

[9] Additional financial exposure can be purchased by buying stocks in firms that are leveraged with debt.

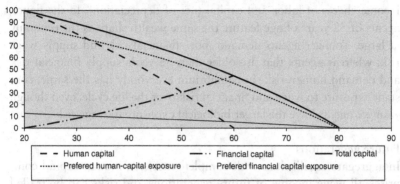

Figure 5.1 Expected exposure to financial and wage risks over the life cycle (initial wealth = 100)

Individuals with too much exposure to human-capital risk trade it for financial risk and the other way around. The demand for additional wage or financial exposure of an agent with a wealth composition that is equal to that of the economy as a whole $\left(\text{i.e., } \dfrac{H^i}{F^i} = \dfrac{H}{F}\right)$ is zero.

Intuitively, the endowment of this agent has the same exposure to risks as the aggregate endowment of the economy, and with homogeneous preferences this agent has no incentive to trade risks. Agents that – in the absence of trade – have a higher (lower) exposure to wage risks than the economy as a whole want to go short (long) on this risk. In equilibrium, everybody has the same exposure to risk, namely the average exposure of the economy as a whole to that risk.[10]

Figure 5.1 illustrates the expected evolution of wealth and its components over the life cycle in this stylized case. We consider an individual that works for 40 years up to the age of 60, and then lives in retirement for 20 years. Consumption is perfectly smoothed over the life cycle. This individual features the average exposure to human-capital risk.[11] This case assumes economy-wide wealth shares of human and financial wealth of 85 percent and 15 percent, respectively, corresponding to the

[10] In the absence of a risk-free production technology, the net supply of risk-free bonds is zero in the aggregate. Hence, risk-free assets are not traded in equilibrium, as everybody holds a wealth share of zero in these assets.

[11] In principle, we could allow for intra-generational heterogeneity by allowing for different occupations that have different exposures to aggregate human capital risk. We abstract from this heterogeneity since this section focuses on intergenerational risk sharing.

income shares of labor and capital (net of depreciation). In the figure, agents of 32 years of age feature the same wealth share as the economy at large. Younger agents demand more financial risk and supply wage risk, whereas agents that are older than 32 years supply financial risk and demand human-risk. In equilibrium everybody has the same, constant exposure to wage and financial risk over the life cycle, even though younger agents have the larger biological exposure to wage risks.

Future generations

In aggregate equilibrium with complete markets, human capital comprises all wage income of future generations and risks can be traded with these generations, which have not yet been born. Any shock, whether it involves present generations (e.g., the current financial crisis) or future generations (e.g., climate change) should be shared among all generations living now and in the future. With human capital making up an even larger share of total wealth, retirees will *ceteris paribus* optimally hold a larger stock of wage-linked assets that are in effect issued by generations that will enter the labor force in the future (see (5.10) with $F^i = 0$ and $W^i = H^i$). These future generations in effect go short in wage-linked bonds and hold positive amounts of financial capital. In this way, they share in capital risks while hedging their wage risks.[12]

Extending risk sharing to future generations thus matters a lot for the base over which to share risks. Indeed, with uniform CRRA preferences and optimal risk sharing, the equity premium λ_r is given by

$$\lambda_r = \theta \frac{F}{(F+H)} \sigma_r, \qquad (5.12)$$

where σ_r is the standard deviation of capital returns and F and H represent aggregate financial and human capital.[13] With also future generations being part of the optimal risk-sharing arrangement,

---

[12] We assume here only one risk factor in the capital market and one risk factor in the labor market. In this rather exceptional case there is no scope for intergenerational risk sharing in human capital. In reality, future generations may be subject to other wage risks than current generations are. In that case they will hedge wage risks during their lifespan and take a position in wage risks before their lifespan. Intergenerational risk sharing will then also reduce the risk premium on human capital. How it changes the optimal portfolio depends on the covariances between financial capital and human capital.

[13] Another reason why human capital may be larger than discounted labor income of current generations has to do with the flexibility to adjust labor

opportunities for risk sharing increase, *ceteris paribus* leading to a lower risk premium on financial assets. How this affects the desired portfolio of current generations, and thus the relative risk premium on current human and financial capital, depends on how risks on these assets co-vary with risks on future human capital.

Financial risks and future generations

With non-overlapping generations, valuation risk of tradable assets is especially important because current generations bear the price risk at which future generations are willing to buy these assets. Mispricing and asset bubbles may aggravate the volatility of financial valuations. From an intergenerational risk-sharing point of view, it makes sense to trade the opposite risks for the selling, older generations and for the buying, younger generations.

The benchmark model assumes that financial values are random walks (with drift). Empirical evidence suggests, however, that valuation risks involve some mean reversion because returns are negatively correlated at the low frequencies relevant for financial planning over the life cycle.[14] This provides another argument to smooth short-run volatility in financial valuations across generations, and to allocate these risks to generations with a long time horizon (i.e., young and future generations). The incorporation of future generations can thus reduce the equilibrium risk premium not only by increasing the basis for risk sharing but also by smoothing short-term deviations from equilibrium prices by lengthening the time horizon for assets returns (i.e., in (5.12) not only aggregate human capital H increases but also the annual standard deviation σ_r declines).

Non-CRRA preferences: habit formation

In addition to mean reversion, also non-CRRA preferences may induce younger agents to invest a larger share of their portfolio in risky assets

---

supply (e.g., Gomes *et al.*, 2008). With the ability to flexibly adjust labor supply, potential wage income (i.e., wage income if no leisure would be consumed) exceeds actual wage income. Accordingly, the stock of human wealth exceeds discounted labor income. As the optimal wealth share f in (5.5) applies now to a larger stock of wealth, the overall demand for financial risk rises.

[14] Campbell and Viceira (2005) show that the annualized standard deviation of real returns of about 17 percent of a diversified stock portfolio is reduced to an annualized standard deviation of only 8 percent on a 20-year horizon.

than will older agents with a shorter investment horizon. The reason is that habit formation implies that younger agents are more risk tolerant because they have more time to adjust their habits to unexpected shocks. They thus can adjust more easily to shocks so that they can invest a larger share of their wealth in risk-bearing assets. With these heterogeneous preferences, risk-free assets are traded even though net aggregate supply is zero. In particular, younger generations are net suppliers and older generations are net demanders of these bonds.

The short-run volatility of returns on assets originates in part in changes in discount rates due to variations in aggregate risk aversion in financial markets. These variations, in turn, may be due to habit formation, which implies that risk aversion varies countercyclically.[15] With optimal risk sharing with future generations, the variations in aggregate risk aversion are smaller because younger and future agents can more easily adjust their habits to current shocks. This allows economies to take more risk, and is a third reason why including future generations in the risk-sharing arrangement may reduce the equity premium (i.e., the aggregate coefficient of risk aversion θ in (5.12) declines). Indeed, with habit formation, it makes even more sense to shift short-run volatility of capital returns to future generations, which can be less risk averse.

Longevity risk

Individual agents face considerable longevity risk as changes in life expectancy are not always associated with similar changes in human capital. This is particularly so for the retired elderly whose human capital has worn out already. The idiosyncratic part is insurable and can be pooled within a cohort, but the non-diversifiable, systematic part should be shared among various generations. In case of standard time-separable utility, shocks in longevity should be distributed such that the change in per capita consumption is proportional to risk tolerance for all individuals. Since the oldest age groups typically face the largest changes in mortality rates and thus the largest relative changes in remaining life expectancy, the impact of unexpected changes in mortality on per capita consumption tend to be much smaller for a young person than for an older person if this risk could not be shared across

---

[15] See Campbell and Cochrane (1999). Habit formation affects not only optimal risk taking but also optimal saving behavior.

generations. Moreover, if increased life expectancy goes together with more healthy years and thus more human capital, younger people can absorb the shock by working more. For those already retired, in contrast, this would be difficult. Hence, increased life expectancy thus yields a larger positive effect on the human capital of younger cohorts than on that of the older cohorts. Habit formation adds to these arguments for reallocating longevity risk from the old to the young. With finite risk tolerance, however, some part of the aggregate longevity risk should be borne by the retired generations as all generations should share in the macroeconomic risks according to their risk tolerance.[16]

Non-traded wage risks

In the absence of trade in human capital, agents have to adjust their life-cycle planning by taking account of this missing market. How agents of different ages then allocate their financial portfolio over financial risk and risk-free assets depends on the correlation of wage risk with financial risk. If wage risks are not correlated with financial risks, the risk-free bonds take the place of wage-indexed bonds and young agents will want to go short in these bonds to get the optimal exposure to financial risks as a share of their overall wealth (including their human wealth). Older people are the buyers of the risk-free bonds.

Benzoni *et al.* (2007), however, indicate that labor income is co-integrated with dividends. This makes human capital a closer equity substitute for younger workers with a longer investment horizon than for older workers and retirees with a shorter horizon. Hence, the optimal exposure (as a share of overall wealth) to financial risks increases with age.[17] Moreover, including future generations in the risk-sharing arrangement may not help to reduce the equity risk premium, as these generations also are exposed to equity risk through their labor income.

[16] Moreover, older generations may experience the largest relative increase in lifetime utility as a consequence of a longer expected remaining lifetime.

[17] The presence of uninsurable idiosyncratic risk may also influence the willingness to take macroeconomic risks. In particular, if preferences exhibit "risk vulnerability," more exposure to risk makes people more reluctant to take on risks that are uncorrelated with the additional risk exposure. Most preferences meet this property of risk vulnerability. The existence of idiosyncratic human-capital risk could thus be a reason for taking less risk in pension savings.

5.3 How to organize intergenerational sharing of macro risks?

Optimal life-cycle investment involves trade in risk between younger and older generations. This section explains that financial markets can accomplish only a limited part of the desired intergenerational risk sharing. Hence, other institutions such as governments or pension funds are needed to help generations share risk optimally. Whereas these institutions may help alleviate the market failures, they typically involve other costs. In the end, therefore, institutional design faces difficult trade-offs.

5.3.1 *Capital markets*

Limited liability of human capital

Capital markets suffer from several limitations in shifting capital market risk to the young. Most importantly, limited liability of human capital constrains the exposure to capital risks that young agents can take on through leverage. The basic problem is that in some states of nature in which the capital market suffers negative shocks, younger agents must transfer some of the rewards of labor to older agents. The promise to transfer wage income to others is difficult to enforce; a large claim on future labor income discourages (formal) work and thus enhances the risk of default. Young agents thus cannot use human capital as collateral for taking on capital market risks and getting rid of human-capital risks. Hence, the participation of young agents in financial markets is constrained by their net financial wealth, which is typically rather small in the early stages of adult life. This puts a floor on the downside risk that younger generations can bear on capital markets.

The non-tradability of human capital thus limits the ability of capital markets to shift (downside) financial risks to the younger generations. Similarly, it also constrains the scope for shifting wage risks to older generations. Even in the presence of markets for wage-indexed bonds, younger agents could go short in these assets only to a limited extent. Whereas young generations can go short in wage-linked bonds to leverage equity, these agents must unwind this position if net financial wealth gets close to zero, due to negative capital market shocks or positive wage shocks.[18] The limited liability of human capital thus

---

[18] This assumes continuous trading. Without that, households can buy call options to mimic this dynamic trading.

constrains intergenerational risk sharing and is the main reason why certain markets do not develop, for example, markets for wage-indexed bonds and longevity bonds. As a result, financial risks remain concentrated at the older generations and wage risks at younger generations. This not only leads to welfare losses, but also hampers economic growth as the equity premium will be relatively high.

Commitment of future generations

Another limitation of capital markets in facilitating intergenerational risk sharing is that capital markets do not work well for generations that are far apart in age. In particular, capital markets cannot commit new generations to an intergenerational risk-sharing contract because these generations cannot trade behind the veil of ignorance (i.e., *ex ante*). When the younger cohorts can start to trade on capital markets, the older cohorts' life risks have been realized and thus are largely known. At that time, risk sharing has become intergenerational redistribution. To illustrate, after World War II, many countries established pay-as-you-go (PAYG) pension systems implying systematic redistribution from the young to the old. One can view this redistribution as insurance of generations who had lost capital in the depression and World War II.

Insurance companies and longevity risk

Capital markets can help shift aggregate longevity risk from older generations to younger ones. In particular, young agents can be shareholders of insurance companies that provide annuities to older generations. The young, however, typically have not accumulated sufficient savings to buy all these shares. Moreover, the limited liability of shareholders limits the risk that the young can take on. Indeed, the insurance industry is owned by the cohorts that approach or are in retirement, i.e., the same generations for which the industry provides insurance. For similar reasons, trade in longevity bonds can play only a limited role in trading longevity risk between generations.

Intergenerational altruism

Intergenerational altruism within families can facilitate intergenerational risk sharing. Older cohorts leaving intentional bequests to their children can help share risks between generations in a dynasty. In the face of limited liability, however, this channel works only for rich households that prefer to leave positive bequests. Whereas inter-generational risk sharing through families may thus be of marginal importance for most families, it may be relevant for a substantial share of non-annuitized financial wealth since this wealth is typically concentrated in the hands of the very wealthy.

5.3.2 Government

Through its power to tax, the government is better equipped to commit young generations to risk sharing and address the limited liability of human capital. It can thus make credible the promise of young agents to transfer wage income to the old in case financial returns for the elderly are unexpectedly low and/or wages are unexpectedly high. Its tax power enables the government to create new tradable or non-tradable assets. For example, the government can issue tradable wage-indexed bonds. Alternatively, it can create implicit, non-tradable wage-linked assets by linking pensions and other transfer payments to wages.

As a long-lived institution, the government can help to also share risks across non-overlapping cohorts. The primary instrument for this is public debt policy. By reducing public debt in good times and increasing it in bad times, debt policy helps to smooth shocks over various generations. Also age-specific instruments, such as public pensions and other age-specific transfers and taxes, can play this role. In fact, age-specific transfers can in theory substitute completely for public debt (Calvo and Obstfeld, 1988).

Intergenerational risk sharing through the tax and transfer system ...
To engage in intergenerational risk sharing, the government should take on capital market and human-capital risks on its balance sheet and redistribute these to the young and old generations respectively. The government participates in financial and human-capital risks by taxing consumption, financial wealth and capital and labor income. Through the tax system, these risks are thus transferred to the government and subsequently redistributed to citizens through public spending. In principle, the tax and transfer system could help share risks across generations by taxing the excess exposure (relative to aggregate exposure) and transforming this into the risk that each cohort is not enough exposed to. For example, the overexposure of pensioners to financial shocks (which is matched by an underexposure of retirees

to human-capital shocks) could be addressed by a tax on financial capital in exchange for a pension benefit that is linked to human capital. Similarly, a tax on wages combined with transfers that vary with financial-market shocks could deal with the excess exposure of young agents to human-capital shocks and their underexposure to financial market shocks.

Another way of looking at this is that the government alters the risk profile of incomes through the stochastic properties of the tax and transfer system. In this way, shocks in both human capital and financial capital are spread out over all wealth components in accordance with (5.1). By levying taxes and providing transfers appropriately over time, the government can implement optimal intertemporal consumption smoothing (e.g., according to (5.2) or, with more general preferences, (5.3)). Such policies go beyond familiar budgetary rules such as automatic stabilization and tax smoothing: these policies require tax rates and transfers to be made dependent on the state of the world.

... and the drawbacks of high marginal tax rates on labor ...
Using the tax system for transferring risks across cohorts comes at a cost. From a risk-sharing and distributional point of view, one would like to share risks in proportion to the amount of human capital, which is unfortunately observable only through actual labor income. Insuring human capital by using taxes on labor income therefore distorts investment in human capital and labor supply; positive marginal tax rates harm incentives to work and enhance the quality and quantity of human capital. If taxes on additional labor income become too large, younger generations renege on their wage-linked obligations to the government, by voting either with their feet or their voice. In this way, moral hazard as a result of the non-tradability and limited liability of human capital continues to complicate intergenerational risk sharing.

... and marginal taxation of capital income
Reducing the financial-market exposure of the elderly through taxation of capital income gives rise to moral hazard problems too. In particular, high marginal tax rates on capital income harm the entrepreneur's incentives for raising profits. The fundamental problem is again that effort in profit making is non-verifiable, so that insuring risk cannot be separated from taxing effort. Moreover, taxing capital

162 Lans Bovenberg and Casper van Ewijk

income reduces the return in savings, thereby distorting the savings decision as well.

The tax distortions on saving can be reduced in two ways. First of all, under the so-called cash-flow treatment (which is sometimes also called consumption-tax treatment) of pension saving, contributions are deductible from the income tax while benefits are taxed under the income tax. In this case, net returns are not taxed (from an *ex ante* point of view) if the tax rate against which contributions are deducted equals the tax rate against which benefits are taxed. At the same time, however, the government shares in the capital risks.

An alternative way to share capital market risks without discouraging saving is to make tax rates state dependent. In particular, high tax rates should be levied if returns are high, while tax rates should be reduced if capital returns are low. In this way, the government can reconcile a low expected tax on capital income (i.e., from an *ex ante* point of view) with a high marginal tax on unexpectedly high capital income.

Taking assets on the government balance sheet ...
In addition to taxing private capital income, the government can assume capital market risks on its balance sheet by directly buying equity. In the same vein, a special social security trust fund can invest in risk-bearing assets. This avoids the moral hazard problems connected to using the tax system but is not free of drawbacks either. In particular, the government directly investing in equity may give rise to political risks, as governments may mix up investment with political interests. Moreover, concentrating ownership of equity in the government may harm the governance of private firms. This could be solved by taking the financial risk only through swaps, while leaving economic ownership with private institutions like pension funds. Also, international diversification may reduce this problem.

... and issuing tradable liabilities
In addition to providing non-tradable wage-linked benefits and annuities, the government may instead issue tradable wage-linked bonds and longevity bonds. Issuing tradable wage-linked bonds has the advantage that pension funds, insurance companies and retired individuals can themselves tailor their portfolios to individual circumstances and preferences. Moreover, tradable assets can be priced objectively, which enhances transparency and discipline in trading risks

across generations. Furthermore, they allow private pension funds and insurance companies to promise wage-linked benefits to retirees. In particular, by matching their wage-linked liabilities with wage-linked government bonds, pension funds and insurance companies can reduce mismatch risks and the associated solvency buffers.

As regards longevity bonds, governments can limit the longevity risk on their balance sheets by transferring this risk in part back to the young through a link between longevity and the size of the annuity in the public PAYG system that one obtains at retirement.[19] In this way, the young are exposed to macro longevity risk until they retire. Indeed, if morbidity and mortality are correlated, the young can absorb mortality risk by using their larger stock of human capital through later retirement. An advantage of such a clear rule for shifting the risk back to young generations is that it mitigates the political risk associated with incomplete closure rules. Note that longevity risk after retirement must still be absorbed in other ways, e.g., by varying the tax rate on labor incomes or retirement incomes.

Political risks
Intergenerational risk sharing through the public accounts helps to relieve market failures but also gives rise to government failures, in particular political risk. To optimally share risk, the generational accounts should vary appropriately with the various risks. Indeed, the closure rule for ensuring that the government finances are stable is crucial for properly absorbing the mismatch risk on the government balance sheet. In fact, this closure rule determines who is the residual risk bearer. Governments, however, find it difficult to commit to such a rule for optimal risk sharing among generations.

The lack of commitment may originate in bounded rationality, which makes it hard to design a complete contract *ex ante* that foresees all possible shocks and which thus would make rules rather than discretion optimal.[20] Indeed, discretion may be viewed as additional

---

[19] Longevity shocks are assumed to be permanent rather than temporary.

[20] In the presence of various types of risks, setting state-contingent taxes and transfers is a challenge. For example, insurance of temporary macroeconomic shocks requires discretionary lowering of tax rates in bad states of the economy and raising taxes in good states. A permanent fall in wages, on the other hand, would require only a modest decline in taxes as it equally affects all current and future generations.

insurance against the so-called unknown unknowns. This may be especially relevant for intergenerational risk sharing, which involves long time periods with substantial uncertainty. This in fact explains the incompleteness of the political process and thus the intransparency about who are the residual risk bearers of mismatch risk on the government balance sheet.

Lack of commitment to rules for sharing risks may also have to do with the political economy of a democracy (i.e., the governance of the government) in which voters can always undo earlier commitments, in particular if these voters belong to young generations that were not represented when the commitments were made. The opposite scenario is also possible if elderly voters are powerful. Accumulating large buffers in good times is politically very difficult. Indeed, the additional power of the government to lay a claim on the human capital may be both a blessing and a curse; additional power can be used for better or for worse. Without limits on the burdens that the government can shift to future generations, current generations may be tempted to abuse risk-sharing arrangements and shift risks onto future generations without properly rewarding them. Limitations on debt burdens aimed at protecting future generations do limit intergenerational risk sharing. The ability of future generations to renege on the obligations that current generations shift to them thus disciplines current generations not to shift too much debt forward. We thus again encounter the trade-off between limiting political risk and government failure, on the one hand, and facilitating intergenerational risk sharing and limiting market failure, on the other hand.

Sharing of risks between generations through generational accounts may thus give rise to additional political risk because property rights of various generations on the government balance sheet are not well defined. In any case, some commitments of governments are stronger than others. To illustrate, explicit public debt may involve a stronger commitment than implicit public debt in PAYG pension promises. Similarly, stable tax rates or stable indexation mechanisms may be ways for governments to make promises more credible. This can be done, for example, by setting up a separate social security trust fund with a clear commitment to offer safe benefits while adjusting the contribution rate to close the budget.

The commitment of the government to its promise to provide wage-linked pensions may vary. In notional defined contribution (NDC) systems, citizens have individual accounts in which they accumulate these claims on the government. These individual accounts may reduce the discretion of the government to default on its promise to link benefits to wages. In many NDC systems, the commitment of the government to provide wage-linked benefits is not open-ended, however. Typically, an automatic balancing mechanism ensures that retirement benefits absorb aggregate longevity risk and employment risks.

5.3.3 *Mandatory occupational pensions*

Occupational pension funds are institutions that organize pension contracts for workers in particular companies (company pension funds), sectors (sectoral pension funds) or professions. Pensions are thus linked to employment, and typically mandatory. The pension funds are private cooperatives that explicitly aim to protect the interests of the participants. Indeed, one can view the pension funds as mutual insurance companies that are owned by the policyholders instead of outside shareholders. They are governed by trustees that administer pensions and decide on investment policies.

Occupational pensions offer an alternative to private savings. By bundling private savings into collective contracts, they can save on transaction costs and benefit from economies of scale in investment and administration. Just as the government does, occupational pensions can facilitate intergenerational risk sharing. In particular, mandatory participation of workers in pension funds facilitates intergenerational risk sharing by easing limited liability constraints of younger agents, introducing new (implicit) assets, and trading on account of future generations.

Closed and open accounts
In this connection, the distinction between closed, open and collectively closed accounts is relevant. These can be defined as follows:

• Closed accounts: Individual pension claims are defined in terms of tradable financial assets. Individuals thus hold claims on financial assets rather than on the pension fund.

- Open accounts: Individual pension claims involve claims on the pension fund, which does not necessarily match its liabilities to current participants with financial assets. The pension fund thus carries mismatch risk and owns buffers, which cannot be claimed by individual participants. Indeed, individual ownership of the buffers is typically not defined through complete contracts with current stakeholders.
- Collectively closed accounts: Individuals hold a net claim on other participants in the pension fund but not on the fund itself. These claims are not all defined in terms of tradable financial assets, which can be priced on financial markets. These claims are completely described by policy rules.

The distinction between closed and open accounts is closely related to that between defined contribution (DC) and defined benefit (DB) pensions but it is more general. Typically, DC contracts are closed individual accounts, but these contracts can be replicated also by explicit pension contracts that are conditioned on known financial variables only. The latter contracts can be considered as closed accounts too, as they leave no unallocated net risk to the pension fund either, and claims are fully described in terms of tradable financial assets that are priced on financial markets. Solvency requirements are therefore not needed.

In contrast to DC contracts, DB contracts are usually open accounts, in particular if the pension promise is in terms of wages. The pension fund holds the residual risk on behalf of the sponsor in case of company funds, or future participants in case of mutual funds. However, wage-linked pensions do not necessarily imply open accounts: in the presence of markets for wage-linked bonds, a wage-linked pension could be organized on the basis of closed accounts as well.

"Closed" and "open" accounts are more general than DC and DB in that they avoid the connotation of DC featuring constant contribution rates and of DB promising constant benefit rates. Both open and closed accounts allow for contribution rates and pension benefits that vary with states of the world. The pension contract determines how macroeconomic shocks affect contribution rates and pension benefits.

In addition to closed and open accounts, we distinguish collectively closed accounts. In these accounts, participants may hold claims on each other but not on the fund. Hence, all property rights are allocated to current members of the pension fund. Accounts are thus closed on a fund level; the fund as a whole does not carry mismatch risk and solvency requirements at the fund level are thus not needed. At the individual level, however, claims are not necessarily matched with financial assets. The individual accounts can thus be viewed as open. This allows individuals to trade risks within the pension fund that cannot be traded in financial markets. In the face of limited liability of stakeholders, solvency requirements at the individual level may be required to ensure that individual promises are credible if they are not matched by financial assets. Indeed, these requirements must reduce the value of the option value of limited liability.

Pros and cons of closed and open accounts
Closed accounts feature the advantage that the pension fund does not take any mismatch risk so that the pension fund is not subject to risk. Solvency requirements limiting the risk that pension funds take on their balance sheets are thus not needed. Another advantage is that individual property rights are well defined in terms of financial assets, thereby reducing political risks.

The drawback of closed accounts is that the pension contract is constrained by the set of instruments available on financial markets. In fact, closed accounts face exactly the same constraints, due to missing markets, as the capital markets do (see Subsection 5.3.1).

The advantage of open accounts is that pension funds can create new (non-tradable) assets. For example, pension funds can provide wage-linked pensions financed by contributions of young and future generations. Accounts of individuals are open in the sense that the pension fund bears residual risk on its balance sheet and can shift that risk to its current and future stakeholders. A long-lived institution such as a pension fund thus can trade on behalf of generations who are not in a position to trade themselves because they are too young or are constrained by limited liability of human capital.

The drawback of open accounts is that the fund takes residual risk on its balance sheet, which must be allocated among its stakeholders. Solvency and discontinuity risk now become an issue; the fund must be able to meet its promises even though financial assets owned by the fund no longer necessarily match its liabilities. The net residue (or buffer) is reflected in the net funding ratio of the pension fund, which can be viewed as a residual account that has not been allocated to its stakeholders. A shortage in funding corresponds to a net transfer of future stakeholders of the fund to current participants, whereas a surplus involves a transfer from current participants to future stakeholders. In case of open accounts, the pension fund may take on capital market risks, longevity risk and human-capital risk so that the fund runs a deficit if capital returns fall unexpectedly and life expectancy, prices or wages rise unexpectedly. Over time, these risks are transferred back to the residual risk bearers of the pension fund. The nature of the residual risk bearer depends both on the pension contract describing how funding disequilibria are allocated over the various stakeholders and the incidence of net transfers.

The pension contract may be either complete or incomplete, depending on whether the closure rule describing the allocation of mismatch risks is made explicit before the shocks in the funding rate actually occur. In company pension funds, the shareholders of the associated corporations are typically the residual risk bearer. However, the limited liability of these shareholders implies that the policyholders[21] end up as residual claimant in case of a bad shock. In mutual sectoral pension funds, in contrast, shortages and surpluses in funding are recouped by levying implicit taxes (or subsidies) on wages of future participants. The ultimate risk bearer then depends also on the incidence of these implicit taxes. In non-tradable sectors, for example, consumers may end up with the risk as workers are able to shift these taxes through compensating wage differentials.[22]

Collectively closed accounts
With collectively closed accounts, the pension funds can create internal markets for risks not traded on the open financial markets (for example, human capital and demographic risks) without giving rise to mismatch and discontinuity risk of the pension fund. To illustrate, longevity risk can be tailored to risk tolerance of the younger and older participants even if longevity bonds are not available in financial markets. The same applies to wage risks.

---

[21] In countries with public insurance schemes, the taxpayer may pick up the tab.
[22] If labor can easily move to sectors without gray pension funds, the owners of the firms may end up as residual risk bearers. This limits intergenerational risk sharing as these owners tend to be of similar ages as the policyholders.

Collectively closed accounts suffer from various weaknesses. First of all, individual property rights may not be well defined, especially if the pension contract is incomplete or not time consistent and thus not credible. Even if the pension contract is complete, the risk contracts cannot be objectively priced on financial markets. This lack of transparency may give rise to intransparent transfers of wealth between participants.

A second drawback of collectively closed accounts is that the scope of intergenerational risk sharing is limited by the demographic composition of the funds. In the absence of tradable assets, trade between generations must occur within pension funds. This works only if all generations are represented in a pension fund. This problem could be alleviated if pension funds could securitize some of the risks that they trade internally or engage in mutual insurance schemes. Unfortunately, the pricing of these contracts would be problematic.

Intergenerational risk sharing: pensions funds versus government[23]
By trading on account of future generations, open accounts contribute to intergenerational risk sharing. The limited liability of future participants limits this risk sharing, however. If the fund puts too much risk on future participants, this may lead to discontinuity risk. Future generations may not only withdraw their labor if implicit taxes in pension contributions become too high, but they may also vote with their feet or their voice. These responses endanger the continuity of the pension fund, and thus the intergenerational risk sharing contract as well.

Compared with intergenerational sharing of risk through the government (see Subsection 5.3.2), risk sharing through pension funds has the advantages of less political risk and more possibilities to tailor arrangements to specific constituencies. In fact, the risk-sharing contracts between generations are typically more complete. Accordingly, pension funds typically provide more transparency about intergenerational risk sharing than the government does. Similarly, investment decisions in pension funds are not politically driven, while governments

---

[23] If the pension fund insures longevity risk, residual longevity risk can be borne by the closed accounts in a particular way. For example, risks may be borne in proportion to the accumulations in the accounts in the insurance pool. Older cohorts facing more uncertain mortality rates may then be charged a market price for this insurance. Alternatively, risks can be pooled on a cohort basis only.

may be tempted to make their investment decisions on the basis of political considerations. Another advantage of trading wage risks is that it may induce trade unions to moderate wages so as to constrain the level of pension contributions.[24]

The disadvantages of pension funds, compared with the government, are more discontinuity risk and possible labor-market distortions limiting the room for intergenerational risk sharing.[25] Pension funds face the exogenous and endogenous risk of discontinuity: the firm or the sector sponsoring the pension fund declines so that a negative funding residue cannot be allocated. Moreover, compared with the government, pension funds have less power to commit future generations to the contract because they face more competition on the labor market; younger generations can choose to work elsewhere in the national economy if the pension fund tries to "tax" them. The compensating wage differentials imply that burden is shifted back to older generations.[26] These tax burdens may also result in endogenous discontinuity risk where resources flee from sectors or firms that are burdened by a substantial debt overhang due to underfunding. In that case, retirees become residual risk bearers after all. In all these ways, competition in effect enforces limited liability of younger generations, thereby providing arguments for solvency requirements. These requirements make transparent the limits pension funds face to shift burdens to these generations.

In choosing between the government and pension funds as long-lived institutions in addressing market failures, we thus face a trade-off between political risk and intergenerational risk sharing. The government has more power, a larger and more diversified pool of participants

[24] Political risks are still present though. Older generations may be tempted to hold on to large buffers in case of positive capital shocks while younger generations may not accept negative buffers in case of negative shocks. Thus, intergenerational risk sharing is limited by political risks.

[25] Another disadvantage is that risk trading can occur only within pension funds. The more limited market constrains welfare-improving trades between various age groups with different exposures to risk. This is especially the case if pension funds differ a lot in terms of the age composition of their participants. Pension funds can address this problem by trading wage risk among themselves.

[26] Depending on the tradability of the produced output, the mobility of capital and the specificity of labor to the firm or sector, this may be the owners of the firm (sectors) or the demanders of the firm's (sector's) output, the workers in the firm (the sector) or the participants of the pension fund.

and more instruments for this risk sharing, but these instruments may also give rise to additional political risks. Indeed, competition between sectors or firms with pension funds is a mixed blessing. On the one hand, competition reduces political risk and puts pressure on pension funds to improve their performance and to properly reward young workers for bearing risk. On the other hand, it limits the possibilities for intergenerational risk sharing.

Hybrid solution: open accounts for the government and closed accounts for pension funds

One can also combine the best of governments and pension funds in the following way. Open accounts are reserved for the government, which issues securities that allow pension funds to limit themselves to closed accounts. In particular, the government issues wage-linked and longevity bonds through which the older generations can buy claims on the human capital of younger and future generations.[27] The government is the most natural party to take on wage-linked liabilities on its balance sheet because it has the largest pool of human capital that it can tax. The financial instruments increase the commitment of the government not to default on its explicit wage-linked obligations and thus reduce political risk. Indeed, older generations hold tradable financial claims on the younger generations (rather than implicit PAYG claims).

The pension funds and insurance companies can then take on these assets on their balance sheets to match their wage-linked annuities and other pension liabilities to older generations. Private parties in effect reinsure these wage-linked obligations with the government against transparent market prices. Without mismatch risk, they do not have to hold solvency buffers and do not have to distort labor markets and labor mobility through non-actuarially fair contribution levels.

---

[27] The government can also issue put options on the stock market and call options on wages. In this way, it allows the pension funds to take on more risk. The young agents participate in these risks first through their net financial accounts. If this wealth is exhausted through high wages or low financial returns, they continue to participate in intergenerational risk sharing as taxpayers through the government balance sheet. The advantage of tradable put options is that they can in principle be priced objectively. However, tail risks are difficult to price, also because the credit risk of governments may be an issue in very bad states.

Moreover open accounts can be replaced by closed accounts, thereby eliminating the first and third drawbacks of open accounts.

Finally, the government participates in the capital market risks of pension funds through the cash-flow treatment of pension saving and other taxes on consumption (including value-added taxes). In this way, the young, future generations hold a claim on the current capital stock.

5.4 Intra-generational heterogeneity and idiosyncratic risks

5.4.1 Intra-generational heterogeneity and life-cycle planning

This section turns to heterogeneity within any generation and the consequences for optimal life-cycle financial planning. Agents of the same cohorts feature heterogeneous preferences and endowment risks as regards preferences, risk attitudes, time preference, bequests and housing preferences, and preferred patterns of work, career and retirement differ across agents. Also endowment risks vary depending on individual circumstances. An important aspect of this intra-generational heterogeneity is the nature of human capital, including its level and the associated risks. Related to human capital is the health status and life expectancy of individuals. Household composition and the ownership of a house or other assets (e.g., due to a bequest) are other relevant characteristics.

Heterogeneity can arise from innate differences in ability and health when people are born, or can arise only when people move through their life cycle. Before they know whether shocks will occur or not, agents can trade voluntarily to smooth consumption over various contingencies. Agents in fact trade more consumption in one state of the world for less consumption in another contingency. After uncertainty is resolved and agents know which state of the world has been realized, however, risk sharing becomes redistribution: some agents transfer resources to other agents. If agents have not been able to contract behind the veil of ignorance, this transfer of resources will not occur voluntarily and the government will have to force agents to give up resources. This holds obviously for heterogeneity inherited at birth. But due to several market failures – limited liability of human capital being one of these – shocks later in life are also often "insured" through redistribution rather than explicit risk contracts.

5.4.2 *Idiosyncratic shocks and intra-generational risk pooling*

Idiosyncratic shocks are closely related to intra-generational hetero-geneity. These shocks differ from macroeconomic shocks in that they hit only one single individual at a time and are thus uncorrelated across individuals. They can in principle be pooled across individuals with the lucky individuals transferring resources to the unlucky agents. The law of large numbers then implies that all uncertainty can be eliminated: the variance of the average of independently and identically distributed random shocks approaches zero if the number of random shocks becomes very large. Risk pooling is the principle of insurance.

Longevity risk illustrates the distinction between idiosyncratic and aggregate risk. Idiosyncratic longevity risk implies that individuals face uncertain life expectancies but that average life expectancy is certain for a large cohort. In that case, aggregate uncertainty can be eliminated by perfectly pooling risks among the members of a cohort. Life insurance and annuities (inverse life insurance) are based on the pooling of idiosyncratic longevity risk. In case also average life expect-ancy of a cohort is uncertain, however, risk pooling cannot eliminate all risk. The remaining macroeconomic risk has to be distributed to someone.

Human capital also involves several major idiosyncratic risks. Examples are disability and health risks, which can be pooled through disability, health and long-term care insurance. Individuals are also hit by idiosyncratic career and wage shocks during their working lives (see Meghir and Pistaferri, 2004). Other important idiosyncratic shocks involve household composition. The probability that relationships are formed and broken up is an important example of this risk.

5.5 How to organize optimal life-cycle planning and intra-generational insurance?

5.5.1 *Capital markets*

Imperfect individual decision making and intra-generational heterogeneity
Heterogeneity, including the exposure to non-insurable idiosyncratic risks, typically calls for consumer sovereignty. Individuals know their

individual preferences and circumstances best. They themselves are therefore in the best position to tailor their market transactions to their own situation.

Empirical evidence, however, suggests that households typically lack the basic financial knowledge, computational ability and willpower to implement financial life-cycle planning involving saving levels, risk management, portfolio decisions, and life and annuity insurance (see Lusardi and Mitchell, 2006). Inadequate decision making by individuals gives rise to excessively low saving rates, underdiversified and inefficient portfolios, and insufficient risk pooling through annuitization. Whereas allowing individuals to trade risks can help them to tailor their risk profile to their specific individual circumstances, it can also lead to major mistakes if individuals lack the required expertise and willpower. Indeed, pension provision involves complex decisions involving a long time horizon and major risks. In view of these complexities, the market for pension products is typically rather intransparent and suffers from high transaction costs. Credible, complete contracts over a long time horizon accounting for many relevant contingencies are complex and expensive to write.

Financial illiteracy and individual heterogeneity combined with the nature of the pension products as an experience good give rise to serious agency issues. Due to imperfect individual decision making, households have to delegate these complex decisions to professionals and financial institutions. These latter parties, however, typically lack the necessary information about the characteristics of the beneficiaries and do not necessarily act in the interests of these clients. Establishing trusted institutions that help individuals in tailoring their financial decisions to their individual situation with only small transaction costs is a major challenge. Among other things, it involves major governance issues ensuring that interests of these institutions as agent of the client are aligned with those of the principal. It also requires that these institutions have access to the information about the individual circumstances of the beneficiaries.

Insurance and moral hazard

Moral hazard constrains the insurance of idiosyncratic risk. If individuals can undertake non-verifiable activities that reduce the probability or damage of adverse shocks, insurance will discourage these activities. As a result, overall damages increase. In the presence of moral hazard, full insurance is not optimal and individuals face some residual risk in order to give them an incentive to contain damages.

Moral hazard is especially relevant in case of idiosyncratic human-capital risk. If these risks are insured, individuals undertake less effort to prevent these risks by investing in and utilizing human capital. Hence, considerable human-capital risk should be left with the individuals. These individuals then optimally engage in precautionary saving so as to accumulate financial collateral that can be used in case of adverse uninsured shocks.[28]

The motives for precautionary saving are particularly strong if borrowing constraints prevent individuals from optimally diversifying uninsurable labor income risks over time through consumption smoothing. These borrowing constraints are due to the non-tradability and limited liability of human-capital, which in fact originate in moral hazard and adverse selection. Limited liability of human capital thus limits the sharing of not only macroeconomic risks (see Section 5.3) but also idiosyncratic human capital risks. Indeed, the behavior of individuals facing borrowing constraints resembles that of a pension fund facing solvency constraints. Both borrowing constraints and solvency constraints originate in the non-tradability of human capital and harm the ability to time diversify risk. They thus reduce risk-bearing capacities and encourage precautionary saving to escape these constraints.

Borrowing constraints are especially relevant if agents with small liquid financial resources face temporary idiosyncratic shocks. With permanent shocks and CRRA preferences, however, optimal consumption smoothing dictates also that consumption is reduced less than income and that saving for retirement is reduced or that people start to dissave by reducing financial wealth originally set aside for retirement. Habit formation, however, gives rise to a need for liquid buffers even in case of permanent uninsurable idiosyncratic shocks. The reason is that people want to reduce their consumption only gradually after an adverse shock. Indeed, precautionary motives rather than saving for retirement tend to be the main reason why young households save (see Cocco *et al.*, 2005).

The combination of borrowing constraints and non-insurable idiosyncratic human-capital risk not only raises saving but also results in more conservative investment behavior and a lack of desire to buy

---

[28] In contrast to retirement saving, this precautionary saving should be liquid.

illiquid (deferred) annuities. Indeed, by investing conservatively and setting aside liquid resources through saving, individuals ensure the presence of a financial buffer that helps them to optimally time diversify temporary risks. Using numerical simulations, Gollier (2008) shows that this may cause young households with small financial reserves to invest less in equity than older households who are less constrained by borrowing constraints in diversifying risks over a longer period. In a similar vein, Cocco *et al.* (2005) find that young investors choose portfolios that are less tilted towards equity than middle-aged investors.

Davis *et al.* (2006) formulate a model in which individuals can borrow, but at a cost that exceeds the risk-free rate of return. As far as investment behavior is concerned, high borrowing rates discourage young households from acquiring a large equity exposure by leveraging their portfolio. As regards consumption smoothing, high borrowing rates discourage dissaving early in life so that agents can build up a stock of financial wealth earlier, which helps to boost equity exposure later on in life. Their model is better able to fit the empirical evidence on borrowing and individual equity holdings over the life cycle.

For older households, non-insured medical and long-term care expenses can be an important source of idiosyncratic risk. This has important implications for saving behavior (i.e., precautionary saving), investment behavior and the willingness to take out illiquid annuities. In particular, these households then also save for precautionary reasons and when they start to be subject to these risks invest more conservatively and are hesitant to take out illiquid annuities.

Insurance and adverse selection

In some cases, agents know more about their own risk features than others. This private information in fact lifts the veil of ignorance for the agents involved. In that case, the agents who know that they have a low probability of suffering damages will not voluntarily pool risks because insurance premia are based on the average risk features of the population as a whole. This phenomenon is called adverse selection and destroys insurance markets.

Insuring longevity and long-term care risk gives rise to adverse selection if individuals with private information about their life expectancy or health prospects can freely choose their insurance level or insurance pool. The individuals who expect to live long will buy annuities and those who project large long-term care expenditures buy long-term care insurance. To prevent losses, insurance companies then have to raise prices so that these insurances become unattractive for those individuals with lower life expectancies or lower long-term care risks. Human-capital insurance also suffers from adverse selection. In particular, insurance companies offering disability or unemployment insurance will end up attracting bad risks with a substantial risk of becoming disabled or unemployed.

5.5.2 Government

Redistribution and moral hazard

If agents have not been able to engage in an insurance contract behind the veil of ignorance, insurance becomes redistribution. Redistribution naturally belongs to the domain of the government because the government can force agents to give up resources. The government can alleviate poverty by providing some sort of basic pension or provision for the elderly who have not been able to save sufficient resources during their working lives. By financing such pensions through income-dependent taxes, the government redistributes income. Just as insurance, redistribution yields moral hazard. To illustrate, redistribution towards the poor harms incentives to escape poverty. If the government fights old-age poverty by providing means-tested benefits, agents are discouraged from not only raising lifetime labor income but also from saving part of this income for old age. Means-tested benefits may also give rise to risky investment choices. In particular, if the government in effect provides a put option by guaranteeing a minimum standard of living, individuals reap the benefits from upside risk but can shift downside risk onto the government.

Imperfect individual decision making and moral hazard

One way to address imperfect willpower and moral hazard in saving due to means-tested benefits in retirement is to simply force people to save during the accumulation stage. Moreover, they can be forced to annuitize their wealth at retirement so that they cannot dissave rapidly during the decumulation phase. Forced annuitization also addresses adverse selection in annuity markets.

In setting the level of forced saving in illiquid form, one must trade off the costs of inadequate saving of those with insufficient willpower against the costs of insufficient flexibility and excessively high saving by those who have high consumption needs during the working life (which may be due to adverse health or human-capital shocks) or already have other means to ensure a comfortable retirement. This trade-off is particularly serious if the government lacks adequate information on individual preferences and circumstances. The risks of inadequate saving due to means-tested benefits in retirement are the largest for those with low lifetime labor incomes. The same probably applies to myopia that is due to lack of financial literacy. Hence, compulsory saving and annuitization rates should be relatively high for low incomes.

Compulsory annuitization makes pension saving illiquid. It should therefore be complemented by public care insurance for high medical costs so that the elderly face only limited idiosyncratic risks and illiquid annuities are an attractive option to insure longevity risk. At the same time, means-tested benefits may be provided to cover additional care costs of vulnerable elderly with low pension incomes. These additional expenses involve moral hazard and should in principle be the responsibility of the individual involved and his social network. The government, however, may provide a safety net for those without a social network or financial means.

Government regulation can help to increase the transparency of markets for pension products through standardized information provision and pension products.

Adverse selection

Whereas government compulsion cannot easily fight moral hazard, it can address adverse selection. In particular, the government can combat adverse selection by forcing the good risks to participate in an insurance pool. By making risk sharing compulsory if the good risks no longer operate completely behind the veil of ignorance and know their risk features, the government in effect redistributes resources from the good risks to the bad risks. If the government forces individuals to take out insurance, individuals can no longer tailor their insurance level to individual preferences and circumstances. This gives rise to a trade-off between preventing adverse selection and attuning the insurance level to the individual situation.

This trade-off emerges if one decides when to annuitize pension wealth and buy long-term care insurance. The longer one waits with buying an annuity, the more one knows about the personal circumstances when one benefits from the annuity and the care insurance but the more the market suffers from adverse selection.

5.5.3 Pension funds

Adverse selection and transaction costs

Forced risk pooling of longevity risks can occur through pension funds. This reduces selection in longevity insurance and decreases marketing costs because competition occurs on a wholesale rather than retail level (see below). The downside is that forced pooling may not tailor to the specific circumstances of homogeneous groups and may involve unwanted systematic solidarity (e.g., from short-lived low-skilled workers to long-lived high-skilled workers). Another drawback may be reduced competitive pressures on insurers if governance structures for disciplining the trustees (sponsor) of the insurance pool are weak. Possible insurance pools are sectors, firms, regions and nations.

Pension funds can reduce transaction and marketing costs in other ways as well. In this connection, the trustees can contract out various financial services to insurance companies, hedge funds or mutual funds. Accordingly, competition occurs on a wholesale level rather than a retail level. This tends to reduce transaction costs for individual beneficiaries, who typically lack sufficient expertise to buy the various services that make up the pension product. Moreover, joining forces in a cooperative pension fund that is run professionally strengthens the buying power of individuals, exploits scale economies in buying complex financial products that are not available to individual investors, and helps to discipline commercial financial service providers to act in the interests of the members of the pension fund.

Imperfect individual decision making

Pension funds can implement optimal investment and saving strategies on behalf of their participants. In the extreme case in which individuals do not trade on the capital market at all, the pension contract should ideally be such that the effective risk exposure for each individual member to each risk factor matches the optimum. Furthermore, pension funds should set contribution rates and pension benefits in such a way that consumption is smoothed optimally over time. These are quite demanding requirements as the pension contract should thus reflect individuals' preferences and circumstances. Agents who have access to financial markets and are capable of making good financial decisions, however, can adjust saving and investment themselves.

In this connection, defaults are a third way between compulsion and unstructured free choice. On the one hand, people have the option to opt out of the default and take choices into their own hands. On the other hand, people do not have to take action themselves. If they do not choose themselves, the choice is made for them.

Defaults should be set by trustworthy parties ("trustees") whose interests are aligned with the beneficiaries. Governance arrangements should instill confidence among beneficiaries that this is indeed the case. The parties who determine the defaults should also have access to sufficient information about the individual circumstances and preferences of the individuals concerned in order to tailor the defaults to individual circumstances. ICT may help in this respect. In some countries, pension registers are set up that collect information on citizens' pension rights. This can be supplemented with other information relevant for life-cycle financial planning.

Empirical research shows the importance of defaults (i.e., what happens if people do not choose themselves) in pension insurance. Defaults are so powerful because financially illiterate individuals see the default as an implicit recommendation for a complex product that they do not fully understand. Defaults are important for the premium level, for portfolio selection and for the way in which the pension is paid out.

Default saving rates

Default saving rates should depend on age, retirement preferences (i.e., preferred age of retirement), risk aversion, and the ratio of financial (and housing) capital to wage income. With habit formation, also consumption in the previous period should be added as a state variable determining optimal saving rates.

At a given age, a higher ratio of financial capital to wage income results *ceteris paribus* in a lower default saving rate. If individual wages are low due to negative wage shock, saving may in fact become negative. This is an argument for integrating precautionary saving and pension saving as part of financial planning over the entire life course. Hence, individuals can be allowed to reduce pension saving or even take up part of their saving in case they face adverse uninsured human capital shocks during their active life. Low default saving may be especially relevant at the beginning of life if the individual concerned buys a home, receives a bequest or temporarily cares for a family member. At the end of the working life, this may be important after a negative uninsured health shock or human-wealth shock due to, for example, being laid off or getting divorced.

After a negative permanent shock in financial wealth or a positive permanent wage shock, the default savings rate should rise. With habit formation, saving is increased gradually after a negative shock in financial wealth. After a positive wage shock, in contrast, saving peaks immediately after the shock and then gradually decreases – even if the wage shock is permanent.

Default annuitization rate

To diversify annuitization risks, agents may gradually buy into deferred annuities. The gains of annuitization occur especially at the end of life when mortality rates are high. If agents are subject to substantial non-insured health risks, they should not transform all their saving into illiquid annuities. Accordingly, default annuitization may be combined with additional medical and long-term care insurance. The timing of default deferred annuitization involves a trade-off between preventing selection (which argues in favor of buying annuity and long-term care insurance early) and flexibility to attune insurance to changing non-contractible individual circumstances (which argues in favor of waiting before buying insurance).

5.5.4 Housing

Housing is an important asset for retirement saving. By buying a house and paying off the mortgage during the life cycle, agents ensure that they do not have housing costs during their retirement. They thus need to save less for their retirement through other means. Moreover, owning your own home is a good way to hedge the risk of changing housing costs. Indeed, owner-occupied housing is an excellent inflation hedge.

In addition to saving on housing costs, homeowners can withdraw equity from their house in order to supplement other retirement income. Moreover, when health starts failing and long-term care is called for, one can sell one's home to pay for a stay in a rented place with care facilities. In this way, the home can help to self-insure idio-syncratic risks during old age.

Saving through one's home may also fight myopic behavior because the home is a rather illiquid asset. More facilities for home-equity loans are thus a mixed blessing. On the one hand, they provide more pos-sibilities for older households to use their home to supplement other retirement income and to self-insure idiosyncratic old-age risks. On the other hand, such loans allow younger agents lacking willpower to tap into their home equity before they reach retirement.

If agents withdraw equity from their home, they are subject to house-price risk. The selling, older generations should ideally trade the systematic part of this risk with the buying, younger generations. Traditionally, this risk is often traded within generations in families. Younger generations receive the equity in the home as a bequest and in return provide home care to the aging frail parents. In this way, par-ents transfer the valuation risk of their homes to their children while insuring their idiosyncratic health risk and hedging the risk of high health care costs.

By taking out mortgages, young agents can take on a substantial amount of house price risk. Leveraging house-price equity by young agents with substantial human capital is exactly what optimal invest-ment behavior during the life cycle dictates. As agents grow older, they should gradually pay off their debts and eventually transfer their valu-ation risk to younger households, for example by moving to rental housing or selling their home to insurance companies in return for annuities and long-term care insurance.

5.6 Conclusion

This chapter has explored the relationship between the three main functions of pension systems (intergenerational sharing of macro risks, intra-generational insurance of idiosyncratic risks and life-cycle financial planning) and three alternative institutions perform-ing these functions: capital markets, governments and pension funds. We showed that each of the institutions has strengths and weaknesses in performing these functions. The design of real-world pension systems thus involves important trade-offs. Moreover, institutions may complement each other in helping to address each other's weaknesses.

References

Benzoni, L., P. Collin-Dufresne and R.S. Goldstein, 2007, Portfolio choice over the life-cycle when the stock and labor markets are cointegrated, *Journal of Finance*, vol. 62(5): 2123–67.

Calvo, G.A., and M. Obstfeld, 1988, Optimal time-consistent fiscal policy with finite lifetimes, *Econometrica*, vol. 56(2): 411–32.

Campbell, J.Y., and J.H. Cochrane, 1999, Force of habit: A consumption-based explanation of aggregate stock market behavior, *Journal of Political Economy*, vol. 107(2): 205–51.

Campbell, J.Y., and L.M. Viceira, 2005, The term structure of the risk-return trade-off, *Financial Analysts Journal*, vol. 61(1): 34–44.

Cocco, J.F., F.J. Gomes and P.J. Maenhout, 2005, Consumption and portfolio choice over the life cycle, *The Review of Financial Studies*, vol. 18(2): 491–533.

Davis, S.J., F. Kubler and P. Willen, 2006, Borrowing costs and the demand for equity over the life cycle, *The Review of Economics and Statistics*, vol. 88(2): 348–62.

Gollier, C., 2008, Understanding saving and portfolio choices with predictable changes in asset returns, *Journal of Mathematical Economics*, vol. 44: 445–58.

Gomes, F.J., L.J. Kotlikoff and L.M. Viceira, 2008, Optimal life-cycle investing with flexible labor supply: A welfare analysis of life-cycle funds, *American Economic Review*, vol. 98(2): 297–303.

Lusardi, A., and O.S. Mitchell, 2006, Financial Literacy and Planning: Implications for Retirement Wellbeing, Pension Research Council, Wharton School, University of Pennsylvania, Working Paper.

Meghir, C., and L. Pistaferri, 2004, Income variance dynamics and heterogeneity, *Econometrica*, vol. 72(1): 1–32.

Obstfeld, M., 1994, Risk-taking, global diversification, and growth, *American Economic Review*, vol. 84(5): 1310–29.

PART II

Intergenerational risk sharing and distribution

6 | Private versus public risk sharing: should governments provide reinsurance?

HENNING BOHN

6.1 Introduction

While markets dealing with financial risks are well developed, markets for dealing with demographic risks and productivity risks are generally lacking. Pension funds play an important role in filling this gap. Defined benefit (DB) and hybrid DB/defined contribution (DC) type occupational pensions can be regarded as insurance mechanisms that deal with just these types of risk. However, as corporations are increasingly exposed to competition nationally and internationally, their ability to make credible long-term pension promises may be declining.

What are the options for reform while maintaining the beneficial aspects of such pension contracts? Should the government take over some of the risks by providing insurance against long-term risks? One option is for the government to issue index-linked bonds that have payoffs linked to longevity or to wage growth. Another option is to provide reinsurance to pension funds, either through customized contracts or insurance agencies, or through index-linked bonds. What forms of indexing are desirable or optimal? What are the consequences for the government portfolio?

This chapter examines alternative arrangements for sharing risks in a stylized small open economy, which is subject to a range of macro-economic disturbances. Labor productivity, the return to capital and longevity are generally stochastic at the individual, national and global level. The integration of capital markets and the mobility of labor

The paper was prepared for presentation at the Netspar Conference on Pension Systems after the Crisis, October 2010. I would like to thank Lans Bovenberg, Casper van Ewijk, Ed Westerhout and the conference participants for their excellent comments. The usual disclaimer applies.

may also vary, creating additional uncertainty. In principle, private pension funds can provide substantial risk sharing across generations and across countries (Ponds, 2003; Teulings and de Vries, 2006; Bovenberg *et al.*, 2007; Gollier, 2008; Cui *et al.*, 2009). Such private risk sharing alleviates the burden on governments to provide insurance.

However, governments have a role in allocating large long-run risks, in effect supplementing private risk sharing. The ability of traditional corporate pension plans to reallocate risk has declined as mobility and financial engineering erodes firms' and workers' ability to enter long-term contracts. Sectoral and industry pension funds face similar pressures as mobility across industries is increasing. Efficient risk sharing then calls for a greater role of government. In summary, private and public risk sharing are complementary in a given setting, but substitutes when there are variations in the scope for private contracts.

A challenge for the future is that as international labor mobility is increasing, governments are less and less able to tie future generations into "social contracts" that share risk. This challenge increases the importance of finding efficient mechanisms that are based on voluntary agreements and not primarily on large tax-financed transfers, and it may shift the public–private trade-off back towards private pension funding.

The analysis is tailored to the pension arrangements in the Netherlands, which has a three-pillar system with strong industry and sectoral pension funds (Ponds and van Riel, 2007; Bovenberg and Nijman, 2008). Pillar one is a basic subsistence benefit provided by government and financed on a pay-as-you-go (PAYG) basis. Pillar two consists of industry pension schemes, which are negotiated by employers and unions and are mandatory for all employees and employers in the relevant sector.[1] Such plans cover more than 90 percent of the workforce and are crucial for most middle-class pensioners to obtain an adequate income replacement in retirement. These occupational pensions are supported by independent funds that invest in capital markets. Pillar three refers to private savings, which have received relatively little attention and seem most important at the upper end of the wealth distribution.

---

[1] For brevity, I will refer to independent multi-employer pension funds as industry pension funds. This includes sector and occupational funds. Many findings also apply to single-employer funds, which are regulated to provide at least the same benefits.

The direct role of government pensions in the Netherlands is remarkably limited, both as compared with other countries and in relation to industry pension funds. Because the government's role is viewed as supplemental, a case for government reinsurance must rest on an argument that private pension funds cannot efficiently provide such insurance on their own. A central question of this chapter is therefore under what conditions current Dutch pension arrangements are efficient, and under what conditions additional government support may be appropriate or even necessary.

Three fundamental arguments justify government insurance or reinsurance. The first is based on a mobility constraint, which refers to the ability of workers to exit a pension plan that tries to collect payments from workers in excess of future benefits. Settlement is essential for insurance. But *ex post*, a demand for settlement acts like tax and induces avoidance. Given laws against forced labor, private plans cannot contractually prevent employees from leaving. Hence their ability to "tax" members is limited by the opportunity cost of exit. The government can overcome this limitation by making the young responsible, through the tax system, for insurance contracts or contingent bonds sold to older generations. Because optimal retirement benefits are partially indexed to wages and longevity, optimal insurance takes the form of wage- and longevity-indexed contracts or bonds.[2]

A second argument is based on incomplete markets. Though the merits of completing incomplete markets seem obvious, the underlying issues are default and the cost of collateral. Pension promises must be backed by assets or by a plan sponsor – a firm or industry. Incomplete markets are unproblematic if a plan sponsor can fill the gaps between optimal pensions and available assets. However, corporate backing is credible only if the plan sponsor is adequately capitalized or if the promises are sufficiently collateralized. Rapid technical change, industrial restructuring and advances in financial engineering have eroded the ability of firms to offer their equity capital as

---

[2] Note that this policy is optimal even if financial markets are complete. Though retirees can then find insurance in the market, the inability of workers to participate implies, in the absence of policy intervention, a welfare loss for workers and an inefficiently low private supply of insurance desired by retirees. Put differently, the problem can be interpreted as resulting from the limited liability of the young, who do not own financial collateral and cannot commit to provide future labor effort (see Bovenberg and van Ewijk, 2010).

collateral; dedicated collateral is costly. Wage- and longevity-indexed bonds would help because a reduced mismatch between typical plan assets and liabilities would reduce a plan's dependence on corporate sponsors.

A third argument is based on imperfections in risk sharing abroad. If most foreign countries fail to integrate young and unborn generations into risk sharing arrangements – through pension plans or by their governments – the systematic risk that is priced in world financial markets largely reflect risks facing the old generation. Capital and longevity risks are priced, but not wage risk. This suggests that protection against longevity risk would sell at a premium and protection against wage risk could be purchased at low cost. Both should be welfare improving for governments acting in the interest of future generations.

Government intervention in risk sharing can in principle take many forms. In the Netherlands, where insurance through private pension plans is well established and generally well working, interventions are most practical and cost effective if they occur through the regular tax system and by providing suitable financial instrument to industry pension plans. The latter is reinsurance in the sense that the government provides instruments for funds to insure themselves, which enables them to provide optimal insurance to their members; but (apart from regular taxes) government does not directly insure employees.[3]

The chapter is organized as follows. Section 6.2 introduces alternative arrangements of public and private risk sharing and identifies key issues for the analysis. Section 6.3 presents a stylized model of pension funding that provides conditions for efficient intergenerational risk sharing and discusses conditions under which young and future generations can be included in private risk sharing. Section 6.4 examines limitations to private risk sharing due to increasing labor mobility and financial engineering, and how government reinsurance can alleviate these problems. Section 6.5 comments on limitations to government risk sharing in a world with increasing international mobility, and on potential remedies. Section 6.6 concludes.

---

[3] By comparison, the US government guarantees certain individual pensions through the PBGC. There is no comparable agency in the Netherlands. The US arrangement seems much less efficient; it is activated only in case of insurer default, it provides insurers no help in managing aggregate risks and the pricing does not adequately adjust for risk.

6.2 Public and private risk sharing: the role of private pension funds

Pension financing everywhere faces two principal challenges. The first is to ensure a sufficient level of funding for retirement. In all developed economies, this is accomplished at least in part through a public pension system. The second challenge is to deal efficiently with the unavoidable economic and demographic risks. The two challenges are linked because lack of insurance jeopardizes funding adequacy and because public tax-transfer systems invariably reallocate risk between contributors and recipients.[4]

Three fundamental risks are the focus of this chapter: shocks to productivity, which are reflected in wages; shocks to the return on capital – reflecting mainly obsolescence but also shocks to productivity – and shocks to longevity (or life expectancy).[5]

A simple intuition about the optimal allocation of risk is that Pareto efficiency calls for risk pooling, which means that aggregate risks should be shared by everyone (Bohn 2006b). Without insurance, workers would be exposed to labor productivity risk. Retirees would be exposed to return and longevity risks. Hence efficient risk sharing means shifting wage risk from workers to retirees; shifting rate of return risk from retirees to workers; and shifting longevity risk from retirees to workers.

Efficient risk sharing is more complicated when aggregate disturbances are correlated over time and across variables. Permanent

---

[4] One should also keep in mind that risk is reallocated through the general tax system, and that a robust risk-sharing mechanism must not create additional risks through instabilities in the risk-sharing mechanism itself (discontinuity risks).

[5] This follows Ponds (2003) and Bohn (2006b). Ponds identifies the same three risks as the main sources of uncertainty. Bohn considers uncertainty about birth rates and about medical spending needs in addition. Birth rate uncertainty is a main driver of fluctuations in capital-labor ratios, wages and returns to capital. But in an open economy, factor returns are determined by the world capital-labor ratio, which is exogenous to a small economy. For this paper, wages and returns are simply treated as considered exogenous, without attempting to investigate the sources of their fluctuations. Because in Europe universal health insurance is well established, medical expense risk deserves less emphasis than in the US; one may reasonably assume that medical risk is shared efficiently by the government. An extension to signals about future productivity might be interesting for future work. Anticipated longevity shocks are examined in Bohn (2001) and disregarded here for simplicity.

shocks impact current and future generations equally whereas temporary shocks have a direct impact only on the living generations. Moreover, if labor and capital are complements in production, workers and retirees start off with correlated exposures to the underlying dynamics of total factor productivity. Empirical work suggests that wages and capital incomes are unit root processes with a common stochastic trend. (See Baxter and Jermann, 1997; Bohn, 1999; Benzoni *et al.*, 2007.) This is consistent with balanced growth models where stochastic productivity growth generates a common stochastic trend in wages and capital incomes. However, the value of capital fluctuates relative to capital income, so there are independent fluctuations in asset returns relative to the productivity trend – valuation risk for short (see Bohn, 1999, 2009), which may be interpreted more fundamentally as stochastic obsolescence. In this setting, efficient risk sharing still calls for shifting wage risk from workers to retirees, but only to the extent that workers' initial exposure exceeds retirees' exposure through capital income. Also, the efficient allocation of return risk requires a separation of capital income risk and valuation risk. Because the former is highly correlated with wages, only the latter should be shifted from retirees to workers.[6] To streamline the discussion of alternative risk-sharing mechanisms, I will use the simple terms wage risk and return risk to refer to workers' and retirees' principal risk exposures.

To understand the value of risk-sharing institutions, it is instructive to start with an economy where the government does not intervene in retirement savings, and then add relevant institutions. In a purely private system, everyone would have to save for his or her own retirement. The government would not be involved. An immediate problem is that those too poor to save and those unlucky in their investment

---

[6] Note that Benzoni *et al.* (2007) come to different conclusions about workers' optimal exposure to stock market risk – notably, that young workers should have zero exposure to the stock market. Whereas Bohn (1999) estimates a cointegrated system with capital income, stock prices and wages, Benzoni *et al.* (2007) estimate only capital income and wages and they *assume* a stable price-dividend ratio. The latter is grossly inconsistent with empirical data, casting doubt on the conclusions. Bohn (1999) shows that valuation risk – the risk generated by fluctuations in equity prices relative to capital income – is a major source of volatility of equity returns, and this should be shared with workers. Implicitly, all disturbances are treated as unanticipated. These assumptions are reasonable at a generational timescale (see Bohn, 2009) and convenient to avoid a proliferation of state variables.

strategies would be destitute in old age. A natural response is a basic means-tested welfare benefit in old age. However, such a benefit would likely destroy saving incentives for workers with low earnings. Low earners would be better off by saving nothing and relying on welfare than to save for retirement. This logic justifies mandatory contributions. A Beveridge-type pension system with mandatory contributions to finance a flat, subsistence-level retirement pension is arguably the minimal government intervention in a civilized society.[7]

In an economy with such minimal public intervention, individuals at the bottom end of the income distribution would rely on public pensions. Everyone else would save individually in financial markets. The aggregate supply of financial assets would consist of claims against the capital stock. In equilibrium, retirement savings would be invested in risky capital assets and thus be subject to considerable rate of return uncertainty. Notably, savers would be fully exposed to fluctuations in the profitability of capital, the risk of obsolescence, and they would be unprotected against uncertainty about their length of life. Annuities might be available, but likely subject to adverse selection. Moreover, the insurance companies issuing annuities would be owned by the same generation that needs insurance; hence there would be no insurance against aggregate longevity risk.

One should acknowledge that there may be some private risk sharing between narrowly defined cohorts (e.g., the age-60 cohort may hold less equity and more corporate bonds than the age-55 cohort). On a broad timescale, however, neighboring cohorts are subject to essentially the same shocks over their lifetimes and therefore have much less scope for risk sharing than temporally more distant cohorts. For clarity, it is instructive therefore to abstract from the fine structure of age cohorts and treat prime-age workers who save for retirement as a single generation (as detailed below). To a first approximation, this generation of retirement savers must hold the capital stock. In addition, one may consider private risk sharing via altruistic bequests, but empirical evidence suggests that dynastic risk sharing is rather weak (see Altonji *et al.*, 1992).[8]

---

[7] In comparison, means testing would raise much broader issues of optimal taxation. Mandatory savings are simpler and they correct the moral hazard problem that motivates the intervention.

[8] Private risk sharing via altruistic bequests might play a greater role in countries where a substantial share of national wealth is held by a small number of very

International risk sharing would help to insure country-specific components of risk (see Shiller, 1999). But international insurance is challenging, because it may be difficult to collect on large settlements due from foreigners – say, in response to a large negative domestic productivity shock – unless the claims are collateralized, which is technically difficult. Shiller's macro markets still do not exist. Moreover, the main risks are likely correlated internationally. Longevity is driven in part by medical innovations that are accessible worldwide. Similarly, labor productivity and the obsolescence of capital are driven by innovations that are shared internationally, at least among the technologically leading economies and especially at the long time horizons relevant for pensions. Even non-technological shocks are propagated internationally, e.g., financial crises. Thus the major macroeconomic risks are best interpreted as global risks factors.

A second layer of public intervention arises through the general tax system. Interest and dividend incomes are commonly included in the tax base for income taxes, and capital gains are included in many countries. This tax treatment creates strong disincentives to save for retirement because returns to savings would be taxed repeatedly (Diamond, 1999). When interest, dividends and capital gains are taxed in nominal currency units, effective real marginal tax rates can easily approach or exceed 100 percent. This problem provides a basic motivation for setting up separate institutions for pensions savings. The segregation of saved labor income from other wealth allows a positive discrimination – encouragement – of "meritorious" retirement savings as compared with, say, inherited wealth.

Retirement contributions are commonly exempted from income taxes. The pay-outs are treated as taxable income. This tax treatment implies that total returns on retirement savings are shared in proportions of "tax rate" to "one minus tax rate" between the government and retirement savers. Because fluctuations in tax revenues are likely recovered over time from taxes on many cohorts of taxpayers, the effect is an intergenerational sharing of total return risk. Moreover, taxes on compensation are effectively deferred to the extent that

wealthy families. Calibration results in Bohn (2006a) suggest that inherited wealth is important in some developing countries, but less relevant in developed economies with aging populations. Moreover, risk sharing between the very wealthy and the rest of the population is likely incomplete.

they are diverted into retirement, which – *ceteris paribus* – raises the government debt and provides safe assets for retirement savers.[9]

The United States comes close to exemplifying a "nearly private" system of this kind. DC retirement plans are now prevalent in major corporations. They assign essentially no risk-sharing role to companies and are best interpreted as pure tax shelters. Though US social security provides wage-linked benefits, the linkage decreases with income and provides insufficient retirement income for the vast majority of wage earners.

A polar opposite is a system of proportional income replacement, e.g., as in Germany in the tradition of Bismarck. In such a system, pensions are wage-indexed and generous enough that most workers do not need supplemental savings. Wage indexing means that the incomes of workers and retirees are subject to the same disturbances – notably shocks to labor productivity. Assuming a relatively stable savings rate, which is empirically plausible, this system yields a high correlation of workers' and retirees' consumption opportunities. Such pooling of consumption risk is the hallmark of efficient risk sharing (Bohn, 2006b, 2009). If there is a maximum contribution level, the system does not fully cover high earners; the important difference to a Beveridge-type system is that the middle classes are fully covered.

Left out of this description is a discussion of who bears capital risks. Implicitly, capital risks are either concentrated in a separate class of entrepreneurs, who are perhaps more risk tolerant than wage earners, or spread through the tax system in ways that are not entirely transparent. Another question is how taxes and benefits should respond to changes in longevity. This is now addressed in some systems, e.g., in Sweden after recent reforms, but often left unspecified, e.g., in Germany.

Tax-transfer systems can in principle share risk efficiently (Bohn, 2006b, 2009). One must worry, however, that financial imbalances in a government-run system are resolved through political processes that are not transparent and not predictable *ex ante*, which may lead to new distortions and inefficiencies. It is worth examining therefore if the same risk sharing can be implemented in a less government-controlled manner.[10]

---

[9] Similar risk-spreading effects arise through consumption taxes and through corporate income taxes.

[10] A technical appendix in the Working Paper version of this chapter, Bohn (2010), shows more formally that a number of alternative risk-sharing

A promising third option is a pension system centered on pension plans with DB sponsored by private employers.[11] The Dutch pension system is a leading example, and it motivates the focus on employer-sponsored systems and their potential in this study. Because the incomes of companies and their employees add up to national income, corporate pension plans have the potential to allocate national income efficiently, and in particular, to share both wage and capital income risks. Because firms are profit oriented, one might expect them to be more effective in managing pensions and in discovering gains from trade between shareholders and workers than a government bureaucracy, and less subject to political pressures. Because a pension plan includes multiple generations of participants – including shareholders who are likely older than most active workers – efficient pension arrangements may include intergenerational risk sharing. In summary, private pensions have a potential for sophisticated reallocation of risk across multiple parties, but one must examine carefully under what conditions the potential can be realized.

Conceptually, a key challenge to risk sharing in pension funds is limited commitment. All insurance requires a settlement after an insured event has occurred, and this requires commitment. The problem has several dimensions. First, workers are typically supposed to make extra contributions when labor productivity is unexpectedly high, when capital held by retirees is unexpectedly devalued, and/or if retirees live unexpectedly long. But workers can always quit if they are paid less than their marginal product in alternative jobs. In the limit, if there was no attachment of workers to their jobs, the allocation of risk with pension funds would reduce to a laissez-faire allocation with no intergenerational sharing. Second, workers expect to contribute less if the opposite contingencies are realized. But in a competitive environment, firms can terminate workers who demand more than the current marginal product of labor. Third,

mechanisms are equivalent under suitable conditions. This suggests that an assessment of various frictions is central for comparisons, notably transactions cost, information problems and commitment problems.

[11] To be specific, a DB pension is a promise by a plan sponsor to pay benefits according to an explicit formula or indexation rule. (A "hybrid" plan would be DB in this sense.) This is in contrast to a DC plan that gives retirees a claim on assets but not an enforceable claim against a sponsor. Not part of the definition is to what extent pension risk is retained by the sponsor or transferred to markets or to other (usually younger) plan members.

firms have the option to declare insolvency. Thus whenever a pension commitment to retirees is less than fully funded, firms have an incentive to avoid responsibility, e.g., by paying out the firm's value as dividends or through share repurchases, or by reorganizing their operations in other ways that reduce the ability of pensioners to enforce their claims. Even without intentional avoidance of responsibility, the limited liability of shareholders places an upper bound on pension commitments.

Regulations that mandate overfunding – a "buffer" above full funding – are a common solution to the insolvency threat. Overfunding is an attractive solution under idealized conditions – when there are no intermediation costs – but likely costly under realistic conditions. Moreover, a fund may have to be vastly overfunded to guarantee funding without recourse to the plan sponsor under all circumstances.

Thus it is not obvious to what extent pension funds can deliver on promises to share risk. As noted by Bulow (1982), these commitment problems cannot be dismissed by reference to contribution formulas that appear to make employers and employees jointly responsible for funding imbalances. Employment decisions are based on total compensation. In a competitive labor market, a company that, say, requires higher contributions from young workers to compensate for a pension shortfall must compensate for this "tax" by paying a higher salary. Cash salary plus pension accruals should add up to the marginal product of labor even if the stated contribution rate differs.

A systematic analysis of risk sharing in pension funds must disentangle the multi-faceted relationship between retirees, current workers, future workers (individually and acting collectively through unions), their employers (individually and collectively) and the government. In the literature, different assumptions are made about these relationships.

One the one side, Bulow (1982) assumes competitive labor markets, which reduce pension plans to a contract between each employee and his or her employer. Funding ensures that employers keep their commitments to intermediate risks on behalf of their workers. If a fund has no ability to tie workers to the firm, there is no intergenerational risk sharing. More generally, Allen and Gale (1997) explain why market competition can constrain financial institutions in a way that makes risk sharing impossible.

On the other side, a substantial European literature examines institutional arrangements where participation in a pension fund is mandatory. Ponds (2003) and Teulings and de Vries (2006) lay out the general issues. Both emphasize that mandatory participation is essential to commit future generations to share risk in pension funds. Intergenerational risk sharing means that a generation receives net payments in some states of nature and must make net payments in other states of nature. Young individuals entering the workforce are naturally reluctant to participate in an underfunded plan that will require net payments to regain solvency. But if the underfunding arises in the context of an *ex ante* efficient funding plan, risk sharing is impossible unless participation can be enforced when net payments are due. A key difference to many other countries – notably the US and UK – is that the regulatory environment in the Netherlands favors mandatory industry and sectoral pension funds.

Several papers in the European literature have examined quantitatively how different rules for pension contributions and benefits influence the allocation of risk across generations and the division of the resulting gains in social welfare. Teulings and de Vries (2006), Bovenberg *et al.* (2007), Gollier (2008) and Cui *et al.* (2011) all examine overlapping generations models with each generation living for 55 annual periods. Hybrid plans mixing DB and DC elements are found to share risk flexibly. Teulings and de Vries (2006) show how risk sharing is improved by the inclusion of young cohorts prior to their entry in the workforce.

Several recent papers discuss systemic changes in Dutch pension plans since the 1990s; see Ponds and van Riel (2007), Kortleve and Ponds (2009, 2010) and van Ewijk (2009). Funding ratios have declined sharply in response to the stock market falls in 2001–2002 and in 2008–2009. These large declines apparently exceeded the pension funds' capacity to allocate risk according to pre-planned formulas. By agreement between unions and employers, benefit formulas have shifted since 2000 from DB to hybrid, and from final wage to average wage indexing – suggesting a burden-shifting onto the young. In addition, Dutch regulators have imposed increasingly stringent funding rules, now requiring a significant overfunding of promised nominal benefits. This contrasts sharply with the US, where underfunding is common.

It appears the 2008–2009 financial crisis had different effects across cohorts than the 2001–2002 downturn. Van Ewijk (2009) provides an insightful case study of how the Dutch pension system responded to the 2008–2009 financial crisis. He finds that the burden of pension adjustments fell primarily on retirees (age 60+) and prime-age workers (about age 40–60), largely due to reductions in indexed benefits. The impact on younger adults (age 20–40), due to higher contributions, was also negative but smaller. These findings suggest that risk sharing was only partial and that the young did not bear a disproportionate burden. One may wonder why the 2008–2009 shocks triggered such different responses. One possibility is that the 2008–2009 shock is considered much more damaging to the labor productivity of the young – but this question remains unresolved.

Mandatory participation can be established either by law or regulation, by collusive agreements between employers, or by agreements between employers and unions. Either way, it gives private pension funds an ability to tax or subsidize entering cohorts that is conceptually equivalent to a government's ability to tax and subsidize future generations. Given the powers of taxation, *ex ante* efficient risk sharing is feasible – subject only to the same tax avoidance incentives that also complicate public risk sharing. Thus a reliance on mandates and similar governmental powers blurs the distinction between private and public pension plans and between private and public risk sharing.

The role of employers is secondary in the Dutch literature. Teulings and de Vries (2006) abstract entirely from employer involvement and focus on risk sharing between different cohorts of employees. According to Ponds (2003), employers and employees typically share contributions in fixed proportions, which gives employers a stake in the plan. The equity of a firm that contributes to a pension plan may be owned by other pension funds or even by the same funds to which the firm contributes. The result is a complex web of cross-holdings that makes net exposures difficult to ascertain. In addition, one must doubt that changes in pension contributions would have no impact on current compensation (wages net of pension contributions). Thus the role of employers is unclear.

The next section sets up an economic model to examine the ability of private pension funds to share risk under different assumptions about the competitive and regulatory environment.

6.3 Optimal risk sharing with industry pension plans

This section presents an overlapping generation model with industry-based pensions. The model describes an idealized setting in which such pensions are efficient in the sense that they yield optimal intergenerational risk sharing with a minimal degree of government involvement. Subsequent sections will examine limitations.

A typical life cycle can be divided into three phases – an education and training period, a work period and a period of retirement. Education is usually subsidized by the government. Income from work is taxed to finance education, retiree benefits and general public services. Retirement is financed at least in part though a mandatory PAYG public pension system. Thus private risk sharing occurs "on top of" the risk sharing implied by the public tax-transfer system.

6.3.1 Individuals

To obtain economic insights, consider a stylized model that captures the essence of retirement. Individuals live for three periods. In the first period – youth – no economic activity takes place except education. The cost of education is inessential here; assume for simplicity that young cohorts' cost of living is included in parental consumption and that education is provided by the government and/or parents at negligible cost.

In the second period of life – working age – everyone works. Assume that the economy is "small" and open. The marginal product of a labor unit in period t is exogenous and can be represented by a wage w_t.[12]

In the third period of life – retirement – individuals do not work and live off working-age savings, public transfers and pensions. Individuals have increasing and concave preferences over second and third period consumption. Assume marginal utility is infinite at zero consumption, so retirement financing is an essential task. To capture changes in longevity, let λ_t denote the (fractional) length of retirement, which may be uncertain and variable over time.

Every period, a new generation of children is born – an exogenous number, large enough that behavior is competitive. The country's

[12] For clarity, assume everyone in a cohort earns the same wage. Though the arguments here apply for a wide range of income levels (except perhaps at the extremes), cross-sectional heterogeneity would be a distracting complication.

population at time t consists of the three generations that overlap in their life cycles.

A parsimonious way to think about financial markets is in terms of a pricing kernel and state-contingent claims. All real or financial assets and liabilities can be interpreted as portfolios of state-contingent claims (Arrow securities). The state of nature is defined by the history of the world up to time t, denoted h_t. The period-t price of a security with unit payoff in state $h_t +_n$ can be written as product of the conditional expectation of the state and a pricing kernel $m(h_{t+n}|h_t)$. In a small open economy, the pricing kernel is exogenous and determined by international financial markets.[13] For now, assume financial markets are complete and frictionless. This means that claims against all states of nature can be traded without cost.

Individuals maximize expected utility subject to the given wage and the given pricing kernel. Working-age consumption c_w equals w_t minus savings and taxes. Retirement income equals the return on savings plus government transfers; it must finance consumption c_r for a period of length λ_t.[14]

A key issue is at what time individuals can first enter financial and insurance markets. Standard overlapping generation analysis assumes individuals become economically active when they start to work. In the stylized three-period setting, this means workers can buy a portfolio of state-contingent claims to finance their retirement. The optimal portfolio aligns the marginal rate of substitution between work and retirement (MRS) with the pricing kernel:

$$MRS_{w,r} = \frac{MU_r\left(c_{rt+1}\left(h_{t+1}\right)\right)}{MU_w\left(c_{wt}\left(h_t\right)\right)} = m\left(h_{t+1} \mid h_t\right) \tag{6.1}$$

for all states of nature h_{t+1}, where MU_r and MU_w denote marginal utilities over consumption in retirement and working age, respectively. A simple proof of (6.1) is by contradiction: If marginal utilities were misaligned, utility could be increased by consuming more conditional

---

[13] One can think of histories or states as generated by a sequence of shocks. History h_{t+n} encompasses h_t plus all new information in period- $(t+n)$, notably about productivity, asset values and longevity.

[14] To the extent that individual mortality is stochastic, this implicitly assumes access to fair annuities. Risk-sharing implications of imperfect annuities and resulting accidental bequests are discussed in Bohn (2001).

on a history with higher marginal utility and reducing consumption conditional on another history by an amount that, under the pricing kernel, has the same present value in the prior period.

Condition (6.1) disregards taxes on income from interest, dividends and capital gains. Implicitly, retirement savings are assumed tax-sheltered, which is a reasonable assumption in relevant applications. Condition (6.1) applies not only in a laissez-faire setting with untaxed individual savings, but also in a setting with DC pensions – even including infra-marginal government pensions – and in optimal actuarially fair DB plans where members enter during working age.

Pareto-efficient risk sharing requires that the marginal utilities of all generations be aligned with the pricing kernel for all periods and all states of nature. Notably, the marginal utility of workers entering in period t should be proportional to $m(h_t|h_0)$, where time zero is an arbitrary starting period.[15] Because workers cannot insure themselves against disturbances that are already known at the time they start working, Pareto efficiency is generally violated in the standard OG model. Put differently, there is no private risk sharing across generations.

This imperfection motivates a role for government. One can show that government can use state-contingent lump-sum taxes and transfers to shift resources across time and histories in a way that perfectly aligns marginal utilities (Bohn, 2009). That is, fiscal policy can achieve perfect risk sharing. The government's task is challenging in practice, however, because optimal state-contingent taxes and transfers must compensate for all shocks to wages and to the return to savings, for all savings responses to shocks, and for all fluctuations in consumption needs due to changes in longevity. This may be feasible in theory but difficult in practice.

6.3.2 Firms and pension plans

Assume production is organized in multiple firms or industries, each of which requires distinct occupational skills. Ideally, there is a perfect correspondence between industries – from a firm's perspective – and

---

[15] An implication is that marginal utilities of different cohorts must be aligned with each other, a condition that applies even without an exogenous pricing kernel. Following Bohn (2009), efficiency refers to *ex ante* Pareto efficiency conditional on initial resources (see appendix in the Working Paper version of this chapter, Bohn 2010 for a formal exposition).

occupations – from the employee's perspective. Firms combine labor and capital to produce output. They hold capital between periods and they maximize profits.

Each young individual chooses an occupation (hence industry) and acquires the necessary skills. In working age, the individual either enters this industry, or the individual may switch industries. Switching industries and firms may incur a cost of reduced earnings and/or expenses for retraining.

Competition between firms and industries in this setting includes competition over compensation packages. If capital income outside of pension plans is taxable, every employer should offer at least a DC plan, which gives employees access to tax-sheltered savings of their own choosing. DC plans have negligible cost to the employers and they are valued by employees, who will prefer employers that offer such pension plans.

Alternatively, a firm can offer a DB plan (or hybrid).[16] If multiple firms in each industry compete for employees and if there are no switching costs within an industry, a single-company DB plan cannot do better than a DC plan. No firm can pay entering young workers less than their marginal product. This precludes risk sharing between entering young and retiring older workers. But without intergenerational sharing, workers themselves can replicate any state-contingent income stream in retirement at a cost no higher than the firm would incur in funding the same income stream within a DB plan. One might quibble if higher management cost and realistic market incompleteness might give DB an edge. Since a DB plan invariably involves credit risks and allows less individual choice than a DC plan, it is difficult to find a compelling argument for single-company DB plans in this setting.

If there are switching costs, firms and employers are facing an imperfectly competitive environment. However, employers still have an incentive to attract new employees by promising competitive career compensation. Workers may also be represented by labor unions, which would strive to protect employees from the (post-entry) monopoly power of employers. Importantly, switching costs serve as a

---

[16] For brevity, the label DB is used for "pure" DB plans and for hybrid plans with DB elements. For the purposes of this chapter, it is not essential if pensions are a combination of a DB plan indexed to longevity and wages plus a separate DC plan invested in stocks and bonds, or a unified hybrid plan.

commitment device and they imply that career employment is efficient. This commitment creates an opening for private intergenerational risk sharing that does not rely on governmental powers. By offering DB pension plans with state-contingent contributions, a firm can offer insurance to entering workers against shocks realized during their work life. A pension plan is optimal if it aligns the marginal utility of workers in a period (*t*) with the pricing kernel from the previous period (*t*–1),

$$MU_w\left(c_{wt}\left(h_t\right)\right) = m\left(h_t \mid h_{t-1}\right) \bullet \mu\left(h_{t-1}\right) \tag{6.2}$$

where $\mu(h_{t-1})$ is a (*t*–1)-dated proportionality factor. The ability of individual firms to insure workers is limited by the cost of moving to a new employer and the cost of terminating the worker. These costs are likely small for separations within an industry.

Industry pension plans promise a major improvement over single-employer corporate pensions because switching costs are – almost by construction – higher across industries than across firms that offer similar jobs. For a plan to satisfy condition (6.2), the required worker contributions must be less than the switching cost in all states of nature. This suggests that industry pension plans are most robust if they cover all jobs that are easily substitutable with each other. The main vulnerability is with respect to large negative shocks that would overtax workers' willingness to stay and contribute.

Optimal DB pension plans must also provide benefits to retirees that ensure condition (6.1) in all periods. If (6.1) and (6.2) hold, the marginal utilities of workers and retirees are perfectly aligned. Firms operate on goods and financial markets to maximize their present value under the pricing kernel. Thus all intertemporal trading opportunities between workers, retirees, the firm and financial markets are fully exploited. If markets are complete, one may assume without loss of generality that pension plans are fully funded and hold assets that match their liabilities; there is no need for corporate plan sponsors to bear risk, and hence no default risk.

Industries must compete for new workers. Hence they cannot insure the youth against shocks or events already known at the time of entry. Formally, marginal utilities of period-*t* workers do not respond proportionally in response to shocks realized in or before period *t*–1. This is a key limitation of industry pension funds with voluntary entry. Risk sharing with industry pension funds is more efficient than risk sharing in the standard setting but not fully Pareto efficient.

Note that optimal DB pensions much simplify the government's problem of designing optimal policies. Because retirees share risk with workers, Pareto efficiency can be achieved without state-contingent retirement benefits and without state-contingent debt. Instead, one may assume without loss of generality that the government imposes state-contingent taxes only in working age and that government liabilities are simple securities such as default-free bonds. To smooth out fluctuations in marginal utilities across cohorts, it suffices to change the level of debt over time. (Formally, the optimal debt policy would align the factors $\mu(h_{t-1})$ with the pricing kernel.) Compared with a setting without private intergenerational risk sharing, the government's task of implementing efficient risk sharing is partially privatized. This avoids both the risk-sharing inefficiencies of laissez-faire and the inefficiencies of a complicated "big" social welfare system that attempts to share all life risks through the government.

There is a monetary aspect to risk sharing with public debt. Nominal government debt can be viewed as a claim contingent on inflation. In a setting without private risk sharing, nominal debt held by retirement savers is a policy instrument that can be used to provide insurance to retirees.[17] The debt service required of succeeding generations would be similarly contingent on inflation and implement risk sharing across generations. In a monetary union or under strict inflation targeting, inflation is not available as a policy tool. The returns on government debt are effectively exogenous (assuming no default). For members of the Eurozone, simplicity in debt policy is therefore a relevant practical advantage.

The improved efficiency of occupational pensions over ordinary corporate pension plans comes at a cost of raising questions about collusion and about corporate versus governmental powers. Firms in an industry collude by offering a common pension plan. Workers would have a credible threat to quit if new companies were to enter an industry without joining the pension plan. Maintaining a stable base of pension contributions likely requires governmental mandates or legal sanctions against uncooperative employers. An obligation to

---

[17] Of course, nominal debt and inflation could also be misused and become another source of risk.

join an existing occupational pension plan – even in a state of nature when prior insurance calls for pay-outs – may even discourage the creation of new firms. Moreover, the natural job market competitors of an innovative new firm may be unclear or subject to change, so clear lines of demarcation between occupations and industries are difficult to maintain.

An additional concern is that occupational plans might collude with each other in a way that eliminates competition for new employees. Regulations that encourage funds to conform might have a similar effect. The occupational pension system as a whole would then be empowered to "tax" entrants just like a government. On the upside, such a system could implement *ex ante* efficient risk sharing without constraints. One the downside, one might suspect that if the young have no choices, the gains from improved risk sharing would be captured by the incumbents – firms and older cohorts. Though the political process does not protect entering generations either, it gives citizens ample (voting) opportunities to express their concerns about the welfare of their children and future generations. Firms and incumbent workers in an industry may be much less concerned about entrants into this particular industry, who are mostly not their children.

Put differently, delegating all risk sharing to pension funds may well yield an efficient allocation of risk, but an allocation that places little or no weight on the welfare of future generations – optimal intergenerational risk sharing with an undesirable intergenerational distribution. Competition at entry is therefore worth protecting. This reserves the task of redistribution to the government and ensures that the resulting allocation maximizes social welfare rather than the incumbents' welfare. (Competition between occupational pension plans at the time of entry – or more precisely, at the time of career choice – is assumed in the following sections.)

An alternative interpretation of Dutch pension regulations is that while entrants are indeed taxed, solvency regulations prevent an abuse of privately imposed taxes. The assumption that occupational pension plans can impose taxes is implicit in most quantitative studies of Dutch pensions. Ideally, full funding means that the fair market value of assets matches the expected present value of benefits promised to current participants. Under- or overfunding at the start of the next period can then only result from unexpectedly low or high returns on assets or unexpectedly high or low realizations of variables that govern the indexation of benefits. If the funding gap equals zero in expectation (adjusted for risk), there is no systematic redistribution at the expense of new entrants.[18]

Remarkably, Dutch regulations demand funding ratios greater than 100 percent. Taken literally, this would suggest redistribution in favor of entrants. (According to Kortleve and Ponds, 2010, regulators require 105 percent minimum, and 125–135 percent are required before benefits are fully indexed.) One problem with funding regulations is that they do not prevent a renegotiation of benefits when conditions are favorable to incumbents. For example, retirees could demand extra benefits in a stock market boom when solvency regulations are unlikely to bind. Van Bommel (2007) characterizes such a scenario as a "raid." After a stock market crash, on the other hand, retirees can insist on their formula-fixed benefits and – perhaps citing unprecedented circumstances and severe underfunding – demand extra concessions by workers to return to full funding quickly. Regulators who worry about funding ratios are likely sympathetic to such arguments.

Asymmetric responses to shocks would have undesirable consequences. They are inconsistent with risk pooling, they provide incentives for incumbents to take excessive risks, and they create a potential for underfunding in expectation despite (seeming) overfunding under a baseline projection.[19] Thus a view of the Dutch system as intergenerational risk sharing with competitive entry is a sympathetic interpretation.

A more cynical view of pension funds as tool for incumbents to tax entrants would have implications for government reinsurance.

---

[18] Funding rules are commonly viewed as protecting retirees from the risk of a plan sponsor's default. In a system with intergenerational risk sharing, an important function of funding is to protect new entrants from incumbents who might attempt to tax them.

[19] Put differently, a formula-fixed benefit means retirees hold a put option on the market underwritten by the next generation. The required overfunding is acting as a put premium. The value of the put is maximized by high-risk investments. A counterforce is that benefits are limited to full wage indexing, which means retirees are short a call option. Depending on funding rules and risks, one or the other option may be more valuable. A softening of the "kinks" in funding formulas would be worth considering. The fact that regulators impose overfunding suggests that they are concerned about redistribution and may have doubts about the effectiveness of their rules.

Notably, it could explain a lack of demand for reinsurance against longevity risk. This is because uninsured longevity risk creates volatility in funding ratios that can be exploited to grant extra benefits in good scenarios (say, no rise in longevity) and to tax entrants in unfavorable scenarios (rising longevity).

The assumption of complete markets is instructive but not realistic. Hence it is worth noting that incomplete markets are unproblematic for a pension plan associated with a well-capitalized corporate sponsor. A plan sponsor's promise to cover any mismatch between pension promises, plan assets and employee contributions can be interpreted as an implicit pension asset that – from the perspective of the plan – completes financial markets. Moreover, if the corporate sponsor is a publicly traded company and the Modigliani–Miller theorem applies, the implicit pension asset is converted into a traded security. In a competitive environment with free entry, a well-fund corporate plan in a setting with incomplete markets is essentially equivalent to an independent and fully funded plan under complete markets. One caveat is that with corporate sponsors as residual claimants, a fund's ability to "tax" new entrants must be strictly supervised to prevent abuse.

Table 6.1 summarizes the interaction of private and public risk sharing under alternative pension systems. Row 1 considers plans with mandatory participation, which means entrants can be taxed. Row 2 considers plans where the youth have a choice of competing plans – so entry is competitive – but members are subsequently locked into their plan. Row 3 considers plans without commitment.

Column A displays choices without organized private pensions: Mandatory public systems (A1); a hypothetical case of commitment to private risk sharing in youth (A2); and private savings in working age (A3). Column B displays allocations with employer-independent pension systems. The defining feature is that the sponsoring employers do not back the plan with shareholder funds. Hence any risk sharing must be between different generations of employees. Such systems can either replace government (B1), if mandatory; provide credibility to risk sharing commitments starting in youth (B2), in effect making (A2) feasible; or replicate individual savings (B3), which is no better than (A3). Column C displays the analogous allocations with employer-backed pension systems, which are discussed in the next section.

Table 6.1 *Pension systems and the role of government*

Membership commitment	Private pension system		
	No system, or pure DC (A)	Employer-independent plans (B)	With employer as residual claimant (C)
			Hypothetical
(1) Mandatory participation (all generations)	Comprehensive Bismarckian social insurance Germany, Sweden Problems: • Cost • Political risk	Risk sharing and redistribution delegated to pension plans Problem: Incumbents taxing future gen.	
(2) Choice of plans in youth (at career entry) Commitment in working age	Individual risk sharing contracts. Gov. redistribution Problem: No collateral. Not credible	Private risk sharing in pension plan. Gov. redistribution The Netherlands Problems: • Incomplete markets • Labor mobility Solution: Reinsurance	Private risk sharing in corporate plan. Gov. redistribution US (old-style) Problems: • Default risk • Labor mobility Solution: Reinsurance
(3) No commitment in youth Choice of plans in working age	Individual savings or DC plan. Gov. risk sharing Problems: • Incomplete markets • No risk sharing except by government	Private savings in pension plan. Gov. risk sharing Problem: No advantage over individual savings	Private savings in corporate plan. Gov. risk sharing Problems: • Default risk • No risk sharing except by government

Note: The table characterizes pension systems by sponsor and effective entry age. "Gov. redistribution" means that government intervention can be limited to reallocating initial (working-age) endowments. "Gov. risk sharing" means that efficiency requires optimal state-contingent taxes and government debt. Country labels are illustrative.

My interpretation of Dutch pensions is that the system has elements of (B2), which has advantages over all the type-A systems, and it minimizes reliance on plan sponsors. Concerns are that the system may drift towards (B3) if there is lack of commitment; and the system may degenerate towards (B1) if new cohorts face systematically unfavorable entry conditions.

6.4 Limitations to private risk sharing

This section examines problems that may limit risk sharing in pension plans. The section focuses on a mixed public-private system, where private pensions provide risk sharing to the maximum extent possible and government enters only when necessary to supplement private arrangement. As benchmark cases, assume the youth enter competitively (setting B2).

An occupational pension plan then involves three parties: the youth entering working age, workers transitioning into retirement (young and old workers, for short) and firms as plan sponsors. Because the old are always creditors of the plan, participation constraints involve young workers or the firm, and any default would be against the old. There are several relevant scenarios of how these parties interact. The emphasis of Dutch occupational pensions on intergenerational risk sharing differs notably from traditional pension analysis, which focuses more on old workers and firms.

6.4.1 The mobility constraint with complete markets

With complete markets, intergenerational risk sharing is essentially about the interaction of young and old employees. One may assume without loss of generality that firms contribute to the pension fund for each current worker an amount equal to the present value of the worker's pension. Because the fund can reinsure all risks on financial markets, there is no need for firms to assume risks or other responsibilities. In effect the firm serves as a platform for intergenerational contracts between employees and the fund.[20]

The most important limitation under complete markets is the *mobility constraint*, which is the ability of the young to exit the pension

---

[20] Cui *et al.* (2011) also make this assumption. It applies only under complete markets.

plan whenever premiums are excessive. Suppose the opportunity cost of exiting is given and known. The constrained optimal risk DB pension plan satisfies condition (6.2) only for states of nature such that the wage minus pension contribution exceeds the marginal product of labor minus the cost of exit. In states of nature for which this condition is violated, pension contributions are bounded by the cost of exit.

Recall that the pricing kernel reflects all aggregate risks – uncertainty about return to capital, longevity risk and labor productivity risk. The weights on labor productivity and on the return to capital are positive, whereas the weight on longevity is negative.[21] Because workers have labor income, the mobility constraint is most likely binding when the marginal product of labor is unexpectedly high, when the return on capital is unexpectedly low and when retiree longevity is unexpectedly high.

A complication is that all three fundamental sources of risk may have global, national and idiosyncratic components. For capital and longevity risk, which the young are buying, only the global components are relevant because only these components are priced and hence optimal for the pension fund to hold on behalf of the young. For productivity risk, the young are endowed with all three components. The idiosyncratic component is traditionally managed by the firm (which is arguably better equipped to deal with moral hazard and adverse selection) and not insured by the pension fund. The national component could be hedged either by the pension fund or by the employer; either way, the ultimate holders should be international investors. Global productivity risk is priced, and hence part of the optimal portfolio of older workers. The pension fund's optimal strategy is to give the young a short position (up to the mobility bound), to give the old a long position and to hedge the difference on financial markets.

The complete markets setting points to a fundamental commitment problem in private risk sharing: the inability of the young to pre-commit their labor effort. This is a fundamental constraint because it would be difficult to correct privately without permitting undesirable

---

[21] The negative weight on longevity risk factor is perhaps counterintuitive because life is valued. However, insurance is needed against the marginal cost of financing a longer life, which is a negative. Improving morbidity, if correlated with longevity, could be an offsetting factor. Note that labor productivity risk is priced in the market only to the extent that the young are integrated by entering a DB pension system in youth. That is, the pricing kernel pools all the risks faced by the economically active cohorts with access to financial and insurance markets.

contracts – contracts resembling slavery. Public risk sharing through taxes can serve as a substitute. Taxes on wage income are an obvious tool to reduce the young generation's exposure to labor productivity. High taxes on the young in response to a stock market crash and to abnormally high longevity would also improve risk sharing. Because of excess burden, tax responses to shocks are only a second-best substitute to private risk sharing. They are warranted only when shocks are so large that private responses would conflict with the mobility constraint. (However, as explained below, very large shocks encounter limitations to public risk sharing.)

A straightforward policy recommendation is that the revenues from unexpected fluctuations in the wage tax should be securitized as wage-contingent bonds and sold on financial markets. They would give retirees a more complete exposure to productivity risk. Similarly, there is a case for government insurance against market crashes and protection against high longevity. Ideally this insurance should be calibrated so that it provides protection to pension funds only against large shocks – large enough that pension plans cannot cover the resulting funding gaps by charging higher premiums to young employees.

From a practical perspective, there are many steps between an endorsement of contingent bonds and the issue of specific, well-designed securities. For indexing to longevity, much detailed work has been done; see Blake *et al.* (2010). There is no comparable work on wage-indexed bonds, and aggregation issues are challenging. Given the long-run stability of the labor share in national income, GDP-indexed bonds should be close substitutes. They may be easier to develop (see Borensztein and Mauro, 2004) and they have advantages over nominal bonds from a tax-smoothing perspective (Bohn, 1990). Thus a practical proposal would be for governments to issue longevity bonds and GDP-indexed bonds.

Insurance contracts sold by the government directly to pension funds could provide similar reinsurance as bonds. Such contracts could even be customized to the needs of a particular funds, e.g., to account for differences in mobility or to provide protection against a combination of shocks. The pricing would lack transparency, however, which is troubling when the buyers include large funds that may have political power. Customized contracts might also encounter moral hazard or adverse selection problems if the funds have better information about their exposure to shocks than the government.

Finally, note that if there is uncertainty about the cost of exit, the mobility constraint creates a form of discontinuity risk. An unexpected reduction in exit cost would leave a plan unable to collect higher contributions in states of nature when the young were expected to cover underfunding. Again, taxes might serve as backup. Moreover, though the labor evidence is unclear, there is a perception that job mobility is rising and industrial restructuring is accelerating. This suggests that the ability of occupational pension funds to bind the young into risk-sharing arrangements is declining as well and suggests a greater role for the government.

6.4.2 *The solvency constraint*

In general, a plan sponsor is needed whenever fund assets and employee contributions do not match pension promises. The need for a plan sponsor introduces a new constraint, *the solvency constraint*: Pensions must be designed so that the plan sponsor remains solvent in all states of nature and committed to make the required contributions.

With complete markets, solvency is not a constraint on pension design. For any given state-contingent profile of pension promises and contributions, plan management can buy financial assets that match the gap between promises and contributions. A funded plan with optimal investment strategy will never become underfunded because of economic shocks. With incomplete markets, funding gaps are generally unavoidable in response to economic shocks even in plans that are fully funded *ex ante*. The only exception would be a plan that uses retirees or workers as residual claimants, but this would severely restrict the allocation of risk. Otherwise, recourse to the plan sponsor can be avoided only by overfunding the plan so much that there is a surplus in all states of nature, even in the worst "worst case" scenario. The required degree of overfunding would depend on the riskiness of assets and on the state contingencies embedded in plan benefits.

Easily traded financial assets include corporate equity securities and bonds, and government bonds. Regular nominal government bonds are state-contingent in principle because they are indexed to inflation and inflation is controllable by monetary policy. Even in the Eurozone, inflation could co-vary with variables of interest, such as productivity. However, the ECB and other leading central banks claim to pursue price stability, i.e., they have disclaimed inflation as contingency. Hence government bonds are reasonably considered safe assets. Corporate securities are always risky. Moreover, because optimal pensions are linked to longevity and labor productivity, pension funds face a mismatch between assets and liabilities unless there are securities indexed to future labor productivity and to longevity. This mismatch provides an obvious argument for government issuance – but perhaps too obvious, because there might be alternatives.

One alternative is overfunding. If intermediation costs are (approximately) zero, the solvency constraint can always be satisfied by sufficient overfunding with government bonds. That is, firms can strengthen their pension fund by issuing equity and contributing the proceeds to the pension funds. If bonds have the same risk-adjusted returns as the firm's equity, shareholders would be indifferent. Optimal pension benefits and contributions would be the same as in a complete markets setting. In terms of Table 6.1, pension plans with corporate sponsors could replicate the risk sharing in independent plans. The mobility constraint would again determine if this risk sharing includes the young (setting C2) or only retiring workers (setting C3).

Zero intermediation costs are unrealistic, however, because issuing equity is costly relative to bonds, there is a cost of managing pension assets and there may be agency costs if the firm's claims on surplus pension assets are imperfect. With intermediation costs, it would be efficient to use the assets of the plan sponsor – the value of corporate equity – as collateral even if markets were complete and a perfect matching of assets and liabilities were feasible.

The question to what extent plans can rely on corporate sponsors depends on the nature and valuation of equity capital. Firms are typically valued for their profit opportunities and for the physical and intangible capital assets they own. Pure profit opportunities require market power. Capital assets are reliable as collateral for pensions only if they cannot be diverted easily. It is no surprise therefore that big industrial firms with monopoly power and a high ratio of fixed physical capital to labor were the first to embrace DB pension plans. In some cases, pensions were simply unfunded promises backed only by the firm's capital. Employees were major corporate creditors. In a setting with underdeveloped debt markets, this was arguably a mutually beneficial arrangement. Funding became more prevalent over time because of two problems: the exposure of employees to firm-specific risk and the vulnerability of employees' claims to financial restructuring.

In the United States, these problems have largely destroyed corporate DB pensions. Costly pension insurance was mandated after some well-publicized defaults and employee confidence in DB plans was undermined by pension terminations. The US pension system has moved from a DB system with career employment that offered risk sharing (setting C2) to a DC system that has essentially no private risk sharing (setting A3).

To understand the solvency constraint, it is instructive to decompose corporations into their basic functions. In the context of pensions and career employment, corporations have four distinct functions. First, they combine labor and capital to produce output. Second, they accumulate capital. Third, they may promise a pension to current workers going into retirement next period. Fourth, they may offer a career employment and pension package to the youth to attract them into the industry. These functions are typically combined in real world firms, but they are important to distinguish because they use and provide collateral in different ways.

A pure production firm would rent capital on spot markets and hire workers on the labor market. Under perfect competition, it would earn no economic profits. Its accounting profits would just suffice to cover the cost of equity capital. Because it owns no assets, there is no collateral to backstop a DB pension plan. Such a firm cannot commit to pay anything but the spot marginal product of labor to its workers. A production firm with monopoly power would earn pure profits that might serve as collateral. However, market power is often based on patents or other intellectual capital that can be stripped off.

A pure capital accumulation firm would hold capital and lease it to production firms at a leasing rate that covers depreciation plus the cost of financing. Because such a firm has essentially no employees (abstracting from managers), pension issues are moot.

Only if production and capital accumulation are combined one obtains a firm with capital assets that might serve as collateral for pension commitments. There is a question, however, to what extent a firm can commit to keeping capital unencumbered. In many countries, the standard for legally permissible asset sales is that the firm is solvent at the time and expected to remain solvent. This leaves contingent claims on unexpected events unprotected, notably, a promise to bear the residual long-run risks of a pension fund. The key lesson is that DB pensions are threatened by the possibility of reorganization events that could extract capital from a firm or establish competing claims on collateral. The spread of financial engineering in recent decades has been damaging to pensions.

If there is equity-financed physical capital, one may consider a production firm with pensions for workers moving towards retirement. The pension fund must in each state of nature cover the gap between the promised pension and the firm's equity value. If the firm's value reflects aggregate equity risk plus idiosyncratic risk, the pension fund should try to sell short the idiosyncratic risk and hold assets that fully support any wage- or longevity-indexed pensions. (Some diversification of idiosyncratic risk is automatic in multi-employer plans where all employers are jointly liable.)

Finally, suppose the same firm provides risk sharing for young workers. Because young workers desire exposure to equity, their claims are well collateralized by the firm's equity, especially if idiosyncratic components can be hedged. Moreover, young workers' willingness to take negative wage and longevity exposures reduces the pension fund's need to hold wage- and longevity-indexed assets. One may conclude that risk sharing on behalf of young workers does not trigger additional funding needs. Instead it simplifies the provision of benefits for older workers.

Put differently, the mobility constraint is again a problem. The wage- and longevity-indexed claims valued by retirees are scarce when a tight mobility constraint prevents young workers from taking material short positions in such claims.[22] Risk sharing would be improved if the government sells wage- and longevity-indexed claims.

6.4.3 Equilibrium considerations

The equilibrium pricing kernel can only pool the consumption risks of individuals and generations represented in financial markets. It is affected by changes in mobility cost and changes in government policy.

In a benchmark case of a non-binding mobility constraint, young and old workers pool their risk. With optimal tax and debt policy, taxes ensure that risks are also pooled with future generations. Then the

---

[22] Another problem is the fund may be unable to insure against negative idiosyncratic shocks to the plan sponsor's equity. It seems plausible, however, that an occupational pension plan could hedge this risk either with over-the-counter (OTC) contracts or indirectly by tilting the fund's equity portfolio away from its own industry.

pricing kernel reflects current and lagged realizations of wage risk, asset return risk and (negatively) longevity risk. In an international context, this would require optimal policy in the home country and abroad.

A polar alternative case is a pricing kernel that reflects zero inter-generational risk sharing. If the young cannot commit to firms and governments do not intervene, all financial assets must be held by workers moving towards retirement. This includes the equity of all the firms that operate pension funds. No matter what the pension plans promise, the total resources available to the retiring generation must add up to the value of corporate capital plus their claims against government – debt and pensions. The pricing kernel is then proportional to retirees' marginal utility, which is declining in the return to capital and increasing in longevity. Unless public pensions or debt are wage-contingent, wages have no weight in the pricing kernel.

Intermediate cases work analogously. With positive but not prohibitive mobility cost for the young, the weight of wages in the pricing kernel is an increasing function of mobility cost, and the weight of equity and longevity risk is reduced accordingly. If the government intervenes by supplying wage- and/or longevity-indexed bonds or taxing capital income, weights on the respective risk factors are shifted in the same direction.

Intergenerational risk sharing appears to be highly imperfect in many countries, not only in developing countries but also in large industrialized countries like the United States. This suggests that the worldwide pricing kernel excludes future generations and a large share of the world's young cohorts, and it implies that governments could sell longevity-indexed bonds at a substantial risk premium. Young and future generations would benefit.

By similar reasoning, retiring generations should be willing to buy wage-indexed bonds without demanding a significant risk premium. The premium is likely positive due to correlation between wages and the return to capital, but lower than the value of the insurance accruing to young workers.

If the government of a small open economy issues contingent bonds on behalf of future generations, the change in the asset pool has a negligible impact on the pricing kernel. Hence domestic policy choices do not alter the risk exposures of cohorts that are already participating in financial markets. Contingent debt increases welfare because it exploits differences between risk premiums in the market and the shadow value of the same risk for those currently excluded.

6.5 Limitations to public risk sharing

Government solutions to market imperfections naturally raise questions about limitations to government intervention. If private risk sharing is limited, what limits public risk sharing? One obvious limitation is the need for taxes that are distortionary. This is well recognized in the public policy discussion. A second constraint has received less attention: Governments are also subject to mobility constraints.

International labor mobility is particularly relevant in the European Union where legal restrictions against work in other member countries are being abolished. Though labor mobility in Europe has traditionally been low, it would be negligent for policymakers to disregard the likelihood of rising mobility. Moreover, individuals with the highest productivity and therefore highest ability to pay taxes have the greatest incentives to move.

The implications of rising cross-country labor mobility are analogous to the implication of rising job mobility for corporate pension funds. Insurance *ex ante* means taxation *ex post*. Even if young workers agree *ex ante* to be taxed in case of high wage realizations, or high longevity, or low returns to capital, they have an incentive to move away if a government attempts to collect. A government that cannot promise state contingent taxes also cannot issue wage- or longevity-indexed bonds or promise expensive wage- or longevity-indexed public pensions.

Furthermore, the relation between the European Union and member countries with regard to risk sharing can be seen as analogous to the relation between an occupational pension fund and member firms. Labor mobility is higher between members than between the group and the outside world. Hence cooperation between members or a centralized risk pool would enlarge the set of feasible insurance contracts. As cross-country mobility increases, it will be increasingly efficient for institutions of the European Union to play a role in coordinating consumption and labor income taxes.

International coordination in the European Union would be another step in a line of thinking that has gradually increased the scope of insurance schemes in an effort to prevent members from exiting when payments would be due. Avoiding substitution is the basic force that makes occupational pension plans superior to single employer pensions. It should make national pension plans superior to occupational pensions as job mobility keeps increasing, and international plans superior to national ones.

Opposing forces are the declining ability to monitor and control tax avoidance in larger risk-sharing systems and an increasing operational and bureaucratic inefficiency. Employers are in a better position to judge their employees' work efforts than a government tax collector. This suggests that whenever efficient risk sharing calls for workers to be taxed, the excess burden is less if the tax is collected by the employer as pension contribution than if it is collected by the government. Instead of expanding the scope of insurance schemes beyond employers and nations as mobility increases, it is worth considering other ways to discourage opportunistic behavior.

A potentially promising area for rethinking is education. Boldrin and Montes (2005) have noted that public pensions and public education are offsetting intergenerational transfer schemes. Pensions require payments from younger to older generations. Education requires payments from older to younger generations. The highly productive workers most capable of moving internationally tend to be the ones that have received the most education in their countries of origin. In Europe, most education is publicly funded and essentially costless to recipients. If the mobility of educated workers makes pension systems fragile and intergenerational risk sharing difficult, it may make sense to consider systems that link risk sharing more directly to education, or perhaps more narrowly, to professional training.

Because college fees are already increasing around the world, one should emphasize that improved risk sharing does not mean a net burden on students. To the contrary, claims of efficiency gains would be dubious unless young cohorts are also better off. Improved risk sharing would require a systemic change that matches notional charges for professional training with mechanisms for how the charges are written off over time. The charges are notional because they would normally be financed by the government or by an employer and because optimal risk sharing would call for repayment linked to time, income or other contingencies.

It is beyond the scope of this chapter to suggest specific systems. It seems likely, however, that financing mechanisms for professional training would involve employers and unions in the relevant industry. An involvement of occupational pension plans would be natural and likely to strengthen such plans. In essence, limitations of public risk sharing increase the potential gains from finding innovative ways to improve private risk sharing.

6.6 Conclusions

The short answer to the question posed in the title is: Yes. Under reasonable conditions, governments should provide reinsurance both against aggregate longevity risk and against the risk of fluctuations in aggregate wages or GDP, especially against large shocks.

A more complete answer must be conditional on the structure of pension plans and on the mobility of labor across firms, occupations and countries. The Netherlands is an instructive example – worth studying by economists elsewhere – because the Dutch system of occupational pension funds has, for many decades, facilitated a remarkable level of private intergenerational risk sharing.

Risk sharing in private pension funds faces two serious limitations. One is the ability of workers to exit firms when large negative shocks to their plan require excessively high future contributions. Industry funds mitigate this problem because exiting from an industry is more difficult than leaving a firm. Mobility of workers across industries is a problem for risk sharing in industry-based private pension funds. A second problem is the mismatch between pension assets and liabilities in a setting with incomplete financial markets. When there is a mismatch, corporate plan sponsors are needed to guarantee the pension fund's solvency. A commitment of equity capital to guarantee pensions is difficult to maintain, however, if firms can restructure their operations and divert capital in the process. Thus financial engineering is a threat to private risk sharing.

Government reinsurance can mitigate both problems and hence stabilize pension funds. Governments can provide insurance that is not available on financial markets because they can enter commitments on behalf of taxpayers – current ones and future generations. Payments enforced through the tax system sidestep the problems of limited liability and of limited commitment in employment relationships. Insurance can be provided in the form of explicit insurance contracts, perhaps issued directly to pension funds, or in the form of contingent bonds; the latter are equivalent to insurance for aggregate risk-sharing purposes but more liquid. Most relevant are contracts contingent on longevity and, because optimal pensions are linked to wages, contracts contingent on aggregate wages. Government provision of longevity- and wage-contingent claims would also help to complete financial markets, so pension plans would be able to hold assets that more closely match their liabilities. Moreover, government intervention may exploit imperfections in risk sharing in other countries. If risk premiums on world financial markets are set by the world's old generations, longevity insurance should command a high risk premium, whereas bonds linked to aggregate wages should have a low risk premium. Future taxpayers would benefit if the government issued debt contingent on longevity and wages instead of fixed debt.

Note that GDP-indexed bonds would be a close substitute for wage-indexed bonds, as the wage share of GDP is nearly constant; both provide insurance against productivity shocks. Though the theoretical analysis suggests wage indexing, GDP indexed bonds have been discussed in the literature (see Bohn, 1990; Borensztein and Mauro, 2004) and may be more easily implementable in practice. Both wage- and GDP-indexed bonds would provide better risk sharing than fixed, non-contingent government debt. (Note that inflation-indexed debt is fixed in real terms and hence undesirable.)

Because government commitments must be backed by taxes, the government's ability to offer insurance is limited by its ability to tax future generations. International labor mobility is therefore a threat to the government's ability to offer insurance. The general principle here is that risk sharing and insurance are constrained by the ability of participants to exit when payments would be due. This constraint limits public risk sharing when labor is mobile internationally just like it limits private risk sharing when labor is mobile across firms and industries. However, moving abroad is more costly than moving between industries. The cost of moving abroad includes cultural and language frictions that are likely to persist in the future. Hence governments can still offer reinsurance to private pension funds, though they must respect the bounds defined by the country's tax base.

Looking forward, as mobility is arguably growing and efficient risk sharing is worth preserving, it would be desirable to strengthen individuals' attachment to private and public risk-sharing arrangements. One promising area is the financing of education. Most education is traditionally provided free under the implicit assumption that students will grow up to be the country's taxpayers. International labor mobility invalidates this assumption. With mobile labor, risk sharing could be improved if education were provided in exchange for a contractual claim against the person's human capital. Such a claim would provide collateral for insurance arrangements – public or private. Occupational

pension plans would be natural financiers for education, because they
have funds to invest and because many students would become plan
members anyway once they start working in the occupation for which
they studied. Though a full analysis of education funding is beyond the
scope of this chapter it is a promising area for future research.

References

Allen, Franklin, and Douglas Gale, 1997, Financial markets, intermediaries, and intertemporal smoothing, *Journal of Political Economy*,
vol. 105(3): 523–46.
Altonji, Joseph, Fumia Hayashi and Laurence Kotlikoff, 1992, Is the
extended family altruistically linked? Direct tests using micro data,
American Economic Review, vol. 82: 1177–98.
Baxter, Marianne and Urban Jermann, 1997, The international diversification puzzle is worse than you think, *American Economic Review*,
vol. 87(1): 170–80.
Benzoni, Pierre, Collin Dufresne and Robert S. Goldstein, 2007, Portfolio
choice over the life-cycle when the stock and labor markets are cointegrated, *Journal of Finance*, vol. 62: 2123–67.
Blake, David, Tom Boardman and Andrew Cairns, 2010, Sharing longevity
risk: Why governments should issue longevity bonds, Discussion Paper,
The Pensions Institute, London.
Bohn, Henning, 1990, Tax smoothing with financial instruments, *American
Economic Review*, vol. 80(5): 1217–30.
1999, Should the social security trust fund hold equities? An intergenerational
welfare analysis, *Review of Economic Dynamics*, vol. 2(3): 666–97.
2001, Social Security and Demographic Uncertainty: The Risk-Sharing
Properties of Alternative Policies, in: John Campbell and Martin
Feldstein (eds.), *Risk Aspects of Investment Based Social Security
Reform*, University of Chicago Press, 203–41.
2006a, Optimal Private Responses to Demographic Trends: Savings,
Bequests, and International Mobility, in: Christopher Kent, Anna Park
and Daniel Rees (eds.), *Demography and Financial Markets*, Sydney:
Reserve Bank of Australia, 47–79.
2006b, Who Bears What Risk? An Intergenerational Perspective, in: David
Blitzstein, Olivia S. Mitchell and Stephen P. Utkus (eds.), *Restructuring
Retirement Risks*, Oxford University Press, 10–36.
2009, Intergenerational risk sharing and fiscal policy, *Journal of Monetary
Economics*, vol. 56(6): 805–16.
2010, Private versus public risk sharing: Should governments provide
reinsurance?, Netspar Discussion Paper, 12/2010–091.

Boldrin, Michele, and Ana Montes, 2005, The intergenerational state: Education and pensions, *The Review of Economic Studies*, vol. 72(3): 651–64.

Bommel, Jos van, 2007, Intergenerational risk sharing and bank raids, Working Paper, Universidad Cardenal Herrera.

Borensztein, Eduardo, and Paolo Mauro, 2004, The case for GDP-indexed bonds, *Economic Policy*, vol. 19(38): 165–216.

Bovenberg, Lans, and Casper van Ewijk, 2010, *Designing the pension system: Conceptual framework*, Mimeo, Netspar.

Bovenberg, Lans, and Theo Nijman, 2008, Dutch stand-alone collective pension schemes: The best of both worlds? Working Paper, Netspar.

Bovenberg, Lans, Ralph Koijen, Theo Nijman and Coen Teulings, 2007, Savings and investing over the life cycle and the role of collective pension funds, *De Economist*, vol. 155(4): 347–415.

Bulow, Jeremy, 1982, What are corporate pension liabilities? *The Quarterly Journal of Economics*, vol. 97(3): 435–52.

Cui, Jiajia, Frank de Jong and Eduard Ponds, 2011, Intergenerational risk sharing within funded pension schemes, *Journal of Pension Economics and Finance*, vol. 10(1): 1–29.

Diamond, Peter, 1999, Taxes and pensions, CESifo Working Paper no. 2636.

Ewijk, Casper van, 2009, Credit crisis and Dutch pension funds: Who bears the shock?, *De Economist*, vol. 157(3): 337–51.

Gollier, Christian, 2008, Intergenerational risk-sharing and risk-taking of a pension fund, *Journal of Public Economics*, vol. 92(5–6): 1463–85.

Kortleve, Niels, and Eduard Ponds, 2009, Dutch pension underfunding: Solving generational dilemmas, Working Paper, Center for Retirement Research at Boston College.

  2010, How to Close the funding gap in Dutch pension plans? Impact on generations, Working Paper, Center for Retirement Research at Boston College.

Ponds, Eduard, 2003, Pension funds and value-based generational accounting, *Journal of Pension Economics and Finance*, vol. 2(3): 295–325.

Ponds, Eduard, and Bart van Riel, 2007, The recent evolution of pension funds in the Netherlands: The trend to hybrid DB-DC plans and beyond, Working Paper, Center for Retirement Research at Boston College.

Shiller, Robert, 1999, Social security and institutions for intergenerational, intragenerational and international risk sharing, *Carnegie-Rochester Conference Series on Public Policy*, vol. 50: 165–204.

Teulings, Coen, and Casper de Vries, 2006, Generational accounting, solidarity and pension losses, *De Economist*, vol. 154(1): 63–83.

7 | The redistribution of macroeconomic risks by Dutch institutions

LEON BETTENDORF AND THIJS KNAAP

7.1 Introduction

Macroeconomic shocks influence the entire economy, but their effects may be different from person to person. Unexpected changes in a rate of return, for instance, have an immediate impact on those who are long or short in the asset. Then there may be secondary effects that are felt throughout the rest of the economy, when those initially affected change their behavior. But the final impact of any shock is not just the result of its propagation through the market economy. The result is modified by the influence of the government, which may wish to redistribute the effects, and by different parts of the pension system. For instance, a young worker without financial assets may still be affected by a financial shock through a change in his pension premium payments. Or a slowdown in the birth rate may affect the income that retirees receive from their pay-as-you-go (PAYG) pension.

This chapter aims to chart the main macroeconomic risks for different cohorts in the Netherlands. We look at both the direct impact of different shocks and at the redistribution and insurance that are offered by the government and the pension system. To do this, we examine the effects of unexpected changes in productivity, demographics and financial returns in a calibrated overlapping-generations (OLG) model of the country. We derive likely shocks from a calibrated stochastic model of macroeconomic risks – one scenario, for instance, is that productivity grows unexpectedly, and then converges back to its original path – and feed the time series of these changes into the OLG model. From the new equilibrium of that model, we can derive the effects on the balances of different generations: How has their

Thanks are due to Lans Bovenberg, Peter Broer, Hans Fehr, Albert van der Horst, Bas ter Weel and Ed Westerhout for their detailed comments on an earlier version of this chapter.

labor income changed, the net transfers from the government and the pension funds, their financial wealth?

Our tools enable us to chart the change in wealth for different generations, as it results from the kinds of macroeconomic shocks that we can reasonably expect. It is possible to describe this as a form of generational accounting (see for instance Auerbach *et al.*, 1999), which concerns fiscal sustainability and the intergenerational distribution of wealth by a country's institutions. For the Netherlands, a recent exercise is in van der Horst *et al.* (2010). It finds that current arrangements are not sustainable and that there is a gap between the actual projected deficits and the maximum sustainable path that amounts to 4.5 percent of GDP.

In this chapter, however, we are not interested in levels of the accounts but rather in their dynamics. Instead of inquiring whether there are any sustainability problems, we assume that the sustainability problem has been solved by a one-time permanent decrease of government material consumption. This gives us a scenario in which government debt (as a percentage of GDP) ultimately stabilizes, which rules out a Ponzi-game. We study the effect of different macroeconomic shocks starting from this base path, and report changes in (lifetime) wealth relative to those in the initial scenario.

Using this approach, we find that both the government and the occupational pension funds act as insurers for most macroeconomic shocks. Insofar as we can summarize their actions across many different cohorts, the general rule seems to be that they transfer away from those who gain from the shocks, toward those who lose. When workers become more productive, for instance, higher taxes and pension premiums dampen their gains while the (initially unaffected) retirees see an increase in their benefits. It is to be noted, though, that the insurance role of the government is much larger than that of the pension funds: often, the size of the government's transfers is several times that of the pension funds. Among the shocks studied in this chapter, there are some cases in which we note a distinct lack of insurance, or even perverse redistribution. This usually involves future, unborn, generations. We will indicate these cases in the text.

While we are not able to give an analysis of the welfare effects of different shocks, we can compute what would happen if each generation would suffer an equal (percentage) change in their consumption levels. This is a well-known benchmark case that, under assumptions, corresponds to optimal risk sharing (see Bohn, 2006). We find that actual consumption changes are usually far away from this ideal, with most of the insurance taking place between the generations that are alive at the time of the shock.

Looking at the kinds of macroeconomic risks that are most relevant, we further find that there is little cross-correlation between different risk classes. That is, a shock in one area (e.g., demography) has only small effects in other areas (e.g., productivity). Only in the case of "rare disasters" do we find that several shocks happen at once. In that case, the insurance mechanism seems to protect current cohorts at the expense of future generations.

Our tools are not perfect, though, and we must compromise on several issues: the OLG model is deterministic with perfect foresight, and thus is ill-suited to analyze an environment in which shocks happen every period. The exclusion of government consumption and public health care from the utility function implies that welfare analysis is problematic. This makes it impossible to do normative analysis on the distribution of the shocks.

Aside from the obvious link with generational accounting, this work also relates to previous studies of the distribution and insurance of macroeconomic shocks. The work of Bohn (2006, 2009) is the most prominent example of this literature. Bohn uses a standard Diamond model of two overlapping generations to assess how different shocks should be shared among the young and the old. He derives the benchmark for risk sharing (an equal response of all cohorts that is proportional to their level of consumption) which represents the unique efficient way to distribute shocks if the degree of relative risk aversion is constant over life.

Bohn (2006) finds that market solutions leave the young over-exposed to productivity risk. He then uses a stylized representation of US fiscal institutions to find that American fiscal policy actually magnifies the generational gap between working-age and retiree exposure to this risk. Demographic shocks (fertility and longevity) are shared through fiscal institutions, but to a degree that is too small compared with the benchmark.

Bohn's simpler framework allows an analysis of welfare, but only gives a coarse characterization of the risk-sharing institutions. Our analysis of the Dutch fiscal institutions and pension funds does *not* find that fiscal rules put extra productivity risk on the young. In contrast to the case studied by Bohn, government benefits to the old (pensions, and in-kind medical benefits) are indexed to wages and thus vary with productivity. This puts part of the risk associated with wages on cohorts that have already retired.

This result fits nicely with the idea that the government and pension funds should be sharing risks across generations, exposing retirees to wage risks and young workers to capital risks. Others have quantified the importance of this role in the case of pension funds: Cui *et al.* (2011), for instance, focus on the role of pension funds in insuring investment risk and inflation risk, and present welfare gains on the order of 1–4 percent from a defined benefit (DB) scheme. While our model does not allow explicit welfare comparisons, we do look at a much larger array of risks and include the government as a second party that provides insurance. In our results, it turns out that the government performs a much larger risk-sharing role than pension funds.

There are several reasons, however, to include pension funds as a special kind of redistribution authority in this paper. Their size is one of them: with assets in excess of Dutch GDP a large part of private wealth is stored in occupational pension funds, and it matters how these funds distribute it. Second, workers cannot opt out of the fund and premiums are usually not actuarially fair. The influence on behavior and wealth distribution is therefore non-negligible. Finally, with their large stake in the financial markets and the labor market, it can be argued that occupational pension funds are one of the most exposed parties when it comes to macroeconomic shocks. It is their role in redistribution that will be of special interest.

When a macroeconomic shock is applied to the baseline scenario, we will need to model how the government sector and the occupational pension funds will deal with the effects of the shock to ensure sustainability once again. For pension funds, it is not hard to find such a policy rule. With their constant exposure to shocks and as the subject of financial supervision, pension funds often explicitly publish their resolution mechanism for solvability problems. The rule in our model is discussed in Subsection 7.2.2.

For the government, such explicit resolution mechanisms do not exist. Decisions are taken in the political arena and do not follow fixed rules. We assume that initial sustainability is achieved through a reduction of general spending, but this might well turn out different in practice. Further on in this study (Subsection 7.4.2), we inspect several mechanisms by which to restore sustainability, each with a different effect on the redistribution characteristics of the government.

The next section discusses the tools of our analysis. It looks at the model for macroeconomic shocks, the OLG model of the Dutch economy and the base path. We map the effects of simple, isolated shocks in Section 7.3 and look at mixed shocks, where several (correlated) risks occur together, in Section 7.4. Section 7.5 concludes.

7.2 The shocks, the model and the base path

If we are to gain insight into the initial impact and redistribution of typical macroeconomic shocks absorbed by the Dutch economy, we need to know more about the shocks, and we need a model of the economy that includes the redistributing agents. For this, we turn to the existing literature. Macroeconomic shocks are the subject of a literature review by Broer (2010), which includes a vector autoregressive (VAR) model of the four main types of shocks. Our model of the economy comes from Draper and Armstrong (2007).

In this section we discuss these background works and set the stage for our analysis. We start below with the study of macroeconomic risks. A description of the economic model that we use to assess the shocks' effects is in Subsection 7.2.2. The base path of the model is discussed in Subsection 7.2.3.

7.2.1 Macroeconomic risks

The defining characteristic of macroeconomic risks is that they cannot be diversified within the period in which they occur. For a *series* of shocks some diversification over time is possible, but any effort to do so is associated with discontinuity risk (see, for instance, Gollier, 2008). Because of their exposure to macroeconomic shocks, pension funds and their supervisors share an interest in the characteristics of these risks.

Our main source of information on the size and likelihood of different macroeconomic shocks is Broer (2010). In this literature survey, four types of shocks are discerned: demographic, financial, shocks to productivity and rare (but influential) disasters. In each of these areas, a large literature is available from which estimates of the underlying process can be obtained. Importantly, the four types of shocks all have effects on the same economy and it is natural that a shock in one area should have effects in another. Indeed, Broer finds that there are many spillovers, for instance from demography to productivity (as workers age, their productivity and their ability to innovate decline) and from productivity to financial markets.

It is these spillovers that are potentially very important for parties that are exposed to multiple risks. Pension funds are vulnerable to low financial returns, but also to higher wages. Their worries would be intensified if the two tend to go together. In most cases, however, Broer finds that these spillovers are not very large. The one exception is the case of "rare disasters," a field of analysis made popular by Barro (2006). With a small but positive probability, economies can experience both a large loss in productivity and severely negative returns on risky assets. Recovery from these disasters can take a long time, and economies may not reattain the old path.

Broer summarizes his findings in a VAR model of the four main processes. Most of it is taken from the literature: it combines the financial model of Campbell and Viceira (2005) with the mortality model of Hári *et al.* (2008) and the disaster characteristics of Barro (2006). Fertility and productivity are estimated using a Kalman filter and cross-correlation coefficients are taken from the literature. While the large number of demographic variables leads to a high-dimensional model (the demographic process uses 100 cohorts), most of the connections between demography and the rest of the economy go through the dependency ratio. This somewhat reduces the size of the "core" model. Nonetheless, to get some insight into the joint distribution of all shocks a simulation study is necessary.

Due to the (auto-) correlation between the different variables, a single impulse in one of them can set off a response across many different dimensions. We will refer to an impulse in one variable, the resulting dynamics and the associated movements in other variables as a "mixed shock." It is the kind of event that we see as typical and likely to occur in the future. Our analysis starts with "simple shocks," in which we look at the dynamics of a single variable only, and the response of other variables is turned off. For instance, a simple shock studies the dynamic pattern of productivity after an impulse without changing the rates of return on the financial markets. The distribution of simple shocks is the subject of Section 7.3.

7.2.2 Gamma

We simulate the economic effects of shocks with the deterministic general equilibrium model Gamma. A detailed description of Gamma can be found in Draper and Armstrong (2007). The model describes a small open economy that is calibrated for the Netherlands. It considers a homogenous, tradable good and a single asset. The price of the good and the interest rate are determined on world markets. The model distinguishes five sectors: households, firms, the government, a pension fund and the foreign sector.

Households are disaggregated into 99 different cohorts. Every generation is represented by one representative household. A household chooses consumption of goods and leisure by maximizing lifetime utility, subject to the lifetime budget constraint. The death rate increases with age. Households insure against the uncertain lifetime income by buying annuities (Yaari, 1965). An individual starts working at the age of 20 years. Labor supply depends on net wages and pension accrual. The net wage is determined by the gross wage minus taxes and pension premiums. The gross wage is age-specific due to an exogenous productivity profile. Pension accrual is calculated as the discounted value of the increase of the benefits from the funded pension scheme. The pension system distorts labor supply incentives only if pension premiums are not actuarially fair. Labor supply does not depend on wealth. We do not consider bequests, implying that an individual is born without any financial wealth.

The representative firm uses labor and capital to produce the tradable good. The rate of labor-saving technical progress is fixed at 1.7 percent on the base path. The demand for inputs is derived from maximizing the value of the firm. Since investment is subject to adjustment costs, the capital stock responds with delay to changes in employment.

The government sector is modeled in detail and captures a generational accounting framework, whereby publicly provided benefits and taxes are attributed to the different age cohorts. Government revenues include taxes on labor income, pensions, capital income and consumption. In reality, progressive taxes (including social premiums) are levied on labor income, transfers and pensions. In the model the progressive system is approximated by a proportional tax, with the specification of deductible pension premiums and of a fixed tax credit. With the modeling of constant marginal income taxes, risks are shared less than with existing institutions. Capital income is not progressively taxed but a flat tax is imposed on the value of financial wealth (above a threshold). In the model capital taxes are proportional to financial wealth. Public expenditures consist of consumption, several transfer schemes, social insurance schemes, education, health care spending and interest. Age profiles are specified for transfers in cash and in kind, including the public PAYG pensions. The public pension benefit is paid starting at the age of 65 and is independent of the labor history and income. The benefit is linked to the aggregate net wage. Since a single retired person gets a higher benefit than a person who still lives with a partner, the average public pension rises with age.

The long-term projections for public spending and taxes are made under the assumption that age-specific expenditures are indexed to wages; non-age-related public expenditures are indexed to GDP and tax rates are held constant (see van der Horst *et al.*, 2010). The inter-temporal budget constraint of the government is closed by a permanent adjustment of the material government consumption. Since material consumption is distributed equally over all living individuals, this implies that the net government benefit changes by the same amount for every individual in every year. Achieving sustainable public finances on the base path requires a reduction of government consumption by 4.5 percent as from 2015.

Supplementary occupational pensions are provided by pension funds. These are based on a funded system. Pension premiums are compulsory for individual workers and tax deductible. Pension benefits are taxed upon realization and indexed to the average wage earned over working life. The replacement ratio depends on the labor history of an individual. Pension rights and benefits are indexed to a combination of wages and prices. Benefits are paid from the age of 65, irrespective when the person retires from the labor market. The assets of the pension fund should cover in each year the projected obligations, or the funding ratio, defined as the ratio between asset holdings and nominal liabilities (i.e., without indexation), should be larger than one. In the case of an initial deficit, the pension fund temporarily raises the premium rate and restricts indexation. We limit the change in the (catching-up) premium to 1 percent per year. When the funding ratio is smaller than 1.35, less than full indexation is applied. In the long run, the premium rate converges to the actuarial fair level and the funding rate equals 1.45 (allowing for full indexation).

Table 7.1 *Key parameters of the Gamma OLG model*

Wage elasticity labor supply	0.14
Intertemporal substitution elasticity	0.50
Substitution capital – labor	0.50
Real rate of return	0.03
Technological progress	0.017

In the small open economy, excess supply of goods can be exported at the given world market price. Similarly, a savings surplus is invested on the world capital market at a fixed interest rate.

The model is calibrated on the Dutch national accounts of 2008. The demographic projections are provided by Statistics Netherlands. The calibration is fully discussed in Draper *et al.* (2010). Some of the key parameters are in Table 7.1.

7.2.3 Net benefit on the base path

Generational accounting exercises usually take place in a world in which there is only (micro-) uncertainty surrounding each person's time of death. A Yaari (1965) arrangement provides perfect insurance against this uncertainty. There is no other risk factor; in the financial sector, only a single asset exists whose rate of return has a predictable path. Agents thus are able to optimize their consumption in each current and future period, bound only by the intertemporal budget constraint

$$\mathrm{PV}(\{c_s\}_{s=t,\ldots,t+T}) = \mathrm{PV}(\{w_s \cdot L_s^s\}_{s=t,\ldots,t+T}) + \mathrm{PV}(\{b_s^G\}_{s=t,\ldots,t+T})$$
$$+ \mathrm{PV}(\{b_s^P\}_{s=t,\ldots,t+T}) + W_t.$$

Here, the present value operator is defined as

$$\mathrm{PV}\left(\{x_s\}_{s=t,\ldots,t+T}\right) = \sum_{s=t}^{t+T} \frac{x_s \Lambda_{s,t}}{\prod_{k=t}^{s}(1+r_k)}. \tag{7.1}$$

The (known) interest rate is r, and the cumulative probability of survival from period t to period s is $\Lambda_{s,t}$. The intertemporal budget constraint says that the present value of consumption c must equal the present value of gross labor income (with observed labor supply, call

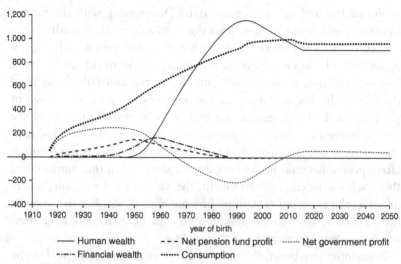

Figure 7.1 Discounted, expected, lifetime net benefit (thousands of euros) Income comes from four sources: labor income, pension fund and government net benefit and private wealth. These four sources add up to expected consumption.

this human wealth), plus the present value of net government transfers b^G (which may be negative in years in which the agent is a net payer), plus the present value of future pension benefits b^p (where b^p is negative in the years that premiums are paid), plus current financial wealth W.[1] The discounting with the probability of survival indicates the presence of the Yaari (1965)-type reverse life insurance scheme.

Figure 7.1 maps out the elements of the right-hand side of this equation on the base path. On the horizontal axis is the year of birth, and plotted are the values of each of the four components in 2016. For those generations that are yet unborn in 2016, the value of their lifetime resources at the time of birth is discounted back to the year 2016 using the rate of technological progress. This has the attractive feature that all unborn generations have the same amount of human wealth ("expressed in 2016 euros") so that we can easily check whether the

[1] Notice that the net government transfers (b^G) at the right-hand side include public consumption, in particular health care expenditures. Therefore, the left-hand side (c) should be interpreted as total consumption. The agents can only choose the level of private consumption. Marginal utility of private consumption is independent of the level of public consumption.

economy has arrived at a steady state. Discounting with the rate of interest would bring all these lines down to zero asymptotically.

Figure 7.1 shows how the importance of the different wealth components differs between ages as the remaining part of the life cycle varies. Discounted labor income is zero for the retired and falls throughout the lifetime for the active part of the population. Those who have not yet entered the labor market see their human wealth increase at the rate of interest as their entry comes near. Expected pension fund benefits increase over the working life as pension rights are being accumulated; premiums paid in the past do not show up in this number. For those who have entered retirement, the value of the pension "asset" drops as the expected remaining lifetime goes down. For the unborn, the actuarially fair pension system with which they have not yet interacted does not represent a net gain or loss.

Remaining net benefits from the government are positive for the retired and the older workers: they expect to receive more than the amount they have left to pay (through taxes on labor, capital, etc.). Note that the expected value of net government benefits declines very slowly for those over 65. Most benefits at this stage consist of health care expenditures, which increase with age and are paid for with public funds. The amounts in the graph are per person and conditional on staying alive. It is not true, in general, that the 90-plus cohorts claim a large part of the government budget.

Young people who have already consumed government services (such as education) in their youth have a negative expected remaining benefit. For the unborn, the expected benefit from the government is positive as they are given ownership of part of the government assets (which, at this time, still exceed the government's liabilities). Financial wealth, finally, is accumulated throughout the working life and decumulated in retirement. As required by the budget constraint, the sum of these four components adds up to the expected value of total lifetime consumption, which completes the graph.

Using graphs that derive from Figure 7.1 we will chart the initial effect of macroeconomic shocks and the subsequent redistribution of this effect by the government and the pension funds. We do this for each wealth component, plotting the change expressed as a percentage of baseline consumption. The four wealth components add up to the net effect that a cohort experiences, which is its (percentage) change in lifetime consumption. One might be tempted to ask how much redistribution is in fact optimal, but it is clear that we cannot answer this question without a social welfare function to weigh the net benefits of different generations. We do not, in fact, make statements about welfare but restrict ourselves to statements about income rather than full consumption.

For comparisons, however, we may use the benchmark case of Bohn (2006). In this case, where agents make optimal saving and portfolio decisions over their lifetime, the relative effect of any shock on yearly consumption should be equal for all generations.[2] If part of the role of government and pension institutions is to help agents in achieving this optimal response, then we can measure the degree to which they succeed by judging whether the distribution of shocks over generations is close to uniform. If that is not the case, we can ask ourselves whether the government and pension institutions at least change the distribution towards uniformity, rather than away from it.

7.3 Initial impact, insurance and redistribution

To understand the response to shocks by agents, pension funds and the government, we initially reduce the shocks' complexity. With many variables moving at once, it becomes harder to pinpoint cause and effect in the OLG model and we therefore start our analysis with four "simple shocks." In these cases, we isolate the sub-VAR model for productivity (or demography, or financial returns) and look at a typical impulse-response pattern in just that submodel, leaving out correlations with other variables. We can more easily analyze the effect of these "simple shocks" in the OLG model. Descriptions of the effects of these shocks should give a feel for the model, without overly going into detail. All shocks discussed below arrive unexpectedly in the year 2016. If the shock also implies changes after this year, these are foreseen by the agents after they learn of the initial shock in 2016.

7.3.1 A shock in productivity

If productivity is hit by a shock, does it stay permanently altered? This question (which was asked about GNP and answered in the

---

[2] Note that this result is derived under the assumption of homothetic utility. If there is habit formation, for instance, it does not hold.

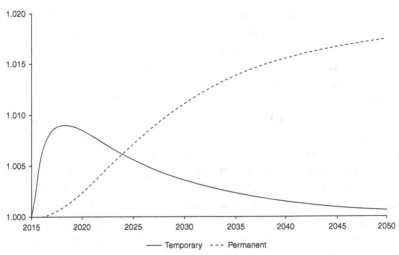

Figure 7.2 Two shocks in the rate of productivity, relative to the base path, administered in the year 2016
With the first shock, the level of productivity eventually drifts back to the base path. The second shock occurs to the latent process that has a unit root. Spillover effects cause the Dutch level of productivity to converge to the new, higher, path where it is permanently 1.87 percent higher than before.

affirmative by Nelson and Plosser, 1982) is discussed at length in Broer (2010, Subsection 2.1.1). At present, the debate on whether GDP has a unit root still continues. We sidestep the controversy by looking at two types of productivity shocks, one of which is permanent and one of which is transitory. Productivity is modeled as a (latent) unit root process with which actual productivity is cointegrated. We apply a one-standard-deviation shock to the productivity process to get a transitory effect, and a one-standard-deviation shock to the latent process to get a permanently higher productivity (in that case, 1.87 percent). The two productivity paths are shown in Figure 7.2.

The initial impact of a shock on productivity is on wages and profits. Since we look at simple shocks in this section, the effect of profits on financial returns has been turned off and the only initial impact is on wages. For the temporary shock, this means that labor income is higher than on the base path for the cohorts that are on the labor market while the shock lasts. For the chosen size and date of the shock, Figure 7.3 shows that generations born between 1945 and 2030 are affected directly. Those with the highest participation rate and age-specific productivity see the largest effect: these are the generations born around 1970 with a gain of around 100 euros per year. This corresponds to 0.4 percent of lifetime consumption and is the result of a shock in which productivity increases just shy of 1 percent, relative to the base path, for a number of years (see Figure 7.2).

The figure also shows how this initial effect is redistributed by the government and the pension funds. The government immediately takes part of the wage increase away through income taxes, and again some through the consumption tax. This accounts for the decline in net government benefits for the cohorts that see their wage income increase. A second effect of the increase in wages is that wage-indexed transfers go up. This benefits all living cohorts, including the elderly who receive first-pillar pensions. This group also sees the value of the health care it gets increase. For the retired, this means that the net benefit from the government goes up. In all, the sustainability of the government budget worsens and public expenditures are decreased somewhat as a result. This shows up as a negative effect on net government benefits for the unborn.

The pension sector also increases benefits to existing retirees, as a result of wage indexing. The decline in solvability caused by this is reversed by increasing premiums. This amounts to a transfer from the working age to the retired, albeit a relatively small one as the dashed line in Figure 7.3 shows.

What Figure 7.3 clearly shows is that both the government and the pension sector actively redistribute the effects of the productivity shock away from the working age who are the initial recipients, towards the initially unaffected retirees. It is the government sector that does the bulk of this redistribution, by disbursing higher pensions and paying for the more expensive health care. The pension system redistributes to slightly younger cohorts, but to a much smaller degree. The total effect of the temporary shock in productivity can be seen from the dashed line in Figure 7.3 that shows the percentage change in consumption. It shows that on an individual level, the main recipients of the shock are the elderly, who feel its effects only through redistribution. A temporary increase in productivity actually makes the unborn generations worse off, as they have to contribute to finance the government's worsened solvability. This is one of the cases, announced in the introduction, where redistributions seem to be perverse, as temporary gain in capacity leads to losses for a number of cohorts.

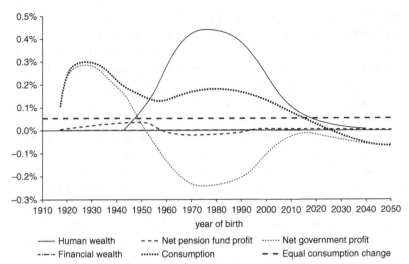

Figure 7.3 Discounted, expected, lifetime net benefit change from a temporary shock on productivity, expressed as a percentage of consumption on the base path

The change is split into human wealth, pension funds and net government profit. Financial wealth is not affected. If each generation responded with the same percentage change in consumption, that level would be at the line Equal consumption change.

It seems odd that a temporary higher productivity should lead to a loss for future generations. This is the result of the current institutional setup: the wage increase leads to higher government expenditures, which are not reclaimed by the increase in the tax intake. In principle, however, it should be possible to use the windfall gain of higher productivity to make everybody better off. The dashed, bold horizontal line in Figure 7.3 shows by how much each generation could have increased their consumption if the shock had been distributed evenly. We compute it by taking the present value of all consumption changes, using the interest rate and mortality after the shock, and dividing evenly over all generations. Relative to this benchmark of 0.05 percent, we see that all generations alive at the time of the shock get more than their share.

The finding that the government redistributes productivity risk to the retired is different from the main result in Bohn (2006), who finds that governments provide too much certainty to the retired vis-à-vis the working cohorts. The reason is that value of government transfers

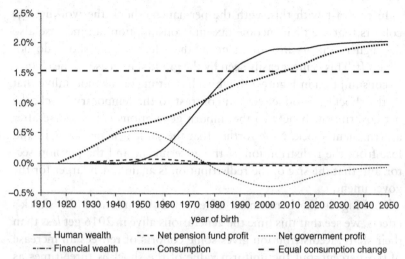

Figure 7.4 Discounted, expected, lifetime net benefit change from an enduring shock on productivity, expressed in percentage change in consumption
The change is split into human wealth, pension funds, government and financial wealth.

to the old in our model is uncertain, rather than certain, and correlates with the shock in productivity. This makes the retirees party to developments in the labor market, which they are not in the Bohn model. Pension funds play the same role on a smaller scale.

In case of a permanent shock to productivity, the change happens gradually and amounts to a 1.75 percent higher productivity level after 35 years (see Figure 7.2). This increases the labor income of all cohorts that are active in the years after the shock, but the effect is skewed towards younger generations. Figure 7.4 shows that those born around the time of the shock can increase their consumption with about 1.75 percent (this is about 400 euros yearly). In this case too, the only direct effect of the increase in productivity is a higher wage rate. Part of this extra income is again redistributed by the government and the pension system, using the same mechanisms as with the temporary shock. The redistribution is, however, much less pronounced. With the temporary shock in productivity, transfers to retirees increase as the wage rate goes up. As the shock fades out, though, transfers decline again. This leads to a number of cohorts that have to pay higher taxes during their working age, but do not get extra benefits in retirement.

In contrast with this, with the permanent shock the working-age cohorts that see their income tax and consumption tax increase also get higher benefits in retirement, as the effects of the shock do not wear off. This is most easily seen by the gradual increase of the change in consumption in Figure 7.4, which has a time profile not unlike that of the shock in productivity. In contrast to the temporary shock, the net government benefit to the unborn generations is not worse after a permanent shock. Note further that the same generations gain and lose from the redistribution of the government and the pension sector, and that the size of the redistribution is again much larger for the government.

Looking at the benchmark of equal distribution of the shock's effects, we see that this time the generations alive in 2016 get *less* than their share. Redistribution gives some cohorts of retirees an increase of 0.5 percent, but the uniform value of the shock is three times as much.

7.3.2 A wealth shock

We next turn to a simple financial shock, in which asset values decline unexpectedly while other exogenous variables stay on the base path. Again, this oversimplifies an actual shock by neglecting the correlations with productivity and future returns. We will turn to realistic shocks later and use this simple shock to understand the workings of the model.

The OLG model works with the assumption of perfect foresight, and as such only has one financial asset. We aggregate the different real-world assets into this measure by assuming a fixed portfolio which holds 25% shares, 25% commercial bonds and 50% in the safe asset. In a disaster, the value of shares can drop anywhere between zero and 70%. Taking the expected value and using the portfolio weight of shares, we model a value decline in the asset of the OLG model as a one-time drop of 8.75%. This shock occurs without affecting the rate of interest, which stays constant at the steady state level both before and after the shock.

Figure 7.5 shows the effects of the drop on the cohorts' wealth components. The affected financial assets are held, in the model, by two parties: individual agents and pension funds, which both see their wealth shrink. For individual agents, the size of the loss is proportional

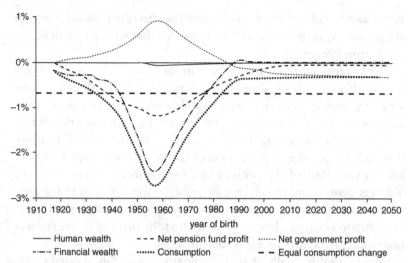

Figure 7.5 Discounted, expected, lifetime net benefit change from a one-time decrease in asset values of 8.75 percent, expressed in percentage consumption change

The change is split into human wealth, pension funds and government net benefit and financial wealth.

to the amount of assets held, which can be seen in Figure 7.1. The loss is felt heaviest by those generations near retirement when the shock occurs, and tapers off toward younger and older agents. This pattern can be observed in Figure 7.5. Note that assets are slightly negative for the youngest generation at the time of the shock; they profit as the value of their debt falls. The effect through private wealth holdings is the largest of the four mechanisms.

Pension funds respond to their deteriorated solvability by decreasing benefit indexation and raising premiums. This primarily affects the same cohorts that were also the largest holders of private wealth, although the effects are a bit more spread out towards the older retirees and include those who do not hold assets at the time of the drop in value. Note that the pension system seems to exacerbate the initial effects of the shock, rather than redistributing them. Without a pension system, however, it is likely that agents would have held even larger personal balances. The much more spread-out profile of the change in pension system benefits indicates that some intergenerational risk sharing is indeed being provided. This result is in line with that of

Bonenkamp *et al.* (2009), who compute the effects per cohort (through the pension system) of the decline in wealth that was the result of the 2008 drop in equity prices.

The government does redistribute in the case of this shock. Taxes on the affected cohorts drop, as do benefit levels for all generations when the government restores solvability after this loss in revenue. Because the latter also includes the unborn, this amounts to a transfer from those too young to suffer from the financial shock to those who did. In size, the redistribution of the government approximately cancels the effect of the pension loss for the most affected cohorts. Younger generations are given a share of the burden by both the government and the pension system. Compared to the benchmark of equal consumption changes, however, we see that the share of future generations under the current rules is too small.

Human wealth, finally, is virtually unaffected by this isolated financial shock since we have purposefully eliminated any real effects on, for instance, productivity. The small drop for the working generations is an indirect effect of higher (distortive) pension premiums.

An aspect of this shock that keeps things simple is that the change in valuation does not involve changes in the rate of interest, which is used to discount the future streams of revenue and consumption. Such a change is the subject of the next section.

7.3.3 A shock in interest rates

We model financial shocks using the five-asset VAR model of Campbell and Viceira (2005). In this model, there are five independent sources of error which hit the return on one asset initially, and then propagate through the values of all five assets. To apply this rich menu of assets in a one-asset OLG model, we work with a fixed portfolio that consists of three of the five assets. Observing how the shocks to different assets lead to a return profile of this portfolio, we find that most tend to generate a similar pattern in returns. When we restrict ourselves to shocks in the real rate of interest, we find that we can reduce the number of independent shocks to two. Keeping inflation constant at 2 percent, the two shocks in Figure 7.6 cover the range of possible dynamics: one is a spike in interest rates that quickly reverses and leads to a slightly lower rate for several years, the other is a prolonged increase with a very slow return to the mean value.

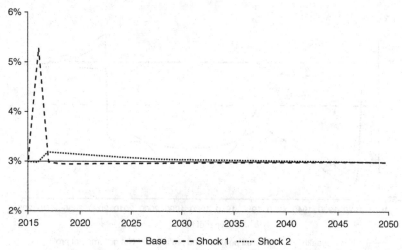

Figure 7.6 Two shocks in the (real) interest rate, administered in the year 2016

A spike, followed by a period of subnormal rates and a long drift upwards.

The effects of a shock in interest rates in our framework of generational accounting work through two channels. The first channel is similar to the other shocks above: the change in interest rates sets off a reaction in economic activity, usually because of a change in the desired capital-labor ratio. This changes behavior and income, depending on the ownership of these factors. The second channel is the computation of net benefits itself. Note that in Equation (7.1) the interest rate is used to discount future receipts and outlays. A change in the interest rate thus directly affects the present value of future transactions. To some extent, this seems artificial: Is someone with a certain, future, income really better off if the interest rate falls, even if prices stay the same? The answer is of course yes, as the interest rate itself is a price. This person could borrow against his future income and consume today; with a lower rate of interest, the amount that he could borrow would increase.

An unexpected change in the rate of interest also affects the holders of fixed income securities through a capital-gains channel; we disregard this effect by assuming that all domestic stocks and bonds are owned by foreigners. This means that a temporary change in the rate of interest has no effect on the *financial* wealth of the agents in this model at the time of the shock.

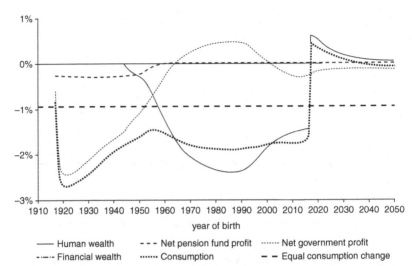

Figure 7.7 A spike in the interest rate in 2016 (see Figure 7.6 above) results in these discounted, expected, net benefits changes
The changes are normalized to cohort consumption, and they compare the previous net benefits (discounted with a constant interest rate) with present net benefits (discounted with the post-shock interest rate).

We illustrate using the first shock in interest rates, the "spike" in Figure 7.6. The changes in net benefit can be found in Figure 7.7. The most important change in the economy is a (temporary) drop in wages of about 2 percent in 2017, when the capital shock adjusts (with a lag of one year) to the new interest rate. The increase in the interest rate leads to a decrease in investments, which has a negative effect on wages as the marginal product of labor falls. This directly affects the value of human wealth for the working cohorts at the time of the shock. The quantitatively more important indirect effect comes about through the interest rate itself: the present value of future wage income falls due to a higher rate of discount. As the graph shows, young workers lose over 2 percent of their consumption (about 200 euros, annualized). The wage recovers after the shock, and marginally exceeds its base path for several decades. Cohorts that are not yet born when the interest rate exceeds its normal level thus see the value of their human wealth increase slightly. That the unborn cohort gains while others lose is inefficient compared to the benchmark, but the redistribution is in the right direction; the government puts part of the costs of compensating current workers on future generations.

With the lower wages income taxes fall as well, which softens the blow for working-age cohorts but deteriorates the government balance. However, the value of government benefits also goes down, both due to the lower wages of those who provide benefits in kind and due to the wage-indexed nature of many benefits. The higher interest costs on the debt tip the balance and make the government slightly worse off. As a result it has to decrease outlays across the board.

Pensioners see no direct effect of the change in wages, but their position vis-à-vis the government declines as their benefits become cheaper, and are more heavily discounted.[3] The working-age cohorts pay less income-related taxes and see the value of their future benefits go up slightly; those outside the labor market are worse off as they suffer the government's actions to restore solvability.

Pension funds use the lower wage rate to scale down their (wage-indexed) benefits. The value of their future obligations falls, which increases solvability and causes the funds to decrease premiums and to increase the pension rights of all participants, spreading a windfall gain over pensioners and the working age alike. The net result is lower pensions for the retired, and slightly higher benefits for the working age.

Figure 7.7 shows that the spike in interest rates is bad for most cohorts. Those that rely on wage (-related) income or future cash flows are made worse off. Higher interest rates also cause a windfall loss for the owners of capital. In the present model however, the parties that bear the risk on capital are assumed to be foreign and so these negative effects do not show up in the analysis.

The alternative shock in interest rates is a modest increase (about 18 basis points maximum) but one that stays positive over a sustained period of several decades. Compound interest being what it is, the total effect can be quite impressive. The effects on net benefits are in Figure 7.8. The main effect of this shock on the economy is that the wage rate drops between 0 and 1 percent for a long period of time.

Figure 7.8 shows that pension funds reduce current pensions and transfer the gains from the increased solvability to the working-age

---

[3] The 99-year-olds see a much smaller effect of this shock than other, slightly younger, retirees. Under the model's assumptions, they are only alive in 2016 and escape the drop in wage-related benefits (in particular, the in-kind health care benefits).

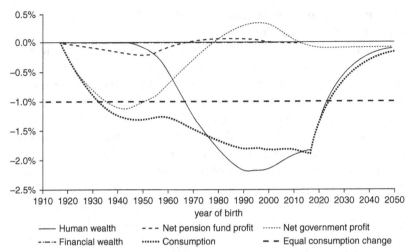

Figure 7.8 A general increase in interest rates starting in 2016 (see Figure 7.6 above) results in these discounted, expected, net benefits changes
The changes are expressed as a percentage of consumption, and they compare the previous net benefits (discounted with a constant interest rate) with present net benefits (discounted with the post-shock interest rate).

cohorts. Human wealth again declines, due to both lower wages and more discounting. With the sustained higher rate of interest, unborn generations also lose from this shock, contrary to the earlier spike in interest rates. The interactions with the government are dominated by the change in wages. This makes indexed financial benefits and benefits in kind worth less, and so all generations are worse off in terms of the value of their benefits. Taxes, however, go down for those whose labor income is diminished and cause those born after 1977 to see an increase in expected government benefits. The overall effect on government solvability is again negative, leading to a lower expected benefit for the unborn.

Summarizing, we see that this long period of elevated interest leads to losses for all cohorts. The government plays a major redistributive role in this scenario, lowering net benefits to the retired generations and compensating the young for their loss in labor income. In the end, both shocks are bad for fiscal sustainability. This stands in contrast to a permanent increase in the interest rate that was analyzed in van der Horst et al. (2010); it shows that temporary changes may have different sustainability effects than permanent changes. Pension funds engage in similar redistribution, but on a smaller scale. The unborn generations do not see much redistribution of the shock, and underpay compared with the benchmark of equal consumption change.

7.3.4 A shock in mortality

The mortality process in Broer (2010) uses the well-known framework of Lee and Carter (1992), which has a latent variable μ_t that influences the probability of death for all cohorts:

$$\log \lambda_{t,\tau} = \alpha_\tau + \beta_\tau \mu_t + \epsilon_{t,\tau}$$

where τ is cohort age and μ_t is a random walk with (downward) drift. $\lambda_{t,\tau}$ is the probability of dying during the age of τ in year t (not to be confused with the survival probability $\lambda_{s,t}$ in Equation (7.1)). Both the constant α and the coefficient on the latent variable β are cohort-specific. A single shock to the latent process means that mortality rates across all cohorts move in the same direction (all β's have the same sign) and that the shock is permanent. The actual model by Hári *et al.* (2008) that is incorporated adds a twist, though, which is that errors to the latent process come from a moving average process and partly reverse themselves. How much of the error is reversed depends on the age of the cohort, with no reversion for the youngest versus two thirds for the very old. Also, the average size of the shock is larger for younger cohorts.

We study the effects of a shock in mortality whereby all cohorts experience a decrease in their mortality that is equal to the standard error of the underlying Lee–Carter process. Shocks are reversed inasfar as that is usual for the age group. This means that two years after the shock, the probability of dying in one particular year goes down by about 10 percent for the middle aged to about 2 percent for the elderly, relative to its previous value. The effect declines slightly over time with the standard drift of mortality rates but stays present in mortality rates for ever.

As with interest rates, the decrease in mortality does two things. First, it has an immediate impact on people's behavior, the balance sheet of the government and that of the pension system. Second, it affects the computation of generational accounts as the rate of mortality shows up in the present-value Equation (7.1). Because mortality acts as a discount factor, lower mortality means that the value of future benefits goes up.

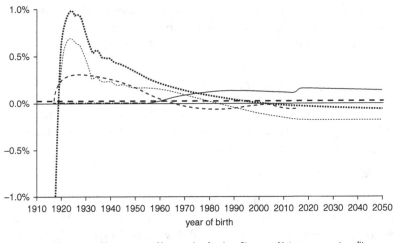

Figure 7.9 Discounted, expected, lifetime net benefit change from a shock in mortality
The change is split into human wealth, pension funds and government.

Figure 7.9 shows these principles in action. A decrease in the mortality rate increases the total amount of wages someone of working age can expect to receive, as the probability of dying before retirement goes down. We thus see a positive effect on human wealth that is proportional to the expected remaining time in the labor force. The marked increase around the year of the shock comes from the relatively high probability of dying in the year of birth.

Retirees, who get benefits conditional on not dying, see the value of their pension rights go up, while pension funds suffer a decrease in their funding ratio. Solvability is restored by charging higher premiums to the working generations, and by lowering the indexation of pension rights. The base premium rate is adjusted for the new expected lifetime and young people who enter the fund after the shock see no effect on their pension wealth.

Finally, net government benefits dominate the effects. A longer expected life means that expected net benefits go up for retirees. There is a second effect, however, which is a consequence of the way health is coupled with expected lifetime. As mortality goes down, the expected health of the old improves along with it. This does not decrease total health care costs over a person's lifetime, but it does move these costs further into the future. The increased discounting of these costs is seen as a decrease in the value of net government benefits. For most retirees, the net effect is positive but for the very old it turns into a loss. The total result of the shock on government sustainability also turns out to be negative, and future generations see about a 60 euro yearly decline in net benefits. This is a case of (mild) overshooting in the redistribution process, as the shock can in principle be used to make each generation better off.

7.4 Mixed shocks

The previous section showed how relatively simple shocks to one exogenous variable are absorbed and redistributed in the Dutch economy. While this is helpful in understanding the mechanisms in the model, we argued in Subsection 7.2.1 that in reality, macroeconomic shocks affect several variables at the same time. In the current section, we turn our attention to these "mixed" shocks. While each originates in one part of the economy, they all spread through several domains. Our analysis of simple shocks will be of great help in understanding the effects of the mixed shocks.

In the current section, our aim is to look at shocks that are all equally likely. For almost all shocks, we start with a one-standard deviation impulse in one random variable. The only exception is the case of a rare disaster, explained below. Since the distributions of the shocks are symmetric, it is also true that the opposite shock is about as likely as the ones we discuss. The reader may find the effects of an increase in mortality, or in productivity, by negating the results in this section.

In this section, we also present the results of two different closure rules for the government. Up to now, any change in the solvability of government finances has been countered by permanently adjusting government material consumption. In Subsection 7.4.2 we close using different instruments after the "rare disaster" shock (see below) and inspect whether different generations shoulder the burden.

7.4.1 *Wealth, productivity and interest: a rare disaster*

Not all macroeconomic shocks follow a standard normal distribution. Barro (2006) notes that with a yearly probability between 1 and 2

Table 7.2 *The parameters of the rare disaster*

Variable	Shock	Dynamics
	%	
Productivity	− 9.50	Permanent effect, arrived at over decades
Interest rate	− 1.50	Immediate, recovery in ten years
Wealth shock	− 8.75	Immediate and permanent

percent, countries experience an economic disaster that results in a large drop in per-capita GDP, falling interest rates and large loss of value on financial markets. This combination of events is exactly the kind of correlation between macro risks that we are interested in, and we start with an analysis of the fallout of such a disaster. First though, a word of warning: as expected, *rare* disasters do not occur with the same frequency as the other shocks that we discuss in this paper. Broer (2010) puts the probability at 1.38 percent each year, which is an order of magnitude lower than the one-standard deviation shocks we discuss in other sections.

The disaster in this section combines the permanent fall in productivity of Subsection 7.3.1 with the asset market drop of Subsection 7.3.2. Interest rates fall by 150 basis points and stay depressed for ten years. An overview of the parameters is in Table 7.2. Note that the shock on productivity is given to the latent productivity variable, which makes it permanent but also introduces a lag of several years before the effect is fully felt.

The first thing to note about Figure 7.10 is the scale of its vertical axis: the effects are much larger than those in previous diagrams. That there are many different things going on at the same time is evidenced by the behavior of the total wage sum: in the first seven years after the shock, this variable goes up as the low interest rate leads to investment that increases the marginal value of labor; after that, the productivity loss kicks in and the wage sum is smaller than on the base path. The (temporarily) higher wages and lower rate of discount explain why human wealth actually goes up after the disaster for the older cohorts on the labor market. Younger cohorts and the unborn see a decline that dominates all other effects for those born after 1985.

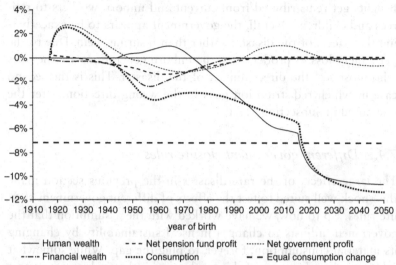

Figure 7.10 Discounted, expected, lifetime net benefit change from a rare disaster that has permanent effects on productivity

The changes are expressed as percentage of consumption and split into human wealth, pension funds, net government profit and financial wealth.

The wealth shock on financial markets is bad for holders of private wealth. Pension funds suffer the same wealth shock plus an increase in the value of their obligations due to the lower interest rates; the effect of the swerving wage rate can go both ways. It turns out that only the very old see an increase in their net benefits from the pension fund; the rest face a loss, whose distribution is similar to that in Figure 7.5: the pension fund spreads the loss over a larger number of cohorts than just the holders of financial wealth.

Those who expect positive net benefits from the government in the future see the present value of that promise increase as interest rates fall. This is true for retirees as well as the very young. When wages start dropping below base case levels, taxes on labor and consumption fall, but so does the value of benefits in kind and indexed pensions. Government interest outlays fall temporarily while the rate is below average. On balance, the effect on the solvability of the government is negative and net government profit falls for future generations. The change in net benefits switches sign several times:

benefits get redistributed from current and unborn workers to retirees and children. Overall, the government appears to be exacerbating the effects of the disaster rather than insuring them. Due to the permanent loss of productivity, the unborn generations are the ones who most feel the direct impact of the disaster. This is the second case in which redistribution goes in the wrong direction, after the one noted in Subsection 7.3.1.

7.4.2 *Different government closure rules*

The large effects of the rare disaster in the previous section make this shock well suited to test the effects of different government closure rules. Up to now, we have worked with the assumption that the government adjusts to changes in fiscal sustainability by changing its material consumption, forever, to plug the gap. While somewhat arbitrary, the advantage of this mechanism is that it does not distort prices and affects all generations equally. In practice, however, changing material consumption may not always be possible. In this case, fiscal sustainability may be brought about by changing one or more tax rates. This introduces (or, with positive shock, reduces) distortions in the economy that influence the distribution of the shock's effects.

We consider two alternative closure rules in this section: using the indirect tax on consumption and investment, and using the direct labor tax. We impose these rules on the base path as well as the after-shock solution, which means that the base path for each shock is different. This follows from the fact that creating a sustainable base path already requires the government to use its closure rule to fix the current fiscal insolvability.

To assess the effects of different closure rules on the division of the shock, consider the three lines in Figure 7.11. They are the change in lifetime consumption, per cohort, after the "rare disaster" shock of Subsection 7.4.1 above. The change in consumption summarizes the effects of the changes in all wealth components, not just net government profit. It is easy to see that other components may also be affected by the closure rule; for instance, changing the direct tax on labor income affects net pension benefits, whose premiums are tax deductible.

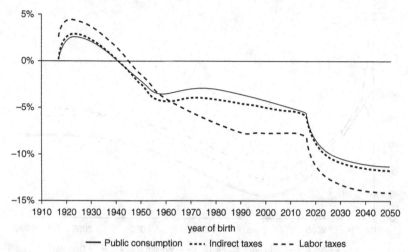

Figure 7.11 Discounted, expected, lifetime consumption change after a rare disaster that has permanent effects on productivity

The government closes using three different instruments: decreasing material consumption (as in Figure 7.10), raising indirect taxes on consumption and investment or by raising direct taxes on labor income.

In the figure, note that using indirect taxes as an instrument leads to little changes in the way the shock is distributed over the different generations. Both workers and retirees regularly pay indirect taxes and are affected by their increase. Cohorts still in their working age appear to be affected slightly less than retirees. The similarity does not hold for the third instrument, direct taxes on wage income. Using this tax rate as an instrument of closure puts the burden of the shock squarely on the shoulders of the workers, the young and the unborn generations. The reduction in human wealth is exacerbated by the reduction in labor supply that follows the lower net wages. Somewhat perversely, using direct taxes on labor as an instrument widens the gap between retirees, who profit from the shock, and younger generations.

Lastly, note that with all these three closure rules we do assume that the government immediately realizes the extent of the fiscal gap and takes action to change the relevant tax rate (or outlays) and put the budget back on a sustainable path. This is a distinct case from a non-forward-looking rule, for instance if the government strives for year-to-year budget balance.

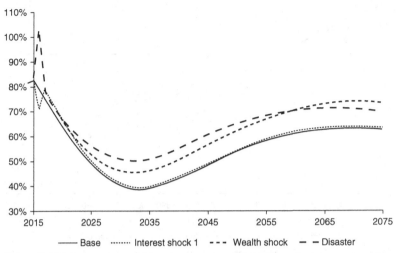

Figure 7.12 Government debt as a percentage of GDP, on the base path and in three scenarios with shocks: the wealth shock from Subsection 7.3.2, interest shock 1 from Figure 7.6 and the rare disaster of Subsection 7.4.1

One reason to deviate from forward-looking rules is that they may cause large, politically infeasible, swings in the budget deficit. If we return to the situation in which government outlays are used as an instrument to guarantee long-run solvency, it follows that government debt becomes an endogenous variable. For all the shocks discussed in this paper, only three cause the debt ratio to deviate from its base path by more than 1.5 percent. These are the interest rate spike, the wealth shock and the rare disaster. The debt paths generated by the standard closing rule after these shocks are in Figure 7.12. The wealth shock results in much higher government profit for the cohorts that live through it, financed by higher taxes in the future. This translates into a gradually increasing debt ratio, up to about 10 percentage points extra in 2075. This path does not seem to violate any constraints on the deficit. In contrast, the rare disaster leads to an immediate jump in the debt level by almost 25 percentage points in the year of the shock. Though not completely unthinkable (in 2008 the Dutch debt ratio jumped by 13 percentage points) this does indicate drastic action by the government. The interest rate shock, lastly, leads to temporary surpluses because of the decreased price of benefits in kind; this is probably not a problematic scenario for politicians.

7.4.3 Mortality and other factors

In this section, we apply the across-the-board decrease in mortality of Subsection 7.3.4 to the full VAR model, taking into account cross-correlations between different macroeconomic risks. As with all demographic shocks, the path of causality to other risk factors is through the dependency ratio. In this scenario, the dependency ratio increases compared with the base path with about 0.6 percentage points in the long run.

The dependency ratio has a direct, negative effect on interest rates (Broer, 2010, Subsection 2.3.8) due to the fact that capital supply varies over the life cycle. The idea is that older people are net capital owners and that a relative increase in their number drives down the rate of return. The effect is small: in the current scenario, the interest rate goes down by two basis points.

A second direct effect of the increased dependency ratio goes through labor productivity. Broer (2010, Subsection 2.2.2) specifies an elasticity of -0.1 between log labor productivity and the dependency ratio. This is caused by relative overpayment of older workers due to implicit contracts and a reduced ability to adapt to innovations. The effect is transitory, though: after several years of slightly lower growth (on the order of 0.1 percentage points) the process reverses and the economy returns to the old growth path.

The two cross-effects cancel each other out when it comes to wages in the first decade. After that, the productivity decrease is reversed but the lower interest rate remains, and wages increase by about 0.11 percent. This can be seen by inspecting the effect of this combined shock on the human wealth of unborn workers, on the right side of Figure 7.13. Note that the left side of this figure is not very different from Figure 7.9, where the cross-correlations are not taken into account. The effect on the consumption of unborn generations changes sign, from negative (without cross-correlations) to positive when cross-correlations are taken into account. Also note that for most cohorts, the effect on consumption is quite close to the benchmark of equal consumption change.

At the same time though, we must conclude that the added effect from letting the other macro-risks vary with a shock in mortality is negligible for most generations, especially the older, living, cohorts. This finding repeats itself across all of the other mixed shocks, which is the reason why we do not report mixed shocks from other sources in this section.

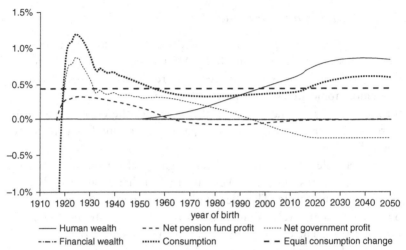

Figure 7.13 Discounted, expected, lifetime net benefit change from a mixed shock in mortality

The changes are expressed relative to consumption and split into human wealth, pension funds, net government profit and financial wealth.

7.5 Conclusion

In this chapter, we study the effects of macroeconomic shocks on different cohorts in the Dutch economy. We aim for realism rather than optimality: the shocks come from a calibrated model of relevant macroeconomic risks and the effects are computed using a large OLG model that contains detailed information on the way taxes and benefits are computed in the Dutch economy. This approach leads to compromises: the OLG model is deterministic, uses perfect foresight and welfare analysis is problematic. We do, however, succeed in showing the impact of different kinds of shocks on the wealth components of different cohorts before and after redistribution.

We find that both the government and the pensions funds engage in the redistribution of shocks. The government does this by taxing the winners and transferring the money to those who lose from the shock. Pension funds also engage in redistribution but their role is more subtle: when financial assets lose value, the effect on private savers is much more concentrated (in terms of cohorts affected) than the effect on current and future members of the pension fund. For the relevant shocks it turns out that the government is by far the most important party in this redistribution. The changes it causes in the wealth of cohorts are several times as large as those caused by pension funds. This is an important lesson that can be taken away from this chapter: while pension funds are often thought to play an important role in intergenerational risk sharing, the importance of their role is trumped by that of the government.

Note however that we take a very kind view of the way in which the government deals with sustainability problems, i.e., by spreading them over all possible cohorts. If the actual response is to fix problems by keeping balances close to zero, the amount of risk sharing decreases. We also neglect bequests and fix agents' portfolios, thus ruling out private risk-sharing arrangements which may overstate the role of the government.[4]

Finally, we find that only in the case of rare disasters do we see a relevant cross-correlation between different kinds of macroeconomic shocks. During these events, financial assets, discount rates and productivity growth are all affected at the same time. Outside of these disasters, shocks in one area can (in theory) have effects in another. We find that the size of these second-order effects does not warrant excessive worrying by researchers or policymakers. The effect of cross-correlations between shocks on generational wealth changes is quite small compared with the initial impact of the shock. It is notable, however, that rare disasters are one of the few cases where the government redistributes the wrong way, i.e., from cohorts that lose substantially towards cohorts that are much less affected.

References

Altonji, J., F. Hayashi and L. Kotlikoff, 1992, Is the extended family altruistically linked? Direct tests using micro data, *American Economic Review*, vol. **82**: 1177–98.

Auerbach, A.J., L.J. Kotlikoff and W. Leibfritz, 1999, *Generational Accounting Around the World*, University of Chicago Press.

Barro, R.J., 2006, Rare disasters and asset markets in the twentieth century, *Quarterly Journal of Economics*, vol. **121**(3): 823–66.

Bohn, H., 2006, Who Bears What Risk? An Intergenerational Perspective, in: D. Blitzstein, O.S. Mitchell and S.P. Utkus (eds.), *Restructuring Retirement Risks*, Oxford University Press, USA, chapter 2: 10–36.

---

[4] Note however that Altonji *et al.* (1992) present empirical evidence which suggests that dynastic risk sharing is rather weak.

2009, Intergenerational risk sharing and fiscal policy, *Journal of Monetary Economics*, vol. 56(6): 805–16.

Bonenkamp, J., C. van Ewijk, H. ter Rele and E. Westerhout, 2009, Herstel dekkingsgraad pensioen-fondsen vergt grote inkomensoffers, *Economisch Statistische Berichten*, vol. 94(4556): 166–69.

Broer, D.P., 2010, Macroeconomic Risks and Pension Returns. CPB Memorandum 241, The Hague. URL: www.cpb.nl/publicatie/macroeconomic-risks-and-pension-returns (accessed January 23, 2012).

Campbell, J.Y. and L.M. Viceira, 2005, The Term Structure of the Risk-Return Tradeoff, CEPR Discussion Paper 4914, CEPR. URL: www.cepr.org/pubs/dps/DP4914.asp (accessed January 23, 2012).

Cui, Jiajia, Frank de Jong and Eduard Ponds, 2011, Intergenerational risk sharing within funded pension schemes, *Journal of Pension Economics and Finance*, vol. 10(1): 1–29.

Draper, D., and A. Armstrong, 2007, Gamma, a Simulation Model for Ageing, Pensions and Public Finances. CPB Document 147. URL: www.cpb.nl/en/publication/gamma-simulation-model-ageing-pensions-and-public-finances (accessed January 23, 2012).

Draper, N., L. Bettendorf, J. Bonenkamp, A. Nibbelink, R. Rosenbrand and H. ter Rele, 2010, Calibration of Gamma 2010. CPB Netherlands Bureau for Economic Policy Analysis, Memorandum 248. URL: www.cpb.nl/en/publication/calibration-gamma-2010 (accessed January 23, 2012).

Gollier, C., 2008, Intergenerational risk-sharing and risk-taking of a pension fund, *Journal of Public Economics*, vol. 92(5–6): 1463–85.

Hári, N., A. de Waegenaere, B. Melenberg and T.E. Nijman, 2008, Estimating the term structure of mortality, *Insurance, Mathematics and Economics*, vol. 42(2): 492–504.

Horst, A. van der, L. Bettendorf, N. Draper, C. van Ewijk, R. de Mooij and H. ter Rele, 2010, Vergrijzing Verdeeld: Toekomst van de Nederlandse Overheidsfinanciën. CPB Bijzondere Publicatie 86 (in Dutch). URL: www.cpb.nl/en/publicatie/vergrijzing-verdeeld-toekomst-van-de-neder-landse-overheidsfinanci%C3%ABn (accessed January 23, 2012).

Lee, R.D., and L.R. Carter, 1992, Modeling and forecasting US mortality, *Journal of the American Statistical Association*, vol. 87: 659–71.

Nelson, C.R., and C.I. Plosser, 1982, Trends and random walks in macroeconomic time series. Some evidence and implications, *Journal of Monetary Economics*, vol. 10(2): 139–62.

Yaari, M.E., 1965, Uncertain lifetime, life insurance and the theory of the consumer, *Review of Economic Studies*, vol. 32(2): 137–50.

8 | The consequences of indexed debt for welfare and funding ratios in the Dutch pension system

ROEL BEETSMA AND ALESSANDRO BUCCIOL

8.1 Introduction

Dutch pension arrangements are rather unique in that they feature a second, funded pillar that is almost as large as the first, pay-as-you-go (PAYG) pillar. The great majority of employees now build up an occupational pension via a company or sectoral pension fund. It is expected that the relative size of the second pillar will rise further, because as a result of rising life expectancy it will become more and more difficult to finance the PAYG part out of workers' contributions. Essential elements of the second pillar are "collectivity" and "solidarity" with a *de jure* or *de facto* obligation to participate. Contribution and accumulation rates are identical across the fund's participants. These elements help to keep the costs of the pension arrangement relatively low, while allowing for risk sharing among the various groups of participants. For example, with indexation of benefits to wages, some of the wage risk is shifted onto the retired, while some of the financial market risk is shifted onto the workers when realized indexation is linked to the market performance of the fund's investment portfolio.

Within the Dutch second pillar workers build up nominal pension rights (expressed in euros) through their contributions to the pension funds. These rights promise a nominally fixed benefit as of the retirement date. In the past, the pension rights were virtually always indexed

Financial support from Netspar is gratefully acknowledged. We are grateful to Lans Bovenberg, Casper van Ewijk, Theo Nijman, Ed Westerhout and the participants of the conference "Macroeconomics of Pension Reform" (October 7–8, 2010, The Hague) for their many useful comments. The usual disclaimers apply.

for price or wage inflation. However, in recent years and in particular as a result of the economic and financial crisis, it has become clear that the financial health of the pension funds, as measured by the funds' buffers, is highly sensitive to a host of shocks. As a result, in many instances indexation has been abolished and the purchasing power of pensions has been eroded through inflation.

It has been frequently suggested that the vulnerability of the pension buffers and, hence, of the future pensions themselves to some of these shocks, such as inflation risk, can be reduced when the pension funds are able to invest in indexed debt. The nominal return on such debt moves up and down with the rate of inflation and, hence, to the extent that the pension fund invests in this type of debt, the value of its assets will be protected against inflation risk.

However, the Dutch government does not issue indexed debt,[1] while only a limited number of foreign governments issue such debt. None of this debt is indexed to the Dutch price level and, hence, pension funds have no other possibility than to hedge against inflation risk through derivative instruments. In this paper, and following Bucciol and Beetsma (2010), we develop an applied many-generation small open-economy overlapping-generations (OLG) model with hetero-geneous agents that is designed to capture the main features of the two pillars of the Dutch pension system. The model is calibrated to the Dutch economy and its unexpected aggregate shocks, which arise from demographic uncertainty (the size of newborn generations and survival probabilities), economic uncertainty (productivity growth and inflation) and financial uncertainty (bond and equity returns, and yield curve). Using stochastic simulations of the model, we explore the consequences for the funding ratio, i.e., the ratio of the fund's assets and liabilities, and welfare of different individuals of replacing nominal with indexed debt in the portfolios of the funds. We consider price-indexed, wage-indexed and longevity-indexed debt. We limit the complexity of the framework by not explicitly modeling a government issuing the indexed debt. Hence, pension funds buy indexed debt on international markets and its returns are exogenously determined.

We find that with the full menu of shocks active the welfare effects of a switch from nominal to any of the aforementioned types

---

[1] A discussion (in Dutch) on the desirability of the Dutch government issuing indexed debt is found in Beetsma and van Ewijk (2010).

of indexed debt are positive for a majority of individuals because consumption variability decreases. However, in most cases the effects are rather modest in size.[2] The effect on the volatility of the funding ratio when the full menu of shocks is present is rather small. The limited size of the effects may not be too surprising. To take the example of debt indexed to price inflation, the return on this type of debt still bears the risk associated with movements in the real interest rate (which, in turn, are linked to movements in the marginal productivity of capital), while the funding ratio continues to be subject to an even much wider range of risks, such as demographic risk, interest risk and stock market risk. Further, the policy rules regulating the funding ratio are identical across the various scenarios. This limits the consequences of a switch from one scenario to another for the volatility of the funding ratio and also for welfare. The implications for the funding ratio of investing in indexed debt are limited even in the presence of only the shock to which the debt is indexed, because pension funds invest only half of their value in debt instruments and at the annual frequency the actual indexation of pension rights to price or wage inflation often deviates substantially from exactly full indexation. In fact, a too large share of wage-indexed debt may destabilize the funding ratio.

The remainder of this chapter is organized as follows. Section 8.2 describes the model. Section 8.3 discusses the model calibration and the rules for the adjustment of the policy parameters. Section 8.4 presents the results of the simulations and compares the cases of the various types of indexed debt with the case of nominal debt held by the pension fund. Finally, Section 8.5 concludes the chapter. Further details are available from an online appendix that can be downloaded at www1.fee.uva.nl/mint/beetsma.shtm.

8.2 The benchmark model

The model is an overlapping generations model with a number of D cohorts alive in any given period t. A period in our model corresponds to one year.

---

[2] This contrasts with Koijen *et al.* (2011), who find that the welfare benefits of introducing indexed debt instruments can be substantial. However, their model substantially differs from ours. In particular, they have fewer sources of shocks.

8.2.1 Cohorts and demography

Index $j = 1,...,D$ indicates the age of the cohort, computed as the amount of time since entry into the labor force. Individuals face an exogenous age-dependent probability of dying in each period. The probability is stochastic and exhibits a downward trend, thereby causing the population on average to become older over time. Further, we assume that the cohort of newborn agents in period t is $1+n_t$ times larger than the cohort of newborn agents in period $t-1$, where n_t is also stochastic.

8.2.2 Skill groups and the income process

Each individual belongs to some skill group i, with $i=1,...,I$, and she remains in her skill group during her entire life. A higher value of i denotes a higher skill level. We assume that all the skill groups are of equal size. The skill level of a person determines her income, given her age and the macroeconomic circumstances. We allow for skill-induced differences in income, because below a certain income level individuals do not build up claims to a second-pillar pension and, hence, groups with low skills will hardly be affected by the policy differences in the second pillar. This may affect the aggregate welfare comparison between different policies. In addition, we want to capture the main elements of the Dutch system in order to be able to compare policies in a realistic setting.

Individuals work until the exogenous retirement age R and live for at most D years. During their working life ($j=1,...,R$), they receive a labor income $y_{i,j,t}$ given by:

$$y_{i,j,t} = e_i s_j z_t, \tag{8.1}$$

where e_i, $i=1,...,I$ is the efficiency index for skill group i, s_j, $j=1,...,R$ is a seniority index (income varies with age for a given skill level), and z_t is an exogenous process:

$$z_t = (1+g_t)z_{t-1}, \tag{8.2}$$

where g_t is the exogenous *nominal* growth rate of the process and $z_0=1$. Hence, individuals in a given cohort in period t only differ in terms of their income, while all individuals in a given skill-group earn the same income per hour worked.

8.2.3 Social security

Social security is based on a two-pillar system that resembles the Dutch pension system. The first pillar is a PAYG DB program which pays a flat benefit to every retiree. It is organized by the government, which sets the contribution rate to ensure that this pillar is balanced on a period-by-period basis. Even though this pillar does not feature explicitly in our analysis, it provides an important part of retirees' income. In particular, because of the franchise for the second pillar (as explained below), for low-skilled individuals the first pillar is (virtually) the only source of income during retirement. Hence, we include it in our model to produce realistic effects of policy changes on income and welfare of the various groups in society. For example, because low-skilled groups receive hardly any income from the second pension pillar, they will also experience hardly any effect of policy changes in the second pillar. The second pillar consists of private pension funds that provide defined benefit (DB) nominal pensions that are usually indexed to some combination of price and productivity changes.

The first pillar of social security

Each period, an individual of working age pays a mandatory contribution $P^F_{i,j,t}$ to the first pillar of the pension system. This contribution depends on the size of his income $y_{i,j,t}$ relative to the thresholds $\delta^l y_t$ and $\delta^u y_t$:

$$
p^F_{i,j,t} = \begin{cases} 0, & \text{if } y_{i,j,t} < \delta^l y_t \\ \theta^F_t\left(y_{i,j,t} - \delta^l y_t\right), & \text{if } y_{i,j,t} \in \left[\delta^l y_t, \delta^u y_t\right] \\ \theta^F_t\left(\delta^u y_t - \delta^l y_t\right), & \text{if } y_{i,j,t} > \delta^u y_t \end{cases}, \quad j \leq R, \qquad (8.3)
$$

where δ^l, δ^u and θ^F_t are policy parameters and y_t is average income across all working individuals. Like those on low income (below $\delta^l y_t$), the retired pay no contributions, while for high-income workers the contribution is capped. In period t a retiree receives a flat benefit that is a fraction ρ^F of the average income in the economy:

$$
b^F_t = \rho^F y_t. \qquad (8.4)
$$

Given the benefit formula in Equation (8.4), in each period the contribution rate θ^F_t is adjusted such that aggregate contributions into the first pillar equal aggregate first-pillar benefits.

Note that under this system an individual earning a low income pays no contributions, but still receives the same benefit as an individual with a high income.

The second pillar of social security

Each period, an individual of working age also pays a mandatory contribution $p_{i,j,t}^S$ to the second pillar if his income exceeds the franchise income level λy_t, where parameter λ denotes the franchise as a share of average income. Specifically,

$$p_{i,j,t}^S = \theta_t^S \max\left[0, y_{i,j,t} - \lambda y_t\right], \quad j \leq R, \tag{8.5}$$

where θ_t^S is a policy parameter. We assume that θ_t^S is capped at a maximum value of $\theta^{S,\max} > 0$. The Dutch pension contract generally imposes a cap on the contribution rate, but this cap may differ across funds. We take account of the presence of such a cap by imposing a maximum $\theta^{S,\max}$ on θ_t^S.

A cohort entering retirement at age $R+1$ receives a benefit linked to its entire wage history. Period t benefits of an individual in skill group i of cohort j are given by:

$$b_{i,j,t}^S = M_{i,j,t}, \quad j \geq R+1, \tag{8.6}$$

where $M_{i,j,t}$ is the "stock of nominal pension rights" in euros accumulated by the end of period t. It is the second-pillar pension that a retiree receives each period from this year and on, as long as this number is not revised. Variable $M_{i,j,t}$ is a stock variable in the sense that a retiree's annual benefit increases for each additional year of work that she has provided. Precisely, $M_{i,j,t}$ evolves as follows:

$$M_{i,j,t} = \begin{cases} (1+m_t)\left\{ \begin{array}{c} \left(1+\kappa_t\pi_t + \iota_t\left(g_t - \pi_t\right)\right)M_{i,j-1,t-1} \\ +\mu\max\left\{0, y_{i,j,t} - \lambda y_t\right\} \end{array} \right\}, & j \leq R \\ (1+m_t)\left(1+\kappa_t\pi_t + \iota_t\left(g_t - \pi_t\right)\right)M_{i,j-1,t-1}, & j > R \end{cases}, \tag{8.7}$$

where parameter μ denotes the annual accrual rate of nominal rights as a share of income above the franchise level. The productivity indexation parameter ι_t and the price indexation parameter κ_t capture the degree of indexation of earlier accumulated nominal rights $M_{i,j-1,t-1}$ to real income growth, $g_t - \pi_t$, and inflation, π_t, respectively. Indexation aims at following total wage growth, in which case $\iota_t = \kappa_t = 1$. However, the actual degree of indexation may depend on the financial position of the pension fund. Further, $m_t < 0$ captures a proportional reduction in nominal rights that is applied when the pension buffer is so low that the other instruments (the indexation rates and the contribution rate) are insufficient to restore the buffer within the allowed restoration period, while $m_t > 0$ when earlier cuts in nominal rights are undone. Each individual enters the labor market with zero nominal claims ($M_{i,0,t-j}$ for any i and t). Notice that, in contrast to the first-pillar pension benefit, the second-pillar benefit depends on both the cohort and skill level of the individual.

As we shall describe below, the pension fund's instrument setting strongly depends on the so-called nominal funding ratio F_t, which is the ratio between the fund's assets, A_t, and its liabilities, L_t:

$$F_t = \frac{A_t}{L_t}. \tag{8.8}$$

At the end of period t the pension fund's assets are the sum of the second-pillar contributions from workers in period t *minus* the second-pillar benefits paid to the retirees in period t *plus* the pension fund's assets at the end of period $t-1$ grossed up by their return in the financial markets:

$$A_t = \left(\sum_{j=1}^{R} \frac{N_{j,t}}{I} \sum_{i=1}^{I} p_{i,j,t}^{S} - \sum_{j=R+1}^{D} \frac{N_{j,t}}{I} \sum_{i=1}^{I} b_{i,j,t}^{S} \right) + \left(1 + r_t^f\right) A_{t-1}, \tag{8.9}$$

where

$$1 + r_t^f = \left(1 - z^e\right)\left(1 + r_t^{lb}\right) + z^e\left(1 + r_t^e\right), \tag{8.10}$$

where r_t^f is the nominal rate of return on the pension fund's asset portfolio with a constant share z^e invested in equities and the remainder in long-term nominal bonds. Later we shall also consider variants in which the pension fund invests in indexed bonds rather than nominal bonds.

We take the standard perspective of a small open economy with perfect capital mobility. All the asset returns, that is the returns on long-term bonds (r_t^{lb}) and equities (r_t^e), are exogenously determined on the international financial markets. Given that we do not model a domestic government sector, we can think of the bonds being issued by foreign governments with foreign taxpayers liable for the repayment of the debt.[3] To avoid complicating the model further, we also assume that the pension fund's portfolio composition z^e is exogenous. Actual data for Dutch pension funds show a stable composition over the years, which may point to pension funds aiming at stable targets for the various asset categories.

We assume that the long-term bonds held by the pension fund always have a ten-year maturity. This implies that at the end of each year bonds of nine-year maturity are sold to purchase new ten-year bonds. In more detail, the fund's annual portfolio rebalancing operation works as follows. In year $t-1$, say, the pension fund buys ten-year zero-coupon bonds for an amount of B_{t-1}. Denoting the return on ten-year bonds by $r^b_{10,\,t-1}$, the value at maturity of the bonds is

$$P_{t+9} = B_{t-1}\left(1 + r^b_{10,\,t-1}\right)^{10}, \tag{8.11}$$

hence, the present value B_{t-1} of the bond holdings in year $t-1$ is:

$$B_{t-1} = \frac{P_{t+9}}{\left(1 + r^b_{10,\,t-1}\right)^{10}}.$$

In year t, only nine years of maturity are left, and the bond return is $r^b_{9,\,t}$. The present value B_t is then

$$B_t = \frac{P_{t+9}}{\left(1 + r^b_{9,\,t}\right)^{9}}.$$

Combining with (8.11) we obtain the following expression:

$$B_t = B_{t-1}\frac{\left(1 + r^b_{10,\,t-1}\right)^{10}}{\left(1 + r^b_{9,\,t}\right)^{9}} = B_{t-1}\left(1 + r^{lb}_t\right).$$

---

[3] Introduction of a domestic government sector would be beyond the scope of the present chapter, as it would introduce many complications. While with perfect capital mobility nominal asset returns would still be exogenous, we would have to introduce taxes that are needed to finance government expenditures and the repayment of debt. Tax policies could be used to affect redistribution and risk sharing among generations. These issues cannot be addressed in the present chapter.

The fund's liabilities are the sum of the present values of current and future rights *already accumulated* by the cohorts currently alive:

$$L_t = \sum_{j=1}^{D} \frac{N_{j,t}}{I} \sum_{i=1}^{I} L_{i,j,t}, \tag{8.12}$$

where $L_{i,j,t}$ is the liability to the cohort of age j and skill level i, which is computed by discounting the projected future nominal benefits resulting from the current stock of nominal rights against a term structure of annual nominal interest rates $\{r_{k,t}\}_{k=1}^{D}$:

$$L_{i,j,t} = \begin{cases} E_t \left[\sum_{l=R+1-j}^{D-j} \left(\prod_{k=1}^{l} \psi_{j+k,t-j+1} \right) \frac{1}{\left(1+r_{l,t}\right)^l} M_{i,j,t} \right], & \text{if } j \leq R, \\ E_t \left[\sum_{l=0}^{D-j} \left(\prod_{k=1}^{l} \psi_{j+k,t-j+1} \right) \frac{1}{\left(1+r_{l,t}\right)^l} M_{i,j,t} \right], & \text{if } j > R, \end{cases} \tag{8.13}$$

When $j \leq R$, we discount all future benefits to the current year t, but of course they will only be paid out once individuals have retired. Importantly, notice that the computation of the liabilities excludes the effects of possible *future* indexation. Hence, the liabilities are less than the total pension wealth accumulation by current generations. This is also the reason why pension funds that aim at maintaining the purchasing power of the accumulated rights need to maintain a funding ratio that is substantially above 100 percent.

8.2.4 Individuals

Period utility of individuals is given by

$$u\left(\tilde{c}_{i,j,t}\right) = \frac{\tilde{c}_{i,j,t}^{1-\gamma}}{1-\gamma},$$

where γ is the coefficient of relative risk aversion for the entire term in square brackets, and $\tilde{c}_{i,j,t}$ is *real* consumption,

$$\tilde{c}_{i,j,t} = \frac{c_{i,j,t}}{\prod_{s=1}^{t}\left(1+\pi_s\right)},$$

where $c_{i,j,t}$ is nominal consumption (the price level at the end of period 0 is unity). Further, $\tilde{y}_{i,j,t}$ is labor or pension income net of contributions:

$$\tilde{y}_{i,j,t} = \begin{cases} y_{i,j,t} - p^F_{i,j,t} - p^S_{i,j,t} & \text{if } j \le R \\ b^F_t + b^S_{i,j,t} & \text{if } j \ge R+1 \end{cases}.$$

To keep matters as simple as possible and enhance intuition, we assume that individuals take no decisions, implying that they simply consume all of their disposable income $\tilde{y}_{i,j,t}$. Hence, their savings are zero. Since they enter the world with zero assets, their assets $a_{i,j,t}$ are zero throughout their life.

The individual's value function is

$$V_{i,j,t} = E_t \left[\sum_{l=0}^{D-j} u\left(\tilde{c}_{i,j+l,t+l}\right) \frac{\beta^l}{\psi_{j,t-j+1}} \left(\prod_{k=-j+1}^{l} \psi_{j+k,t-j+1} \right) \right].$$

8.2.5 The shocks

We assume that there are only aggregate, hence no individual-specific, shocks. Seven types of aggregate exogenous shocks hit the economy. Specifically, we allow for demographic shocks (to the growth rate of the newborns cohort and to the survival probabilities), inflation rate shocks, nominal income shocks (which, together with the inflation shock, produce a shock to the productivity growth rate) and financial market shocks (to bond returns, equity returns and the yield curve). The shocks are collected in the vector $\omega_t = \left[\varepsilon^n_t, \varepsilon^\psi_t, \varepsilon^g_t, \varepsilon^\pi_t, \varepsilon^b_t, \varepsilon^e_t, \varepsilon^b_{2,t}, ..., \varepsilon^b_{D,t} \right]'$ with elements

- ε^n_t: shock to the newborn cohort growth rate n_t,
- ε^ψ_t: a vector of shocks to the set of survival probabilities $\{\psi_{j,t-j+1}\}^D_{j=1}$,
- ε^g_t: shock to the nominal income growth rate g_t,
- ε^π_t: shock to the inflation rate π_t,
- ε^b_t: shock to the one-year nominal bond return r^b_t,
- ε^e_t: shock to the nominal equity return r^e_t,
- $\varepsilon^b_{k,t}, k=2,...,D$: shock to the yield curve at maturity $k>1$, $r^b_{k,t}$.

All these shocks affect the size of the funding ratio (Equation (8.8)), whereas only the demographic shocks affect the first pillar of the pension system. As a consequence, the key parameters of the pension system have to be adjusted to restore the balance in the first pillar and to maintain sustainability of the second pillar. Below we give a brief description of each shock process.

The demographic shocks are independent of each other and of all the other shocks (at all leads and lags). The growth rate n_t of the newborns cohort depends on deterministic and random components:

$$n_t = n + \varepsilon_t^n, \tag{8.14}$$

where n is the mean and ε_t^n the innovation at time t, which follows an AR(1) process with parameter φ:

$$\varepsilon_t^n = \varphi \varepsilon_{t-1}^n + \eta_t^n, \quad \eta_t^n \sim N(0, \sigma_n^2). \tag{8.15}$$

The survival probabilities evolve according to a Lee and Carter (1992) model:

$$\ln(1 - \psi_{j,t-j+1}) = \ln(1 - \psi_{j,t-j}) + \tau_j (\chi + \varepsilon_{t-j+1}^\psi),$$
$$\varepsilon_{t-j+1}^\psi \sim N(0, \sigma_\psi^2), \quad j = 1, ..., D, \tag{8.16}$$

with τ_j an age-dependent coefficient, χ a constant growth factor (to describe the historical trend increase in survival probabilities) and ε_{t-j+1}^ψ an innovation at time $t-j+1$ that follows an i.i.d. process with variance σ_ψ^2.

We allow the shocks to the inflation rate, the nominal income growth rate, the one-year bond return and the equity return to be correlated with each other and over time. These variables feature the following multivariate process:

$$\begin{pmatrix} \pi_t \\ g_t \\ r_t^b \\ r_t^e \end{pmatrix} = \begin{pmatrix} \pi \\ g \\ r^b \\ r^e \end{pmatrix} + \begin{pmatrix} \varepsilon_t^\pi \\ \varepsilon_t^g \\ \varepsilon_t^b \\ \varepsilon_t^e \end{pmatrix}, \tag{8.17}$$

with annual means $(\pi, g, r^b, r^e)'$ and innovations $\left(\varepsilon_t^\pi, \varepsilon_t^g, \varepsilon_t^b, \varepsilon_t^e\right)'$ following a VAR(1) process,

$$
\begin{pmatrix} \varepsilon_t^\pi \\ \varepsilon_t^g \\ \varepsilon_t^b \\ \varepsilon_t^e \end{pmatrix} = B \begin{pmatrix} \varepsilon_{t-1}^\pi \\ \varepsilon_{t-1}^g \\ \varepsilon_{t-1}^b \\ \varepsilon_{t-1}^e \end{pmatrix} + \begin{pmatrix} \eta_t^\pi \\ \eta_t^g \\ \eta_t^b \\ \eta_t^e \end{pmatrix}, \quad \text{with} \quad \begin{pmatrix} \eta_t^\pi \\ \eta_t^g \\ \eta_t^b \\ \eta_t^e \end{pmatrix} \sim N\left(\underset{4x1}{0}, \underset{4x4}{\tilde{\Sigma}}\right). \tag{8.18}
$$

For the estimation of (8.17) and (8.18) we use inflation and income data for the Netherlands (source is OECD, 2009) and one-year bond and equity data for the US (sources are, respectively, Federal Reserve, 2009; Datastream, 2009).

We finally turn to the term structure of annual nominal interest rates (the yield curve). We set the interest rate at one-year maturity equal to the one-year bond interest rate arising from the above multivariate process. To describe the remaining components of the yield curve, we focus on the rates in excess of the bond interest rate at maturity 1, $\tilde{r}_{k,t}^b$. Following the prevailing literature (see, e.g., Evans and Marshall, 1998; Dai and Singleton, 2000), we model the excess interest rates as a vector autoregressive distributed lag (VADL) process with lag 1:

$$
\begin{pmatrix} \tilde{r}_{2,t}^b \\ \tilde{r}_{3,t}^b \\ \vdots \\ \tilde{r}_{D,t}^b \end{pmatrix} = \Gamma_0 + \Gamma_1 \begin{pmatrix} \tilde{r}_{2,t-1}^b \\ \tilde{r}_{3,t-1}^b \\ \vdots \\ \tilde{r}_{D,t-1}^b \end{pmatrix} + \Gamma_2 \begin{pmatrix} \pi_{t-1} \\ g_{t-1} \\ r_{t-1}^b \\ r_{t-1}^e \end{pmatrix} + \begin{pmatrix} \varepsilon_{2,t}^b \\ \varepsilon_{3,t}^b \\ \vdots \\ \varepsilon_{D,t}^b \end{pmatrix}, \tag{8.19}
$$

with

$$
\left(\varepsilon_{2,t}^b \quad \varepsilon_{3,t}^b \quad \cdots \quad \varepsilon_{D,t}^b\right)' \sim N(0, \Sigma). \tag{8.20}
$$

Each period t, the excess interest rate at maturity k, $\tilde{r}_{k,t}^b$, $k \geq 2$, is a linear combination of deterministic and random components. The deterministic part is a function of several variables at time $t-1$: the excess interest rates at all maturities $k \geq 2$ and the four macro and financial variables whose shocks follow the VAR(1) process (8.18). The random part is given by the innovations $\varepsilon_{k,t}^b$, which may be correlated across maturities.

Actual yields at any maturity $k \geq 1$ are then built as the sum of the VADL(1) realizations and the realization to the one-year bond interest rate:

$$
\begin{pmatrix} r_{1,t}^b \\ r_{2,t}^b \\ r_{3,t}^b \\ \vdots \\ r_{D,t}^b \end{pmatrix} = \begin{pmatrix} 0 \\ \tilde{r}_{2,t}^b \\ \tilde{r}_{3,t}^b \\ \vdots \\ \tilde{r}_{D,t}^b \end{pmatrix} + \begin{pmatrix} r_t^b \\ r_t^b \\ r_t^b \\ \vdots \\ r_t^b \end{pmatrix}.
$$

The average yield curve $\left\{ r_k^b \right\}_{k=1}^D$ is given by:

$$
\begin{pmatrix} r_2^b \\ r_3^b \\ \vdots \\ r_D^b \end{pmatrix} = \begin{pmatrix} r^b \\ r^b \\ \vdots \\ r^b \end{pmatrix} + \left(I - \Gamma_1 \right)^{-1} \left(\Gamma_0 + \Gamma_2 \begin{pmatrix} \pi \\ g \\ r^b \\ r^e \end{pmatrix} \right), \tag{8.21}
$$

where we have applied $E\left[\tilde{r}_{k,t}^b \right] = E\left[\tilde{r}_{k,t-1}^b \right]$ to (8.19) because of stationarity.

We estimate (8.19) using US data (source is Federal Reserve, 2009).

8.2.6 Welfare comparisons between policies

We are interested in welfare comparisons based on simulations with one or more shocks. Generally speaking, welfare differences measured in this way are the sum of a "redistribution effect" of a shift from the benchmark scenario A to the alternative scenario B in the absence of shocks and a "risk-sharing effect" that captures the difference between the total welfare effect of the shift from the benchmark to the alternative under shocks and the redistribution effect. In the comparisons that we will consider below, only the risk-sharing effect will be present.

Welfare comparisons are made at the aggregate level by reporting the share of individuals alive at $t=1$ in favor of the alternative. At the individual level (i.e., based on the combination of skill and age) welfare comparisons take place at the start of period $t=1$ of our simulations (see below) for those cohorts alive at that moment and at the start of the first year of life for the cohorts that are born later. Individual welfare is measured as the certain "consumption equivalent change" (CEC), as is standard in the literature of life-cycle models (see, e.g., Cocco *et al.*, 2005; Krueger and Kubler, 2006). It is defined as the change in certainty-equivalent consumption over the remainder of the individual's life under scenario B relative to scenario A. That is, if $V_{i,j,t}(s)$ is the welfare for skill group i of the generation aged j in year t under scenario $S \in \{A, B\}$, we compute[4]

$$CEC_{i,j,t} = \left(\frac{V_{i,j,t}(B)}{V_{i,j,t}(A)} \right)^{\frac{1}{1-\gamma}} - 1.$$

We consider $CEC_{i,j,1}$ for the alive generations and $CEC_{i,1,t}$ for the unborn generations with $t > 1$.

8.3 Calibration, simulation details and the policy rule

8.3.1 Benchmark calibration

We assume that the economically active life of an agent starts at age 25. Individuals work for $R = 40$ years until they reach age 65. They live for at most $D = 75$ years, until age 100. The discount factor β is set to 0.96, as is common practice in the macroeconomic literature (see, e.g., Imrohoroglu, 1989; Krebs, 2007). The coefficient of relative risk aversion γ is set to 3. While there is substantial uncertainty about the size of this parameter, this assumption accords quite well with the assumed risk aversion in much of the macroeconomic literature (see, e.g., Imrohoroglu *et al.*, 2003) as well as estimates at the individual level (for example Beetsma and Schotman, 2001). Further, we assume a rather large number of $I=10$ different skill groups in order to be able to also capture the consequences of the lowest skill groups not participating in the second pillar. The efficiency index $\{e_i\}_{i=1}^{I}$ is given by the income deciles in the Netherlands for the year 2000 taken by the World Income Inequality Database (WIID, version 2.0c, May 2008). We normalize the index to have an average value of 1. The seniority index $\{s_j\}_{j=1}^{I}$ uses the average of Hansen's (1993) estimation

---

[4] Certainty-equivalent consumption c_S under scenario S, i.e., the constant consumption level at all future dates of life and under all states of the world under this scenario, follows from

of median wage rates by age group. We take the average between males and females and interpolate the data using the spline method.

The social security parameters mimic the institutional framework in the Netherlands. For the first pillar, the Dutch Tax Office (*Belastingdienst*) reports for 2008 a maximum income assessable for contributions of 3,850.40 euros per month. We therefore set our upper income threshold for contributions to $\delta^u = 1.10$, which is roughly equal to 3,850.40*12/42,403, where 42,403 euros is our imputation for the economy's average income for 2008.[5] The lower income threshold is set to $\delta^l = 0.4685$, so as to generate an initial contribution rate of $\theta_1^F = 12.77\%$, identical to the initial second-pillar contribution rate $\theta_1^F = \theta_1^S$, which is calculated assuming that aggregate contributions at time 1 coincide with aggregate benefits in the absence of shocks. This value of θ_1^S is close to the actual value in the Netherlands. In our simulations we will cap θ_t^S at $\theta^{S,max} = 25\%$. We finally set the benefit scale factor at $\rho^F = 0.2435$.

For the second social security pillar, we set $z^e = 0.50$ for any level of the funding ratio F_t. Our choice roughly corresponds to the balance sheet average for Dutch pension funds over the past ten years (source: DNB, 2009). Because the bond and equity investments in the pension fund's portfolio generally have different realized returns, at the end of each period t the portfolio is reshuffled such that the system enters the next period $t+1$ again with the original portfolio weight $z^e = 0.50$. We set the pension accrual rate μ at 2% and the franchise parameter

$$V_{i,j,t}(S) = k_0 u(c_S) = k_0 \frac{c_S^{1-\gamma}}{1-\gamma},$$

where k_0 is some constant involving the individual's discount factor, survival probabilities and inflation rates. Hence,

$$CEC_{i,j,t} = \frac{c_B}{c_A} - 1 = \left[\frac{(1-\gamma)V_{i,j,t}(B)/k_0}{(1-\gamma)V_{i,j,t}(A)/k_0} \right]^{\frac{1}{1-\gamma}} - 1 = \left(\frac{V_{i,j,t}(B)}{V_{i,j,t}(A)} \right)^{\frac{1}{1-\gamma}} - 1$$

$$= u^{-1} \left(\frac{1}{1-\gamma} \frac{V_{i,j,t}(B)}{V_{i,j,t}(A)} \right) - 1.$$

[5] In Eurostat the most recent number on average income in the Netherlands refers to year 2005. The same source also provides the minimum income until year 2008. Exploiting the correlation between average and minimum income, we run an OLS regression of average income on minimum income. As a result, we predict the average income for year 2008 to be 42,403 euros.

λ at 0.381.[6] The choices of ρ^F and λ are meant to generate realistic replacement rates that on average are equal to 30.40% for the first pillar and 37.60% for the second pillar. The first-pillar replacement rate is higher for less skilled groups and ranges on average between 12.06% and 63.33% across the skill groups, while the second-pillar replacement rate is higher for more skilled groups and ranges on average between 3.78% and 56.64%. Overall, the total replacement rate from the two pillars is higher for more skilled groups and ranges on average between 67.11% and 68.70%.

Given the initial value of the second-pillar contribution rate $\theta_1^S = 12.77\%$, we choose initial assets A_0 so as to generate an initial funding ratio F_1 of 1.25 in the absence of shocks.[7]

The deterministic component of the growth rate of the newborn cohort, $n = 0.2063\%$, is the average annual growth rate based on the estimation of an order-one moving-average model for the annual number of births in the Netherlands over the period 1906–2005 (source: Human Mortality Database, 2009). Our calibration of survival probabilities is based on the estimation of a Lee and Carter (1992) model using Dutch period survival probabilities.[8] The combination of survival probabilities and birth rates determines the size of each cohort. The starting value of the old-age dependency ratio (i.e., the ratio of retirees over workers) is 20.99%, in line with the OECD (2009) figures for the Netherlands in 2005.

Crucial is the calibration of average price inflation, average nominal income growth and the average bond and equity returns. The

[6] The maximum accrual rate that is fiscally facilitated in the Netherlands is 2.25 percent for pension arrangements linked to average lifetime wages and 2 percent for pension arrangements linked to final wages.

[7] Initial assets A_0 are 1.4731 times aggregate income in the economy. This is on the high side compared with the actual Dutch situation. However, in our model every worker participates in the pension fund, while in the Netherlands this is only part (though a majority) of the employed. Moreover, a substantial fraction of the workers has its pension arranged through insurance companies, while the self-employed do not participate in pension funds either (they have the possibility to build up their own pension through an insurance company, but the financial reserves of insurance companies are not considered part of the pension buffers).

[8] With these probabilities, the average population age is initially set to 48.21 years and the remaining life expectancy is 33.54 years, as opposed to 33.23 years for a 48-year old in 2005 according to the actual data (see Human Mortality Database, 2009).

Table 8.1 *Benchmark calibration of the parameters*

Symbol	Description	Calibration
General setting		
D	Number of cohorts (= maximum death age -25)	75
R	Number of working cohorts (= retirement age -25)	40
β	Discount factor	0.96
γ	Relative risk aversion parameter	3
$\{e_i\}_{i=1}^{I}$	Efficiency index	WIID (2008)
$\{s_j\}_{j=1}^{I}$	Seniority index	Hansen (1993)
First-pillar pension parameters		
$\{\vartheta^l, \vartheta^u\}$	Income thresholds in the contribution formula	{0.469,1.10}
ρ^F	Benefit scale factor	0.2435
Second-pillar pension parameters		
z^e	Equity share in fund portfolio	0.5
$\{K^S, K^L\}$	Restoration periods	{5,15}
μ	Second-pillar pension accrual rate	0.02
λ	Franchise share	0.381
F_1	Initial funding ratio	1.25
$\theta^{S,\max}$	Upper bound on contribution rate	0.25
Annual averages of the random variables		
π	Inflation rate	2%
g	Nominal income growth rate	3%
r^b	One-year nominal bond return	3%
r^e	Equity return	5.5%

calibrated averages are reported in the final four lines of Table 8.1. We loosely follow the literature in this regard (see, e.g., Brennan and Xia, 2002; van Ewijk *et al.*, 2006) and set the average inflation rate at $\pi = 2\%$, the average nominal income growth rate at $g = 3\%$ (which corresponds to an average real productivity growth of 1% per year), the average one-year bond interest rate at $r^b = 3\%$ and the average equity return at $r^e = 5.5\%$.[9]

8.3.2 Simulation details

We simulate $Q = 1,000$ times a sequence of vectors of unexpected shocks over $2D - 1 + 250 = 399$ years, drawn from the joint distribution of all the shocks. Our welfare calculation is based on the economy as of the Dth year in the simulation. Hence, we track only the welfare of the cohorts that are alive in that year, implying that those that die earlier are ignored, and we track the welfare of cohorts born later, the latest one dying in the final period of the simulation. In other words, the total number of years of one simulation run equals the time distance between the birth of the oldest cohort that we track and the complete extinction of the last unborn cohort that we track. At each moment there are D overlapping generations. For convenience, we relabel the Dth year in the simulation as $t = 1$. The purpose of simulating the first $D-1$ years is to simply generate a distribution of the assets held by each cohort at the end of $t = 0$.

In each simulation run, we assume that the aging process stops after $t = 40$, by setting the trends in newborn growth rates and in survival probabilities to zero after $t = 40$, while the shocks to both processes and thus the demographic uncertainty still remain. Hence, also mortality rates at any given age no longer fall. For two reasons we stop the aging process after 40 years. First, it is hard to imagine that mortality rates continue falling for many more decades at the same rate as they did in the past. In particular, important common mortal diseases have already been eradicated, while it will become more and more difficult to treat remaining lethal diseases. Second, some important aging studies, such as those by the Economic Policy Committee and European Commission (2006) and the United Nations (2009), only project aging (and its associated costs) up to 2050 (hence 40 years from now), because the uncertainty in the projections becomes too great over larger horizons.

To allow for the cleanest possible comparison among the various policies, during each simulation run we use the same shock series for

---

[9] With these assumptions, the funding ratio, which is initially set at $F_1 = 1.25$, is equal to 1.16 after 75 years in the absence of shocks and policy intervention.

all policies, while, moreover, during the initialization phase of each simulation run no policy responses occur. Hence, the situation at the start of $t = 1$ (before choices are made) is identical in each run under the various policies. Specifically, at the start of the initialization phase all policy parameter values are set at their $t = 1$ levels (complete price indexation, zero productivity indexation and a constant contribution rate) and they remain unaffected during this phase. Further, at the start of the initialization phase the pension rights of all individuals are set to zero. During the initialization phase individuals accumulate pension rights according to (8.7), with zero indexation to productivity growth and full indexation to price inflation ($\iota_t = 0$ and $\pi_t = 1$), under the assumption that there are no shocks and income evolves according to Equations (8.1) and (8.2), with g_t thus being constant. After the initialization phase, at the end of $t = 0$, the process z_t is rescaled to unity and the nominal pension rights of all the individuals are rescaled by the same factor. Using (8.12) and (8.13), we can then compute total pension liabilities at the end of $t = 0$. Because welfare depends on the size of the buffer after the initialization period in the simulation run, we reset the stock of pension fund assets such that the buffer at the end of $t = 0$ equals 1.25. In other words, the assets and liabilities of the pension fund at the end of $t = 0$ are identical across all policy variants.

8.3.3 The policy rule

The baseline and the alternatives to be considered below are subject to various sources of suboptimality. First, instead of optimizing their decisions, individuals consume their disposable income. Second, we consider rules for the adjustment of the policy instruments that are not necessarily optimal, but that are intended to capture the main features of the policies imposed by the Dutch pension supervisor and followed by Dutch pension funds.

The government automatically adjusts the contribution rate $\theta_t^F \in [0,1]$ to maintain a balanced first pension pillar. On average, this contribution rate increases over the years along with the aging of the population.

More policy options are available to affect the funding ratio of the second pillar. There are three key parameters, whose period $t + 1$ values are determined on the basis of the funding ratio F_t in period t: the contribution rate $\theta_{t+1}^S \in [0, \theta^{S,\max}]$, the two indexation parameters $\{\kappa_{t+1} \in [0,1], \iota_{t+1} \geq 0\}$ and, as a last resort, a reduction in the nominal pension rights ($m_{t+1} < 0$). The board of the pension fund selects the contribution rate and the indexation parameters, but can only reduce nominal rights under special circumstances, as described below.

Policymakers start with a benchmark parameter combination $\{\theta_1^S, \kappa_1, \iota_1\}$ and a funding ratio equal to $\xi^m = 1.25$. We set $k_1 = 1$ (complete price indexation) and $\iota_1 = 0$ (zero productivity indexation). We define two threshold values for the funding ratio, ξ^l and ξ^u, with $\xi^l < \xi^m < \xi^u$ and $\xi^l > 1$. In particular, we set $\xi^l = 1.05$ and $\xi^u = 1.50$. All policies are identical when the funding ratio F_t is above ξ^m. In that case, after restoring possible earlier cuts in nominal rights, the fund's board sets the contribution rate at its initial level θ_1^S, price indexation to $k_{t+1} = 1$ and productivity indexation to $\iota_{t+1} = \dfrac{F_t - \xi^m}{\xi^u - \xi^m}$. Hence, productivity indexation increases linearly in F_t and becomes complete at θ^u; it continues to increase at the same rate as F_t rises above ξ^u. This way the funding ratio is stabilized from above.

As mandated by the Dutch Pension Law, when the funding ratio falls below ξ^m, but remains above ξ^l, a long-term restoration plan is started, while when it falls below ξ^l a short-term restoration plan is started. The latter situation is termed "underfunding." The long-term restoration plan requires a restoration of the funding ratio to at least ξ^m in at most $K^l = 15$ years (ignoring possible future shocks), while the short-term restoration plan requires its restoration to at least ξ^l in at most $K^s = 5$ years (ignoring possible future shocks). In the case of both a short-term or a long-term restoration plan, productivity and price indexation are always reduced first. If the adjustment is insufficient, the other instrument is also adjusted. Conform Dutch Law, when there is underfunding ($F_t < \xi^l$) and the adjustments in the indexation parameters and the contribution rate are jointly insufficient to eliminate the underfunding, nominal rights are scaled back by whatever amount is necessary to eliminate the underfunding within the allowed restoration period. In the case of a long-term restoration plan, nominal rights remain untouched.

8.4 Simulation results and comparisons

Financial instruments potentially help to protect against some specific risks. In principle, including such instruments in the pension fund's asset portfolio may reduce the overall volatility of the funding ratio and, therefore, limit the need for adjustments of the policy parameters. In this section, while keeping everything else unchanged, we compare the benchmark of a pension fund portfolio with long-term nominal debt with alternatives in which this nominal debt is replaced by, respectively:

- *price-indexed debt and inflation shocks only*, of which the yields depend on the actual inflation rate plus a fixed spread, $r_t^{lb} = \alpha^p + (\pi_t - \pi)$;
- *wage-indexed debt and wage shocks only*, of which the yields depend on the actual nominal wage growth rate plus a fixed spread, $r_t^{lb} = \alpha^w + (g_t - g)$;
- *longevity-indexed debt and demographic shocks only*, of which the yields depend on the difference between the actual and expected remaining life expectancies (which we denote by, respectively, T_t and $\tilde{T}_t$) of the population, $r_t^{lb} = (1 + \alpha^l)^{1-(T_t - \tilde{T}_t)}$. This way of modeling the return on longevity-indexed debt follows that in Blake and Burrows (2001).

We choose the parameters α^p, α^w and α^l so as to generate an average return on indexed bonds equal to the return on long-term nominal bonds, r^{lb}. This way our analysis is purely devoted to comparing the consequences of a reduction in the mismatch between the funds assets and liabilities, while keeping the expected path for the value of its assets unaltered. Hence, on purpose we ignore the potential difference in risk premia paid on the various types of debt instruments. Notice that the respective instruments provide high (nominal) returns when there are upward shocks in price, wage growth and life expectancy. As mentioned earlier, all asset returns are exogenous.

Below we first investigate separately the use of each type of indexed debt in the presence of only the shock that it is supposed to hedge against. That is, we focus on price-indexed bonds when there are price shocks only, wage-indexed bonds when there are wage shocks only, and longevity-indexed bonds when there are demographic shocks only (shocks to survival probabilities and the growth rate of the newborn cohorts). Finally, we explore the role of all types of indexed debt in the presence of the full menu of shocks.

8.4.1 Price-indexed debt and inflation shocks only

We first investigate the use of price-indexed debt in the presence of inflation shocks only. In such an environment price-indexed debt should be beneficial. After all, price-indexed debt is often promoted as an instrument to reduce the inflation risk of pensions. Figure 8.1 shows the median funding ratio under the benchmark and with price indexed debt. During the first ten years it rises, because income through contributions and asset returns dominates the outlays in the form of pension benefits. Due to the aging process after ten years the fund's outlays start to dominate the fund's income and the funding ratio starts to decline. Its decline is halted at the 125 percent level due to the restoration plans imposed by the supervisor. The median funding ratio remains essentially unaffected by the inclusion of price-indexed debt in the pension fund's portfolio. Comparing the volatility of the funding ratio under the two scenarios, we see that its median coefficient of variation is indeed quite a lot (one fifth to a quarter) lower with price-indexed debt.

Table 8.2 reports statistics on the funding ratio under the baseline and with price-indexed bonds. The volatilities of both assets and liabilities, as measured by the median coefficient of variation, are highest under price-indexed debt while, as expected, the volatility of the funding ratio is lowest. These facts are reconciled by the observation that the increases in volatility under price-indexed debt result from the density functions of both assets and liabilities becoming more skewed to the right, implying a larger frequency of relatively small values of assets and liabilities and, hence, less volatility in the ratio of assets over liabilities. The second panel of Table 8.2 reports the frequencies with which the funding ratio is below certain thresholds.

We observe that the likelihood of the funding ratio falling below $\xi^l = 105\%$ is zero, which is the result of the fact that inflation shocks alone are a relatively minor source of volatility in the funding ratio. The likelihood that the funding ratio falls below ξ^m is slightly lower under price-indexed debt than in the baseline case. In the third panel of the table we dissect the frequency of the funding ratio being below ξ^m into cases in which only the indexation rate needs to be adjusted, cases in which both the indexation rate and the contribution rate need to be adjusted and this adjustment is enough and cases in which the indexation and contribution rates are both adjusted, but this is insufficient for a (long-term) restoration plan. The cases are reported as frequencies of all the simulation observations. The fourth panel of the table reports average (over all observations) values of the policy

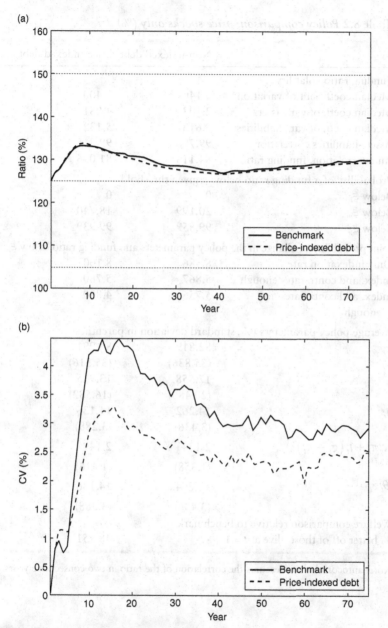

Figure 8.1 Fund properties: price shocks only
a. Median funding ratio b. Median coefficient of variation

Table 8.2 *Policy comparison: price shocks only (%)*

%	Non-indexed debt	Price-indexed debt
Funding ratio volatility		
Median coefficient of variation	3.140	2.400
Median coeff. of var., assets	2.103	4.081
Median coeff. of var., liabilities	3.613	5.132
Assets-liabilities correlation	99.796	99.815
Autocorrelation, funding ratio	84.118	81.046
Probability of a funding ratio below a given threshold		
Below ξ_l	0	0
Below ξ_m	20.199	18.740
Below ξ_u	99.859	99.939
Joint probability of change in the policy parameters and funding ratio below ξ_m		
Only indexation rate	8.586	8.100
Index. and contr. rates enough	5.867	5.760
Index. and contr. rates not enough	5.756	4.880
Average policy parameters (%, standard deviation in parenthesis)		
κ_t	82.819	83.991
	(35.836)	(35.316)
ι_t	17.558	13.925
	(20.480)	(16.582)
θ_t^s	14.262	14.136
	(3.436)	(3.288)
$\kappa_t \pi_t + \iota_t \left(g_t - \pi_t \right)$	2.134	2.147
	(1.358)	(1.416)
$\theta_t^s \tilde{z}_t$	14.264	14.136
	(3.436)	(3.288)
Welfare comparison relative to benchmark		
% better off of those alive at $t = 1$	-	48.751

Note: autocorrelation measures the correlation of the ratio in two consecutive years.

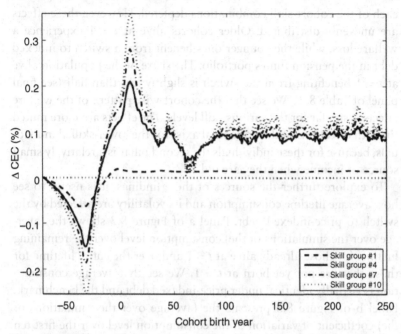

Figure 8.2 Welfare comparison: price-indexed bonds versus benchmark

parameters. The averages for the contribution rate and the rate of indexation to price inflation under price-indexed debt are rather similar to the benchmark, while the average rate of indexation to productivity improvements is somewhat lower. The volatilities of all instruments are smaller under price-indexed debt than under the alternative. However, the differences are small, except in the case of indexation to productivity.

Figure 8.2 depicts the cohort-specific welfare consequences under price-indexed bonds relative to the benchmark of non-indexed bonds. We are interested in separating the risk-sharing effects of switching to indexed bonds from the pure redistribution effects that may arise in the absence of shocks. However, the redistribution effects are zero, because in the absence of shocks the benchmark and alternative cases are identical. After all, in the absence of shocks, the returns on indexed debt are identical to those on long-term nominal debt. Therefore, Figure 8.2 displays the pure risk-sharing effects. We see that the welfare effects of using price-indexed debt are on average rather small for each of the cohort-skill combinations depicted. However, these effects are unevenly distributed. Older cohorts alive at $t = 1$ experience a welfare loss, while the younger ones benefit from a switch to indexed debt in the pension fund's portfolio. The share of the population alive at $t = 1$ benefiting from the switch is slightly less than half (see final panel of Table 8.2). We see that the cohort-wise pattern of the welfare effects is similar for the various skill levels. The effects are more muted (in both directions of the horizontal axis) for the lower-skilled individuals, because for these individuals the second pillar is a relatively small source of income when they are old.

To explore further the sources of these findings, it is useful to see how average lifetime consumption and its volatility are affected by the switch to price-indexed debt. Panel a of Figure 8.3 shows the (average over the simulations of the) consumption level over the remaining lifetime for those already alive at $t = 1$ and over the entire lifetime for those that are not yet born at $t = 1$. We see that average consumption is virtually identical under price-indexed debt and the benchmark. Panel b of Figure 8.3 presents the (average over the simulations of the) coefficient of variation of the consumption level over the first ten years of life for those not yet born at $t = 1$ and the first ten years of the remaining lifetime for those already alive at $t = 1$. Consumption variability is relatively high for the retired and the older workers. The reason is that the funding ratio starts at 125 percent, which implies a high chance that the older generations at $t = 1$ are confronted with restoration plans that involve reduced indexation of their pension rights and, hence, lower pension benefits. Table 8.2 reports the average pension contribution $\theta_t^p \tilde{z}_t$ (the contribution rate times its base) and its volatility.[10] Both are lower under price-indexed debt. As individuals consume their disposable income, changes in pension contributions translate directly into changes in consumption of workers. Hence, because pension contributions are more stable under price-indexed debt, consumption variability for those born after $t = 1$ is lower under this type of debt, which explains why those individuals benefit from the switch to price-indexed debt. The same pattern is observed if we

---

[10] Here, $\tilde{z}_t$ is "detrended income," given by $\tilde{z}_t = \left(1 + \varepsilon_t^g\right)\tilde{z}_{t-1}$, where we recall that ε_t^g is the shock to the nominal income growth rate. Because nominal income is growing at a positive average rate, we consider the product of the contribution rate and detrended income as a more suitable indicator of the impact of the pension system on disposable income.

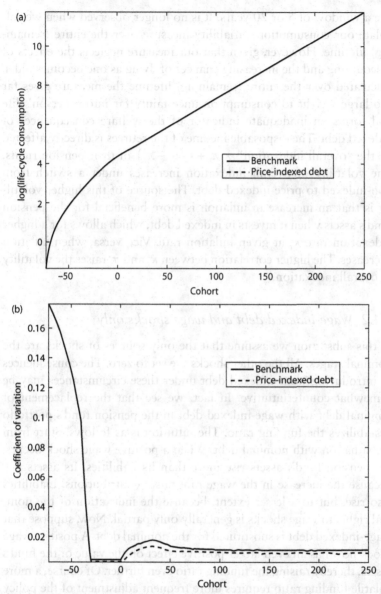

Figure 8.3 Household consumption
a. Average over lifetime b. Coefficient of variation over the next ten years

use a window of 5 or 20 years. It is no longer observed when we calculate our consumption variability measure over the entire (remaining) lifetime. However, given that our measure neglects the effects of discounting and the increasing chances of dying as one becomes older, calculated over the entire (remaining) lifetime the measure gives far too large weight to consumption uncertainty far into a person's life and forms an inadequate indicator of the welfare consequences of indexed debt. The disposable income of the retirees is directly affected by the "overall indexation" $\kappa_t \pi_t + \iota_t (g_t - \pi_t)$ of their pension rights. The volatility of overall indexation increases under a switch from non-indexed to price-indexed debt. The source of this higher volatility is that an increase in inflation is more beneficial for the pension fund's assets when it invests in indexed debt, which allows for a higher indexation rate κ_t at given inflation rate. Vice versa, when inflation decreases. The higher correlation between κ_t and π_t raises the volatility of overall indexation.

8.4.2 Wage-indexed debt and wage shocks only

In this subsection we assume that the only sources of shocks are the nominal wages. All the other shocks are set to zero. The consequences of introducing wage-indexed debt under these circumstances may be somewhat counterintuitive. In fact, we see that the replacement of nominal debt with wage-indexed debt in the pension fund's portfolio *de*stabilizes the funding ratio. The intuition is as follows. Start from the situation with nominal debt. When a positive wage shock occurs, the pension fund's assets rise more than its liabilities. Its assets rise because the increase in the wage rate raises contributions. Liabilities also rise, but to a lesser extent, because the indexation of the nominal rights to wage shocks is generally only partial. Now, suppose that wage-indexed debt is substituted for the nominal debt. A positive wage shock now has an even larger positive effect on the value of the fund's assets, thereby raising the funding ratio even further. Of course, a more volatile funding ratio requires more frequent adjustment of the policy parameters. However, this offsets only part of the increase in the volatility. The welfare effects of the switch from nominal to wage-indexed debt are again generally small for the various individuals in the economy and will not be discussed any further. Figures for the behavior of

Table 8.3 *Average remaining life expectancy*

t	$\bar{T}_t$	T_t, 90% conf. int.	r_t^{lb}(%), 90% conf. int.
1	27.3	(27.2, 27.3)	(2.82, 3.18)
20	28.9	(28.8, 28.9)	(2.73, 3.12)
40	30.5	(30.4, 30.5)	(2.75, 3.17)

the funding ratio, welfare and household consumption are available in the online appendix.

8.4.3 *Longevity-indexed debt and demographic shocks only*

In this subsection, we assume that the only shocks are those to the number of newborns and to the survival probabilities, which affect life expectancy. An unexpected increase in life expectancy raises the fund's liabilities and, hence, has a negative effect on the funding ratio. In the benchmark case with nominal debt assets are unaffected. However, by substituting the longevity-indexed debt for nominal debt the mismatch between assets and liabilities is reduced, because the value of assets rises in case of a positive life-expectancy shock. Indeed, the volatility of the funding ratio falls with the use of longevity-indexed debt. The profiles of average lifetime consumption and consumption variability are very similar to those under price-indexed debt and are not discussed here. The uncertainty of life expectancy around its average is rather limited, implying that the welfare effects of a switch to longevity-indexed debt for the various individuals are generally small. Also in this case, figures for the funding ratio, welfare and household consumption are available in the companion online appendix.

The small size of the welfare effects may not be surprising given that the amount of uncertainty to be hedged away is only small. Table 8.3 above reports the average remaining life expectancy $\bar{T}_t$, as well as the 90 percent confidence bands around this average. While $\bar{T}_t$ rises quite substantially (more than three years) over a period of four decades, the confidence band is very narrow compared with this increase. The confidence bands on T_t are also translated into confidence bands for the return according to the formula $r_t^{lb} = \left(1 + \alpha^l\right)^{1-\left(T_t - \bar{T}_t\right)}$. In view of the historical movements in nominal interest rates these confidence bands are also narrow.

8.4.4 Simulation results for full set of shocks

We now turn to the simulations of each type of indexed debt under the full set of shocks. The format in which the results are reported follows that in the previous subsections. Figure 8.4 shows the median funding ratio (panel a) and its volatility as captured by its median coefficient of variation (panel b) under the benchmark scenario and the three alternative cases. Again the median funding ratio tends to increase during the first ten years. However, the increase is much sharper than in the presence of a single shock only. The median funding ratio also remains higher over the median run and stabilizes at around 140 percent. Although the averages of the shocks are zero, the funding ratio is a nonlinear function of those shocks and, hence, the median with the full menu of shocks differs from that with a single shock only. In particular, because the funding ratio is regulated more strictly at its lower bound than at its upper bound negative shocks are more strongly offset than positive shocks, thereby on average pushing up the funding ratio upwards. While the median funding ratio exhibits rather similar patterns under the various scenarios, the figure shows that it tends to be somewhat less volatile under the alternatives to the benchmark of nominal debt.

Importantly, the volatility of the funding ratio is substantially higher than in the presence of a single shock only. The reason is that the various individual shocks feature low or zero correlation. In particular, shocks or groups of shocks do not offset each other. Hence, the presence of each of the individual shocks adds to the volatility of the funding ratio.

Table 8.4 reports statistics on the funding ratio under the benchmark and the three alternative cases. For the reason laid out above, the volatilities of both assets and liabilities, as measured by the median coefficient of variation, are higher under the alternatives than under the benchmark, while the volatility of the funding ratio is lower under the alternatives. The second panel of Table 8.4 reports the frequencies with which the funding ratio is below certain thresholds. Not surprisingly, there is now a non-negligible chance that the funding ratio falls below 105 percent. This likelihood is somewhat lower, though, under the

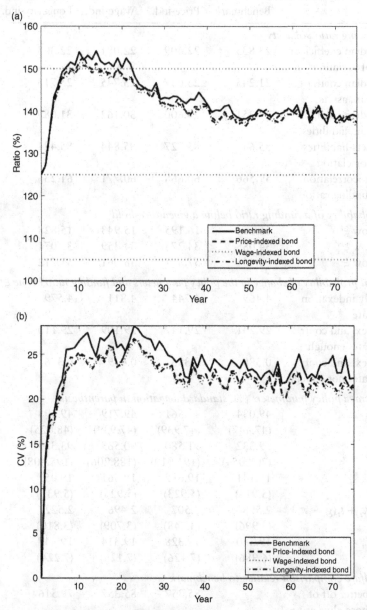

Figure 8.4 Fund properties: full set of shocks
a. Median funding ratio b. Median coefficient of variation

Table 8.4 *Policy comparison: full set of shocks*

%	Benchmark	Price-ind.	Wage-ind.	Longevity-ind.
Funding ratio volatility				
Median coefficient of variation	23.835	22.409	22.081	22.303
Median coeff. of var., assets	21.245	23.047	23.745	25.713
Median coeff. of var., liabilities	27.251	29.600	30.162	31.089
Assets-liabilities correlation	85.641	85.727	85.844	85.484
Autocorrelation, funding ratio	59.566	60.668	60.771	61.236
Probability of a funding ratio below a given threshold				
Below ξ^l	16.664	16.195	15.943	15.828
Below ξ^m	34.088	34.273	34.359	34.071
Below ξ^u	56.431	57.817	58.061	57.712
Joint probability of change in the policy parameters and funding ratio below ξ^m				
Only indexation rate	4.469	4.744	4.811	4.579
Index. and contr. rates enough	29.231	29.147	29.109	29.116
Index. and contr. rates not enough	0.388	0.383	0.439	0.376
Average policy parameters (%, standard deviation in parenthesis)				
κ_t	49.034	49.561	49.719	49.498
	(47.447)	(47.939)	(47.939)	(48.025)
ι_t	99.332	91.580	90.569	93.329
	(208.054)	(191.010)	(188.206)	(195.408)
θ_t^S	19.141	19.082	19.061	19.057
	(5.914)	(5.923)	(5.925)	(5.931)
$\kappa_t \pi_t + \iota_t(g_t - \pi_t)$	2.598	2.507	2.496	2.522
	(3.996)	(3.748)	(3.709)	(3.810)
$\theta_t^S \tilde{z}_t$	19.340	19.328	19.314	19.347
	(6.986)	(7.126)	(7.126)	(7.224)
Welfare comparison relative to benchmark				
% better off of those alive at $t = 1$		85.357	85.357	79.516

Note: autocorrelation measures the correlation of the ratio in two consecutive years.

alternatives than under the benchmark. Again, the fourth panel of the table reports average values (over all observations) of the policy parameters. The averages for the contribution rate and the rate of indexation to inflation are very similar over the various cases, while the average rate of indexation to productivity is somewhat higher under the benchmark. Also the volatilities of the contribution rate and the rate of indexation to inflation are very similar in the various cases. However, the alternatives to the benchmark benefit from a more substantial reduction in the volatility of the rate of indexation to productivity.

The final line of Table 8.4 reports the aggregate welfare consequences of including indexed debt in the fund's portfolio, as measured by the percentage of those alive at $t = 1$ that strictly prefer the alternative scenario to the benchmark one. The measure shows that around 80 percent or more of these individuals prefer a scenario in which the pension fund invests in indexed debt.

Panel a of Figure 8.5 considers the specific case of price-indexed debt and shows the welfare effects per cohort for some specific skill groups. The welfare consequences of moving from the benchmark situation to one in which the pension fund invests in price-indexed debt are positive for most cohort-skill combinations. Even most retirees are now better off. While the average overall indexation rate is lower under indexed debt, this effect is dominated by the reduced volatility of the overall indexation rate. The benefit of the shift to indexed debt is smaller for lower-skilled groups, because for them second-pillar income is relatively smaller compared with first-pillar income. Some skill-cohort combinations are worse off. This happens only for relatively low-skilled groups. In the absence of shocks the lowest-skilled group would be indifferent about the type of debt the fund invests in, because the wage of this group would never exceed the franchise. However, in the presence of shocks it sometimes does and the lowest-skilled group suffers from the slightly increased uncertainty about the pension contributions which for this group dominates the reduced uncertainty about indexation leading to a more stable benefit once they are retired. We find that the welfare effect is quantitatively never large, with a maximum CEC effect of 0.8 percent. In most instances the effect is rather modest. Panel b of Figure 8.5 shows the welfare effects per cohort for some specific skill groups for the case of wage-indexed bonds, while Panel c of Figure 8.5 shows those effects for the

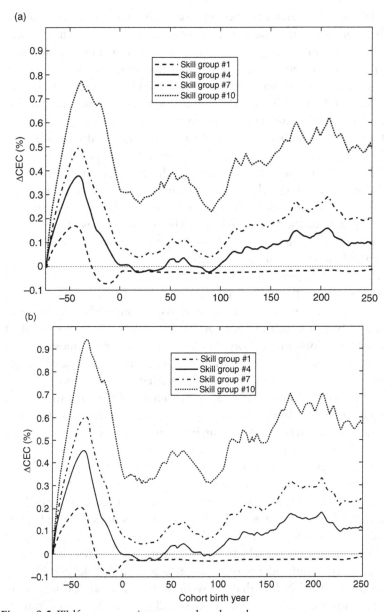

Figure 8.5 Welfare comparison versus benchmark
a. Price-indexed debt   b. Median funding ratio   c. Median coefficient of variation

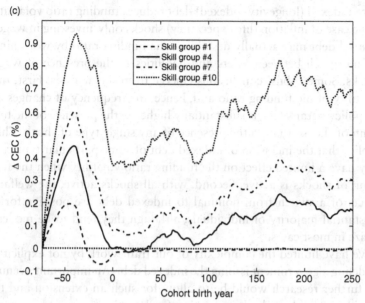

Figure 8.5 (*cont.*)

case of longevity-indexed debt. The patterns of the welfare implications are very similar to those for a switch to price-indexed debt.

8.5 Conclusions

In this chapter we explored the implications of replacing nominal debt with indexed debt in pension fund portfolios for both the behavior of the fund's funding ratios and the welfare of (groups of) individuals. We considered three types of indexed debt: price-indexed debt, wage-indexed debt and longevity-indexed debt. Our simulations were conducted using an overlapping-generations model of a small-open economy that was calibrated to the Dutch situation both in terms of pension arrangements and the shocks hitting the economy. To gain more insight into the effects of including indexed debt in the fund's portfolios, we first considered the different types of shocks (inflation shocks, wage shocks and demographic shocks) individually, before moving on to simulations in the presence of the full menu of shocks. The consequences of including indexed debt may appear somewhat counterintuitive to the proponents of investing in indexed debt. While price-indexed (longevity-indexed) debt reduces funding ratio volatility in the case of inflation (life expectancy) shocks only, investing in wage-indexed debt may actually destabilize the funding ratio by worsening the mismatch between assets and liabilities in the presence of wage shocks. Some robust conclusions emerge from the analysis. First, the volatility of the funding ratio and, hence, the frequency of changes in the policy parameters, is substantially higher in the presence of the full menu of shocks than in the presence of any single type of shock. This implies that the inclusion of indexed debt of some particular type can only have a limited effect on the funding ratio volatility when the full menu of shocks is active. Second, with all shocks active, the welfare effects of a switch from nominal to indexed debt are positive for a substantial majority of individuals, although they tend to be modest in size in most cases.

We have limited the complexity of our framework by not explicitly modeling a government issuing the indexed debt. An important avenue for further research would be to allow for such an extension and to consider individuals both as pension fund participants and payers of taxes to a government whose budget constraint is affected by inflation risk. In such an analysis we need to integrate the consequences of inflation risk for retirement benefits, pension contributions and tax benefits and we need to investigate how the overall effect of inflation risk on individuals' resources can be potentially mitigated if the government issues indexed debt that is (partially) held by pension funds.

References

Beetsma, R., and C. van Ewijk, 2010, Over de Wenselijkheid van de Uitgifte van Gendexeerde Schuld door de Nederlandse Overheid, Netspar NEA Paper 30.

Beetsma, R., and P. Schotman, 2001, Measuring risk attitudes in a natural experiment: Data from the television game show LINGO, *Economic Journal*, vol. 111(474): 821–48.

Blake, D., and W. Burrows, 2001, Survivor bonds: Helping to hedge mortality risk, *The Journal of Risk and Insurance*, vol. 68(2): 339–48.

Brennan, M.J., and Y. Xia, 2002, Dynamic asset allocation under inflation, *Journal of Finance*, vol. 57(3): 1201–38.

Bucciol, A., and R. Beetsma, 2010, Inter- and intra-generational consequences of pension buffer policy under demographic, financial and economic shocks, *CESifo Economic Studies*, vol. 56(3): 366–403.

Cocco, J.F., F.J. Gomes and P.J. Maenhout, 2005, Consumption and portfolio choice over the life-cycle, *Review of Financial Studies*, vol. 18(2): 491–533.

Dai, Q., and K. Singleton, 2000, Specification analysis of affine term structure models, *Journal of Finance*, vol. 55(5): 1943–78.

Datastream, 2009, www.datastream.com (accessed April 4, 2012).

DNB, 2009, www.statistics.dnb.nl (accessed April 4, 2012).

Economic Policy Committee and European Commission, 2006, The Impact of Ageing on Public Expenditure: Projections for the EU25 Member States of Pensions, Health-Care, Long-Term Care, Education and Unemployment Transfers (2004–2050), European Economy, Special Reports, 1.

Evans, C., and D. Marshall, 1998, Monetary policy and the term structure of nominal interest rates: Evidence and theory, *Carnegie-Rochester Conference Series on Public Policy*, vol. 49(1), 53–111.

Ewijk, C. van, N. Draper, H. ter Rele and E. Westerhout, 2006, Ageing and the Sustainability of Dutch Public Finances, CPB Special Publication 61.

Federal Reserve, 2009, www.federalreserve.gov/releases/H15 (accessed April 4, 2012).

Hansen, G.D., 1993, The cyclical and secular behaviour of the labour input: Comparing efficiency units and hours worked, *Journal of Applied Econometrics*, vol. 8(1): 71–80.

Human Mortality Database, 2009, www.mortality.org (accessed April 4, 2012).

Imrohoroglu, A., 1989, Costs of business cycles with indivisibilities and liquidity constraints, *Journal of Political Economy*, vol. 97(6): 1364–83.

Imrohoroglu, A., S. Imrohoroglu and D.H. Joines, 2003, Time inconsistent preferences and social security, *Quarterly Journal of Economics*, vol. 118(2): 745–84.

Koijen, R.S.J., T.E. Nijman and B.J.M. Werker, 2011, Optimal Annuity Risk Management, *Review of Finance*, vol. 15(4): 799–833.

Krebs, T., 2007, Job displacement risk and the cost of business cycles, *American Economic Review*, vol. 97(3): 664–86.

Krueger, D., and F. Kubler, 2006, Pareto improving social security reform when financial markets are incomplete!? *American Economic Review*, vol. 96(3): 737–55.

Lee, R.D., and L.R. Carter, 1992, Modeling and forecasting US mortality, *Journal of the American Statistical Association*, vol. 87(419): 659–71.

OECD, 2009, www.stats.oecd.org (accessed April 4, 2012).

United Nations, 2009, www.un.org/esa/population (accessed April 4, 2012).

WIID, 2008, version 2.0c, www.wider.unu.edu/research/Database/en_GB/database (accessed April 4, 2012).

PART III

Pensions and financial planning over the life cycle

9 Rational pensions for irrational people: behavioral science lessons for the Netherlands

ZVI BODIE AND HENRIËTTE PRAST

9.1 Introduction

This chapter argues that the pension system in the Netherlands should use insights from behavioral economics as well as financial technology when making the necessary changes for a sustainable pension scheme. Starting with Kahneman and Tversky (1979), behavioral scientists have convincingly demonstrated that many – perhaps most – people make serious cognitive mistakes that are systematic and predictable. In saving, investing and insuring for retirement, some mistakes can have very damaging consequences for these people and for society at large. In this chapter we analyze the most consequential of these mistakes, and we consider possible public policies to correct them or adapt to them. We focus on the Dutch context, drawing lessons from other countries where appropriate. We argue that it is the responsibility of institutions, including the government, employers and pension funds, to guide people in realizing adequate financial planning. We add to the existing literature by proposing the use of sensible defaults in both the second pillar and in retirement saving for the self-employed, and by arguing that employees should get limited choice not in input (portfolio) but in output (real living standard).

Throughout the industrialized world, pension systems are becoming unsustainable in their current form. They must adapt to longer

The authors would like to thank Richard Fullmer, Kent Smetters, Jan Snippe, Lans Bovenberg, Casper van Ewijk, Ed Westerhout, Jan Potters, two anonymous referees and the participants of the CPB-Netspar conference in The Hague in October 2010, for their comments on an earlier version of this chapter; the usual disclaimer applies.

life expectancies and a predictable increase in the ratio of benefits to contributions. Unless retirement investments can be made to yield higher rates of return, pension systems can be fixed only by lengthening working lives or increasing the rate of saving for retirement. The biggest obstacle to making the necessary changes in the system is wishful (even magical) thinking by the people directly concerned: the tendency to pretend that the problem does not exist or that some powerful entity – the government, the trade union, the employer or some other organization – will take care of it at little or no cost to them personally. Wishful thinking must be replaced with pragmatism. People must be made to understand and accept the need to save more, postpone retirement or both.

In the US and the UK, businesses that in the past have sponsored pension plans are shifting the responsibility to individuals. Investment companies, insurance companies and other financial service firms have responded with products and advice that have been hard for consumers to understand or trust. In the Netherlands the same demographic factors and behavioral patterns are creating a need to induce people to save more or postpone retirement. It has also been suggested that plan participants should bear more risk, and that guarantees should be reduced. In order to help citizens make sound decisions, institutions in the Netherlands are focusing on financial education and providing better pension information. Will this effort succeed? What can be learned from the experience in the US? What other approaches based on sound behavioral science might work?

The chapter is organized as follows. In the next section, we briefly describe the Dutch pension system and the challenges facing it now. In Section 9.3 we present the relevant behavioral findings about life-cycle saving and investing. In Section 9.4, these behavioral lessons are applied to the Dutch system and are used to assess current policy and to make suggestions for improvements. Section 9.5 summarizes and concludes.

9.2 Retirement plans in the Netherlands: a bird's eye view

The typical employee in the Netherlands has a career-average defined benefit (DB) pension. During the active working period accrued pension rights are still indexed to negotiated wage increases.

However, full indexation of pension claims to cost-of-living increases is not guaranteed, and even nominal "guarantees" are conditional on the coverage ratio of the pension fund meeting the government's minimum requirement. Hence employees are somewhat exposed to asset market risk.

The 2008 global financial crisis has made clear to policymakers that the current system – even with the changes introduced earlier in the decade – is unsustainable. Even those who support the social goals of the system point to some fundamental problems that have to be addressed. Changes are unavoidable.

Two committees of experts have produced reports and recommendations for reform. The Frijns committee recommended replacing the current focus on the nominal funding ratio by a framework in real terms (Frijns *et al.*, 2010). The Goudswaard committee concluded that either the target pension benefit level should be lowered, or workers should accept a higher risk of not reaching it. At any rate, it should be made clear to participants what risks they are bearing (Goudswaard Committee, 2010).

The latest reform proposals have tackled the issue of raising the age of eligibility for the first pillar of pension benefits – social security. In 2010, employers and employee organizations launched a plan to make changes to the current system in order to make it sustainable (Stichting van de Arbeid, 2010). As for the first pillar, the organizations have proposed increasing the eligibility age starting in 2020. For the second pillar they have reached an agreement to shift more of the cost from younger to older employees by putting a ceiling on premiums and reducing the level of guaranteed benefits.

Another challenge in the Netherlands is the growing group of self-employed who are not covered by an occupational plan – indeed, pension coverage among the self-employed is rather low. There are pension funds for traditional groups of independent professionals (by category, for example for specialized doctors), and all professionals are required to become a plan member if 60 percent of the profession agrees. However, there is no equivalent for the new self-employed who as a group are very heterogeneous and do not belong to a professional organization (as compared, e.g., to the traditional "guild"). This group is growing quickly for a number of reasons (de Jong, 2009; van der Lecq and Oerlemans, 2009). Digital technology and the Internet enable individuals to start a company from their "kitchen table" at low cost. Working mothers prefer the flexibility of their own business to the rigidity of being an employee. Employers like to hire the self-employed ad hoc in order to have flexibility and avoid the contractual rigidity associated with hiring employees. In 2009 the estimates of the self-employed vary (depending on the definition) between 250,000 and 810,000, out of which the majority have no employees and hence run their own business on their own. In 2007 the largest trade union in the Netherlands foresaw an increase of 50 percent within ten years (FNV, 2007)

9.3 Behavioral economics findings

With his remark that "God must love those folks that behavioral scientists write about because She created so many of them," the late Paul Samuelson underscored that the people described by behavioral economists are the rule, not the exception (Samuelson, 2006). Core findings in psychology and economics are that both in experiments and in the field people consistently deviate from the rational choice model in all of the following respects: they have nonstandard *preferences*, nonstandard *beliefs* and exhibit systematic and predictable biases in decision making.

Several excellent recent surveys of the behavioral economics literature have been published; see for example Camerer (2006) and DellaVigna (2009). The aim of this section is therefore not to provide a comprehensive review; instead, we focus on those behavioral economics findings that provide lessons for the Dutch pension system.

For the subject of this chapter, nonstandard time preferences and biased decision making are especially relevant.

As for *nonstandard time preferences*, the findings on self-control problems suggest that the discount factor in intertemporal choice is time-inconsistent. Under standard exponential discounting the relative utility of A over B in period t does not differ according to whether it is evaluated in period t or any other period $t–k$. Under hyperbolic discounting, the utility of A as compared to B does differ according to the time between the period of evaluation and the period of "consumption."

As for *biased decision making* in the pension domain, the status quo bias, default sensitivity, the omission-commission bias and the distortive effect of complexity on choice are particularly relevant.

Beshears *et al.* (2008) identify five circumstances that make it likely that revealed preferences – tastes that rationalize observed actions – do not correspond to normative preferences – what people would like to choose/should choose, given their preferences. These circumstances are the following:

(1) There is intertemporal choice with an immediate gratification option;
(2) Choice is complex;
(3) Passive choice (a "silent consent" option);
(4) Limited experience/little opportunity to learn from mistakes;
(5) Third parties take advantage of psychological biases of their clients.

In the field of personal finance in general, and in that of saving and investing for retirement in particular, these factors play a prominent role.

In addition to these circumstances, there are other behavioral biases and inconsistencies that are relevant for the domain of retirement. Inconsistent risk preferences (notably, myopic loss aversion) may lead to a portfolio that is not risky enough given long-run risk preferences, while the "gospel of stocks" – the conventional "wisdom" that stocks are safe in the long run – may lead to too much risk taking. Money illusion may distort perceptions in the pension domain and make people sensitive to the framing of guarantees. In the remainder of this section we discuss these biases.

9.3.1 *Intertemporal choice with immediate gratification*

Saving for retirement implies sacrificing current consumption. The notion that people find it difficult to stick to their plans is not new in economics. Paul Samuelson derived the optimal strategy for an individual who seeks to maximize lifetime utility. However, he made it clear that he regarded the assumption of time-consistent preferences as completely arbitrary:

[I]t is extremely doubtful whether we can learn much from considering such an economic man, whose tastes remain unchanged ... who seeks to maximize consumption only ... in a perfect world where all things are certain. (Samuelson, 1937, p. 160)

In *The Theory of Moral Sentiments* Adam Smith, when discussing intertemporal choices involving short-term gratification, described the willpower problem as a conflict between the "passions" that lead to short-sighted behavior, and the farsighted "impartial spectator" (see Ashraf *et al.*, 2005).

Yet, it is only recently that economists have systematically incorporated lack of willpower and self-control problems in their models of microeconomic behavior. The first to do so were Thaler and Shefrin (1981), who described decision making as a conflict between a planner, who aims at maximizing lifetime utility, and a doer, who behaves as a one-day fly. The self-control model and the hyperbolic discounting approach explain the empirical evidence that people delay saving for the distant future for much longer than their long-term preferences would suggest (Frederick *et al.* 2002).

Bounded willpower in the field of personal finance implies that even if people are well informed and have the intention to save more for retirement, they delay doing so. Obviously, this has implications for any policy aiming to help people make good choices (see Section 9.4 below). In fact, information and education seem at best to influence intentions only. Choi *et al.* (2002) find that after a financial education seminar 100 percent of participants announce that they will enroll in the companies' pension plan; in the end, a mere 14 percent actually enrolled.

Behavioral economics distinguishes between sophisticates – people who are aware of their willpower problem and look for self-commitment strategies – and naïves – people who believe they will have no difficulties changing their behavior, "tomorrow." An example of a commitment strategy in the pension domain is the SMaRT mechanism, whereby employees can sign a contract now in which they agree to start saving more for retirement two years from now (Thaler and Benartzi, 2004). The program resulted in a large increase in retirement savings, and Vanguard has adopted it (Stewart, 2005).

9.3.2 Complex choice

Economists have traditionally assumed that more choice is better. This view is now challenged, as it is clear that when there is "too much" choice, people are discouraged from choosing anything, or, if they are forced to choose, simply pick something (Schwartz, 2004). Complexity delays choice, increasing the fraction of consumers who adopt default options – see below (O'Donoghue and Rabin, 1999) – and it biases choice, since people tend to avoid complex options (Iyengar and Kamenica, 2010).

Research into pension portfolio allocation documents the "paralyzing" effect of increased choice. Huberman and Jiang (2006) study the records of more than half a million participants in more than six hundred pension plans that differ in the number of funds they offer (ranging from four to 59). They find that the median number of funds used is between three and four, and does not depend on the number of funds offered by the plans. Moreover, participants tend to allocate their contributions evenly (1/n) across the funds (the "1/n heuristic").

Not only does more choice hardly provide any advantages: it even reduces participation. Huberman *et al.* (2004) study participation decisions in retirement saving plans. They find that participation in plans offering ten or more funds is lower than that in plans that offer only a handful of funds. From a rational perspective this is counterintuitive, as a higher number of funds would increase the probability that the plan offers allocation possibilities in line with employee preferences. From a behavioral perspective, it confirms the relationship between complexity on the one hand and choice avoidance on the other.

That people tend to avoid choices when they are complex has to do with anticipated regret and the omission bias: the more options to choose from, the more people anticipate regret if they make the wrong choice (Schwartz, 2004). Providing more information and education does not solve this psychological problem. Or, as Redelmeier and Shafir (1995) put it: "Thinking harder will not eliminate a cognitive bias any more than staring harder will make a visual illusion disappear." Moreover, as Herbert Simon (1955) has pointed out, people may be distracted instead of helped by information.

9.3.3 Passive choice

People often choose not to choose. As a result, defaults (what you choose if you do not take action, silent consent) affect behavior. There are several explanations for the default effect. People may regard a default as the recommended choice by experts. They may interpret the default as the social norm (in the descriptive sense: what most people do, or in the injunctive sense: what most people approve of). Deviating from the default requires an effort, either in terms of time, money or psychologically. People may forget the deadline for taking action, or lose the form they need to fill in. People have an omission/commission bias: an active choice (act of commission) results in more regret if things turn out wrong, than a passive choice (act of omission (Potters and Prast, 2009)). As we have seen above, people tend to delay choice if it is complex, which in the case of passive choice implies choosing the default (O'Donoghue and Rabin, 1999).

The default effect exists for a wide range of domains, but it is especially prominent in life-cycle saving and investing decisions. It plays an important role in decisions regarding pension plan participation, the retirement savings rate, asset allocation and in the withdrawal of pension wealth when changing jobs or upon retirement. If the default is to not enroll – that is, the scheme is opt-in – employees are slow in becoming a plan member. If enrollment is the default, over 90 percent of new employees immediately participate in the company pension plan. The difference in participation is still high at two years of tenure: 25 percentage points higher under automatic enrollment as compared to a default of non-enrollment (Beshears *et al.*, 2005).

Automatic enrollment requires a default savings rate set by the employer. Madrian and Shea (2001), Choi *et al.* (2003) and Beshears *et al.* (2005) find that the default rate attracts a high fraction of employees. Note that because of this default rate effect, defaults can also reduce savings. If the default rate is set below the level that active participants would have chosen, the effect on total savings of an increase in the fraction of employees participating can be (more than) offset by the effect of a lower average savings rate per participant (Beshears *et al.*, 2005).

Defaults also affect behavior in the decumulation of retirement savings. In Switzerland, employees in DB schemes have no discretion in the accumulation phase. Upon retirement, however, they can choose between an annuity and a lump sum. Bütler and Teppa (2005) find that the company default has a major effect on the choice between the two.

9.3.4 Limited experience/little opportunity to learn from mistakes

People learn from their mistakes. By getting feedback, they invest in their choice capacity. However, there are domains and types of choice where the opportunities to learn are virtually absent. Saving for retirement is one of them. The 70-year-old who finds out that he has saved too little for retirement has no opportunity to benefit from this knowledge. Moreover, people hardly learn from others' mistakes. Choi, Laibson and Madrian (2005) show that the experience with Enron, Worldcom and Global Crossing – employees who lost both their job and their pension savings – did not affect the pension asset allocation of workers outside these firms. This may be due to cognitive dissonance – people will not face inconvenient truths – and to over-confidence – "it won't happen to me" (Akerlof and Dickens, 1982). A final reason why people do not learn from their mistakes is that private parties tend to exploit psychological biases (see below).

9.3.5 Third-party marketing

Behavioral economics argues that profit-maximizing firms can and do exploit the predictable inconsistencies and biases of their customers. Through contract design, pricing schedules and marketing techniques they exploit their customers' self-control problem, their status quo bias and their sensitivity to defaults and choice complexity (Samuelson and Zeckhauser, 1988; DellaVigna and Malmendier, 2004; Gabaix and Laibson, 2006; Agarwal *et al.*, 2009).

Automatic renewal of contracts and non-monetary transaction costs of switching exploit the status quo bias and default sensitivity of the customer.

Partitioned prices reduce consumers' perceptions of their total purchase costs (total cost of ownership, in business terms) and increase demand (Morwitz *et al.*, 2009). Moreover, even if the cost of add-ons were visible, naïve customers are attracted by the low base price because of their present bias.

"You can fool all of the people some of the time, and some of the people all of the time. But you can't fool all of the people all of the time." Well, perhaps you don't need to. If all customers were rational, firms would choose to unshroud their prices in equilibrium. However, as Gabaix and Laibson (2006, p. 509) put it:

Educating a myopic consumer turns him into a (less profitable) sophisticated consumer who prefers to go to firms with loss-leader base-good pricing and high-priced (but avoidable) add-ons. Hence, education does not help the educating firm.

Third-party marketing strategies abound in the financial services industry (Ausubel, 1999). Agarwal *et al.* (2009) show that life-cycle patterns in credit behavior follow a U-shaped pattern, with the cost-minimizing performance occurring around age 53. A likely explanation is that financial companies benefit from the fact that young borrowers are relatively inexperienced, and elderly borrowers have limited fluid cognitive abilities. Financial institutions compete for the "sophisticates," who are cross-subsidized by the "weaker" customers.

9.3.6 Further complications to retirement planning

In addition to the five circumstances mentioned above taken from Beshears *et al.* (2008) there are several other bias issues that complicate retirement planning.

Myopic loss aversion may lead to portfolio choices that are inconsistent with long-term risk preference, notably in the retirement planning domain (Prast, 2004).

Money illusion – defined as a tendency to think in terms of nominal rather than real monetary values – influences the way people react to variations in inflation and prices (Shafir *et al.*, 1997). The term nominal guarantees used in the Netherlands exploits money illusion, as it suggests that a guaranteed nominal pension income has meaningful economic value. The power of money illusion in the pension domain is obvious from the different reactions to the indexation implications of the low coverage ratio of pension funds on the one hand, and the protests against the announcement of nominal cuts to deal with the underfunding on the other (Prast and Snippe, 2010).

The time diversification fallacy

Time diversification is the idea that the riskiness of stocks diminishes with the length of an investor's time horizon and therefore the young should invest more heavily in stocks than the old. It is regarded as "gospel" among financial advisors and results in a bias towards investing in equities even for investors who ought to avoid them.

Finance theory indicates that no such simple rule applies in all cases. If investors act so as to maximize the expected utility of consumption over their lifetimes, then an investor's age per se has no predictable effect on the optimal proportion to invest in stocks. Robert C. Merton and Paul A. Samuelson have written many articles over the years explaining the fallacy (Merton and Samuelson, 1974; Samuelson 1963, 1989, 1994, 1997). Bodie (1995) uses option pricing theory to show that the riskiness of stocks – measured by the cost of insuring against the risk of earning less than the risk-free rate of interest – increases rather than decreases with the length of that horizon. Bodie's proof is valid both under the assumption of a random walk process for stock returns and for the mean-reverting processes reported in the economics and finance literature.

Rational asset allocation for individuals should be viewed in the broader context of deciding on an allocation of *total* wealth – human and financial – between risk-free and risky assets. A critical determinant of optimal asset allocation for individuals is the time and risk profile of their human capital. A person faces an expected stream of labor income over the working years, and human capital is the present value of that stream. One's human capital is a large proportion of total wealth (human capital plus other assets) when one is young and gradually decreases as one ages. From this perspective, the optimal strategy may be to start out in the early years with a high proportion of one's investment portfolio in stocks and decrease it over time as suggested by the conventional wisdom. The conventional wisdom, however, may not apply to broad classes of individuals who face substantial human-capital risk early in their careers. For such individuals, the *opposite* policy may be optimal – that is, to start out with a relatively low fraction of the investment portfolio in stocks and increase it over time.

Another critical determinant of the optimal investment in stocks is how close people are to some minimum *subsistence* level of consumption. People should be expected to insure against falling below such a level through their asset allocation policy.

9.4 Behavioral economics lessons for the pension system in the Netherlands

Behavioral economics has demonstrated that people often and predictably fail to make good decisions. In the previous section we have discussed under which circumstances people do not do what they would like to do/what they should do, given their preferences. We have also made it clear that those circumstances apply to life-cycle saving and investment behavior, and hence are of high relevance to the domain of pension savings. In this section we will discuss what these behavioral lessons imply for the pension system in the Netherlands. We address the following questions:

- Can financial education assist people in making better decisions in their life-cycle financial planning?
- Does it make sense to have a very large semi-compulsory pillar without much freedom of choice for employees and with a high level of mandatory annuitization?
- Should the second pillar make more use of defaults and, if so, how should they take account of differences in individual circumstances and preferences?
- What would this imply for the relationship with the third, voluntary pillar and how can we design better pension arrangements for the self-employed?
- What should be the role of the "pension register" that will provide information on individual pension rights by 2011, and what is the role of government regulation in this respect?

9.4.1 Education

In the past, both the government and the pension industry in the Netherlands have made it clear that they feel responsible for informing and educating citizens about financial decisions in general and pension issues in particular. Examples are the establishment of the Centiq platform on financial education and the – since 2008 – mandatory Uniform Pension Overview. The Pension Register is meant to give people easy access to information about their pension rights.

The assumption underlying a policy aimed at helping individuals make good choices by informing them is that well-informed individuals make choices that are consistent with their preferences. However, as we have seen in the previous section, revealed and normative preferences differ consistently in the domain of life-cycle saving and investing. In fact, the behavioral evidence indicates that information may affect intention, but is hardly enough to influence behavior. Some studies even suggest that education may be counterproductive. Instead of turning financial consumers into market players who are both motivated and competent to make financial decisions that maximize their own welfare, it may increase confidence without improving ability, leading to worse decisions (Willis, 2008). At any rate, education and information provision *by themselves* cannot address most behavioral problems.

Some argue that in a compulsory system it is important that trustees disclose to the participants why they select certain investment strategies, disclosure of information being essential to gain trust. In this view, efforts to provide more pension information in the second pillar are not so much driven by the desire to have people make better choices but rather by the desire to retain the trust and confidence of participants so that the second pillar keeps its legitimacy. However, most of the information provided focuses on individual pension rights, not investment strategies. Moreover, if the intention is to gain support, in our view the pension sector would have done better by avoiding terms like "nominal guarantees" which, as we have pointed out, set people on the wrong foot. Just as consumers are not expected to be their own doctors, they should not be their own financial experts, especially given the enormous gap between actual consumer skills on the one hand, and what would be needed to benefit optimally from today's (and tomorrow's) financial technology on the other. Nor can we expect to, or should we aim at, making people rational (Merton and Bodie, 2005).

The evidence presented in the previous section has made it clear that the institutional *design* of pension schemes matters very much for the pension choices people make, while information and education have a much smaller role – if any – to play when it comes to assisting people in making better decisions in their life-cycle financial planning. In our view any institutional design of pension saving should take these behavioral lessons into account.

Some might argue that Dutch employees have been "pampered" by a generous system of social security, and that if left to themselves, they will learn to become competent financial market participants. Van Rooij *et al.* (2007) find that risk aversion is especially high in the pension domain, and that the typical employee considers himself to be financially illiterate. Lack of exposure to self-directed savings plans and investments may go some way in explaining both the low level of self-assessed financial expertise and the high level of self-assessed risk aversion. However, US evidence indicates that financial illiteracy has not disappeared with the widespread introduction of individual defined contribution (DC) plans (Lusardi and Mitchell, 2005). Few participants in the US have really been successful in realizing their pension targets and many of them fall victim to agency problems, including the third-party marketing techniques described in Section 9.3 of this chapter. The US approach – government regulation of consumer credit, insurance and investment products based on disclosure and unfettered choice, accompanied by financial literacy campaigns – has not been successful. Moreover, it is important to keep in mind that where decisions are taken infrequently or even once in a lifetime, there is little scope to learn from mistakes. In fact, the behavioral evidence underscores that a carefully designed choice architecture does much more to help people.

9.4.2 Income differentiation

An important question is whether behavioral biases, such as the present bias and lack of willpower, are distributed uniformly over income groups or, alternatively, are more heavily concentrated among low-income groups. In the latter case, the optimal institutional design might differ across income groups. First of all, behavioral biases do not seem to disappear with higher education and/or higher income. Illustrative in this respect is the outcome of an experimental study by Choi et al. (2006) among Harvard staff (white-collar non-faculty employees) with many years of experience managing their personal finances, 88 percent with a college degree and 60 percent with graduate school education as well. Each subject was given $10,000 to allocate across four S&P 500 index funds and could keep the subsequent return net of fees. Harvard staff members failed to minimize fees, even after they had been given some specific financial education.[1] Performance was only slightly improved by education. As for automatic enrollment, US evidence indicates that the effect differs between income groups in the US: the increase in participation is higher for the lower income groups. Agarwal et al. (2009) find that, after accounting for default probability, income and education, economic mistakes show strong age-based patterns, even among prime borrowers, with the middle-aged doing better than the old or young. Their explanation is that firms compete

---

[1] I.e., one page of answers to the following questions: (1) What is a mutual fund? (2) What is an S&P 500 index fund? (3) What is the S&P 500 Index? In the basic treatment fees paid were on average.

for the sophisticate middle-aged consumer, who is then subsidized by the young who are inexperienced, and the old whose analytical abilities are lower.

As for the Netherlands, the Dutch Nibud institute for budgetary education, in cooperation with Wageningen University, has studied whether people regard their financial buffers as adequate. Although there are differences across income groups, with a higher fraction of lower incomes having buffers that they regard "too low," the study concludes that 10 percent of the *highest* income quartile in the Netherlands does not have the financial buffer that they think they should have (Nibud, 2005). Lessons regarding the relationship between income and portfolio choice can also be learned from the Swedish experience, which concludes that high-income employees who opted out of the safe default did choose highly biased portfolios with high management fees (Cronquist and Thaler, 2004).

Hence from a *behavioral* point of view there is no reason to differentiate the institutional design according to income groups. Obviously, financial mistakes hurt low-income groups more than high-income groups, and that might be a consideration to keep in mind when thinking of the optimal pension arrangement. That falls out of the scope of the present chapter, however.

9.4.3 Policy options for the Netherlands

What then are possible arrangements for the Netherlands that take account of behavioral issues, make optimal use of available technology and are in line with financial consumers' individual circumstances and preferences?

In answering this question, we distinguish between employees and self-employed. The proposed arrangements for these groups are somewhat, but not extremely, different. This should come as no surprise, as both groups suffer from the same behavioral biases, and the complexity of financial planning is also similar.

Employees
As we have seen in Section 9.2, for employees the current second pillar in the Netherlands is semi-compulsory. If an employer offers an occupational pension plan, employees have no choice but to participate, and as almost all firms offer a plan, over 90 percent of employees are "forced"

to be an occupational plan member.[2] Only nine out of 30 OECD countries have mandatory private pension schemes, and it is a fact that these countries show a high participation compared with countries with voluntary private pension schemes (van Els *et al.*, 2007).

From a rational economics perspective, one would conclude that the participation in countries with voluntary schemes corresponds to true preferences. However, one of the behavioral economics lessons is that the majority of people need and welcome mechanisms that help them overcome their lack of willpower and tendency to procrastinate. In fact, in the Netherlands a mere 20 percent of the self-employed (that is, those who are not forced to save) believe that they save enough for retirement, against 75 percent of employees (van Rooij *et al.*, 2007).

Does this imply that participation by employees should in the future continue to be mandatory? The evidence suggests that there may not be much difference in outcomes between making participation mandatory or making it the default option. Of the possible commitment mechanisms, a mandatory arrangement is the most "distortionary" compared with alternatives that take account of self-control issues and procrastination, like automatic enrollment and/or a SMaRT contract, or an even softer alternative, mandatory active choice: requiring employees to actively decide whether or not they wish to become a plan member. Choi *et al.* (2005) show that a mandatory active decision increases participation in pension schemes as compared to automatic non-enrollment (opt-in) by around 25 percent. Madrian and Shea (2001), Choi *et al.* (2003) and Beshears *et al.* (2005) find that the default rate attracts a high fraction of employees.[3] This implies that the design of defaults is crucially important.

Before the financial crisis, the majority of Dutch employees declared themselves in favor of the current mandatory system, the two main reasons being that they do not want to think about

---

[2] The only way that employees can choose between plans is by choosing the firm that they work for.

[3] Note that because of this default rate effect, defaults can also reduce savings. If the default rate is set below the level that participants would have chosen, the effect on total savings of an increase in the fraction of employees participating can be (more than) offset by the effect of a lower average savings rate per participant (Beshears *et al.*, 2005).

retirement saving, and that they are afraid that if plan participation were not compulsory, they would not save enough – the latter being evidence of awareness of a willpower problem (van Rooij *et al.*, 2007). Although the financial crisis and the pension problems that it has revealed no doubt have reduced trust in the current system and institutions, the typical employee still has a willpower problem, and does not want to think about his pension. Moreover, the typical Dutch employee feels he would not be able to manage a pension portfolio. He considers himself financially unsophisticated and is reluctant to take control of managing his retirement fund, even when offered the possibility to increase expertise (van Rooij *et al.*, 2007). Given that employees are happy with the current system being semi-mandatory, this could be the preferred solution over automatic enrollment and softer arrangements. As far as information and education are concerned, the evidence shows that they affect intention, not behavior.

As for the high mandatory annuitization, this seems to have the obvious advantage of preventing people from taking out too much money at retirement age due to the present bias. In our view introducing reverse mortgages for retirees would be more attractive.

Given the behavioral evidence, what we know about employee preferences in the Netherlands, and the risk shift to employees which exposes them to asset market risk, the optimal arrangement should help people deal with their present bias while at the same time give them some choice. This could be either by mandatory participation combined with some choice as to the level of risk, by automatic enrollment with a carefully designed default, or by a mandatory active decision with limited choice.

Assuming a "behaviorally sound" institutional design, we recommend use of financial technology to design mass customized personal pension contracts at the lowest possible cost. Current debates on financial products tend to focus on complexity of products as something to be avoided, at least for people who are not experts. In our view, having people make complex choices is indeed to be avoided both because of the behavioral issues outlined in the previous section, and because making optimal choices in the domain of retirement planning is too difficult. But this does not necessarily imply that individuals saving for retirement cannot benefit from financial technology – on the contrary (Prast, 2007). Given that the current mandatory participation meets with much support by employees, we would suggest keeping the current arrangement. However, in our view the employee should be offered meaningful choice regarding the minimum target income that he would like to see guaranteed, an income ambition combined with the risk that the ambition is not met, and his retirement age (Bodie, Ruffino and Treussard, 2008). This way, employees would have downside protection while benefiting from upside potential. Moreover, high-income employees (or those with a lot of financial wealth) would be free to choose a low minimum target combined with a high risk level (as well as a low retirement age) if they feel they can take care of pension saving and investing by themselves. This way they are not constrained by the mandatory participation. The risk of not realizing the (individually selected) minimum income level would be minimized by allocating the available assets and expected future contributions to the portfolio of fixed income investments that minimizes the mismatch between the expected asset returns and future contributions on the one hand and the cash flow requirements resulting from the selected minimum post-retirement income (or purchasing power) target on the other.

The second question that participants have to answer is about the desired income level that they wish to achieve as well as the risk tolerance with respect to this income. The optimal composition of the portfolio of more risky assets maximizes the probability of realizing that desired income level. This probability may be increased by selling the upside above the desired income level. In this case, participants would select their minimum required level (or replacement ratio). This results in a requirement on available assets and contributions, depending on the (real) interest rate. The distinction between a minimum income level that should be relatively safe and a desired income that may or may not be attained depending on asset performance is not with CRRA preferences, but it is consistent with a preference for protecting the downside (e.g., buying insurance) while at the same time keeping open the possibility of benefiting from the upside (buying a lottery ticket). Employees would not have to decide upon a frequency distribution, as they should be offered two alternatives to the safe default (e.g., the risk of not reaching the desired level is X percent).

Note that in this solution, the plan sponsor would not be the residual risk bearer, as it would be in a classic DB plan. Note also that the system combines individual contracts with mandatory participation as well as collective management and administration.

Smetters and Lin (2010) show how financial technology can be used to limit losses while benefiting from upside potential even when account is taken of behavioral finance findings and of fat tails/shocks that are not normally distributed. A strategy which caps maximum losses implies a portfolio that underperforms during small bulls, but outperforms a stock-bond blend with similar downside risk. As the purpose of investing for retirement is not to get rich, but to reach a standard of living at retirement, this is an appropriate strategy which is in line with the science of finance. Bodie, Ruffino and Treussard (2008) describe a mass customization process for the design and production of pension contracts based on Contingent Claims Analysis. Within such a mandatory arrangement with meaningful individual choice, there would not be much need for a third pillar, as employees can already choose their optimal solution within the mandatory plan.

Self-employed

The self-employed are, by choice, not part of a collective labor agreement. Hence it is difficult, if not impossible, both from a practical and principle point of view to make participation mandatory. However, their (self-assessed) savings rate is too low and they cannot be expected to make optimal saving and portfolio decisions. Their welfare could be improved either by enrolling automatically in a default plan, or by making active choice mandatory. This could be done when they apply to the Chamber of Commerce (*Kamer van Koophandel*) to set up their business in order to get a VAT number. For those who have initially chosen not to participate, the mandatory active choice could be repeated each time they fill in their tax statement.

We would be in favor of a single "public" plan, with administration and investment auctioned off to the private sector. As we have seen, more choice hardly provides any advantages: it even has been shown to reduce participation, due to the relationship between complexity and choice avoidance. We therefore recommend offering those self-employed who have indicated that they want to become a plan member (or, alternatively, who have not opted out) a plan with limited choice, in line with the meaningful choice which in our view should be offered within the occupational pillar that we envisage (see above).

Our solution differs from the proposal by the Goudswaard committee, which suggests that for the second pillar the Dutch choose between either a lower, but guaranteed pension income for all, or a higher, but risky pension for all. A low guaranteed income will not be sufficient for many (if not all) employees. In order to prepare optimally for retirement, these employees would have to search individually for an additional pension (third pillar). The behavioral evidence indicates that not much good is expected to come out of this. As for the alternative, a higher but riskier pension, it is in our view suboptimal to expose employees to asset market risk without giving them a say in how much risk they find acceptable. Moreover, given the low risk tolerance in the pension domain (Prast *et al.*, 2005) many employees would have to go out to search for insurance, which we know they wouldn't. The lower incomes would be the most vulnerable in this system.

A behaviorally sound design would be to enroll participants in a sensible default with a lot of protection, and give them two riskier alternatives. The effect of myopic loss aversion – a level of risk that is too low given preferences – can be prevented if participants are not given the possibility of evaluating their portfolio. Most people never look at their DC plans again anyway, after setting them up (Merton, 2010). Our institutional arrangement would enable participants to benefit from scale advantages. Additional efficiency gains may also be realized through the collective purchase and/or insurance of annuities. The guarantees should be in real terms or in replacement rates rather than nominal amounts; this requires more supply of index-linked bonds than is currently available

It is sometimes argued that individually tailored contracts would be prohibitively expensive: employees would not be willing to pay the premiums needed. Bovenberg *et al.* (2007) argue that the costs of collective plans are usually lower than the costs associated with individual pension plans. They point to the time-consuming search by customers and the marketing costs incurred by financial intermediaries, indicating that the additional costs amount to almost 1 percent of financial wealth.

We would like to point out that collectiveness does not automatically imply solidarity. The present system in the Netherlands is a case in point: by pooling resources, the system makes sure that higher incomes (with on average higher life expectancy) are subsidized by lower incomes (who on average live shorter).

We agree that customized contracts provided at the individual level by intermediaries are costly. However, the institutional arrangement for the personal pensions that we envisage does not have to entail higher costs and lower efficiency. Semi-customized fully hedged contracts designed and guaranteed by low transaction cost financial intermediaries can be offered at a low price to high transaction cost financial consumers (Bodie, Ruffino and Treussard, 2008). If these contracts are offered to groups of employees as defaults, they can be designed to take account of needs and circumstances shared by all members of the group. In doing so, the default sensitivity in the retirement planning domain can be put to good use in the interest of the financial consumer (Beshears *et al.*, 2005, 2008; Kooreman and Prast, 2010). Similarly, the plan for the self-employed could offer a basic minimum target pension as default, and an additional ambition level combined with the risk tolerance not to reach it. At first sight the group of self-employed is perhaps more heterogeneous than that of employees in a given firm or industry (de Jong, 2009). However, the self-employed have many characteristics in common: they tend to be mostly of a below-average age, are more often women and have partners who earn a labor income. Some of them may have deliberately chosen to become self-employed, others may have been forced to do so because they did not find a job. They typically tend to prefer flexibility in contribution levels and may prefer liquid saving over illiquid pension saving given that they have no contract rights, a volatile income and no social insurance. However, they state that their pension savings are too low and need to save for retirement anyway. Moreover, by having them enroll automatically and then choose their minimum target income, they have flexibility while at the same time the threshold for starting to save for retirement is low.

The powerful effect of choice architecture requires that this architecture is designed carefully. As Bovenberg and Nijman (2009) correctly point out, to make further progress here, more research needs to be done, for example by using microeconometric data to document heterogeneity across individuals.

For the collectively managed individual personal pension plans that we envisage, defaults could be designed for relatively homogeneous groups depending on relevant objective and easily observable characteristics that are relevant for optimal saving and investing. Goda and Manchester (2010), study the effect of an age-based default rule for the choice between remaining in a DB plan or switching (irrevocably) to a DC plan within the same firm, using data from a large employer that transitioned from a (DB) plan to a DC plan and offered existing employees a choice of plans. Employees who did not make an active choice were defaulted according to the following rule: switch to the DC plan if under age 45, remain in the DB plan if age 45 or older. The default had a considerable effect: it increased the probability of enrolling in one plan over the other by 60 percentage points. Moreover, for a broad range of levels of risk aversion, conditioning the default for the choice between pension plans on age can substantially improve welfare as compared to a uniform default. Other welfare gains are possible by varying defaults according to observable characteristics. In the case that the Netherlands would like to switch from the current system to an infrastructure where risks are more explicitly shifted toward pension rights, one way of doing so would be to offer an age-based default rule for enrollment in the new system.

In addition to easily observable and objective characteristics, additional relevant characteristics may be used to further improve the "match" between default and plan participants. Goldstein *et al.* (2008) and Dinner and Goldstein (2010) distinguish between the following types of defaults:

- Simple defaults: A default configuration set by the policymaker;
- Forced choice: Ask user one or more questions to determine the default;
- Random defaults: Choose a default randomly from several alternatives;
- Sensory defaults (If-then rules): Choose among multiple defaults based on any available data.

Clearly, simple defaults can be applied if the population that the default it is meant for is very homogeneous. Random defaults are unlikely to optimize welfare for any type of population, although it may be an improvement relative to a non-participation default. Forced choice requires an effort from the employee, but should be an improvement relative to non-participation. Employers already have some information available about their employees – age, income, type of job (hence riskiness of human capital and exposure to stock market risk) and usually some additional information as well either directly or through

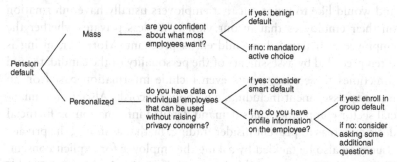

Figure 9.1 Pension plan decision tree

collective arrangements (health insurance, which would reveal whether the employee has a spouse and/or children). Therefore, sensory defaults should not be too difficult to offer, and once employees are defaulted into a plan based on these data, further refinement and personalization could be applied by asking additional questions (does your spouse work? do you have financial capital exceeding amount X? do you own a home ...).

Goldstein *et al.* (2008) suggest a decision tree for firms which would like to optimally and efficiently service their customers. Figure 9.1 is inspired by their idea, and adapted to pension defaults. It can be used for participation, premium, portfolio and decumulation defaults.

For participation, it is most likely that the decision tree will lead to a benign default of standard enrollment. For the saving rate and portfolio choice, either (with mass default) mandatory choice or (with personalized default) one of the other options. For decumulation, depending on general preferences either an annuity default or mandatory choice (mass default) or a more personalized default. Depending on the available information to the employer or pension fund personalized choices may be feasible.

In the Netherlands, the pension register would be helpful in bringing together individual pension wealth accumulated in various occupations. Efficiency might be further improved by obtaining data on income and wealth through tax data (after consent from individual employees). This suggestion often meets with criticism because of privacy issues: the employer or other institution taking care of the pension administration would be informed about, for instance, the wealth status of the plan participant. We are not convinced by this argument and would like to point out that employers usually have information on their employees that in our view is no less private: whether the employee is married, has children, is pregnant. Moreover, hiring is often preceded by assessments of the personality of the candidate, and sometimes these assessments even include information based on an integrity assessment including, e.g., police records. Also, in the financial sector compliance rules demand detailed information on financial decisions so as to prevent insider trading. Be that as it may, the privacy issue may also be tackled by asking the employee for explicit consent. The pension register that is being set up in the Netherlands could also be used to this end. Given the behavioral evidence on education, intention and actual behavior, we do not expect much from the register if it is not accompanied by default-type mechanisms to facilitate additional pension saving by those who do not save adequately.

Summing up, we envisage a pension plan which has the simplicity the participant needs given both his behavioral biases and the fact that making optimal life-cycle saving and investment decisions is highly complicated, but within a DC-type institutional structure (Merton, 2006).

9.5 Conclusion

In this chapter we have addressed a number of questions relating to the future of the pension system in the Netherlands. In doing so, we have benefited from the insights of behavioral economics. Core findings in psychology and economics are that people deviate from the rational choice model in *all of the following respects*: they have nonstandard time, risk and social preferences; they are systematically biased in the gathering and processing of information; and they exhibit systematic and predictable biases in decision making. In addition to behavioral biases that would complicate decision making even among simple products, the area of life-cycle saving and investing is too complex to provide financial consumers with information, and then leave it to them to make good decisions. At the same time, financial technology could (and, in our view, should) be used to design optimal (semi-) individual contracts at low cost.

The first question was whether financial education assists people in making better decisions in their life-cycle financial planning. First of all, the evidence indicates that financial education often has merely an effect on intention, not behavior. This has to do with the behavioral fact that people tend to lack willpower to follow up on their plans. Worse even, a growing number of studies find a counterproductive effect of financial education. This has to do partly with the fact that overconfidence increases with education. Moreover, in our view it is as unrealistic to make employees and self-employed their own pension experts as it is to make patients their own doctors. At the same time, much is to be gained from more secondary education on risk and risk management as well as on psychological biases and decision making.

The second question we addressed was whether it makes sense to have a very large semi-compulsory pillar without much freedom of choice for employees, and with a high level of mandatory annuitization. In our view, the large semi-compulsory pillar has the "behavioral" advantage that employees cannot procrastinate in saving for retirement. The international evidence makes clear that not much good is to be expected from leaving it to individual employees to take action to save and invest for their pension. No doubt the system of semi-compulsory saving in the second pillar leads to higher saving rates than would be the case in the absence of such a system. However, this is not because employees are forced to save more than they want, but because in the absence of this pillar they would save less than they want. Mandatory annuitization is likely to improve welfare for the vast majority of employees, because upon retirement the self-control problem might induce people to take out their savings as a lump sum and spend more than is in line with their normative preferences.

The third question was whether the second pillar should make more use of defaults and, if so, how defaults should take account of differences in individual circumstances and preferences. Despite the advantages that mandatory participation offers for the reasons stated above, the current second-pillar plans in the Netherlands have the flaw that they are not tailored to individual needs and preferences, are less attractive for younger employees, are not robust to an aging labor force, and expose employees to asset market risk even up to the point where nominal claims are not guaranteed. Evidence shows that ample choice does not improve the match between employees' preferences and portfolio characteristics. Therefore, within this mandatory (at the firm or industry level) system we propose limited, meaningful choice for the employee. He should be able to choose his retirement age, minimum target income and aspirational income consistent with his tolerance for a shortfall. Within this framework there could be a carefully designed default (both for minimum and aspirational income levels, retirement age and risk tolerance). In our view a mandatory system requires that employees be protected against stock market risk. One way to do so is by making a safe portfolio (guaranteed real pension) the default. This default will require a relatively high level of contributions. For those opting out of the default in the second pillar, a limited number of alternatives regarding risk should be available. These offer the expectation of lower contributions, but carry the risk that contributions will turn out higher or benefit levels lower than with the safe option.

A semi-compulsory second pillar with meaningful choice is likely to offer enough possibilities for most employees to adequately save and invest for retirement. However, some employees may want to save more, or invest differently, than is possible in the second pillar. Moreover, the self-employed do not have access to an occupational second pillar. Behavioral biases and the complexity of financial decision making apply no less to the self-employed than to employees. In the latter case, choice should be limited in order to increase participation. Better pension arrangements in the third pillar for the self-employed would make use of either default participation or mandatory active choice, e.g., upon request of a VAT number. This would require a default contribution rate and portfolio composition. These would have to take into account similar data as those that are to be used for sensible employee defaults in the third pillar, but also the fact that the returns on human capital of the self-employed are less steady than those of employees.

The Pension Register contains information regarding individual employees' retirement savings at different employers. The Register is meant to inform employees. However, given the behavioral evidence it is extremely unlikely that individual employees will (be able to) make optimal use of it. However, the information in the Register could be used as a source of information to construct optimal defaults in the second and third pillar, especially if combined with tax statements. The role of the government would be to facilitate data collection and disclosure in this respect. An example would be the provision of tax data on a silent consent basis. Combining these data with those in the Pension Register would provide a rich database for designing defaults at a group and even individual level.

References

Agarwal, S., J.C. Driscoll, X. Gabaix and D. Laibson, 2009, The age of reason: Financial decisions over the life cycle and implications for regulation, *Brookings Papers on Economic Activity*, vol. 40(2): 51–117.

Akerlof, G., and W.T. Dickens, 1982, The economic consequences of cognitive dissonance, *American Economic Review*, vol. 72(3): 307–14.

Ashraf. N., C. Camerer and G. Loewenstein, 2005, Adam Smith, behavioral economist, *The Journal of Economic Perspectives*, vol. 19(3): 131–45.

Ausubel, L.M., 1999, *Adverse Selection in the Credit Card Market*, Mimeo, University of Maryland, College Park.

Beshears, J., J.J. Choi, D. Laibson and B.C. Madrian, 2005, The Importance of Default Options for Retirement Savings Outcomes: Evidence from the United States, NBER Working Paper 12009.

2008, How are preferences revealed?, *Journal of Public Economics*, vol. 92(8–9): 1787–94.

Bodie, Z., 1995, On the risk of stocks in the long run, *Financial Analysts Journal*, vol. 5(3): 18–22.

Bodie, Z., D. Ruffino and J. Treussard, 2008, Contingent claims analysis and life-cycle finance, *American Economic Review: Papers & Proceedings*, vol. 98(2): 291–96.

Bovenberg, A.L., and T.E. Nijman, 2009, Developments in pension reform: The case of Dutch stand-alone collective pension schemes, *International Tax and Public Finance*, vol. 16(4): 443–67.

Bovenberg, A.L., T.E. Nijman, C. Teulings and R. Koijen, 2007, Saving and Investment over the Life Cycle: The Role of Individual and Collective Pension Funds, Netspar Panel Paper 1 – July.

Bütler, M. and F. Teppa, 2005, Should You Take a Lump-sum or Annuitize? Results from Swiss Pension Funds, CEPR Discussion Papers 5316.

Camerer, C., 2006, Behavioral Economics, in: R. Blundell, W. Newey and T. Persson (eds.), *Advances in Economics and Econometrics: Theory and Applications*, Ninth World Congress of the Econometric Society, Vol. II.

Choi, J.J., D. Laibson and B. Madrian, 2005, Are empowerment and education enough? Under-diversification in 401(k) plans, *Brookings Papers on Economic Activity*, vol. 2: 151–98.

2006, Why Does the Law of One Price Fail? An Experiment on Index Mutual Funds, NBER Working Paper 12261.

Choi, J.J., D. Laibson, B. Madrian and A. Metrick, 2002, Defined Contribution Pensions: Plan Rules, Participant Decisions, and the Path of Least Resistance, in: J. Poterba (ed.), *Tax Policy and the Economy*, vol. XVI: 67–114.

2003, Passive Decisions and Potent Defaults, NBER Working Paper 9917.

2005, Optimal Defaults and Active Decisions, NBER Working Paper 11074.

Cronquist, H., and R. Thaler, 2004, Design Choices in Privatized Social-Security Systems: Learning from the Swedish Experience, American Economic Association Papers and Proceedings, May.

DellaVigna, S., 2009, Psychology and economics: Evidence from the field, *Journal of Economic Literature*, vol. 47 (2): 315–72.

DellaVigna, S., and U. Malmendier, 2004, Contract design and self-control: Theory and evidence, *Quarterly Journal of Economics*, vol. 119(2): 353–402.

Dinner, I., and D. Goldstein, 2010, Partitioning Default Effects: Why People Choose Not to Choose, paper presented at the Transforum Conference on Multiple Selves and Sustainability, Amsterdam, November.

Els, P.J.A. van, M.C.J. van Rooij and M.E.J. Schuit, 2007, Why mandatory retirement saving?, in: O.W. Steenbeek and S.G. van der Lecq (eds.), *Costs and Benefits of Collective Pension Systems*, Springer, Berlin, 159–86.

FNV, 2007, De Dynamische Driehoek, zzp'ers en de FNV, February.

Frederick, S., G. Loewenstein and T. O'Donoghue, 2002, Time discounting and time preference: A critical review, *Journal of Economic Literature*, vol. 40(2): 351–401.

Frijns, J.M.G., J.A. Nijssen and L.J.R. Scholtens, 2010, Pension: Uncertain security, Investment Policy and Risk Management Committee, An analysis of the investment policy and risk management of Dutch pension funds, Eindhoven/The Hague/Wognum.

Gabaix, X., and D. Laibson, 2006, Shrouded attributes, consumer myopia, and information suppression in competitive markets, *The Quarterly Journal of Economics*, vol. 121: 505–40.

Goda, G.S., and C.F. Manchester, 2010, Incorporating Employee Heterogeneity Into Default Rules For Retirement Plan Selection, Working Paper Crr Wp 2010–6, Center for Retirement Research at Boston College/NBER Working Paper 16099.

Goldstein, D.G., E.J. Johnson, A. Herrmann and M. Heitmann, 2008, Nudge your customers toward better choices, *Harvard Business Review*, vol. 86(12): 99–105.

Goudswaard Committee (Committee on the Sustainability of Supplementary Pension Schemes), 2010, A Strong Second Pillar – Toward a Sustainable System of Supplementary Pensions, The Hague.

Huberman, G., and W. Jiang, 2006, Offering versus choice in 401(K) plans: Equity exposure and number of funds, *Journal of Finance*, vol. 61(2): 763–801.

Huberman, G., S.S. Iyengar and W. Jiang, 2004, How Much Choice Is Too Much: Determinants of Individual Contributions in 401K Retirement

Plans, in: O.S. Mitchell and S.P. Utkus (eds.), *Pension Design and Structure: New Lessons From Behavioral Finance*, Oxford University Press, 83–96.

Iyengar, S.S., and E. Kamenica, 2010, Choice proliferation, simplicity seeking, and asset allocation, *Journal of Public Economics*, vol. 94(7–8): 530–39.

Jong, Frank de, 2009, Towards a Flexible Pension Scheme for Self-employed Workers, NEA Paper 23, Netspar.

Kahneman, D., and A. Tversky, 1979, Prospect theory: An analysis of decision making under risk, *Econometrica*, vol. 47(2): 263–91.

Kooreman, P., and H. Prast, 2010, What Does Behavioral Economics Mean for Policy? Challenges to Savings and Health Policies in the Netherlands, *De Economist*, vol. 158(2): 101–22.

Lecq, Fieke van der, and Alwin Oerlemans, 2009, Zelfstandigen zonder pensioen, NEA Paper 24, Netspar.

Lusardi, A., and O.S. Mitchell, 2005, Financial Literacy and Planning: Implications for Retirement Wellbeing, DNB Working Paper 78.

Madrian, B.C., and D.F. Shea, 2001, The power of suggestion: Inertia in 401(k) participation and savings behavior, *The Quarterly Journal of Economics*, vol. 116(4): 1149–87.

Merton, R.C., 2006, Observations on innovation in pension fund management in the impending future, *PREA Quarterly*, Winter.

2010, Solutions for the future, *Pension Insight*, February.

Merton, R.C., and Z. Bodie, 2005, Design of financial systems: Towards a synthesis of function and structure, *Journal of Investment Management*, vol. 3(1): 1–23.

Merton, R.C., and P.A. Samuelson, 1974, Fallacy of the log-normal approximation to portfolio decision-making over many periods, *Journal of Financial Economics*, vol. 1(1): 67–94.

Morwitz, V.G., E. Greenleaf, E. Shalev and E. Johnson, 2009, The Price does not Include Additional Taxes, Fees, and Surcharges: A Review of Research on Partitioned Pricing (February 26). Available at SSRN: http://ssrn.com/abstract=1350004 or doi:10.2139/ssrn.1350004 (accessed April 4, 2012).

Nibud, 2005, *Geldzaken in de praktijk*, March, www.nibud.nl (accessed April 4, 2012).

O'Donoghue, T., and M. Rabin, 1999, Doing it now or later, *American Economic Review*, vol. 89(1): 103–24.

Potters, J.J.M., and H.M. Prast, 2009, Gedragseconomie in de praktijk, in: T. Tiemeijer and H. Prast (eds.), *De menselijke beslisser- over de psychologie van keuze en gedrag*, WRR/Amsterdam University Press, The Hague/Amsterdam, 47–62.

Prast, H.M., 2004, Investor Psychology: Six Puzzles of Finance, Research Series Supervision 64, De Nederlandsche Bank, March.

2007, Complexe producten: wat kunnen ze betekenen en wie moet ze begrijpen? Over financiële educatie en de verantwoordelijkheid van instituties, De Nederlandsche Bank, Amsterdam.

Prast, H., and J. Snippe, 2010, De kruik gaat zo lang te water tot zij barst, *NRC Handelsblad*, September 6.

Prast, H., M. van Rooij and C. Kool, 2005, Werknemer kan en wil niet zelf beleggen voor pensioen, *Economisch Statistische Berichten* vol. 90(4458): 172–75.

Redelmeier, D., and E. Shafir, 1995, Medical decision making in situations that offer multiple alternatives, *Journal of the American Medical Association*, vol. 273(4): 302–5.

Rooij, M.C.J. van, C.J. Kool and H.M. Prast, 2007, Risk-return preferences in the pension domain: Are people able to choose?, *Journal of Public Economics*, vol. 71(3–4): 701–22.

Samuelson, Paul A., 1937, A note on measurement of utility, *The Review of Economic Studies*, vol. 4(2): 155–61.

1963, Risk and uncertainty: A fallacy of large numbers, *Scientia*, vol. 57(6): 1–6.

1989, The judgement of economic science on rational portfolio management: Timing and long-horizon effects, *The Journal of Portfolio Management*, vol. 16(1): 4–12.

1994, The long-term case for equities and how it can be oversold, *The Journal of Portfolio Management*, vol. 21(1): 15–24.

1997, Dogma of the day, invest for the long term, the theory goes, and the risk lessens, *Bloomberg Personal Finance Magazine*, January/February.

2006, *Is Personal Finance a Science? Keynote Address, The Future of Life Cycle Saving and Investing*, Boston University, Boston, October 25.

Samuelson, W., and R. Zeckhauser, 1988, Status quo bias in decision making, *Journal of Risk and Uncertainty*, vol. 1(1): 7–59.

Schwartz, B., 2004, *The Paradox of Choice: Why More Is Less*, Ecco/HarperCollins, New York.

Shafir, E., P. Diamond and A. Tversky, 1997, Money illusion, *Quarterly Journal of Economics*, vol. 112(2): 341–74.

Simon, H., 1955, A behavioral model of rational choice, *Quarterly Journal of Economics*, vol. 69(1): 99–118.

Smetters, K., and B. Lin, 2010, Elastic Option Overlays, White Paper.

Stewart, S., 2005, Can behavioral economics save us from ourselves?, *The University of Chicago Magazine*, vol. 97(3).

Stichting van de Arbeid, 2010, Pensioenakkoord 2010, June 4.

Thaler, R.H., and S. Benartzi, 2004, Save more tomorrow: Using behavioral economics to increase employee saving, *Journal Political Economy*, vol. 112(1): S164–S187.

Thaler, R.H., and H. Shefrin, 1981, An economic theory of self-control, *Journal of Political Economy*, vol. 89(2): 392–410.

Willis, L.E., 2008, Against financial literacy education, *Iowa Law Review*, vol. 94; U. of Penn Law School, Public Law Research Paper No. 08–10; Loyola-LA Legal Studies Paper 2008–13.

10 Opportunities for improving pension wealth decumulation in the Netherlands

JEFFREY R. BROWN AND THEO NIJMAN

10.1 Introduction

An important element in the design of any national retirement system is the set of rules, products and institutions that provide for the decumulation of wealth. The academic literature in economics has long emphasized the important role of annuitization in providing retirement income security by insuring that individuals cannot outlive their resources. However, there are few experts who would claim that full mandatory annuitization of all retirement wealth would be a characteristic of any optimally designed retirement system. After all, while some risks (most notably longevity risk) are indeed best addressed through life annuity products, other risks (e.g., unexpected liquidity needs) and/or preferences (e.g., a strong desire to leave bequests) are best served by non-annuitized financial wealth. Unfortunately, beyond a general consensus that neither zero nor complete annuitization is optimal, it is difficult to pin down an optimal level of annuitization that is appropriate for any one individual, let alone every individual in a heterogeneous population.

This lack of consensus on the optimal level of annuitization may explain, at least in part, the wide variation in retirement wealth decumulation policies across developed countries. While virtually every OECD country provides a minimum floor of annuitized income through a first-pillar pension system, the similarities often end there. In the United States, most workers have little, if any, annuitization outside of the first-pillar Social Security system, which itself provides an average replacement rate of just over 40 percent of average lifetime income (with considerable variation around this average based on lifetime income). At the other end of this spectrum is the Netherlands, where virtually all retirement wealth in the first, second *and* third pillars is subject to mandatory annuitization. Most other countries fall at intermediate points along this spectrum.

Public policy towards annuitization is also a current "hot topic" in many countries. For example, the UK is currently considering loosening its annuitization requirements, while the US is considering how to promote further annuitization. While these potential policy shifts are in opposite directions, it can also be argued that this represents a convergence of policies because both countries are discussing a movement toward an intermediate solution. Both of these cases will be discussed in more detail below.

In this chapter, we draw upon the existing body of economic theory, empirical analysis and international experience with annuitization to develop some general guidelines as to what might constitute a well-designed decumulation policy. We then compare this benchmark policy with the actual annuitization policy in place in the Netherlands today.[1] Based on this comparison, we suggest several avenues for reform of the decumulation policies in the Dutch retirement system.

Our benchmark policy would promote sufficient annuitization to provide a real (i.e., inflation-indexed) lifetime income floor that is adequate to meet one's (and one's spouse's) most basic needs, such as food and housing. Beyond this, our benchmark policy would strongly encourage – but not mandate – additional annuitization in order to provide individuals with a high likelihood of being able to maintain their pre-retirement standard of living (which, we assume, is a higher level of consumption than simply meeting basic needs). We recognize that economists and other policy experts will disagree on what level of income is required to meet basic needs and/or maintain pre-retirement living standards. We also recognize that there may be important heterogeneity across the income distribution with regard to income replacement rates that would meet these objectives. We do not try to resolve this issue for the Netherlands in this chapter. Rather, in order to move forward and provide a general framework that can be adapted based on future work and/or societal preferences, we will

---

[1] We use the term "benchmark" rather than "optimal" because our view is based on the authors' synthesis of the academic literature, as tempered by political and practical realities in the Netherlands, rather than on a formal optimization model.

somewhat arbitrarily assume that in order to meet basic needs, one needs to replace approximately 50 percent of pre-retirement income, and that in order to maintain one's standard of living, one needs to replace approximately 70 percent of pre-retirement income. To the extent subsequent research can more rigorously justify different standards, our suggested reforms could easily be adapted to reflect those changes. We will discuss the implications of these benchmarks for our policy recommendations in more detail below.

Many retirees in the Netherlands currently have replacement rates that are quite high, largely because the Dutch system has historically targeted a replacement rate of 70 percent of pre-retirement income. Research by Eenkhoorn and Zijlmans (2010) indicates that the first and second pillars of the Dutch system together provide replacement rates of approximately 68 percent for active workers, and this is without consideration of third-pillar assets.[2] Given these numbers, and given the heterogeneity that these averages mask, it is likely that many Dutch citizens may be overannuitized relative to what is individually optimal. Indeed, the Netherlands may be one of the few countries (perhaps even the only) where moving in the direction of providing more financial flexibility and less annuitization may enhance average welfare, as it would allow individuals to address liquidity issues, precautionary motives and bequest motives.

We offer several potential avenues for reform. First, we suggest moving away from a requirement that all retirement wealth be annuitized and to a requirement that individuals annuitize enough to have a real income floor that is sufficient to cover basic needs. Second, we argue that this minimum floor needs to have more secure inflation protection, and that the unnecessary degree of purchasing power uncertainty that is introduced due to the second pillar's "conditional indexation" approach should be reduced. Third, above this minimum floor, additional annuitization should be encouraged, but not mandated. One avenue for achieving this would be to rely on automatic annuitization with an opt-out (i.e., an annuity default) rather than mandates

---

[2] There are a few important caveats to these numbers, in addition to the exclusion of the third pillar. First, it is much higher for employees, and substantially lower for self-employed individuals (who are not subject to mandatory participation). Second, these projections assume that pension benefits will always be indexed for inflation, which as we will discuss below, has not been true in recent years.

in the second pillar. Fourth, we argue that above the minimum floor, retirees should have more flexibility in their choice of annuity products, including having access to nominal, variable, deferred and other annuity pay-outs. However, we note that the recently introduced "bank saving" products should not be viewed as substitutes for life annuity products, as these products offer no longevity insurance and are essentially the exact opposite of a deferred life annuity. We also discuss the protection of spouses, and note that the "guaranteed income floor" requirement be applied to spouses as well as to retired workers. We specifically note that the ability to convert joint-and-survivor income into single life income be constrained sufficiently to protect elderly widows/widowers. Relatedly, we observe that couples might be given more flexibility to allow the primary pension amount to be reduced upon the death of either the worker or the spouse in order to allow for a more equal allocation of resources across various survival states.

This chapter proceeds as follows. In Section 10.2, we briefly review the academic literature on the optimality of annuitization as well as research on reasons why individuals so often appear to be averse to annuitization. In Section 10.3, we outline our benchmark annuitization policy. We contrast the Dutch system with this benchmark in Section 10.4. International experience is presented in Section 10.5. In Section 10.6, we outline several possible avenues for reform. Section 10.7 concludes.

10.2 The academic perspective of literature on the pros and cons of annuities

10.2.1 The "optimality" of annuitization

Life annuity products (by which we mean products that offer a stream of payments that will last for as long as one lives) exist to help solve a consumer problem that arises due to uncertainty about one's length of life. Put simply, financial planning for retirement would be much easier if individuals knew exactly how long they would live, as this would allow them to simply spread their wealth over a fixed time horizon. In reality, individuals face several significant sources of uncertainty, including uncertainty about length of life, future expenditure needs (such as for uninsured medical expenses) and future real rates of return, among others. The financial implication of this length-of-life uncertainty is that an individual must balance the risk of consuming too aggressively, which runs the risk of resulting in a large consumption drop at advanced ages, against the risk of consuming too conservatively, which will subject him to a lower of level of consumption than he could otherwise afford.

Life annuities eliminate longevity risk by allowing an individual to exchange a lump sum of wealth for a stream of payments that continue so long as the individual (and possibly a spouse) is alive. At least since Yaari's (1965) seminal paper, economic theory has shown that life annuities can substantially increase individual welfare by eliminating the financial risks associated with uncertain lifetimes and providing consumers with a higher level of lifetime consumption. Indeed, Yaari showed that risk-averse individuals would find it optimal to annuitize 100 percent of their wealth, although this result was based on a number of assumptions that may not hold in practice – including the absence of bequest motives, time-separable utility and exponential discounting, to name a few.

More recently, Davidoff *et al.* (2005) extended the results of Yaari by showing that full annuitization remains optimal even after many of these restrictive assumptions are relaxed. Indeed, they showed that as long as one does not value bequests and markets are relatively complete, full annuitization remains optimal. The basic intuition can be seen through an oversimplified case in which an individual without a bequest motive cares only about his consumption in the current period and one period hence. If this individual invests $1,000 in a non-annuitized asset with a rate of return of 4 percent, then next period he will be able to consume $1,040. On the other hand, if the individual invests $1 in an annuity, and if with 0.03 probability the individual will not survive to receive the payment next period, then the insurer is able to pay $1,040/(1–0.03) = $1,072 to the annuitant, conditional on survival. The extra return provided to surviving annuitants is sometimes called the "mortality premium" or "mortality credit," because it is provided in return for giving up one's right to the wealth upon death (Milevsky, 2005). Conditional on surviving, the rate of return on the annuity is greater than the rate of return on the non-annuitized asset, and thus individuals who do not care about bequests would rationally annuitize all wealth.

Similarly, Peijnenburg *et al.* (2010a) show that if agents save opti- mally out of annuity income, full annuitization can be optimal even in the presence of liquidity needs and precautionary motives. Peijnenburg *et al.* (2010b) extend these results and derive a simple rule of thumb that shows that only if agents risk substantial liquidity shocks early after annuitization, and only if they do not have liquid wealth to cover these expenses, would full annuitization be suboptimal. This result is shown to be robust to the presence of significant loads.

While most of the literature on the optimality of annuitization has focused on rational utility-maximizing models, annuities can also be welfare-enhancing in at least some models that account for behavioral biases. For example, annuities can serve as a very effective commit- ment device for individuals who exhibit hyperbolic discounting and who are aware of their tendency to do so.

10.2.2 So why not mandate full annuitization?

The various conditions under which full annuitization has been shown to be optimal rarely hold in reality. As a result, there are a large num- ber of rational and behavioral reasons that individuals may choose not to fully annuitize. In this subsection, we quickly review some of the reasons, and provide references to papers that explore each of these topics in more detail.

Bequests
The academic literature has long debated the salience of bequest motives in influencing both wealth accumulation and wealth decumu- lation. For example, Hurd (1989) finds little evidence of bequests in terms of how they differentially influence wealth decumulation pat- terns of households with and without children. Brown (2001b) finds that stated importance of bequest has little impact on intended annui- tization behavior in the Health and Retirement Survey, conditional on controlling for the life-cycle value of annuitization. On the other hand, Lockwood (2010) suggests that bequests are the factor most able to explain patterns of wealth decumulation, annuitization and long-term care insurance in the US. Despite the difficulty coming to a consensus view on the salience of bequest motives, it is well understood that even small bequest motives render 100 percent annuitization sub-optimal.

Pricing

In private annuity markets, there are three reasons that prices for annuities may deviate from actuarially fair levels. First, private annuity providers must cover their expenses (including selling expenses, underwriting expenses, etc.) and earn a reasonable market return on their capital. Second, there is considerable evidence that annuity markets are subject to the forces of adverse selection (i.e., longer lived individuals are more likely to buy annuities). A third potential reason that annuity prices may exceed actuarially fair levels is that insurance companies who provide the annuities may demand a risk premium due to exposure to aggregate, non-diversifiable mortality risk.[3]

As with most countries, the administrative and selection costs are quite low in the Dutch first pillar. They also appear low in the second pillar (in the range of 30–70 basis points), especially for large pension funds (Bikker and de Dreu, 2009).[4] In the third pillar, however, the costs are much more substantial, as is true in the third pillar of most countries that have been studied. Indeed, bank saving products (which we will discuss in Subsection 10.6.6) were introduced in part to provide an alternative to third-pillar annuity products that were deemed to be too expensive.

Inflation risk

There are two aspects of inflation that are important to retirees. First, even relatively low, stable rates of inflation can cause significant deterioration of purchasing power over the typical length of retirement. For example, an annual rate of inflation of 3 percent will halve the purchasing power of a nominal annuity stream in roughly 23 years.

The second and more important aspect of inflation is the *uncertainty* about the future rate. Inflation uncertainty introduces an undesirable fluctuation in the real purchasing power of a fixed nominal annuity stream. Simulation work shows that fully rational, risk-averse consumers should value inflation-indexed annuities more highly than nominal annuities (Brown *et al.*, 2001).

---

[3] Brown and Orszag (2006) discuss ways that insurance companies can partially hedge aggregate risk.

[4] Note however that participation in the second pillar can be unattractive because of the fact that accrual and contribution rates are not age dependent. One can become self-employed, for example, and thereby avoid expensive annuities when young.

Lack of equity market exposure

A reasonably large literature has shown that the inability to diversify into equities when mandated to purchase fixed annuity contracts may be welfare-reducing. For example, Inkmann *et al.* (2007) study the demand for annuities in a life-cycle model in which consumers can access equity market returns only by investing in stocks because only fixed life annuities are available. They report that "the flexibility associated with investment in the stock market rather than locking into the fixed annuity pay-out seems to be an intuitive explanation for a number of households choosing not to buy an annuity."

Horneff *et al.* (2008) derive the optimal portfolio choice in a life-cycle model when households face mortality risk, capital market risk and labor market risk. In a stylized model, they find that individuals will begin investing in annuities at very early ages (20) as long as they have sufficient financial wealth, and that by age 50, annuities crowd out bond investments. By age 78, they find that annuities crowd out stocks as well.[5] Relevant for the Dutch system is the fact that the complete conversion from stocks into annuities is not optimal until well into the retirement years.

As noted by Davidoff *et al.* (2005), there is no theoretical reason that equity exposure cannot be provided in an annuitized form. Indeed, the leading annuity provider in the United States – TIAA-CREF – has long provided annuity products with payments that are linked to underlying diversified portfolios.[6] Such products provide longevity insurance, while still maintaining exposure to broader equity markets.

In the past few years in the US, there has also been a growing demand for variable annuity products that offer minimum retirement income guarantees, such as a "guaranteed minimum withdrawal benefit" (GMWB). These products have witnessed substantial growth in recent years.[7] Unlike a true life annuity, these products allow account balances (if any) to be left to one's heirs after death, and therefore do not pay a "mortality premium." As a result, the amount of income that is

[5] When they account for actuarially unfair prices, annuity purchases are postponed until closer to retirement age (or beyond if the person has limited financial wealth).

[6] Disclosure: one of the authors of this study (Brown) is a Trustee of TIAA.

[7] For example, Prudential Financial reports that the GMWB option was available on nearly 80 percent of the variable annuities sold in the first quarter of 2006, up from 44 percent in 2003.

guaranteed by variable annuities with a GMWB is lower than what a fixed life annuity would provide. Nonetheless, there is a "life-annuity" aspect to these products to the extent that they provide a floor of guaranteed lifetime income.

Illiquidity of annuities

Primarily due to concerns about dynamic adverse selection, it is difficult to allow annuitants to substantially alter the timing of annuity pay-outs once they have begun or to undo the choice to buy annuities. Agents that annuitize all their wealth may therefore experience significant welfare losses if they are hit by liquidity shocks, such as the need to pay for health care expenditures or other high and unexpected costs (see, e.g., Turra and Mitchell, 2008; Pang and Warshawsky, 2010; Peijnenburg *et al.*, 2010a).

Incomplete annuity markets

Koijen *et al.* (2011) emphasize the role of access to a menu of annuities in a life-cycle model. In a model that allows for time-varying interest rates, inflation and risk premia, along with mortality risk, they show that consumers optimally will allocate wealth at retirement to a mix of nominal, inflation-indexed and variable annuities depending on the state of the economy. They show that the welfare costs of annuity market incompleteness are quite significant. Relative to an optimal annuity portfolio that provides access to all three types of annuities, the authors find that if the portfolio choice is restricted to inflation-indexed annuities, even conservative investors suffer a welfare loss of nearly 10 percent. Restricting choice to only nominal annuities results in even greater losses, ranging from 22 to 55 percent.

Reverse solidarity/redistribution

It is well known that mortality rates and life expectancy are not identical across the population. For example, individuals with lower education have a life expectancy that is several years shorter than that of high educated individuals of the same sex.[8] Thus, one implication of a policy that mandates the annuitization of all pension wealth at a

---

[8] While we are focusing on mortality differences by education, there are mortality gradients across a range of demographic characteristics, including income, race and ethnicity, to name a few.

uniform conversion rate is that it creates financial transfers from lower to higher education groups based on differences in life expectancy (see Brown, 2002 for the US; Bonenkamp, 2009 for the Netherlands).[9] Such "reverse redistribution" is a particularly important political and policy reason to limit the amount of mandatory annuitization.

Behavioral factors

A growing literature is raising questions over the extent to which consumer aversion to annuities is fully rational. For example, a recent paper by Brown *et al.* (2008) suggests that individuals might be easily influenced by how the features of annuities, in comparison with alternative investments, are framed. They show that when annuities are presented in an investment frame, about 80 percent of respondents believe that annuities are inferior to traditional savings products. In contrast, when annuities are presented in a consumption frame, nearly 70 percent prefer the annuity product. Numerous other behavioral explanations have also been suggested, although few of them have yet been tested empirically.

10.3 A benchmark decumulation policy

As discussed at length by Einav *et al.* (2010), it is difficult to accurately assess the social welfare consequences of social insurance programs in a heterogeneous population, thereby making it quite difficult to determine an "optimal" annuitization policy. Based on our knowledge of the academic work and industry practice around the world, however, we feel comfortable outlining a few broad-based principles that we think should guide any well-designed decumulation policy. As noted above, for illustrative purposes we will arbitrarily use a 50 percent replacement rate as a benchmark for a minimum income floor to cover basic needs, and a 70 percent replacement rate as a benchmark

---

[9] Of course, as noted by Brown (2003), consideration of utility consequences partially mitigates some of this financial redistribution. The intuition is that because low education/high mortality rate individuals have smaller probability of living to advanced ages, saving for such a small probability outcome is very inefficient. Thus, an annuity – even one that is not actuarially fairly priced for that individual – is quite beneficial in terms of allowing this individual to avoid saving for an unlikely outcome. This partly offsets the actuarially unfairness of having to annuitize at unfavorable rates and makes the welfare loss smaller than the loss in market value.

for smoothing lifetime consumption (and thus maintaining one's living standard in retirement). As additional data and research provides clearer guidance on the appropriate levels of income in the future, these benchmarks can and should be adjusted. However, we believe the broader conceptual principles which we outline below are robust and can be easily adapted to changes in the benchmark levels of income.

10.3.1 A minimum annuity floor

Standard life-cycle models of consumer behavior suggest that rational individuals will maximize their lifetime well-being (i.e., utility) by allocating money across different time periods and states of the world to equate the marginal utility of consumption across periods and states. If a consumer's utility function (i.e., the happiness they derive from spending on consumption) is not time-varying, then this implies smoothing of consumption levels (i.e., equal consumption each period) over one's lifetime.[10]

In practical terms, this suggests that a natural starting point for policy is to think in terms of providing a level of income in retirement that is defined in relation to the amount of consumption that individuals had during their working lives. A replacement rate of 70 percent appears to be widely accepted in the Netherlands as a reasonable benchmark, and thus we use this as our benchmark for maintaining one's pre-retirement standard of living.

However, we believe that it is not necessary for policy to mandate a 70 percent replacement rate. First, the academic literature itself is quite split on the question of what constitutes an optimal replacement rate (see, for example, the very different views of Scholz *et al.*, 2006 and Munnell *et al.*, 2007). Additionally, these studies have primarily focused on a US context, which is quite different from the Netherlands along a number of salient margins. For example, differences in both the level and the variance of uninsured health expenditures, or

---

[10] While there is some evidence that the marginal utility of consumption depends on health (e.g., Finkelstein *et al.*, 2008), the magnitude of the effect on overall consumption is small. Note that it is quite possible that the composition of the consumption bundle may change over the life cycle. What matters for consumption smoothing is that the marginal utility of another dollar spent on an optimal consumption bundle is the same across ages.

differences in the progressivity of the tax system, may lead to very different optimal replacement rates across countries. Furthermore, the direction of these effects is complex: for example, to the extent that the Netherlands provides more comprehensive health insurance in retirement than does the US, this may lower the income required to maintain living standards in retirement. On the other hand, it also suggests that one of the arguments against annuitization – the cost of an annuity's illiquidity in the face of uninsured shocks – is less salient in the Netherlands than in the US. Thus, more work is needed to determine a reasonable replacement rate that is specifically appropriate to the Netherlands.

Second, we recognize that there is substantial heterogeneity in society, and 70 percent will be too high for some and too low for others, especially when one considers the complications of a progressive tax system, heterogeneity in household composition, etc. Ideally, target replacement rates would be based on after-tax income both before and after retirement. Thus, to the extent that retirement income receives certain tax advantages relative to pre-retirement income, this would call for lower replacement rates than those we have chosen as our benchmark case.

Third, as a practical concern, mandating that individuals annuitize enough to provide an inflation-indexed replacement of 70 percent of average lifetime income may require even higher savings rates than are currently required in the Netherlands. Thus, we set a lower benchmark – for discussion purposes, we use 50 percent – as a level that should be sufficient to cover a retiree's most basic needs, i.e., food and shelter.

Fourth, as noted above, excessive mandatory annuitization can lead to "reverse solidarity" outcomes due to the expected financial transfers that flow from lower education/income individuals to higher education/income individuals as a result of mortality differences.

In contrast to what we believe is a suboptimal requirement to annuitize all retirement wealth, we believe that there is substantial rationale for mandating sufficient annuitization to ensure a guaranteed, real income stream sufficient to cover basic needs. Among other reasons, mandatory annuitization overcomes problems with adverse selection (and thus improves pricing), and also prevents households from gaming the welfare system by spending their resources too quickly and then falling back on public assistance.

Before continuing, it is worth discussing the consequences for our conclusions of using admittedly arbitrary 50 percent and 70 percent income replacement benchmarks. In general, most of the arguments made in this chapter would still follow if, for example, one were to use 40 percent and 60 percent instead. An important exception would be that if it were determined that the first pillar were sufficient to meet the basic needs of most of the population, then this would obviate the need for our proposal to strengthen inflation indexation in part of the second pillar. Indeed, with a sufficiently large first pillar, many of the arguments that we have made about the third pillar (e.g., the desirability for more flexibility, etc.) would apply to the second as well.

It is also worth noting that an alternative to our replacement rate approach would be to mandate annuitization up to a fixed real euro floor, rather than basing it on a fraction of income. Such an approach would arguably be less burdensome from an administrative perspective, especially if it were implemented by adjusting the size of the first pillar to match the desired floor. While conceptually appealing, however, a difficulty with this approach is that it would be difficult to find a floor that was meaningful for middle and higher income households while not providing an income floor that was "too high" relative to the lifetime consumption needs of those at the lower end of the income distribution. Estimating an appropriate replacement rate target for the Netherlands would require substantial empirical work that is beyond the scope of this chapter.

10.3.2 Indexing this annuity floor for inflation

Economic theory (and common sense) is very clear that individuals receive their well-being from consuming real goods (not from the nominal euros used to buy those goods). Thus, the theory of consumption-smoothing over the life cycle is typically thought of in terms of real (inflation-indexed) consumption. Indeed, research (Brown et al., 2002) shows quite clearly that in the presence of inflation uncertainty, inflation-indexed annuities improve welfare to a greater degree than fixed, nominal annuities.

Of course, we recognize that many individuals suffer from "nominal illusion," and thus fail to understand the value of accepting a lower initial payment in return for being protected from inflation. Thus, the political sustainability of an emphasis on real rather than nominal annuities may require that individuals be continually educated on the value of such products.[11]

10.3.3 *Default annuitization above the floor*

Above this minimum floor of inflation-indexed annuitization – and at least up to the 70 percent target that we have set as an appropriate goal for maintaining one's living standard – additional annuitization should be encouraged, although not required. This could be achieved, for example, through the use of annuities as a default distribution option in which individuals have the right to opt out.

There is reason to believe that default annuitization would be effective at promoting annuitization, while still preserving individual choice. For example, Beshears *et al.* (2006) note an important change in the regulations about annuitization options with defined benefit (DB) plans in the US. The Employee Retirement Income Security Act (ERISA) of 1974 required that the default annuity option from DB plans be a joint-and-one-half survivor annuity, unless the individual opted out of this by choosing a single life annuity with higher monthly benefits. In 1984, the regulations were amended to require an annuitant to obtain a notarized signature of his or her spouse in order to opt out of the joint-and-survivor annuity requirement. Holden and Nicholson (1998) show that before 1974, less than half of married men chose a joint-and-survivor annuity. Following the passage of ERISA in 1974, use of the joint-and-survivor annuity rose by roughly 25 percentage points. Aura (2001) reports that the adoption of the spousal consent regulations in 1984 further increased the use of joint-and-survivor options by up to 10 percentage points.

Bütler and Teppa (2007) provide evidence that is strongly suggestive of the importance of default options on annuity choice in Switzerland. They examine the annuitization decisions of over 4,500 individuals in

---

[11] An often heard argument suggests that habit formation might justify nominal annuities. This implicitly assumes inflation to be constant. In most habit formation models, the habit is thought to be a "real" and not a nominal habit. As shown in Davidoff *et al.* (2005), depending on whether the habit level of consumption is high or low relative to the initial annuity amount can cause annuities to be more or less attractive. Nominal annuities can be damaging to the welfare of an individual with a "real" habit, because inflation would impose real deviations away from the habit level of consumption.

ten company pension plans. In nine of the ten companies, the annuity is the default pay-out option (with a partial or full lump sum as alternative options). The remaining company "provides a lump sum payment (amounting to the last working year's salary) as the standard option." Annuitization rates are quite high in these plans overall: in eight of the ten plans, annuitization rates exceed 50 percent. In the one company that does not use the annuity as the default option, the annuitization rate is only 10 percent.

10.3.4 More flexibility in options above the minimum income floor

Simple textbook financial theory indicates that even risk-averse individuals benefit from having some exposure to equity markets. Importantly, there is really no reason that the optimality of having some equity market exposure suddenly changes as one exits the labor force. As noted above, research indicates that the optimal portfolio of retirees includes equity exposure as well as annuities. Given heterogeneity in financial literacy, risk preferences, and so on, we believe it is very important that individuals be able to choose the mix of annuity and non-annuity products that best meets their needs. Ideally, individuals would have access to a rich market of fixed, inflation-indexed, variable and deferred annuity pay-out products from which to choose.

In particular, we believe that variable annuities (with lifelong income linked to an underlying diversified portfolio) have a potential role to play. Under the current system, retirees only have equity exposure quite indirectly through the loss of inflation protection when funding ratios fall. It may be advantageous to provide additional options for investing in annuities that are linked to equity market performance, akin to the variable pay-out annuities offered by TIAA-CREF in the United States.

Another type of product that may be a useful addition to the menu of products available over and above the minimum annuity floor are delayed pay-out annuities (e.g., an annuity purchased at an early age, such as 65, that does not begin paying out until a later age, such as 85). Scott *et al.* (2006, 2009) show that such products can be an efficient approach, because individuals can provide a higher income floor at advanced ages by allocating only a small part of their pension wealth to delayed pay-out annuities.

Of course, in recommending that individuals be given more options, we are cognizant of the behavioral economics research indicating that there is such a thing as "too much" choice. Botti and Iyengar (2006), for example, in an article reviewing the literature on choice proliferation, discuss how "decision makers' happiness with the outcomes of their increased choices depends not only on their ability to preference match but also on their social values ... their mispredicted expectations during the decision process ... and their feelings of responsibility associated with the act of choosing" (p. 35). Thus, if policymakers move toward an environment in which more choice is provided, it is important to think about structuring the choice set in a manner that maximizes the possibility of welfare-improvement by thinking carefully about choice architecture.

10.3.5 *Protection of spouses*

In many countries, the protection of elderly widows or widowers is an important policy concern. Poverty rates among widows/widowers are often higher than for married individuals of the same age. A straightforward way to reduce the likelihood of poverty upon entering widowhood is to ensure that annuities provided through retirement plans are joint-and-survivor annuities that continue to provide payments for as long as either spouse is alive. Of course, economic evidence on "equivalence scales" suggests that the ratio of survivor benefits to couples benefits need not be 100 percent, but neither is it likely as low as 50 percent. In other words, while there are some economies of scale in consumption within a household, these economies are not one-for-one. From the perspective of designing a decumulation policy, it is critical to ensure that the minimum income floor will still be available to widows/widowers after the death of the primary retiree.

There are several policy approaches that are helpful in providing adequate spousal protection. First, minimum annuity rules can be written in such a manner that they provide a minimum income floor that is adequate not only when one spouse is alive, but also upon the death of either spouse. Second, for annuities above this amount (such as automatic enrollment in annuities), a joint-and-survivor pay-out stream can be the default. Individuals should only be allowed to deviate from this default if the spouse agrees. Third, both the minimum annuity floor and any default rules should specify that spouses are treated symmetrically. For example, the ratio of survivor benefits to couple benefits should be the same regardless of whether it is the primary worker or the spouse who dies first. In many plans around the world, there is asymmetric treatment: often, the primary worker gets unreduced benefits after his or her spouse dies, while the dependent spouse sees a reduction if the primary worker dies first. While there is good economic rationale for allowing for survivor benefits to be less than couple benefits, there is really no economic rationale for an asymmetry based on which member of the couple dies first.

10.4 Current decumulation policy in the Netherlands

The Dutch pension system consists of three pillars, each of which provides annuities with few exceptions. Here, we discuss the decumulation policy in each of these pillars.

10.4.1 Annuitization in the first pillar (AOW)[12]

The first pillar (AOW) provides basic income above the level of the minimum wage as of the age of 65 until death for singles, and about 170 percent of this amount for couples. AOW income is not means tested, and it is financed on a pay-as-you-go (PAYG) basis. Full AOW income is available for everyone who lived in the Netherlands for 50 years as of the age of 65.[13] People who lived in the Netherlands for a shorter period (e.g., immigrants, Dutch knowledge workers who worked abroad) get the analogous fraction of full AOW.[14] The current proposal for adjusting the eligibility age for AOW to improved life expectancy states that for every year that one postpones benefit the annual income will be increased by 5 percent.[15] In the spring of 2010 there was an active policy discussion whether or not people should be allowed to take AOW income before the extended

---

[12] Algemene Ouderdomswet.
[13] In 2020 and 2025 the age at which people will be entitled for full AOW income is likely to be increased to 66 years and 67 years respectively.
[14] They might be entitled for additional social benefits if they fell below the poverty line.
[15] This raises many issues, some of which are analyzed in Sanders *et al.* (2010). The 5 percent compensation is low and in many cases it will be beneficial to take the money early and buy additional annuities in the market if one likes to have more income at higher ages. Of course this depends on the prevailing interest rates as well as on other factors.

entitlement date. Decreases in lifelong income of 6.5–8 percent were quoted for people who would use that option. In some proposals taking this option would only be allowed for low-income workers, in the government proposal only for physically or mentally demanding professions (a list of these professions would have to be agreed on). The most recent consensus in the policy debate seems to be that all individuals will be allowed to take AOW as of the age of 65 but with actuarially fair (for the average recipient) adjustments for taking AOW before the statutory age which will increase in 2020 and 2050 as indicated. AOW will have to be claimed no later than at the age of 70.

10.4.2 Annuitization in the second pillar

The second pillar of the Dutch pension system consists of (almost always) mandatory[16] contributions to a pension fund or insurer. A typical arrangement is to have two thirds of the contributions paid for by the employer, and the remaining third by the employee. Social partners (i.e., employers and employees) set the percentage of labor income[17] that is to be contributed to the fund, and are also responsible for fund governance. Most second-pillar entitlements are typically characterized as DB plans and we will follow that convention. However, one should keep in mind that because real pension income is not guaranteed, but rather is dependent on the funding status of the pension fund, the contract is sometimes characterized as a hybrid.

The binding (or "hard") pension rights generate a nominal annuity income as of the target date. The standard annual accrual is 1.75 percent for final wage schemes and 2.0–2.25 percent for career average schemes. After 40 years of participation in the labor force the total annuity income would be 70 percent in final wage schemes and 80–90 percent of average wage in career average schemes.[18] The target date currently is 65 years. Social partners (i.e., labor unions and employer organizations) have agreed that the target date will be linked to life expectancy and will therefore be increased roughly simultaneously with the AOW age. Every individual can claim second-pillar benefits

---

[16] Both the level of payments and the selection of the pension fund are mandated.
[17] After correcting for AOW income.
[18] Many funds shifted from final wage to career average wage in the years 2002–2004.

as early as age 62, or can delay beyond age 65, and the adjustment is actuarially fair for the average participant.

Second-pillar pension income comes in the form of annuities and individuals are generally not allowed to convert pension income to a lump-sum payment. There is a (limited) possibility to have higher or lower annual income in earlier than in later years (but the lower income should at least be 70 percent of the higher income). Second-pillar pension wealth can also be used to generate an income stream at the level of AOW income to "bridge" AOW income in an actuarially fair way for people who retire before the statutory age.[19]

With regard to spousal benefits, the standard offering is to provide spousal and survivor benefits that are equal to 70 percent of the pension benefit. However, before the first pension payment, and upon the agreement of both spouses, individuals have the opportunity to convert these partner pensions to additional "own" old-age pensions.[20]

With regard to inflation protection, an unusual but important feature of the second-pillar Dutch DB pension entitlements is the annual decision of the pension fund whether or not to compensate the pension entitlements for (price or wage) inflation. Many funds have announced that they will fully compensate inflation if the nominal funding ratio (i.e., the market value of assets divided by the present value of liabilities) exceeds 140 percent. No indexation will be given if the funded rate is less than 110 percent; partial indexation will be given in the intermediate range. Missed compensations for inflation will usually be compensated in subsequent years. This system, which is often referred to as "conditional indexation," was introduced in 2003. In the years before 2003, inflation indexation was almost universal. Since 2003, however, funds have failed to index several times, including in 2009 when nearly all funds chose not to index. This occurred because, in the spring of 2009, the nominal funded rates of many funds were below 100 percent. While many funds recovered somewhat by the end of 2009, in mid-2010 and since mid-July 2011 the nominal funded rates were again less than 100 percent on average (driven largely by low interest rates and therefore high value of the liabilities). In January 2012 the supervisor (De Nederlandsche Bank,

---

[19] Note that this option is not available for low-income workers and that it can exhaust all pension wealth in the second pillar for people with small pensions.

[20] The conversion factor depends on the average age of men and women in that fund, not on individual characteristics.

or DNB), has announced that about 100 funds might have to cut nominal benefits as of January 2013. A few funds have already actually cut benefits in 2012.

While this "conditional indexation" has a benefit of helping to stabilize the funding of the plan, it also generates uncertainty in the real income stream available to retirees. Not only does it not guarantee the real income level, but its structure is such that the real income reductions will come at exactly those points in time when such cuts are most harmful (e.g., when the marginal utility of income is high because the economy is performing poorly, other assets are down in value, etc.). In essence, this conditional indexation can be viewed as a combination of a nominal annuity with a complicated call option that can increase the income by up to the rate of inflation if the pension funding ratio is high enough. It is worth considering whether retirees might be better off receiving a lower initial level of annual income, in return for more secure inflation-indexation.

In June 2010 the social partners reached an important agreement on the future of the Dutch pension system. In order to support the sustainability of the system and to stabilize the required contribution rates it was agreed that the level of guarantees ("hard" pension rights) will be reduced. As of 2010, a larger fraction of the benefits of the system will be dependent on the investment returns in ways which are currently under discussion. Technically the promise will be close to that of a variable annuity. Likewise, as discussed before, the target date for pension income generated by second-pillar products will be linked to life expectancy.

While most second-pillar schemes are DB, a limited number of firms offer defined contribution (DC) schemes in the second pillar. Like the more prevalent DB plans, these DC plans are mandatory and are also required to be annuitized. In these schemes the participants usually have ample choice opportunities, in particular with respect to the investment strategy. Unlike in DB schemes the participant faces investment, interest and longevity risks directly. The rules and legislation for these second-pillar DC funds are close to those for third-pillar products.

Transparency is currently an important second-pillar policy issue in the Netherlands. Pension providers in the second pillar already have to classify the "indexation quality" of their schemes in five categories. This "indexation label" is computed using asset-liability matching

(ALM) models and reports the expected loss of purchasing power of pay-outs from the scheme on a 15-year horizon as well as the loss of purchasing power in a pessimistic scenario. Recently, an advisory committee[21] to the Dutch government proposed to report expected purchasing power and an outcome in a pessimistic scenario on an individual basis. Moreover this transparency requirement would apply to all pension providers, be they first, second or third pillar.[22] The same committee has also proposed to allow more general pension products to be offered in the Netherlands. Their proposals include variable annuities in the second pillar, deferred annuities which provide monthly income as of a future date that would depend on life expectancy, and life-cycle accumulation in the second pillar so that young participants would invest a larger fraction of their wealth in equities.

10.4.3 *Annuitization in the third pillar*

The third pillar of the pension system, which is essentially a DC system, consists of tax-exempt, voluntarily purchased pension products from insurers or banks. This pillar of the system is particularly important for 5 percent of the working population that is self-employed and who do not have second-pillar coverage. The third pillar is also used by participants in pension funds who judge their first- and second-pillar coverage as insufficient, such as those with more limited work histories. The rules governing the tax deductibility of contributions require that the accrued pension is less than a certain percentage of income.

Generally speaking, the legislation allows two forms of decumulation of pension wealth: life annuities purchased through insurers, and "bank saving" products, which essentially return principal and interest to the participant over a fixed number of years. These bank saving products allow for bequest, but do not offer any longevity insurance.[23]

---

[21] Committee on the sustainability of supplementary pension schemes (the Goudswaard committee). One of the authors of this chapter (Nijman) was a member of this committee.

[22] This will be technically possible once the new pension register, which provides a portal to the administration of all pension providers, has been realized.

[23] Another possibility is a temporary (additional) income for at least five years. This is restricted to 20,000 euros annually. It resembles the flexibility of the 100%: 75% income levels in the second pillar.

In this third pillar, individuals choose their own contributions and bear the investment and conversion (interest and longevity) risks. Some of the products that are offered contain rate-of-return guarantees during the accumulation phase. A few years ago, duty of care legislation was introduced which forces insurers to offer only investment strategies that manage the conversion risks to annuities. These regulations require that, close to the target date, the exposure to equities be reduced and the duration of the fixed income portfolio be approximately that of the annuity to be bought.

Another distinguishing feature of the third-pillar products is that no inflation protection is offered. The pay-outs are nominal, although they sometimes increase annually with a fixed percent. While this is not unusual when compared with other countries, it is nonetheless an unfortunate feature, as it subjects individuals to uncertainty in the real purchasing power of their retirement income stream. Generally two reasons are put forward to explain this lack of inflation protection in the Netherlands, as well as in most other countries where annuities lack inflation protection. The first potential driver is "money illusion" on the side of individuals who are not willing to accept the lower initial payment in return for the long-term preservation of purchasing power. The second potential driver is the lack of bonds indexed to Dutch inflation. Issuers of real annuities in the Netherlands would have to use bonds linked to European inflation to hedge their risks and the corresponding basis risk makes it unattractive for insurers to issue such products.

The legislation allows for variable annuities in which the level of the annual payments would depend on the investment returns. As noted above, these are potentially important as they allow individuals to potentially benefit from the higher expected returns to equities. This is attractive as the life expectancy at the annuitization date can be as large as 20 years, and much research is supportive of the notion that the optimal equity share should not fall to zero just because someone enters retirement. In reality, though, hardly any variable annuity products are offered in the Netherlands at this time.

After much media attention, the cost level of third-pillar pension products has become a major policy concern in the Netherlands. Many insurers charge annual fees in the order of 150 basis points (in contrast to the largest second-pillar provider's charge of 30 basis points). When this cost difference is compounded over many decades, the impact can be quite substantial. In response, "bank saving" products were introduced in 2007. These products carry the same fiscal incentives but differ in two crucial aspects from the annuities offered by insurers. First, these products are fixed term (minimum 20 years) rather than lifelong and therefore do not provide insurance against outliving one's assets if one gets very old. Second, in case of premature death of the insured the money is transferred to the heirs rather than to the pool of annuitants.

10.5 Pension wealth decumulation around the globe

When looking around the globe, there are significant differences in the extent of overall annuitization of retirement wealth, arising primarily in the treatment of assets in the second and third pillars.[24] In this section we provide a brief summary of the key features of the legislation in six countries. More details and analysis for more countries is provided, e.g., in Mitchell *et al.* (2011). First-pillar systems appear to be almost universally annuitized. There is tremendous heterogeneity in the extent of annuitization in the second pillar. In the third pillar, the Netherlands is a notable exception to the general rule that annuitization is typically voluntary – and quite rare – in most countries.[25]

10.5.1 The United States

The first pillar in the US, covering over 90 percent of workers, is Social Security. Paid out in the form of a mandatory life annuity, Social

---

[24] In what follows, we provide a very brief overview of second-pillar arrangements in a sampling of OECD countries. This is far from an exhaustive overview, but rather is meant to simply help place the Netherlands into a comparative context.

[25] As noted by Lindeman and Yermo (2002, p. 3), "except in a few OECD countries, annuities markets either do not yet exist or are still in an incipient stage of development." Mitchell *et al.* (1999) report on the small size of the voluntary market in the US. Mackenzie (2006, p. 27) reports that "annuities markets in France, Germany, Italy and Japan are small." In a study examining the Australian annuity market, Knox (2000) reported that "the market for private life annuities with longevity insurance is very small." An IMF (2007, p. 10) study of the pension annuity market in Mexico in the decade following the 1997 pension reform reports that "the pension annuity market in Mexico is very small." A study of annuity markets across the OECD comes to the general conclusion that there is an "apparent paradox in the findings: despite

Security benefits are automatically indexed to inflation each year.[26]
Social Security provides an average replacement rate of approximately
42 percent of income, although it is much higher for lower income
households, and much lower for higher income households. Social
Security is considered by most economists and financial planners to
be insufficient, by itself, to maintain pre-retirement living standards
through retirement, except possibly for those at the low end of the
lifetime earnings distribution.[27]

The second pillar in the US consists primarily of employer-provided
retirement plans. Coverage in the second pillar is far from universal:
even when one considers not only current pension coverage, but also
pensions from prior jobs, Gustman *et al.* (2010) report that approximately
two thirds of respondents aged 51–56 have some employer-
provided pension coverage. Over the past three decades, the private
pension system in the US has witnessed a dramatic decline in second-
pillar annuitization for two reasons. First, the private sector DB plan
is all but disappearing in the US and being replaced with 401(k) plans
and other forms of DC plans. Whereas, historically, annuitization was
the standard distribution option from DB plans, most DC plans do
not even offer participants an opportunity to annuitize. According to
Hewitt Associates, the fraction of 401(k) plans (currently the most
common employer-provided plan in the US) offering annuities as a
pay-out option fell from 31 percent in 1999 to only 17 percent in
2003. Second, among those DB plans that still exist, Salisbury (2002)
points out that over half of them now offer a lump-sum benefit at
retirement. In addition, he reports that "nearly all of the over 500"
cash balance, or hybrid, plans offer lump-sum distributions as a
pay-out option. As a result of these two trends, the Congressional
Research Service (2005) reports that 85 percent of the 61.1 million
workers aged 21 or older who were included in a retirement plan at

good value for consumers, demand for annuities remains weak" (Lindeman
and Yermo, 2002, p. 1).
[26] The overwhelming majority of those not covered by Social Security are public
sector workers covered by various federal, state and local pension plans which
also pay benefits primarily in the form of annuities.
[27] While the view that Social Security is inadequate as a sole source of
annuitization for most households is widely held, it is not universal. Bernheim
(1991) argued, on the basis of extensive life insurance holdings among the
elderly, that many households were over-annuitized by Social Security. Brown
(2001a) provides contrary evidence using more recent data.

work participated in a plan that offered a lump-sum distribution as a payment option.[28]

Like many countries, annuitization in the third pillar – namely, the system of both tax-deferred and taxable private savings – is extremely rare.

Concern over low and declining levels of annuitization has led the Obama Administration's Treasury and Labor departments to issue a joint "Request for Information" (RFI) in February 2010, seeking input on ideas related to promoting annuitization within 401(k) plans. Indeed, a key US Treasury official – prior to joining the Obama Administration – coauthored an influential policy paper that called for treating annuitization as the default pay-out option from 401(k) plans (Gale *et al.*, 2008).

The Gale *et al.* paper, as well as a paper discussing how one might implement an automatic annuitization policy (Brown, 2009b), suggest several rationales for default annuitization. The current incarnation of the US system is best thought of as a "quasi-accidental" design. In particular, section 401(k) of the Internal Revenue Code (the US tax code) was originally designed in the late 1970s as a way to provide tax benefits to supplemental retirement plans that were "elective" on the part of participants. Because they were designed as supplemental, rather than as core plans, little attention was paid to decumulation issues: after all, the 401(k) was not intended as a primary source of retirement income. Over the past three decades, however, the US retirement system evolved in such a way that the 401(k) is now the single most common type of plan. However, it is a system based on wealth accumulation, not a system based on providing retirement income security. For example, very few 401(k) plans offer annuities: indeed, until the passage of the Pension Protection Act of 2006, most pension lawyers advised plan sponsors to avoid annuities due to the additional fiduciary risk that they created for the sponsors.

The "accumulation culture" that has built up in the US over the past three decades has created an environment in which most citizens do not fully understand annuities, how they operate, or the benefits they

---

[28] In contrast, the second pillar in the public sector – namely, pensions for federal, state and local workers – continues to be dominated by DB plans. However, there is currently a politically charged debate in the US about the sustainability of these plans due to the large unfunded liabilities that they present, a situation that has been exacerbated by the recent economic downturn.

provide. Thus, they do not demand them from their employers. This lack of demand – combined with the fiduciary risks that employers have historically faced if they offer them – means that employers have traditionally been very happy to avoid offering annuities altogether. Thus, a primary rationale for those promoting automatic annuitization is to "change the conversation" in the US back to one focused on retirement income security. Proponents believe that policy action is needed to achieve this.

While the Obama administration initially appeared supportive of automatic annuitization and/or requiring that 401(k) plan sponsors at least offer annuity options, it appears to have backed off of this position recently. In part, this may be because the public response to the "Request for Information" resulted in a surprising degree of negative feedback from the public at large. Indeed, some high-profile politicians used it as an opportunity to politicize the discussion. Possibly as a result, in September 2010, high-ranking administration officials stated that while the administration is still interested in seeing more annuitization, it would prefer to see firms do this on their own without compulsion on the part of policymakers.

10.5.2 The United Kingdom

The UK annuity market has long been better developed, both in terms of the size of the market and in terms of the selection of products available, than markets in the US and many other countries. As discussed by Finkelstein and Poterba (2002), the development of the UK annuity market is due in large part to the fact that the UK has long required partial annuitization of DC pension schemes in the second pillar by the age of 75. To be more specific, individuals can draw down from their pension wealth before the age of 75 up to a maximum of 120 percent of the annual income that a fair annuity would offer. At the age of 75, at least 75 percent of the remaining annuity wealth has to be annuitized.

Interestingly, at the same time that the US has begun policy discussions about whether to promote additional annuitization, discussions in the UK lead to adjustments in the opposite direction. As discussed in Blake, Cannon and Tonks (2010), the Conservative–Liberal-Democrat Coalition Government that came to power in May 2010 announced that it was going to end the requirement for pension scheme members to purchase annuities by the age of 75. The rules have actually changed in April 2011. A minimum income requirement (MIR) of £20,000 was introduced and the obligation to annuitize is dropped if one can show that a lifetime minimum income is assured. The use of the MIR emphasizes that people should not be allowed to run down their wealth and then become eligible for social assistance (see Buetler *et al.* (2010) for evidence of this in Switzerland). The so-called 'age 75 rule' has been replaced in the UK by 'capped drawdown' and 'flexible drawdown'. With capped drawdown, if your total sources of lifelong income come to less than the MIR, you cannot withdraw from your DC pension plan each year more than the amount that you would receive from a single life annuity for your age. With flexible drawdown, if your total sources of lifelong income come to at least £20,000 annually, you can withdraw as much as you like from your DC pension plan.

10.5.3 Germany

Cannon and Tonks (2008) refer to the German pension system as a "traditional continental model," consisting of a first-pillar PAYG system that provides relatively high replacement rates. Because of these high replacement rates, second-pillar pensions are quite small, comprising only 5 percent of average retirement incomes.

The Riester reforms of 2001 were designed in part to stimulate second- and third-pillar plans through the use of tax subsidies. At least 80 percent of accumulations in these "Riester plans" must be annuitized before the age of 85, although these plans are new enough that there is insufficient data to analyze the extent of annuitization that will occur (Cannon and Tonks, 2008).

10.5.4 Sweden

Sweden undertook a significant reform of its pension system in 1998, at which time it changed its second pillar from a fairly standard DB system to a notional defined contribution (NDC) system. The notional account provides annuities, and may do so as early as age 61. The Swedish system incorporates an "automatic rebalancing mechanism" to protect system finances, meaning that annuity rates are adjusted to keep the system in fiscal balance. The annuity level is dependent on shocks in fertility and longevity, not on financial markets.

Sweden also has an additional second pillar – known as the Premium Pension Plan – which offers hundreds of investment funds through a DC account. Accounts accumulated under this system also face mandatory annuitization at rates set by the agency which regulates the plan.

10.5.5 *Switzerland*

Switzerland's second pillar is mandatory, but is organized through various occupational schemes. At retirement, the Swiss can choose either to annuitize or to take a lump sum. The decision taken is highly dependent on the default option that is offered, as documented by Bütler and Teppa (2007). An important aspect of this choice is also that social benefits are mean tested in Switzerland. Bütler *et al.* (2010) show that this affects annuity choice in that lower income groups are more inclined to take lump sums as they have lifetime protection for their consumption level anyway.

10.5.6 *Australia*

In terms of the prevalence of annuitization, Australia bears similarity to the US. As discussed by Bateman *et al.* (2001), Australia has a universal first pillar that provides an average replacement rate of 37 percent (Cannon and Tonks, 2008, p. 98). The second pillar – known as the Superannuation Guarantee, which was introduced in 1992 – provides tax incentives to take pay-outs as an annuity. Despite this, Bateman *et al.* (2001) report that 75 percent of benefits were taken as a lump sum in 2001.

10.5.7 *Some general lessons from abroad*

Taking into account the lessons of the six countries analyzed above, plus the experience of other nations, there are a few general lessons that appear to hold across countries.

First, as noted at the outset, annuitization is virtually universal in first-pillar systems. Second, when annuitization is voluntary, few individuals choose to purchase them, despite the substantial benefits that academic research suggests should accrue to risk-averse consumers. Third, the Netherlands is an "outlier" in terms of mandating annuities in all three pillars of its retirement system. Fourth, with the exception of the US (which has very limited annuitization outside of Social Security), most policy discussions appear to be in the direction of providing more flexibility in the upper pillars.

10.6 Possible avenues for reform of the Dutch decumulation system

In this section, we use our benchmark design, as well as international experience, to suggest a few avenues for reform in the Netherlands.

10.6.1 Reduce the mandated annuitization amount to an amount sufficient to meet basic needs

As discussed above, Dutch legislation imposes that all pension wealth be converted to annuities at (or close to) retirement.[29] Some mandated annuitization is beneficial, in that it helps to overcome information problems that might otherwise unravel a private market in annuities. It might also be beneficial if individuals are failing to recognize or fully value the insurance aspects of annuities, as might be the case according to some behavioral explanations.

However, the current requirement that all retirement wealth be annuitized is likely welfare-reducing for many Dutch citizens. As argued above, in case of bequest motives, liquidity concerns, incomplete annuity menus or significant costs of purchasing annuities it can be attractive to annuitize only part of the pension wealth. This is because annuity income and liquid wealth can be viewed as serving different economic purposes. Annuitized income provides a minimum consumption floor and is the most efficient way to provide guaranteed consumption for life in the presence of longevity risk. On the other hand, financial wealth provides liquidity which can be quite important in the presence of uncertain and potentially "lumpy" expenditure items. In the academic literature, uninsured health expenditures are usually referred to as the prime example of such risks, as these are

---

[29] Bank saving (fixed term "annuities") is the exception to this rule and will be discussed in Section 10.6.6 below.

quite dominant in the US. For countries like the Netherlands where health costs are largely insured, other expenditure categories such as expenditures for housing and house maintenance, or intervivos transfers to children, or bequests, might be equally important. In short, an optimal retirement portfolio should include both annuitized and unannuitized resources.

10.6.2 Provide more secure inflation-indexation for the mandated annuity income

Essentially, true inflation-protection in the Netherlands is limited to the first pillar. In second-pillar DC plans, as well as in the third pillar, annuity choices are typically limited to fixed nominal annuities (although the Dutch legislation does not impose this; Dietvorst *et al.*, 2010). In the second-pillar hybrid DB plans, the "conditional indexation" is a way of indirectly providing retirees with equity market exposure on top of their pension benefit. More specifically, the conditional indexation approach provides individuals with a *nominal* annuity plus a rather complicated call option. This option is one that makes a partial or full inflation adjustment only if the funding status of the pension – which in turn depends on contributions, pay-outs, portfolio allocations and asset prices – exceeds certain thresholds. If equity returns are not highly correlated with inflation rates, the inflation protection can be low.

As discussed above, when it comes to meeting basic needs through the 50 percent annuitization requirement, the case for more reliable inflation-indexation is strong. While the first-pillar AOW is inflation-indexed, the first-pillar income (identical for all who are fully eligible) is sufficient to meet the 50 percent replacement rate that we recommend only for low-income workers. As such, we would suggest that at least *part* of the second pillar – that which would be sufficient to meet the 50 percent replacement rate – be required to be explicitly inflation-indexed to the extent that adequate investment products are available to implement these pension promises.[30] In conjunction with this, the appropriate way to handle pension funding would be to calculate at least this part of the funding liability based on real – not

---

[30] Currently there is no market for indexed-linked bonds tied to Dutch inflation. There is a small over-the-counter market for inflation swaps.

nominal – pension pay-outs, and to ensure that there is sufficient asset-liability matching to have high confidence that these payments will be made.

Above this "guaranteed" level of income, social partners should have the flexibility to design the risk-and-return characteristics that best suit the needs of the employers and employees. We will discuss this more below. However, for these benefits above the minimum floor, we would still recommend that when pension funding falls short relative to what was promised, such adjustments ought to be made in a manner that is concentrated more on younger workers, and less on retirees. Younger workers have many more years during which to adjust labor supply, saving and investment behavior to offset future benefit changes. Current retirees have few such options, and thus the loss of benefits has a larger utility consequence.

10.6.3 Encourage, but do not require, additional annuitization above the minimum

An emerging strand of research in behavioral economics suggests that people may be averse to annuitization for reasons that are not fully rational (see, for example, Brown, 2009a, 2009b; Brown *et al.*, 2008). As such, we are sympathetic to the view that individuals may need to be "nudged" in the direction of annuitization. One way to do this would be to offer annuitization as the default pay-out option for second-pillar balances that are in excess of what is minimally required.

As noted earlier, there are reasons to believe that default annuitization rules would still result in a high level of annuitization. However, it has the obvious advantage over compulsory annuitization of maintaining consumer choice. In particular, those individuals for whom additional annuitization would clearly be welfare-reducing (e.g., those with short remaining life expectancies, those with particularly strong bequest motives, etc.) would have the ability to opt out of the default.

10.6.4 Provide more flexibility in annuity and non-annuity choice above the minimum amount

As noted above, a large and growing body of research suggests that retirees may be better off with a more broadly diversified portfolio than one consisting solely of fixed nominal or real annuities. Most life-cycle simulation models, for example, suggest that some continued equity exposure into retirement years remains optimal.

While the current Dutch system provides equity exposure indirectly through its conditional indexation model, this approach obfuscates the link. In addition, it does not allow individuals to adapt their portfolio to their own preferences. An advantage of offering a richer array of products during the retirement phase is that it allows for customization that reflects the preference heterogeneity in the population.

10.6.5 *Keep an eye on spousal protection*

In general, we believe it is important to ensure that the minimum annuitized income floor is sufficient to meet minimum needs of both a retired worker and his or her spouse, including possible states of widowhood after the death of the retired worker. It appears that the Dutch system has a reasonable approach in place for protecting spouses in the form of providing spousal and survivor benefits. In Dutch DB plans the default is that the insured gets a level of old-age pension income and that if he or she passes away while the partner is alive, the partner will receive 70 percent of that income until death.

At retirement, however, the couple has the right to swap old age and partner pension. If both agree, the partner pension can be dropped and converted in an actuarially fair way to an additional old-age pension for the insured. One might question the policy rationale for allowing this. From a paternalistic perspective, one cannot help but wonder if a decision to trade-off survivor benefits for "own" benefits is driven less by an optimal reallocation and more by a misunderstanding of the value of survivor annuities.

Related to this, the actuarial compensation for converting between spousal and own benefits is computed for the average participant in the fund, rather than on population mortality rates. This implies that the actuarial adjustment depends on the relative fraction of women versus men in the fund. It seems worthwhile to consider replacing this rule by an adjustment that is actuarially fair using population-wide survival probabilities. This would, of course, make the funding status sensitive to such conversions, as the gender mix of survival rates that is used to value liabilities is fund specific. But doing so would at least provide economically appropriate incentives for individuals making the choice.

The existing conversion rules also exhibit an important asymmetry. Specifically, the income of the primary worker is not affected by the death of his spouse. However, the death of the primary worker does affect the income of his or her spouse. As noted above, there does not seem to be any economic reason for such an asymmetry to be the norm. In effect, the rule can generate a mismatch, such that the insured gets too much income if he were the only survivor, and too little income in states of the world in which both partners are alive or the spouse is alive.[31] Sanders (2010) argues that the welfare effect of this can be as large as 10 percent.[32] A simple way to adjust the legislation would be to have the default rule be one in which the annuity amount is calculated on the basis of a joint and (symmetric) survivor annuity for couples.

10.6.6 Removing special treatment for bank savings products

As explained above, the general rule for decumulation of pension wealth in the Netherlands is that the pension wealth is to be converted to an annuity. The exception to the rule is "bank saving," which was introduced recently. These third-pillar products carry all the tax benefits of annuities but differ from them in two crucial aspects. First, these products are fixed term (minimum 20 years) rather than lifelong and therefore do not provide insurance against outliving your assets if one gets very old. Second, in case of premature death of the insured the money is transferred to the heirs rather than to the pool of annuitants. Historically the main motivation to introduce these products in 2007 was to promote competition and to reduce cost levels in the third pillar which was dominated by a small number of providers of annuities.

To the extent that policymakers are trying to ensure that individuals have adequate insurance against the risk of outliving their assets, bank saving products make little sense as a product choice. Two arguments are available that support the use of bank saving for retirement: lower

---

[31] The same issue arises with US DB schemes where both partners initially have single life annuities that can be converted to survivor pensions. If one of them has all the accrued rights the income level for this individual will not be affected if his spouse passes away. These are sometimes called "joint and contingent" annuities (Brown and Poterba, 2000).

[32] The 10 percent number assumes that the pension wealth is generated by only one of the partners and the level of joint consumption is low.

cost levels than third-pillar annuities and its role as a commitment device, i.e., it makes it less attractive to spend more in later years than planned. However, these products do not offer insurance benefits, and do nothing to protect individuals against outliving their income. In an important sense, they are the "anti" delayed pay-out annuity. That is, instead of providing income during advanced ages where individuals are at risk of experiencing consumption declines, bank savings products pay out all the income during the earlier period of retirement, thereby increasing the longevity risk that individuals face. Scott *et al.* (2006, 2009), for example, show that allocating only a small part of pension wealth to delayed pay-out annuities generates very sizable welfare gains under the standard assumptions. The counterpart to this is that it is quite inefficient to lock pension wealth in illiquid accounts that cannot be invested in the stock market or protected against inflation risk while at the same not covering the risk of outliving your assets at advanced ages. In short, bank savings products are *not* substitutes for life annuities. Indeed, they appear to have some of the worst aspects of annuities (i.e., imposing illiquidity) without any of the benefits of annuities (i.e., guaranteed income for life).

To the extent that policymakers wish to provide more flexibility in the third pillar, as we have endorsed here for those with adequate lifetime income, a better approach would be to open the set of allowable investment options to the full array of financial products (e.g., mutual funds, direct holdings of stocks, bonds, etc.). We see little reason to favor bank-saving products over other savings and investment vehicles.

10.6.7 *Managing conversion risk*

While many Dutch pension plans generate annuities by construction, in third-pillar plans and in second-pillar DC plans pension wealth is to be converted to pension income. Pension providers are subject to "duty of care" legislation. In order to avoid a situation in which the pension income is strongly affected by financial market shocks shortly before conversion to annuities, the Authority for the Financial Markets (AFM) has published guidelines to manage the conversion from capital to annuities.[33] AFM expects the exposure to equities to be

---

[33] Note that even if no equity exposure is present at conversion a 1 percent drop in interest rate just before conversion can have a 5 percent impact in pension

reduced to zero close to the conversion date. Moreover, AFM suggests the duration of the overall portfolio should be equal to the duration of the (nominal) annuity to be bought in order to manage interest rate risk. In spirit these are adequate guidelines to check whether pension providers manage pension wealth adequately in the interest of the individual.

To the best of our knowledge other countries do not have similar "duty of care" rules to protect individuals. In some cases, the financial crisis has had very significant impact on the pension income of many individuals in these countries. Despite being "ahead of the curve" in this regard, the Dutch recommendations still have some limitations. For example, AFM seems to assume that pension wealth will always be converted to fixed annuities. In the previous section we argued that this is not necessarily optimal (and also not imposed by current legislation). Such standards may not be appropriate – as written – if a wider selection of annuity products (e.g., variable or deferred) are part of the plan. Regulation may be better suited to specifying the degree of "risk tolerance" around the conversion, rather than specifying the precise mechanism that must be followed prior to conversion.

10.7 Conclusions

The Dutch system for the decumulation of pension wealth is to be commended for placing a high priority on ensuring that individuals are provided with sustainable levels of lifelong income. This emphasis on annuitization stands in stark contrast to many other countries – such as the US – in which the retirement system is more focused on wealth accumulation than on retirement income security.

However, the Dutch system may be a case of "too much of a good thing is a bad thing." The requirement that virtually *all* retirement wealth in the first, second and third pillars be annuitized has the effect of likely overannuitizing many citizens relative to what would be individually optimal for them. While mandating some level of annuitization is sensible, excessive annuity mandates can reduce welfare by imposing liquidity constraints and by making it more costly to leave bequests.

income if the difference in the duration of the annuity and that of pension wealth would be 5. The shocks in equity markets can obviously easily be of similar magnitude, even if only part of the wealth is invested in equities.

In this chapter, we propose that the amount of compulsory annuitization be scaled back, and only mandated to the extent necessary to ensure that retirees' basic needs are covered. This minimum annuity requirement should provide adequate inflation protection and adequate spousal protection. Above this, we argue that additional annuitization should be encouraged, but not mandated, and we discuss "automatic annuitization with an opt-out" as a promising policy approach. We also suggest that above the minimum annuity amount, consumers be provided with a richer set of options, including variable annuity products, deferred pay-out products and even non-annuity products.

References

Aura, Saku, 2001, Does the Balance of Power Within a Family Matter? The Case of the Retirement Equity Act, IGIER Working Paper 202, Milan, Italy: Innocenzo Gasparini Institute for Economic Research.

Bateman, Hazel, Geoffrey Kingston and John Piggott, 2001, *Forced Saving*, Cambridge University Press, New York.

Bernheim, B. Douglas, 1991, How strong are bequest motives? Evidence based on estimates of the demand for life insurance and annuities, *Journal of Political Economy*, vol. 99(5): 899–927.

Beshears, John, James J. Choi, David Laibson and Brigitte C. Madrian, 2006, The Importance of Default Options for Retirement Saving Outcomes: Evidence from the United States, NBER Working Paper 12009.

Bikker, Jacob A., and Jan de Dreu, 2009, Operating costs of pension funds: The impact of scale, governance and plan design, *Journal of Pension Economics and Finance*, vol. 8(1): 63–89.

Blake, David, Edmund Cannon and Ian Tonks, 2010, Ending Compulsory Annuitization: What are the Consequences? Pensions Institute Report, July.

Bonenkamp, Jan, 2009, Measuring lifetime redistribution in Dutch occupational pensions, *De Economist*, vol. 157(1): 49–77.

Botti, Simona, and Sheena S. Iyengar, 2006, The dark side of choice: When choice impairs social welfare, *Journal of Public Policy and Marketing*, vol. 25(1): 24–38.

Brown, Jeffrey R., 2001a, Are the Elderly Really Over-Annuitized? New Evidence on Life Insurance and Bequests, in: David Wise (ed.), *Themes in the Economics of Aging*, 91–126, University of Chicago Press.

2001b, Private pensions, mortality risk, and the decision to annuitize, *Journal of Public Economics*, vol. 82(1): 29–62.

2002, Differential Mortality and the Value of Individual Account Retirement Annuities, in: Martin Feldstein and Jeffrey Liebman, *The Distributional Effects of Social Security Reform*, 401–446, University of Chicago Press.

2003, Redistribution and insurance: Mandatory annuitization with mortality heterogeneity, *The Journal of Risk and Insurance*, vol. 70(1):17–41.

2009a, Financial Education and Annuities, Report prepared for the OECD.

2009b, Understanding the Role of Annuities in Retirement Planning, in: Annamaria Lusardi (ed.), *Overcoming the Saving Slump*, 178–206, University of Chicago Press.

Brown, Jeffrey R., and Peter R. Orszag, 2006, The political economy of government-issued longevity bonds, *Journal of Risk and Insurance*, vol. 73(4): 611–31.

Brown, Jeffrey R., and James M. Poterba, 2000, Joint life annuities and the demand for annuities by married couples, *The Journal of Risk and Insurance*, vol. 67(4): 527–53.

Brown, Jeffrey R., Olivia S. Mitchell and James M. Poterba, 2001, The Role of Real Annuities and Indexed Bonds in an Individual Accounts Retirement Program, in: John Campbell and Martin Feldstein (eds.), *Risk Aspects of Investment-Based Social Security Reform*, 321–60, University of Chicago Press.

2002, Mortality Risk, Inflation Risk, and Annuity Products, in: O. Mitchell, Z. Bodie, B. Hammond and S. Zeldes (eds.) *Innovations in Retirement Financing*, 175–97, Philadelphia: University of Pennsylvania Press.

Brown, Jeffrey R., Jeffrey R. Kling, Sendhil Mullainathan and Marian Wrobel, 2008, Why don't people insure late life consumption? A framing explanation of the under-annuitization puzzle, *American Economic Review*, vol. 98(2): 304–9.

Bütler, Monika, and Frederica Teppa, 2007, The choice between an annuity and a lump sum: Results from Swiss pension funds, *Journal of Public Economics*, vol. 91(10): 1944–66.

Bütler, Monika, Kim Peijnenburg and Stefan Staubli, 2010, Do Means Tested Benefits Reduce the Demand for Annuities: Evidence from Switzerland?, Netspar Discussion Paper.

Cannon, Edmund, and Ian Tonks, 2008, *Annuity Markets*, Oxford University Press.

2011, Compulsory and Voluntary Annuity markets in the UK, in: Olivia Mitchell, John Piggott and Noriyuke Takayama (eds.), *Revisiting Retirement Payouts*, Oxford University Press.

Congressional Research Service, 2005, Pension Issues: Lump-Sum Distributions and Retirement Income Security, CRS Report for Congress.

Davidoff, Thomas, Jeffrey R. Brown and Peter A. Diamond, 2005, Annuities and individual welfare, *American Economic Review*, vol. 95(5): 1573–90.

Dietvorst, Gerry, Carel Hooghiemstra, Theo Nijman and Alwin Oerlemans, 2010, Decumulatie van pensioenrechten, NEA Paper 34 (in Dutch).

Eenkhoorn, Elisabeth, and Gerrit Zijlmans, 2010, Normen voor de pensioenaanspraken-satistiek, NEA Paper 29, Netspar (in Dutch).

Einav, Liran, Amy Finkelstein and Paul Schrimpf, 2010, Optimal mandates and the welfare cost of asymmetric information: Evidence from the UK annuity market, *Econometrica*, vol. 78(3): 1031–92.

Finkelstein, Amy, and James Poterba, 2002, Selection effects in the United Kingdom individual annuities market, *Economic Journal*, vol. 112(476): 28–50.

Finkelstein, Amy, Erzo F.P. Luttmer and Matt Notowidigdo, 2008, What Good is Health Without Wealth?, The Effect of Health on the Marginal Utility of Consumption, NBER Working Paper W14089.

Gale, William G., J. Mark Iwry, David C. John and Lina Walker, 2008, Increasing Annuitization in 401(k) Plans with Automatic Trial Income, The Retirement Security Project Paper 2008–02, available at: www. retirementsecurityproject.org (accessed January 2011).

Gustman, Alan L., Thomas L. Steinmeier and Nahid Tabatabai, 2010, *Pensions in the Health and Retirement Study*, Cambridge, MA: Harvard University Press.

Holden, Karen, and Sarah Nicholson, 1998, *Selection of a joint-and-survivor pension (IRP Discussion Paper 1175–98)*, Madison: University of Wisconsin Institute for Research on Poverty.

Horneff, Wolfram J., Raimond Maurer and Michael Z. Stamos, 2008, Life-cycle asset allocation with annuity markets, *Journal of Economic Dynamics and Control*, vol. 32: 3590–3612.

Hurd, Michael D., 1989, Mortality risk and bequests, *Econometrica*, vol. 57(4): 779–813.

Inkmann, Joachim, Paula Lopes and A. Michaelides, 2007, How Deep is the Annuity Market Participation Puzzle?, Netspar Discussion Paper 2007–011.

International Monetary Fund, 2007, Mexico: Financial Sector Assessment Program Update – Technical Note – The Pension Annuity Market, IMF Country Report 07/163, May. www.imf.org/external/pubs/ft/scr/2007/cr07163.pdf (accessed January 2011).

Knox, David M., 2000, The Australian Annuity Market, World Bank Policy Research Working Paper 2495. Available at SSRN: http://ssrn.com/abstract=632565 (accessed January 2011).

Koijen, Ralph S.J., Theo E. Nijman and Bas Werker, 2011, Optimal Annuity Risk Management, CentER Working Paper Series 2006–78, *Review of Finance*, vol. 1594: 799–833. Available at SSRN: http://ssrn.com/abstract=890730 (accessed January 2011).

Lindeman, David, and Juan Yermo, 2002, Private Annuity Markets, Paper presented at the OECD and INPRS Korea Conference on Private Pensions in Asia, Seoul, October 23–25. Available at www.oecd.org/dataoecd/51/39/2763708.pdf (accessed January 2011).

Lockwood, Lee, 2010, The Importance of Bequest Motives: Evidence from Long-Term Care Insurance and the Pattern of Saving, Mimeo.

Mackenzie, George A., 2006, *Annuity Markets and Pension Reform*, Cambridge University Press.

Milevsky, M.A., 2005, Advanced life delayed annuities: Pure longevity insurance with deductibles, *North American Actuarial Journal*, vol. 9(4): 109–22.

Mitchell, Olivia S., John Piggott and Noriyuke Takayama, 2011, *Revisiting Retirement Pay-outs: Market Developments and Policy Issues*, Oxford University Press.

Mitchell, Olivia S., James M. Poterba, Mark J. Warshawsky and Jeffrey R. Brown, 1999, New evidence on the money's worth of individual annuities, *American Economic Review*, vol. 89(5): 1299–1318.

Munnell, Alicia H., Anthony Webb and Francesca Golub-Sass, 2007, Is There Really a Retirement Savings Crisis? An NRRI Analysis, Boston College Center for Retirement Research Issue Brief #7–11 July.

Pang, G., and M. Warshawsky, 2010, Optimizing the equity-bond-annuity portfolio in retirement: The impact of uncertain health expenses, *Insurance: Mathematics and Economics*, vol. 46(1): 198–209.

Peijnenburg, Kim, Theo Nijman and Bas Werker, 2010a, Optimal Annuitization with Incomplete Annuity Markets and Background Risk During Retirement, Netspar Discussion Paper.

2010b, Health Cost Risk and Optimal Retirement Provision: A Simple Rule for Annuity Demand, Netspar Discussion Paper 05/2010–018.

Prudential Financial, 2006, Learning the Two-Step: A New Approach to Asset Allocation for the Retiree, Prudential Financial white paper.

Salisbury, Dallas, 2002, June 20 Statement Before the Committee on Ways and Means, Subcommittee on Oversight, United States House of Representatives. Hearing on Retirement Security and Defined Benefit Pension Plans.

Sanders, Lisanne, 2010, The Impact of Incomplete Annuity Markets on the Demand for Joint and Survivor Annuities, Mimeo.

Sanders, Lisanne, Anja De Waegenaere and Theo Nijman, 2010, When Can Insurers Offer Products That Dominate Delayed Old-age Benefit Claiming, Netspar Discussion Paper 04/2010–011.

Scholz, John Karl, Ananth Seshadri and Surachai Khitatrakun, 2006, Are Americans saving "optimally" for retirement?, *Journal of Political Economy*, vol. 114(4): 607–43.

Scott, Jason, John Watson and Wie-Yin Hu, 2006, Efficient Annuitization with Delayed Payout Annuities, Mimeo.

2009, What Makes a Better Annuity?, Mimeo.

Turra, Cassio, and Olivia S. Mitchell, 2008, The Impact of Health Status and Out-of-Pocket Medical Expenditures on Annuity Valuation, in: John Ameriks and Olivia S. Mitchell (eds.), *Recalibrating Retirement Spending and Saving*, 227–50, Oxford University Press.

Yaari, Menahem E., 1965, Uncertain lifetime, life insurance, and the theory of the consumer, *Review of Economic Studies*, vol. 32(2): 137–50.

PART IV

The future of multi-pillar pension systems

11 | *The future of multi-pillar pension systems*

LANS BOVENBERG AND CASPER VAN
EWIJK

11.1 Introduction

This final chapter takes stock of the evolution of the pension system and the challenges remaining for the future. It describes how pension systems in the industrial world have been facing similar challenges. As a result, pension contracts in various countries have developed in similar directions. At the same time, however, the way pensions are organized still differs substantially between countries. This international heterogeneity is likely to remain in the future. A unique answer to what is the optimal pension system does not exist; several alternative solutions exist alongside each other, depending on the specific historical, political and institutional context of each country. We therefore derive a typology of pension systems, discuss the strengths and weaknesses of alternative systems, and sketch some important challenges for the future.

The rest of this chapter is organized as follows. Section 11.2 describes trends in pension insurance and the key remaining issues and trade-offs based on the analysis in this book. This section concludes that the reform of pension systems in response to common trends is underway but by no means finished. In order to answer the normative question how alternative institutional designs should ideally develop in the future, Section 11.3 develops a typology of pension systems. Section 11.4 investigates how the various pension systems identified in this typology can enhance intergenerational risk sharing. It considers also how these alternative pension designs can better tailor life-cycle planning and intra-generational insurance to individual heterogeneity.

11.2 Challenges to pension systems: functions, trade-offs and trends

For each of the three main functions of pensions described in Chapter 5 and briefly reiterated here, this section discusses the most important trade-offs in the institutional design of the functions. It then indicates how various trends affect these trade-offs and how institutions have responded to these trends. Finally, the remaining challenges for each of the functions are explored. Table 11.1 below summarizes the trade-offs, trends, responses and challenges. This table may serve as a starting point for our discussion of the challenges of the pension system; we consider each of the functions in turn.

11.2.1 Life-cycle planning

To take account of intra-generational heterogeneity, pension arrangements should be tailored to specific idiosyncratic circumstances and individual preferences. Heterogeneity typically calls for consumer sovereignty. Unfortunately, however, empirical evidence suggests that households typically lack the basic financial knowledge, computational ability and willpower to implement optimal life-cycle planning and the associated intertemporal financial decisions under uncertainty. Accordingly, various "internalities" complicate efficient individual intertemporal decision making under uncertainty. Moreover, delegating these complicated decisions to others may give rise to serious agency and governance problems, especially because financially illiterate individuals are poorly equipped to discipline suppliers.

Institutions for life-cycle planning
The government can address myopia and other "internalities" that give rise to poor individual decision making in life-cycle financial planning by forcing agents to participate in public earnings-related pension schemes. Alternatively, the state can make private pension schemes mandatory for workers. It can also mandate workers to take out pension insurance while allowing individuals to select their own insurance pool. The drawback of compulsion is that it typically cannot account for heterogeneity between consumers, especially because governments are reluctant to use information on specific features of individuals in setting compulsory insurance levels. To accommodate intra-generational heterogeneity, pension schemes can be tailored to groups of workers with the same specific features (e.g., the same type of human capital). Personal pension plans provided by insurance companies and other financial institutions can accommodate individual idiosyncratic features. These retail products, however, are typically

substantially more costly than standardized wholesale products, in part due to substantial marketing costs and adverse selection.

Trade-off: choice versus individual failure

A fundamental trade-off bedeviling life-cycle planning is between tailoring to intra-generational heterogeneity (in terms of individual preferences and circumstances), on the one hand, and containing individual imperfections, on the other hand. To illustrate, high compulsory saving levels with mandatory pooling of longevity risk may prevent myopic behavior and fight inadequate longevity insurance (see Section 11.2.3 below). At the same time, however, such a measure may force people with low preferences for old-age consumption or those facing temporary borrowing constraints to save too much and to take out too much longevity insurance.

Trade-off: competition versus mandatory pooling

More individual choice increases competitive pressure on pension providers to better accommodate preferences of consumers and to contain costs. However, the more the scope for individual choice is increased and the more the market for pensions becomes contestable, the more suppliers tend to spend on public relations and marketing costs. This raises transaction costs passed on to consumers. Hence, as an instrument to discipline pension providers, the effect of more individual choice raising competition on costs is ambiguous. Indeed, individuals who suffer from imperfect decision making raise difficult governance issues.

Trends: more heterogeneity, more demanding consumers and better ICT

In the face of growing heterogeneity and more demanding consumers, the first trade-off shifts towards tailoring to individual circumstances. The financial crisis, however, has shown that many individuals are poorly equipped to make financial decisions, thereby increasing the awareness of individual foibles. This increased awareness has shifted the trade-off towards containing individual failures. More individual elements require pension agencies to gather more information about specific relevant features of participants – not only the individual's work history and family status, but also health, financial portfolio, housing status (home-owner or renter) and preferences. Better ICT

Table 11.1 *Trade-offs, trends, responses and challenges*

Function	Trade-offs	Trends	Responses	Remaining challenges
Life-cycle planning	• Tailoring to heterogeneity versus containing personal failures • Competition versus lower transaction costs	• Increasing heterogeneity • More demanding consumers • Better ICT	• More choice options • Guided choice (defaults)	• Design choice architecture • Integral financial services
Intergenerational risk sharing	• Risk sharing versus political risk and labor-market distortions	• Aging and maturing of pension funds • Increasing competition on labor and commodity markets	• More complete risk-sharing contracts • Risk-bearing pensions • Increased and more flexible retirement ages	• Labor market for older workers • Design optimal risk-sharing scheme • Risk management by the government
Intra-generational risk sharing	• Fighting selection versus accommodating heterogeneity • Insurance versus moral hazard	• Increasing heterogeneity in skills and longevity • More elastic labor-market behavior	• Actuarially fair pension systems • Tighter disability and unemployment insurance	• Employability of older low-skilled workers • Optimal mix between saving and insurance

has improved the possibilities to collect more information about individuals. However, privacy considerations and fears about a "big brother" type of pension agency may prevent the potential of ICT from being fully exploited. Moreover, financial intermediaries are often not allowed to use individual information in the context of market regulation aimed at preventing risk selection or at ensuring a level playing field with other suppliers that do not have access to this information. ICT, however, may allow other providers to more easily get access to this information if the individuals concerned assent to this. Furthermore, ICT can improve information on pension products and enhance the transparency of markets. In addition to more transparent information, better education may facilitate better individual decision making. Also new insights from behavioral economics may help. To illustrate, properly designed defaults based on information of individual features may assist individuals to tailor their pension arrangements to their specific circumstances.

Response to trends

In response to these trends pension systems have moved in the direction of accommodating more choice. Most pension systems now allow for a flexible choice of the retirement age with more or less actuarially fair adjustments. This applies to public, occupational and individual schemes alike. Many European pension systems have reduced or eliminated altogether generous early retirement incentives introduced in the 1970s and the 1980s. Moreover, the tendency to limit the mandatory contribution rates in the face of the growing financial burden of pensions has increased the scope for individual choice in determining the ambition level of pension insurance. Furthermore, some countries have introduced flexibility in choice of provider (Chile, UK), flexibility in contribution rates (KiwiSaver in New Zealand) and the portfolio mix with defaults (UK). With more financial risks being shifted to individuals in occupational schemes, some of these schemes may allow for more individual portfolio choice in the future, albeit with carefully designed defaults.

To contain individual failures, experiments with defaults (see Bodie and Prast in Chapter 9 of this book) are increasingly popular in countries that traditionally heavily treasure individual discretion. Defaults maintain the freedom of individuals to opt out while at the same time addressing individual failures by assisting those who are not able or willing to choose themselves. To illustrate, the US introduced a pension law in 2006 that facilitates default enrollment in pension plans, automatic default escalation of pension contributions and default portfolios (see Beshears *et al.*, 2008).

Remaining challenges

Although empirical research shows that choice architecture has a powerful impact on actual choices, structuring choice in pension insurance in an optimal way is still in its infancy. Defaults may take into account personal characteristics. However, defaults face similar problems that mandatory systems do. In particular, defaults cannot be tailored to individual features without pension agencies gathering information on individuals. Hence, also here privacy considerations limit the scope for tailoring pensions to the individual level, even though the cost of imperfectly tailoring pension contracts may be smaller than in mandatory systems because individuals can opt out. Furthermore, just as mandatory provisions, defaults raise governance and agency issues. How does one ensure that the agency setting the default settings acts in the interests of the pension consumers?

Whether pensions, which typically benefit from a favorable tax treatment compared with other type of savings, will be integrated more with other facilities for life-cycle planning is unclear, and may depend on the pension model chosen. If governments force workers to participate in pension funds, they may not allow these mandatory pension funds to compete for supplementary financial services in order to not distort financial markets. Indeed, at present, pension insurance is often quite separate from other parts of life-cycle financial planning, such as housing finance and health insurance.

Financial intermediaries (including pension funds), however, can help individuals with their financial planning over the life cycle. In particular, they can advise workers in accumulating and insuring human and financial capital during their working lives. In this regard, disability and unemployment insurances are closely related to pension insurance. Indeed, the optimal retirement age depends on idiosyncratic health and labor-market risks, which tend to increase with age. Disability and unemployment insurances involve moral hazard; better insurance reduces the incentives to maintain human capital. Pension funds may help to find the optimal mix of saving and insurance. Moreover, integration of part of pension saving with precautionary saving for idiosyncratic human-capital risks may be optimal (see Stiglitz and Yun, 2005; Holzmann and Hinz, 2005).

During the retirement phase, the elderly need integrated advice with regards to housing, health care, the type of annuity (possibly of the escalating type) and, possibly, part-time labor income. Linking reverse life insurance through annuities to health care insurance can combat selection; bad risks for an annuity company tend to be good risks for health insurers, and the other way around. Moreover, by providing health insurance, an insurance company reduces the need for liquidity, thereby making annuitization more attractive. Also in health and care insurance, moral hazard may be important, especially for relatively small risks such as personal services required around the home. For these risks, precautionary saving may thus be appropriate. This implies that annuities should be complemented by liquid private saving.

11.2.2 Intergenerational risk sharing

From a welfare point of view, risks should be shared as broadly as possible over various generations. Sharing current risks with future and young generations is especially valuable with regard to habit formation[1] and volatile capital markets as a result of mispricing and bubbles. Two fundamental constraints, however, limit intergenerational risk sharing. First, the limited liability of human capital (and the resulting non-tradability of human-capital risks) constrains the ability of young agents that have not yet accumulated financial collateral to voluntarily trade risks with older agents. Second, when younger cohorts start to trade on capital markets and can begin to conclude voluntary contracts, the older cohorts' life risks have been realized and are thus largely known. By that time, intergenerational risk sharing has become intergenerational redistribution. Generations do not voluntarily commit to a risk-sharing contract that involves risks that have already been realized; whereas young cohorts do not accept debts that older generations have run up in the face of adverse shocks, older cohorts do not transfer to younger generations the surpluses that these older

---

[1] This applies both to external and internal habit formation. With internal habits, people are more risk averse in the short run than in the long run because they need time to adjust their habits in response to shocks. With external habits, the pain of adverse shocks is softened if social reference groups share in these shocks.

cohorts have been able to accumulate in good times. Hence, in both good and bad times, intergenerational risk sharing may break down. This so-called discontinuity risk of the risk-sharing contract limits the credibility of sharing large risks across generations.

Institutions for intergenerational risk sharing

Private capital markets can help to share risks between generations who are close in age. To illustrate, by buying bonds, older agents may try to shift risk to younger generations who hold primarily equity claims. The limited liability of equity implies, however, that in case of large shocks bond holders will still be residual risk bearers. Private intergenerational risk sharing may occur also in rich dynasties that leave financial bequests.

As emphasized by Bohn in Chapter 6 of this volume, some limited private risk sharing may occur also through private pension funds, which may alleviate the burden on the government in accomplishing intergenerational risk sharing. Bohn shows, however, that private risk sharing through occupational pension funds is feasible only if specific human capital or other factors (such as the limited portability of pension rights or implicit labor contracts involving deferred wages) tie workers to the insurance pool of the pension fund. Quasi rents that originate in specific human capital thus allow occupational pension funds to tax workers to some extent. Competition and mobility on the labor market, however, limit the tax power of occupational pension funds and therefore give rise to discontinuity risk as workers who are taxed heavily move to a different place of employment. Private and public risk sharing may be complements if the government either provides longevity and wage-linked bonds to private funds and insurance companies or engages in reinsurance of private pension schemes.

The government wields more tax power than pension funds because it controls the entire labor market of a country so that workers cannot escape taxation by moving to another sector or by becoming self-employed. Taxes on labor income can include in risk-sharing arrangements also the non-tradable human wealth of young generations who have little financial collateral. Even the government, however, is limited in its ability to commit generations to risk sharing because younger generations vote with their feet or their voice. In particular, if taxes are very high, agents avoid taxes by reducing labor supply in the formal sector or evade taxes by no longer declaring their labor income; the associated labor-market distortions limit the scope for intergenerational risk sharing.[2] Moreover, voters may not be willing to finance high government debts. Anticipating the limited liability of the citizens of a country, financial markets constrain the ability of older generations to keep up their consumption level in the face of adverse shocks.

The state suffers from other weaknesses as well. First, the government is subject to political risk. Second, and related to this, the state may have difficulty in taking a diversified portfolio of financial assets on its balance sheet. Indeed, political considerations may distort investment decisions if the state owns most firms in the economy.

Trade-offs: risk sharing versus limiting political risk, discontinuity risk and labor-market distortions

The fundamental trade-off bedeviling intergenerational risk sharing is the trade-off between risk sharing and limiting political risk. Forcing workers to participate in intergenerational risk sharing reduces the discontinuity risk that young generations escape the risk-sharing contract by voting with their feet. At the same time, however, lack of competition may give rise to political risks. In particular, older generations who wield the political power in a democracy may be tempted to abuse risk-sharing arrangements and shift risks onto younger and future generations without properly rewarding younger agents; incumbents grant themselves additional benefits in good times while they try to tax new entrants in bad times.

This trade-off between intergenerational risk sharing and containing political risk[3] thus involves market failure versus government failure; whereas markets cannot sustain voluntary risk sharing between generations that differ a lot in age, governments suffer from political risks as older generations that lack market discipline may abuse political power. The conflict between the economic power of workers who control their human capital, on the one hand, and the political power

---

[2] Bonenkamp and Westerhout (2010) find that these distortions are only small compared with the welfare gains of risk sharing. Mehlkopf (2011), in contrast, argues that the costs of risk sharing may be larger in current pension contracts.

[3] A related trade-off is that between rules and discretion. Rules reduce political risks by limiting the discretionary powers of politicians but at the same time these rules constrain the flexibility of governments to respond to contingencies that were not anticipated when the rules were formulated.

of older agents, on the other hand, complicates intergenerational risk sharing.

A related trade-off is between risk sharing and limiting discontinuity risk. Risk sharing involves *ex post* redistribution, which threatens the continuity of the contract. Solvency regulations, for example, constrain intergenerational risk sharing but limit both political and discontinuity risk. Depending on the economic power of the young and the political power of the old, these regulations protect old or young cohorts. They protect younger generations by preventing older generations from shifting substantial unfunded liabilities onto the younger generations. If labor mobility is high or disincentives are important, these regulations limit discontinuity risk in the face of adverse shocks and thus protect the older generations.

This trade-off can also be stated as risk sharing versus labor-market efficiency.[4] In view of the limited liability of human capital, intergenerational risk sharing occurs through taxes on labor income, which distort the labor market. Accordingly, the price of intergenerational risk sharing is a less efficient labor market. Moreover, intergenerational risk sharing may require limiting the mobility of labor, for example by restricting the portability of pension rights across sectors. Also this may hurt the efficiency of the labor market.

Trends: aging, more labor mobility, more competition and the financial crisis

Various trends move the trade-off of risk sharing versus limiting discontinuity risk and labor-market distortions away from risk sharing. First of all, aging increases the weight of older compared with younger generations. In other words, the risk-bearing capital of younger agents is leveraged with more numerous older generations. This limits the scope for protecting older generations from risks by shifting risks onto future generations. To illustrate, aging of the membership of occupational pension funds has expanded the obligations of the funds compared with the premium base. Accordingly, unanticipated shocks in financial markets and longevity require larger changes in pension contributions in order to shield pension rights from these shocks. Guaranteed pension obligations have thus become more expensive in

---

[4] See also the trade-off between insurance and incentives discussed in connection with intra-generational risk sharing below.

that these defined benefits (DB) result in more volatility in pension contributions. Also increased mobility of workers[5] and the reduced importance of firm-specific human capital move the trade-off between risk sharing and limiting discontinuity risk away from risk sharing because taxing workers in the event of a bad shock becomes more difficult.

Aging also affects corporate pension funds in which the residual claimants are primarily the shareholders of the corporation involved; for many corporations, financial and actuarial risks of pension guarantees start to dominate those of their core business. New accounting rules (FRS 17/IAS 19/FAS 87), which force corporations to disclose pension risks, make this increasingly transparent. The volatility of financial markets in the recent decade has also confronted corporations with the risks of corporate pension funds. At the same time, more intense competition implies that companies exhibit shorter lifespans and enjoy smaller rents. Moreover, increased debt finance has increased bankruptcy risk and has reduced the quality of the debt claims, including the pension obligations of the corporate pension funds. In the face of increased discontinuity risk and the limited liability of the shareholders, firms can thus offer less security to the participants of their occupational pensions. Retirees end up as residual risk bearers because companies often are in trouble when the pension fund is experiencing financial distress. In the recent financial crisis, for example, several corporations had to close their pension funds.

Response to trends: pension rights become risk bearing
As the capacity of sponsors, (future) workers and (future) taxpayers to absorb pension risks has become more limited in the face of aging and increasing competition on commodity and labor markets, those who have accumulated pension claims become risk-bearing stakeholders and are thus confronted with more risks. Whereas traditional DB plans protect pension rights from financial-market and demographic risks, pension claims are increasingly being made contingent on shocks in longevity and on developments in financial markets. In other words, guaranteed debt claims have become risk-bearing capital. Also in the Netherlands, sectoral DB schemes are being transformed into hybrid

---

[5] The increased portability of pension rights aimed at a more efficient allocation of labor also enhances the mobility of labor.

systems, which explicitly put financial-market risk on those holding pension claims (both workers and retirees). In fact, risk-sharing contracts are becoming more complete in the sense that the pension contract is more explicit about who bears risks in case of unexpected macroeconomic shocks.

Earnings-related pay-as-you-go (PAYG) systems also put more macroeconomic risk on participants themselves, sometimes in an explicit fashion as in the notional defined contribution (NDC) systems and sometimes in an implicit way as retirees share the pain of budget cuts if the public finances are hit by adverse shocks. In fact, PAYG schemes are becoming more explicit *ex ante* on how demographic and output shocks are allocated over various stakeholders to ensure the financial sustainability of the scheme, for example through automatic balancing mechanisms. Accordingly, not only in funded but also in PAYG schemes, the risk-sharing contract is becoming more complete in the face of a smaller base to absorb ever-larger macroeconomic risks. Accordingly, DB systems that suggest that pension benefits can be shielded from macroeconomic risks are being replaced by pension systems that put these shocks on the participants in a predictable manner. Individual property rights on risky assets are clarified by separating the public pension system from the rest of the budget. This shift away from discretion to predictable rules reduces political risks.

Response to demographic changes

Aging is the result of increased longevity and lower fertility. Increasing life expectancy challenges both funded and PAYG systems; at a given retirement age, it increases the length of the retirement period that needs to be financed. More and more pension systems are explicitly shifting the costs of higher longevity onto the participants of the pension plan – at least during the accumulation phase. Hence, workers have to delay their retirement if they want to maintain their standard of living in retirement in the face of increased longevity. This may not be problematic if lower mortality goes together with lower morbidity and people can maintain their labor productivity up to an advanced age. Indeed, whether increased longevity leads to lower consumption level depends on whether human capital rises at a slower speed than the life span.

As regards fertility risk, PAYG schemes especially seem to be vulnerable to lower fertility because PAYG schemes rely on human capital of the young to finance the pensions of older generations. Indeed, in the face of lower fertility, funded pensions may replace part of the PAYG pensions as cohorts that raise fewer children rely more on financial capital than on investments in the human capital of children to safeguard their retirement incomes (see Sinn, 2000). However, as global aging may reduce rates of returns on capital markets, also funded schemes may come under pressure as a result of lower fertility. Indeed, aging is likely to increase the return on human capital and reduce the return on financial saving. Hence, lower fertility may result in more labor supply per capita and more investment in the quality of human capital rather than in more saving.

In response to the growing burden of aging, many countries have cut back the cost of pensions in an attempt to put a ceiling on pension contributions. In line with defined contribution (DC) schemes, most of the burden of adjustment is thus put on the benefit side by raising the retirement age, restricting the eligibility for benefits in other ways, or reducing replacement rates. Some countries with large PAYG systems have limited the indexation of benefits in payment. This may facilitate a move towards a multi-pillar scheme, which includes not only a public PAYG scheme but also occupational pension plans and personal pension schemes (see European Commission, 2010, 365/3, Figure 10).

Remaining challenges

The primary remaining challenge concerns the optimal sharing of labor-market and financial-market risks across generations. PAYG systems typically link pension rights to wages (most NDC systems), while pension rights in funded systems typically depend on financial-market risks. A more optimal pension system would implement optimal life-cycle investment. In particular, the government, which taxes labor income, would provide wage-linked retirement benefits to older generations so that wage risks are shifted away from workers to pensioners, who are then protected against standard-of-living risk. Alternatively, the government could issue wage-linked bonds, which pension funds and insurance companies can buy to hedge wage-linked retirement benefits. At the same time, workers would absorb financial-market risk by holding equity in their own retirement accounts. Moreover, the government can take financial-market risks on its balance sheet on behalf of younger generations with non-tradable human capital (e.g., through taxes on capital income and consumption). There is no unique solution to these challenges; different pension systems can take different routes. We return to this in Section 11.4 below.

Important demographic risks are aggregate mortality and morbidity risk. In the optimal pension system, the tail mortality risk (i.e., the survival probabilities at very advanced ages) should be absorbed by younger generations rather than by the cohorts concerned. This in effect amounts to a DB aspect in the pension system: younger generations insure the macro longevity risk of the oldest generations. One way to implement this in the face of the limited liability and non-tradability of human capital is for the government to issue longevity bonds for these tail risks while at the same time reducing its longevity risk by not allowing the public pension claims of younger cohorts to rise with longevity. In this way, both the government and the private sector are involved in providing pension insurance.

With participants of funded schemes bearing more financial-market risks, private pension funds must find optimal ways to allocate risk over the participants,[6] to communicate this risk and to help participants absorb the risk. To illustrate, current Dutch occupational pension plans impose uniform investments and indexation rules on all participants but are currently investigating whether indexation rules can be differentiated across age groups. Workers can then take more risks on their pension savings and benefit from the associated risk premiums, whereas the contract for the retirees is geared primarily towards protection of the purchasing power of the pension entitlements (see, e.g., Molenaar and Ponds, 2009). These reforms can be complemented by more flexibility in contribution rates. In fact, flexible contribution rates allow workers to bear more financial risks and thus to benefit more from the rewards of risk taking. Indeed, after an expected shock, it is optimal to adjust consumption levels during the rest of one's lifetime and not only during retirement. Hence, both premium levels and benefit levels should respond to risks, although habit formation may dictate smaller adjustments in the short run than in the long run.

There are other challenges as well. Due to the longevity adjustments, many countries project substantial declines in the replacement rates

---

[6] This involves also the function of life-cycle planning and the associated individual failures. Individuals are typically not able to select optimal portfolios during the life cycle.

at the fixed retirement age over the coming decades. These declines help to ensure fiscal sustainability in the face of an aging population. However, these cuts in replacement rates are credible only if older workers remain more productive and are able to continue to find work beyond current effective retirement ages. If these labor-market conditions are not met, governments will face political pressures to raise replacement rates so that the living standard of the older population does not decline too far below that of the rest of the population. Indeed, intertemporal consumption smoothing then demands higher pension contributions. Alternatively, the public finances will be burdened by higher costs of other social insurance programs, such as the disability insurance, unemployment insurance or means-tested guaranteed pensions. Financial sustainability therefore depends on whether human capital of older citizens can be protected and utilized better. Only if lower mortality goes together with more durable earning power are stable contribution rates credible in the face of increased longevity.

11.2.3 Intra-generational risk sharing

Before they know which idiosyncratic shocks they will be subject to, agents can voluntarily pool risks in insurance markets. In some cases, however, agents feature private information about their risk features. Agents who know that they have a low probability of suffering damages will then not voluntarily pool risks because insurance premia are based on the average risk features of the population as a whole. This phenomenon, which originates in private information about one's risk features when one first can take out insurance,[7] is called adverse selection and undermines voluntary insurance markets. More generally, after uncertainty is resolved and agents know their type, intra-generational risk sharing becomes redistribution: some agents must transfer resources to other agents. If agents have not been able to sign an insurance contract behind the veil of ignorance about their type, this transfer of resources will not occur voluntarily.

---

[7] Just as the function of life-cycle planning, the function of intra-generational risk sharing is complicated by asymmetric, private information about an individual's idiosyncratic features. Just like intergenerational risk sharing, intra-generational risk sharing becomes more complicated and does not occur through voluntary market transactions if agents cannot sign insurance contracts when they are still ignorant about their risk features.

Institutions for intra-generational risk sharing and redistribution
By making risk sharing compulsory, the government in effect redistributes resources from the good risks to the bad risks. More generally, after uncertainty is resolved and insurance has become redistribution, the state has to force the lucky agents to give up resources. Indeed, the state has a leading role in facilitating intra-generational distribution. The state has the monopoly power to tax because democratic control provides the legitimacy to intervene in private property rights.

Private insurance schemes controlling a group of workers may also fight selection and implement some limited redistribution. If workers feature specific human capital in specific sectors, for example, pension schemes that cover the entire industry may be able to pool workers facing different risk levels. However, competition and mobility on labor markets limit the scope for compulsory pooling of workers who exhibit different risk levels. To illustrate, if some workers pay contributions that exceed an actuarially neutral level, the employers involved may have to pay higher wages to attract these workers.

Government regulation and private risk pooling are complements if government regulation forces workers with specific human capital in a particular sector to pool their risks in a single pension scheme. Moreover, private pension funds can help to redistribute if the government regulation ensures that individuals cannot escape the redistribution by moving to a different place of employment. To illustrate, regulation that forces financial institutions to charge the same price for annuities to both genders may be able to redistribute from males to females.

Trade-off in longevity insurance: combating selection versus accommodating heterogeneity
Forcing people to pool their risk prevents them from selecting their own level of insurance. This gives rise to a trade-off between combating selection and accommodating individual heterogeneity. To illustrate, some people may not want to take out longevity insurance through forced annuitization because they prefer to keep their wealth liquid during retirement in the face of either idiosyncratic risks or spending preferences that differ from the average preferences.

Another illustration of this trade-off involves the choice of the age at which one wants to start receiving an annuity. Offering people more discretion to select this age on the basis of uniform actuarial adjustments results in selection as short-lived agents choose to retire early while long-lived agents are better off retiring later.

Combating selection in longevity insurance also yields a trade-off between efficiency and equity. In regular social insurance, compulsory insurance benefits both equity and efficiency as it protects the bad risks, which tend to be the persons with little human capital. In pension insurance, however, the bad risks are long-lived agents, who tend to have substantial human capital as well. Accordingly, by forcing people to take out pensions, the government helps to create efficient longevity insurance but at the cost of perverse solidarity between short-lived vulnerable agents and long-lived richer agents.

Trade-off in human-capital insurance: insurance versus incentives
Another trade-off affects the insurance of idiosyncratic human-capital risks such as disability, health problems and unemployment: the better people are insured against loss in human capital and the associated decline in labor productivity, the fewer incentives they face to prevent this loss. This trade-off between insurance and incentives is closely related to the trade-off between equity and efficiency: more redistribution by providing more income to those with less human capital and less labor income harm the incentive to work and to accumulate skills.

The trade-off between insurance and incentives applies to the design of retirement incentives. Older workers who suffer from idiosyncratic health shocks affecting their labor productivity want to retire early. Providing generous early retirement benefits thus helps to insure these adverse human-capital shocks. At the same time, however, such benefits erode labor-supply incentives and the incentives to treasure human capital. In other words, making retirement benefits more actuarially neutral by compensating workers for delaying retirement serves labor-supply incentives but removes the insurance of human-capital shocks at the end of the working life. Adverse labor-supply incentives associated with human-capital insurance can be mitigated by providing benefits only on the basis of verifiable health problems. However, disability and pension insurance often cannot be separated because health shocks and the impact on labor productivity are not verifiable.

The insurance-incentives trade-off is quite relevant in the last part of the working life. On the one hand, people face more idiosyncratic productivity risk at the end of the working life due to loss of specific human capital or the accumulation of adverse health shocks. On the other hand, retirement decisions are quite sensitive to incentives, thereby raising the efficiency costs of policies that protect those who have to retire early due to non-verifiable health and ability shocks.

A related insurance-incentives trade-off involves the commitment of the government not to let older agents starve. This implicit public insurance discourages agents from saving. If the government combats moral hazard in saving by forcing workers to save out of their labor income, it discourages labor supply. The better the government thus insures its citizens against old-age poverty through means-tested programs, the more saving and labor supply are discouraged.

Trends: more heterogeneity and more moral hazard

Trends complicate the insurance-incentives trade-off by both raising the need for insurance and increasing the efficiency costs of insurance. As regards the benefits from insurance, heterogeneity among older workers increases due to growing cultural and economic diversity. To illustrate, the gaps in mortality, morbidity and health between various workers is growing. Moreover, along with increased competition, insurance in implicit labor contracts is decreasing, thereby raising idiosyncratic human-capital risk. A more dynamic world economy and a decline of the extended family as an insurance device have increased the demand for such insurance as people experience more substantial economic insecurity.

As regards the costs of insurance, various developments increase the dangers of moral hazard and hence make insurance of human-capital risks more costly. As the economy shifts from blue-collar work in industrial sectors to white-collar work in service sectors and knowledge-intensive activities, mental causes of sickness and disability become more prominent. These types of sickness and disability can be less easily verified than physical disabilities. Moreover, more heterogeneity of work patterns in general and at the end of the working life in particular makes it more difficult to separate voluntary periods of inactivity from involuntary unemployment. Retirement decisions, for example, are becoming more flexible now that mandatory retirement and pension systems with fixed retirement ages are being phased out.

At the same time, individuals can increasingly affect the probability that they become unemployed by investing in their own employability. In other words, the dividing line blurs between the contingencies that people are responsible for and those for which they are not. These changes in the nature of social risks make it more costly to insure human capital in terms of harming the incentives to accumulate and maintain that capital.

Another reason why redistribution has become more distortionary is that age is no longer a good indicator of poverty, because many elderly individuals have accumulated substantial financial wealth. Hence, information on age should increasingly be supplemented by other information (in particular on incomes and family status) to identify those most in need of income support. This increases the efficiency costs of redistribution because individuals can affect this information (in contrast to information about age) by changing their behavior. Another aspect of intra-generational redistribution is that between genders. In many countries, the labor-market position of women has strengthened, which reduces the burden on pension systems to provide generous survivor benefits. At the same time, however, family structures have typically become less stable. The associated higher risk of divorce has put many women at risk, thereby increasing the pressure on redistributive programs.

Response to trends

To reduce labor-market distortions, occupational pension systems and earnings-related PAYG systems have become more actuarially fair. In particular, many countries have improved incentives for later retirement by raising actuarial adjustments for later retirement. Moreover, several countries have at the same time tightened eligibility criteria for unemployment and disability schemes in order to prevent these schemes from being abused as early retirement programs. In particular, the duration of unemployment benefits has been shortened and disability benefits are granted only for verifiable losses in earnings capacity. More generally, disability programs are more and more separated from old-age pension programs. Indeed, as longevity increases, the purposes of disability insurance and retirement insurance are increasingly distinct.

Earnings-related pension schemes have improved labor-market incentives during the working life by linking benefits more tightly to contributions during the entire working life. In occupational pension schemes, for example, final-pay schemes (in which benefits are based on wages in the last years before retirement) have been replaced

by career-average schemes so that pension rights are based on earnings during the entire life cycle. Moreover, in contrast to many older
Bismarckian earnings-related PAYG schemes, NDC systems link benefits more tightly to contributions during the life cycle.[8] Improved ICT
systems facilitate the registration of the entire labor-market history.
The function of redistribution and poverty alleviation is separated
from the earning-related pension system and put in a separate zero
pillar (see Chapter 3 by Hinz).

In view of a more heterogeneous older population, some countries
are replacing generic tax privileges for the elderly by means-tested
tax benefits. Indeed, as age is no longer a good indicator of poverty,
tax privileges should be based on not only age but also income and
wealth.

Remaining challenges

In setting retirement incentives, pension systems as a whole do not
escape the fundamental trade-off between insurance and incentives
that is the result of substantial heterogeneity at the end of the working life. In particular, more actuarially neutral pension pillars that are
aimed at consumption smoothing during the life cycle are typically
supplemented with special provisions for low-income groups in order
to avoid old-age poverty. Helping groups with low human capital
escape old-age poverty inevitably harms the incentives to accumulate, maintain and utilize human capital. To illustrate, means-tested
pensions impose a marginal tax rate on labor income for those who
benefit from these pensions. Moreover, disability and unemployment
insurance programs inevitably give rise to moral hazard as a result of
human-capital insurance.

Compared with other workers, workers with low earnings typically face substantially smaller incentives to delay retirement for at
least two reasons. First of all, various means-tested programs discourage low-skilled workers from continuing to work because additional labor income is taxed away in the form of lower means-tested

---

[8] Despite the stronger link between contributions and benefits, mandatory
earnings-related schemes still imply an implicit tax on workers if these workers
are myopic. In that case, workers discount the value of the additional savings
that are being accumulated. Accordingly, forced saving may help to address
saving distortions, but at the same time introduce labor-supply distortions.

benefits. Second, actuarial adjustments of pension benefits are based on average mortality rates, while low-skilled workers generally feature higher mortality rates and lower life expectancy. Low-skilled workers are thus not compensated adequately for later retirement and thus face incentives to start receiving retirement benefits as early as possible.

An important challenge in this respect is whether countries succeed in addressing the labor-market challenges of low-skilled and high-skilled workers alike. The less countries succeed in raising the earning powers of low-skilled workers in line with those of high-skilled workers, the more they will be forced to have additional means-tested DB social programs for low-skilled workers whose human capital depreciates earlier in life. These programs typically harm incentives to maintain human capital, increasing the likelihood of a vicious circle in which human capital does not become more durable. Accordingly, the main challenge for aging economies in which longevity increases is to address the weak labor-market position of elderly workers in general and that of vulnerable older low-skilled workers in particular.[9]

Individual saving accounts can improve the trade-off between insurance and incentives by facilitating self-insurance over the life course. For each type of human-capital risk, another combination between insurance and precautionary saving is optimal. Stiglitz and Yun (2005) show that saving should play a more prominent role if risk aversion is low, moral hazard is important, various risks are uncorrelated across time and among each other, and these risks are only small in a lifetime perspective. They also demonstrate that the optimal extent to which agents use precautionary saving to buffer shocks depends on the history of an individual. Self-insurance should optimally be the most important for those individuals who have not experienced adverse shocks early in life so that they are not likely to end up being lifetime poor. Saving schemes thus can play a more important role in enhancing incentives for the middle and higher incomes than for the lifetime poor.

---

[9] Similar issues arise for women. The more countries succeed in strengthening the labor-market position of women, the less they have to rely on social programs that protect women (e.g., partner pensions) but that at the same time harm labor-market incentives faced by women.

11.2.4 Conclusions

We identified similar tendencies in all pension systems, irrespective of whether they are mainly state oriented and PAYG or more privately oriented and funded. One could even speak of convergence in many important respects as distinct pension systems respond to the same trends by reforming pension contracts in similar ways. As regards tailoring to heterogeneity in life-cycle planning, pension systems accommodate more individual choice but at the same time more carefully structure the choice architecture, for example through defaults. As far as intergenerational risk sharing is concerned, more pension systems determine *ex ante* how major macroeconomic risks (wage and employment risks, demographic risks, financial-market risks) will be allocated over the various stakeholders. In the resulting risk-sharing contracts, more macroeconomic risks are put into pension rights and pension benefits instead of pension contributions in view of the limited liability of the sponsors of the pension schemes. Also retirement ages have been raised and made more flexible, early retirement benefits have become more actuarially fair, and pension benefits are linked more tightly to lifetime contributions in an attempt to make pensions and their financing more transparent and less distortionary. Other functions, such as redistribution and poverty alleviation, have been moved outside of earnings-related pension systems to the tax and welfare system or social insurance (e.g., disability and unemployment insurance).

These similar responses to common trends faced by all retirement systems do not mean that all systems can be expected to evolve toward one unique "optimal" system, for two reasons. First, underlying the design of the pension system are fundamental trade-offs, with countries taking different positions on these trade-offs. Second, the institutional design of a particular position on the trade-off has no unique solution. The same functions can be performed by alternative institutions. Which institutions fit best in a particular country depend on the country's specific circumstances and history.

The transformation of pension systems in response to trends is underway but is by no means finished. We have identified a number of challenges for future reforms. The next section will turn to the normative question how the pension system under alternative institutional designs should ideally develop in the future.

11.3 Alternative pension systems

Pension systems can be organized in different ways. Each system performs the same functions and faces the same challenges that were identified in Section 11.2. Nevertheless, important differences remain between countries with regard to the organization of the pension system, depending on the specific history and institutions in a particular country. These differences involve especially the earnings-related part of the pensions. We therefore develop a typology of earnings-related pension systems. This typology is based on two dimensions (see Figure 11.1).

The first dimension involves the governance of pensions. Does the state administer and control earnings-related pensions or are these responsibilities left to the private sector through group insurance (occupational pension plans) or individual decisions (personal pension plans)? As pure public and private systems do not exist, we will rather speak of state-oriented and private-oriented systems. Indeed, government versus private control has various dimensions. For example, the government can mandate individuals to take out pension insurance from a specific insurance pool, which is administered privately (e.g., sectoral pension funds). Alternatively, the state can provide the longevity insurance but contract out certain tasks (administration, investment) to private parties. Yet another possibility is that private insurance companies provide voluntary pensions but that the government provides financial instruments to allow private parties to hedge important macroeconomic risks (such as wage inflation risk and longevity). This illustrates that the various tasks involved in earnings-related pension insurance (administration, investment, insurance, intergenerational and intra-generational risk sharing, marketing, assisting individuals in complicated life-cycle financial planning) can be distributed in alternative ways over the government and the private sector.

The second dimension distinguished in our typology involves the scope for individual choice in pension insurance. Also here, we speak of choice-oriented and mandatory-oriented systems because the extent of choice is multi-dimensional as well. Indeed, choice has more aspects than mandatory versus voluntary participation in pension insurance. In particular, during the working life, individuals may be able to select the level of the contributions, the investment portfolio or the sensitivity of the accumulated pension rights to macroeconomic risks,

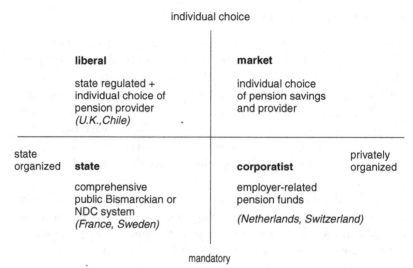

individual choice

liberal	**market**
state regulated + individual choice of pension provider *(U.K.,Chile)*	individual choice of pension savings and provider

state organized

state	**corporatist**	privately organized
comprehensive public Bismarckian or NDC system *(France, Sweden)*	employer-related pension funds *(Netherlands, Switzerland)*	

mandatory

Figure 11.1 Typology of pension systems

the extent and type of survivor and other insurances (e.g., disability insurance), the insurance pool, the provider and the retirement age (i.e., the age at which pension income is received for the first time). At or during retirement, they may choose the type of annuity (unit-linked, linked to price or wage, or lump-sum payments), additional insurances (e.g., health or care insurance) and the insurance company or the insurance pool. Finally, in addition to individual choice, employer choice is an issue. For example, are employers free to select their own insurance pool and insurance company or pension fund for their workers?

The typology of earnings-related pensions in Figure 11.1 leads to four prototype models. The classical juxtaposition is that between, on the one hand, a mandatory state system (in the southwest corner of Figure 11.1) and, on the other hand, a market-based system with free choice of savings and insurance in private capital markets (in the northeast corner of Figure 11.1). The typology distinguishes also two more hybrid systems: a corporatist system with mandatory participation in private pension funds (in the southeast corner of Figure 11.1) and a liberal system, which leaves scope for individual choice in publicly regulated systems (in the northwest corner of Figure 11.1). The Dutch and Swiss pension systems with an important role for employer-provided earnings-related pensions provide an example of the corporatist system. The Chilean system with mandatory pension savings together with free individual choice between private pension funds and insurance companies is an example of the liberal system. Also the pension reforms of the State Second Pension in the UK with automatic enrollment with the option of opting out can be viewed as an example of a liberal system.

These prototypes bear some resemblance to the classification of the welfare state by Esping-Andersen (1990), who distinguishes the Scandinavian, Anglo-Saxon and Corporatist systems. The three prototypes of state, market and corporatist correspond more or less to the Scandinavian, the Anglo-Saxon and the Corporatist models, respectively. Our fourth prototype – the liberal system – relies on extensive government regulation but leaves ample scope for individual choice and market competition.

The World Bank (see Holzmann and Hinz, 2005) distinguishes three pillars in earnings-related contributory pensions.[10] The first pillar is a publicly managed and mandated pension plan. The second pillar involves mandatory, private pension plans. Voluntary private plans make up the third pillar. The first dimension of our typology – state versus private systems – thus involves the distinction between the first public pillar, on the one hand, and the private second and third pillars, on the other hand. The second dimension – individual choice versus mandated systems – relates to the borderline between the mandatory first and second pillars, on the one hand, and the voluntary third pillar, on the other hand. In our typology in Figure 11.1, the first pillar is the dominant form of pension provision in the state model while in the market model the third pillar is dominant. With regard to the second pillar, our typology distinguishes between two alternatives: first, the traditional corporatist model in which participation is mandatory and linked to the employer or industry through occupational pension plans controlled by corporations and possibly representatives of workers and, second, the liberal model in which the government determines the pension contract and

[10] In addition, the World Bank identifies a basic pension (the so-called "zero" pillar) aimed at poverty alleviation and a fourth pillar involving informal family support, formal social programs for the elderly (e.g., health care insurance and social housing) and individual assets (including home ownership). These two pillars are not directly related to earnings.

enforces participation but at the same time leaves the administration, investment and insurance to private sector parties. The second model creates scope for individual choice and competition in the market for personal pension plans.

These four prototypes can be expanded upon in more detail as follows.

State model

The classical state is associated with the traditional welfare state that provides social insurance for its citizens from cradle to grave. The pension system is controlled and administered by the state and is comprehensive and largely mandatory. The state organizes not only the basic pension aimed at poverty alleviation but also earnings-related pensions for the middle class. Most households thus do not need to save voluntarily for their retirement income. Not only the function of life-cycle planning but also that of intergenerational risk sharing is conducted by the government. Intergenerational risk sharing sometimes relies on separate rules such as automatic balancing in NDC systems but can also be integrated with the rest of the public finance, including public-debt policy. Funding of future pension liabilities is ensured through fiscal policy aiming at debt reduction or building up some reserve fund within the government (Norway, Sweden).

These state systems are typically mandatory, but may leave some scope for individual choice, for example regarding the retirement age. However, this scope is limited in order to avoid adverse selection in insurance and individual failures in life-cycle planning. This prototype encompasses both the classical Bismarckian systems (in Germany and France, for example) and the more modern NDC systems (in Sweden and Norway, for example).

Market model

Earnings-related pensions are the responsibility of the private sector through either employer-provided plans or individual pension plans. Participation in pension savings is voluntary, or can be part of the labor contract of individual employers. The state provides a basic flat social pension to avoid poverty in old age. The government also regulates the private sector. Solvency regulation ensures that the promises of pension funds and insurance companies are credible. Moreover, regulation helps to make financial markets more transparent for individual consumers. Individuals are not forced to participate in mandatory earnings-related plans, can take their own portfolio decisions and are free to take out their retirement capital as a lump sum rather than an annuity. The government may encourage pension savings or annuitization by using subsidies and tax benefits.

In the Esping-Andersen terminology, the Anglo-Saxon welfare state conforms to the market model. With respect to pensions, however, the state in the main Anglo-Saxon countries – the UK and the US – plays an important role in providing earnings-related pensions. Moreover, over and above these public systems, these countries are starting to employ defaults to guide individual decisions and stimulate privately provided pensions to supplement their public systems. The planned reforms in the UK, for example, move this country further towards the liberal model.

Corporatist model

In the corporatist prototype, pension funds organize earnings-related pension insurance for workers of specific firms or sectors. Earnings-related pensions are considered to be part of the labor contract. Pensions are thus employment related and provided by the employer. Pension funds are organized on an occupational or sectoral basis, for example, as collective DC or DB systems or as mutual insurance companies. As cooperatives, pension funds are typically governed by representatives of the employers and the unions, which play an important role in corporatist countries. Together with the basic pension provided by the state, the system is comprehensive and mandatory, leaving little scope for individual choice in terms of the level of saving or the portfolio choices. Typical examples are the Dutch and Swiss pension systems. The government may support the private pension funds by providing tax advantages and enforcing mandatory pooling of individual firms and their workers in industry-wide pension funds.

Liberal model

Just like the corporatist solution, this prototype aims to synthesize the state model and the market model. But rather than relying on employer-provided pensions negotiated between social partners, it combines state regulation with individual responsibility. The state both organizes the basic pension and controls earnings-related pensions, but leaves room for private administration and insurance as well as individual choices. In particular, the government can mandate earnings-related pensions by forcing workers to enroll in personal pension plans, while leaving workers free to select their own investment and insurance companies. Individuals are thus not constrained by agreements between unions and employers. The Chilean system is an example of this model.

Rather than forcing people to enroll, a more liberal version of this prototype model is to automatically enroll workers while giving them the discretion to opt out of earnings-related pension insurance. This model thus takes to heart the lessons of behavioral economics and can be characterized as "libertarian paternalism" as distinct from "old paternalism" and the associated mandatory systems. An example is New Zealand's KiwiSaver plan, which combines automatic enrollment with some degree of individual choice of contribution rate (within some range), including the option to take contribution holidays and withdraw capital before the retirement age under special circumstances. People can opt to save also through mortgage repayment rather than a pension plan. Another interesting case is the UK where the State Second Pension (S2P) allows for contracting out with an employer-based occupational pension. From 2012 on, a new system of centrally administered personal accounts is being introduced, the so-called National Employment Savings Trust. Enrollment will be automatic for all employees, who are not enrolled in a suitable occupational pension, but opting out or making additional contributions are possible.

11.4 Optimizing the four pension models

Significant further improvements are possible within each of the four models identified in Section 11.3. This section focuses on two major issues: first, how each of the systems can improve upon intergenerational risk sharing (Subsections 11.4.1 to 11.4.3) and, second, how each system should balance the increasing need to tailor individual arrangements to individual heterogeneity with the desire to combat adverse selection and to combat individual foibles in life-cycle planning (Section 11.4.4).

11.4.1 *Intergenerational risk sharing*

As in Chapter 5, we distinguish human capital of current generations H, human capital of unborn generations U and financial capital F, which matches physical capital and may consist of equity and debt. Total wealth W is the sum of these three wealth components. We focus on macroeconomic risks related to financial and human capital, and for the moment neglect demographic risks. Under the assumption of constant relative risk aversion (CRRA) preferences, optimal risk sharing requires that each agent i holds a portfolio in which the share of each asset corresponds to the aggregate fraction of that asset. This could be taken as a starting point for the optimal distribution of macroeconomic risks across generations.[11] We thus have in the optimum

$$W_{it} = H_{it} + U_{it} + F_{it},$$
$$\frac{H_{it}}{W_{it}} = \frac{H_t}{W_t} = h_t, \frac{U_{it}}{W_{it}} = \frac{U_t}{W_t} = u_t, \frac{F_{it}}{W_{it}} = \frac{F_t}{W_t} = f_t.$$

For reasonable values of growth-corrected interest rates (1.5%) – uniform for human capital and physical capital – and a steady population, the fractions h_t, u_t and f_t, are about 20 percent, 65 percent and 15 percent. The fraction of financial capital in total wealth equals 15 percent, which is in line with the observed share of capital income (net of depreciation and investment) in total income. Of human capital less than a quarter is held by current generations in their working age (20 to 65) while the largest part belongs to future generations. These figures correspond to actual data found for the Netherlands.[12] For example, total financial wealth including housing and net claims on the government amounts to some 550 percent of GDP in the year 2009. Human capital can be estimated at some 3000 percent of GDP, in accordance with the 85–15 division between human wealth and

---

[11] With habit formation, older generations will want to take less risk than younger and future generations. Mean-reversion in stocks works in the same direction. Labor-supply incentives related to the limited liability of human capital, however, is an argument for absorbing risks in the short term rather than the longer term (see Mehlkopf, 2011). Similarly, if financial shocks are cointegrated with wage shocks, current generations may want to absorb a large share of the current financial shocks as they are over time absorbed by younger generations through their human capital.

[12] Calculated on the basis of long-term projections in van der Horst *et al.* (2010).

financial wealth. Optimal risk sharing requires that shocks in each asset are smoothed among all individuals. For example, a relative drop in the value of financial assets of 1% should cut individual consumption levels by no more than 0.15% if human capital is unaffected. We measure shocks in terms of stocks of wealth rather than momentary flows of income because we focus on permanent shocks only.[13]

Human capital and financial capital are aggregates that are subject to different underlying risk factors. Whereas they may be subject to similar underlying risk factors (such as productivity risk), human and financial capital are also subject to some uncorrelated risks. For example, human capital may be subject to – labor augmenting – productivity shocks, while physical capital faces depreciation and valuation risk. Also the time frame may differ across asset categories: financial assets generally feature a longer time horizon than human capital of current generations (H), but a shorter duration than human capital of future generations (U).

Risk sharing and the size of pension pillars

An important implication of our normative analysis is that pension wealth of retirees who have depreciated their human capital should be exposed to financial risks for only 15 percent and to human-capital risks for 85 percent. Human capital here includes human capital of future generations. If wages follow a random walk, all shocks are permanent so that current and future human capital is subject to the same shocks. Indexing pensions to current wages then ensures optimal risk sharing. If the process of wages is more complex, pensions should be linked to the permanent component of wage shocks. Hence, current shocks are smoothed and current pensions depend also on current news about future wages.

This optimal pension contract for retirees is hard to realize through tradable financial assets only because financial markets typically do not trade claims on current and future human capital. Markets in wage-linked bonds would be an adequate substitute, but also these markets

---

[13] If temporary shocks can be smoothed over time, they exert only a negligible impact on welfare. Intertemporal smoothing is a reasonable assumption for owners of financial capital, but may be disputable for younger households facing borrowing constraints. This could be an argument for state-dependent taxation conditional on flow rather than stocks. In particular, tax rates can be reduced in bad states when wages are low and increased when wages are high.

do not yet exist and will probably require government intervention in light of the limited liability of human capital. In the absence of wage-linked assets, tradable financial claims can take care of only 15 percent of total pension income, namely the part corresponding to physical capital. The government or pension funds should take care of the remaining 85 percent of the retirees' pension portfolio, which should be related to human capital. This could take the form of pension payments indexed to wages. The pension funds could match these wage-linked promises by buying wage-linked bonds issued by the government. Alternatively, occupational pension funds can promise wage-linked benefits to retirees if they can tax workers who earn quasi rents in the insurance pool covered by the pension fund.

Our model of intergenerational risk sharing thus yields a normative theory about the optimal share of wage-linked pension benefits, which can consist of non-tradable PAYG pensions and wage-linked private pensions on the basis of tradable wage-linked debt issued by the governments (or derivatives thereof). Aging of the population decreases the portfolio share of human capital in total wealth so that the optimal share of wage-linked assets declines. Aging should thus result in a larger exposure to financial risks and a smaller exposure to human-capital risk in retirement.

Taking account of risk sharing through the tax system
In determining the optimal size of the pension pillars, one should take account of the redistribution of risks already present in the tax system. By taxing wages of the young to finance wage-linked pensions for the old, the government shifts human-capital risks from workers (i.e., the young) to retirees (i.e., the old). Taxing capital or capital income (including taxes on bequests,[14] imputed rents from owner-occupied housing and property) redistributes risks in the opposite direction, i.e., from the old to the young. How the tax system affects the distribution of risks across generations depends on the tax and transfer system and the way taxes and transfers are changed if shocks hit the government budget. Precise analysis of intergenerational risk

---

[14] Bequests shift capital-market risks from the older to the younger generations. Taxing these bequests helps to spread these risks over a larger population rather than focus these risks on the relatively small group of agents that benefits from large bequests. Taxation of bequests thus facilitates intra-generational rather than intergenerational risk sharing.

sharing through the public sector is beyond the scope of this chapter, but that it can be substantial is evident from the contribution of Bettendorf and Knaap to this book (Chapter 7) and the related study by Bohn (2009).

One important aspect that deserves attention, however, concerns the taxation of private pension savings. In the absence of public pensions, optimal risk sharing would require a capital income tax on life-cycle saving of retirees equal to the share of human wealth in aggregate wealth $(H+U)/W$. According to our benchmark, this would amount to a tax rate on life-cycle savings of no less than 85 percent. Such a high tax rate on life-cycle saving is clearly out of the question. Yet, in the case of a cash flow treatment (EET) of private pension savings and consumption taxation (such as VAT) actual tax rates may come close, even without causing overly large distortions in pension savings (see Chapter 5). Another way in which the government can insure capital-market risks on pension saving is by providing a minimum guarantee, as is the case in the US. Alternatively, the tax rate on pensions can depend on the rate of return. In particular, by offering a tax reduction if returns are low and raising tax rates if returns are high, the government mitigates the downward risks of private savings.

If financial wealth is concentrated in the hands of very wealthy individuals, this may also mitigate the problem of inadequate intergenerational sharing of financial risk in a market system. Most of the wealthy may be expected to leave intentional bequests. The size of these bequests varies with financial shocks so that future generations owning human capital bear financial risks. In other words, these dynasties own both human capital and financial capital and can engage in optimal risk sharing between various members of such a dynasty.

11.4.2 Risk sharing in the four alternative systems

How risk sharing is organized depends on the pension system. We consider each of the alternative systems distinguished in the typology of Figure 11.1. Table 11.2 summarizes the results with regard to the magnitudes of the pension pillars distinguished by the World Bank. We start with the market model and the liberal model and then turn to the more complex cases of the state model and the corporatist model.

Table 11.2 *Optimal risk sharing and the size of pillars in alternative pension models during the decumulation stage*

	State	Market	Corporatist	Liberal
Pillar 0	30%	30%	30%	30%
Basic pension, public	wage-linked	wage-linked	wage-linked	wage-linked
Pillar 1	55% wage-linked	[a]		55% wage-linked[b]
Earnings-related, public				15% financial risk
Pillar 2			55% wage-linked[c]	
Earnings-related, private			15% financial risk	
Pillar 3	15% financial risk	55% wage-linked bonds		
Individual savings		15% financial risk		

[a] Optional: limited wage-linked first pillar up to modal income.
[b] Through limited first pillar, or private pensions backed by wage-linked bonds.
[c] Open accounts or wage-linked bonds + wage-linked bonds.

Market model

In the market model, individual savings in financial markets are typically invested in tradable financial assets representing physical capital, while the basic PAYG pension provided by the state (zero pillar) takes care of the human-capital exposure of retirees. Optimal risk sharing would then require PAYG pensions representing 85 percent of total pensions, which is quite substantial. To illustrate, in the Netherlands, the basic public pension currently represents about 50 percent of total pension income, but this figure is declining due to population aging and the maturing of funded pensions. A rough indication of the desirable size of the zero pillar can be derived from the difference between the social minimum (as a measure of the poverty line) and average wage income. In Europe, average wage income is about three times larger than the income of the poorest 10 percent of the population. Applying this to the size of the basic pension, this would lead to a zero pillar of only 30 percent of total pensions, leaving an overexposure of 55 percent to financial risks, matched by the same underexposure in absolute terms of the younger generations. If pensions are means tested, the zero pillar would be even smaller.

Also the tax and welfare system contributes to risk sharing, however. In particular, by taxing funded pension benefits,[15] the government in fact takes over financial risk from the retirees. At the same time, the government subjects the elderly to human-capital risk because taxes and transfers other than pensions depend on wages and the general state of the government budget.

To fill the gap between the human-capital exposure through the basic pension and the optimal exposure to human-capital risk, the government could issue wage-linked bonds up to 55% of total pension wealth – on account of the younger generations and to be held as part of the pension wealth of the retirees. This is quite substantial, however. In the Netherlands, for example, total pension wealth can be roughly estimated at 200% of GDP (65% for the public pension and 125% wealth of pension funds, neglecting individual pension savings). A share of 55% wage-linked debt would represent about 110% of GDP well above actual public debt, and also by far exceeding the ceiling of 60% for public debt in the EMU area. Naturally, this 55% concerns gross debt in wage-linked bonds. This exposure can also be reached by buying equity and corporate bonds and issuing wage-linked bonds, or equivalently by swapping fixed interest payments with wage-linked payments.

There are several qualifications to these figures. First, these calculations may overestimate the actual need for wage-linked bonds as the desired 85 percent wage-linked share of financial wealth concerns the decumulation phase only. However, also older workers demand positive amounts of human-capital exposure in their pension wealth,

---

[15] This assumes that the government taxes pension savings on a cash-flow basis, i.e., according to the so-called EET system. The EET system exempts (E) contributions and returns and taxes (T) benefits.

which may be quite substantial. As we saw in Chapter 5, all individuals of 32 years and older feature a net underexposure of human capital according to the standard life cycle using the same shares of aggregate financial and human capital. Second, a substantial share of financial wealth is not related to life-cycle saving but is owned by rich individuals who intend to leave bequests. These dynasties can engage in optimal risk sharing. To illustrate, in case of an adverse financial shock, these wealthy individuals could reduce bequests by 85 percent of the shock in accordance with the optimal exposure of future generations. Third, corporate bonds are a good substitute for wage-linked bonds in case of the pension wealth of retirees who typically hold pension claims with only a short duration. And finally, as mentioned above, also the tax system may contribute to the redistribution of risks across generations.

Liberal model
In the liberal model, earnings-related pension savings are typically modeled as individual accounts managed by the private sector. Consumers can choose between alternative pension providers. Accordingly, pension funds cannot commit workers to intergenerational risk sharing and cannot tax quasi rents. Hence, pensions are based on financial assets traded in the financial markets only, so-called "closed accounts" (see Chapter 5). This model thus faces similar constraints as the market model in creating the optimal exposure of retirees to human-capital risk (and the corresponding optimal exposures of workers and future generations to current financial market risks).

Several alternative options facilitate intergenerational risk sharing by increasing the human-capital exposure of pensioners. First, as in the market model, the government can issue wage-linked bonds up to 55 percent of total pension wealth of the retirees to be held by pension funds that provide wage-linked pensions or individuals in personal pension plans. Second, the government could organize a substantial part of earnings-related pensions, which are linked to wages, or provide other types of benefits to the elderly that are linked to wages (e.g., health benefits). This "first pillar" should then comprise 55 percent of total pension income (and almost 80 percent of earnings-related pensions) for those income earners who do not leave intentional bequests to their offspring. Third, the government can increase the human-capital exposure of retirees by having tax rates on retirees decline with wage income. At the same time, the exposure of the retirees to financial risks can be reduced by taxing the pension benefits from funded systems according to the EET system and using the revenues to provide wage-linked benefits.

These options are by no means exclusive; all kinds of combinations are possible. For example, the government may provide a small earnings-related public pension (first pillar) up to, for example, the modal wage. This is in fact close to the actual US system. The idea is that those earning more than the modal wage can engage in intergenerational risk sharing through their bequest behavior.

State model

In the state model, life-cycle saving is fully mandatory and managed by the state. Individual savings in the private sector are limited to bequest saving only. The government raises taxes on wages, profits and private capital income, and uses the proceeds to provide pensions to the retirees. For optimal risk sharing the government should use the tax system to eliminate the overexposure to human-capital risk of the young and the overexposure of financial market risk of the old. Pensions should be linked to human-capital risk and financial risk in proportion to the shares of H, U and F to total wealth, in our example 20, 65 and 15 percent. For generations with positive human capital the role of the government to raise the exposure of human capital (H) decreases accordingly, and it will become negative for the younger generations.

For the youngest generation with no financial capital at all, the government should increase their exposure of financial risks to F/W (here 15 percent), and decrease the exposure to permanent shocks in human capital by this same amount. This can be done by taxing wages by 15 percent and providing to the same generation a transfer that is linked to the return on financial capital. For temporary shocks limited to human capital of current generations, higher marginal tax rates are necessary. Alternatively, taxes (and transfers) should depend on the state of the economy. Marginal tax rates on wages are often already quite high for reasons of intra-generational distribution – often 50 percent or higher. This is too high from the perspective of permanent shocks, but this can be compensated when also transfers to these generations are linked to wages. For temporary shocks, the overexposure of younger generations to these wage shocks can be eliminated by making the net benefit of these cohorts dependent on the state of the economy.

Aggregate risk on the state's balance sheet matches the aggregate under- and overexposure of the current generations. This implies that the government should take sufficient risk of future generations on its balance sheet, while it should go short in human capital of current generations. Furthermore, it should take sufficient financial risks on its balance sheet. As private life-cycle savings are absent in such a world with state-organized pensions, the government should have accumulated sufficient financial wealth,[16] part of which could be invested in risk-bearing assets. In the same vein, a special social security trust fund[17] could hold part of its portfolio in equity.

Taking capital market risk on the government balance was the first step; the next step is to transfer this risk to young workers. This can be done by financing shocks in the government's net wealth by adjusting labor-income taxes or spending categories that benefit the young. Alternatively, the government can adjust the pension accumulations of the workers in NDC accounts. Agents with human capital thus become the residual risk bearers of the capital risks that the government takes on. The government in effect acts as the representative of the younger households in taking on more capital risks, which young individuals cannot take on directly.

Corporatist model
In the corporatist model, earnings-related pensions are mandatory and organized by private occupational pension funds. The role of the state is limited to providing a basic pension (zero pillar). Voluntary individual pension plans (third pillar) play a minor role because occupational pension plans, which are part of the labor contracts of workers, provide quite ambitious earnings-related pensions. In the Netherlands, for example, occupational pension plans aim at a replacement rate that

---

[16] We assume the intergenerational distribution to be equal for all pension models. That means that government savings in the "state model" should be equal to private savings in the "market model."

[17] The government fund does not have to be earmarked for public pensions and can also be used for general revenue purposes.

exceeds 70 percent at the age of 65. If retirees do not have other types
of saving and do not plan to leave bequests, optimal intergenerational
risk sharing implies that the financial risk exposure of the pension
wealth of pensioners should amount to only 15 percent. With a basic
pension representing 30 percent of pension wealth, this implies that
occupational pensions paid to retirees should be linked to (permanent) wages for 55/70 and to financial risk for 15/70. For workers who
still have human capital the share of pension wealth linked to financial
returns can be larger. Indeed, young workers may want to bear substantial equity risk.

11.4.3 Three types of accounts

As discussed in Chapter 5, this hybrid system of wage-indexed pensions, and pensions indexed to financial returns, can be organized
through "closed accounts," matched by wage-linked bonds provided
by the government, or by "open accounts." In the latter case, pension
funds bear the residual risk on account of future generations. This
allows pension funds to engage in intergenerational risk sharing even
in the absence of wage-linked bonds. Pension funds can exploit the
rent on specific human capital to tax workers, but only up to the maximum of these rents. Imperfect portability of pensions or intransparency of pensions may impede mobility of workers, and thus increases
the scope for risk sharing. By way of compromise, collectively closed
accounts allow for trade of risk between current participants of the
pension fund, while leaving no net mismatch risk to the fund in the
aggregate. This reduces the danger of discontinuity – and the consequential need for solvency requirements – which is intrinsic to open
accounts. We will briefly discuss each of these alternatives.

Closed individual accounts
With closed individual accounts, pension funds do not take any risk
on their balance sheets. Intergenerational risk sharing occurs by taking the optimal amount of financial assets and (wage-linked) bonds in
individual portfolios. The share of (wage-linked) bonds increases with
age. For pensioners it should be 55/70 in our example, assuming that
additional individual savings in the third pillar are absent, and that the
government provides a basic pension up to 30 percent of total pensions. If these third-pillar savings are present, the investment behavior

of pension funds is less relevant because agents use their third-pillar investments to achieve optimal risk exposures. For closed individual accounts to accomplish optimal intergenerational risk sharing, governments, which tax labor income and thus address the limited liability of human capital, must issue wage-indexed bonds.

Open accounts

In the absence of wage-indexed bonds, pension funds can contribute to risk sharing by issuing wage-linked assets on their own account in the form of pension promises that are (partly) indexed to wages. In this case, individual accounts are open in the sense that individual property rights of participants take the form of claims on the pension fund rather than tradable financial securities. The risk features of individual pension claims are now implied by the policy of the pension fund with regard to premiums, pension payments and investments. By issuing liabilities on their own accounts, pension funds are involved in the transformation of risks. Indeed, the risk characteristics of the liabilities of the pension funds are not spanned by tradable financial assets.

The optimal mismatch risk on the balance sheet of the pension fund may be substantial. To illustrate, taking the distribution of 85% human-capital risk and 15% financial risk as starting point, an unexpected decline of 10% in financial assets that is uncorrelated to human-capital should ideally reduce the claims of retirees on the pension funds by only 1.5%. The rest of the shock is shifted to younger generations and future generations: a share of 20% of the shock is borne by younger generations, and as much as 60% of the decline in wealth is shifted to future generations in the form of a lower buffer. The pension funds, however, can trade risks with future generations up to the limit that is implied by rents on specific human capital of the workers. It seems therefore natural that also the government engages in intergenerational risk sharing, and takes the larger part of the burden.

Solvency requirements should find a balance between minimizing discontinuity risk and thus ensuring that funds can meet their promises while at the same time maximizing the scope for intergenerational risk sharing. Risk sharing requires that shortages (and surpluses) can be carried over to the future as much as possible. Containing discontinuity risk, in contrast, requires that the largest burden of recovery should be put on the short term or medium term, as current workers – who have already built up their specific human capital – can be taxed more easily than future workers. In view of its power to tax labor income in the country as a whole, the government seems typically more powerful than pension funds in facilitating intergenerational risk sharing. Nevertheless, pension funds may play a welcome, complementary role in assisting intergenerational risk sharing because pension funds and the government may exhibit different strengths and weaknesses.

Collectively closed accounts
Under collectively closed accounts, the pension fund may organize risk sharing between participants of the fund but without taking any net aggregate risk on its balance sheet. The pension fund can thus trade for example human-capital risk and longevity risk between its current younger and older members, even in the absence of wage-linked bonds and longevity bonds on open markets. This may fulfill the need for wage-linked bonds and longevity bonds to some extent, but far from what is needed in total, leaving an important role for the government. In particular, pension funds are unable to organize risk sharing with future generations; this becomes an exclusive task for the government under this solution.

11.4.4 *Optimizing life-cycle planning and insurance*

The second dimension of pension systems involves the trade-off between compulsion and choice (or containing personal failures versus tailoring to heterogeneity; see Table 11.1). All systems face growing heterogeneity and more demanding consumers (see Section 11.2). There is no easy way to get around the trade-off between choice and compulsion. Yet there may be scope for improvement. First, mandatory pensions (i.e., the first and second pillars, which are dominant in the state and corporatist models) could be tailored more to individual heterogeneity. This requires governments and pension funds to gather information on individual circumstances such as household composition, career and housing status. Second, one could allow for more elements of choice within mandatory systems, for example in adjusting contributions, investment portfolio, moment of retirement and type of annuity. Third, the literature on behavioral finance (see Thaler and Sunstein, 2008; Bodie and Prast in Chapter 9) suggests that scope for substantial improvement exists by guiding individual choice using defaults. Structured choice through defaults may result in some convergence of various pension systems; defaults may guide individual choice in individual schemes (which are dominant in the market and liberal models) while also allowing some degree of choice in collective schemes that previously did not allow any individual choice (these systems are dominant in the state and corporatist models). Fourth, the government can support private savings and investment decisions through the tax system. Finally, flexible retirement systems and housing arrangements could also contribute to life-cycle planning.

Integrating pensions with life-cycle savings

The ICT revolution, which is still in its infancy, will open up vast new opportunities to collect data on the features of individuals, thereby allowing mandatory systems to tailor pensions and social security to the individual. However, privacy considerations and fears about a "big brother" type of pension agency may prevent the potential of ICT from being fully exploited under all models. At the same time ICT may also improve individual decision making by making markets transparent and supporting complex decisions on life-cycle planning by, for example, expert systems (see also Ter Weel *et al.* (2010), who sketched alternative scenarios for future social security systems depending on information and communication technology).

Heterogeneity, borrowing constraints and size of the pillars

Despite the scope for improving individual information, it will be impossible to tailor pensions perfectly to individual features and preferences. Some information may remain hard to observe by pension agencies, and agents may be reluctant to sacrifice privacy. Therefore, mandatory systems will continue to be subject to asymmetric information. This implies that there should be some scope for individual choice. With incomplete markets, individuals cannot undo the public arrangements (except redistribution) by private transactions in financial markets. In particular, many agents – especially with lower incomes – face borrowing constraints and thus have little or no access to financial markets. These individuals will therefore be unable to tailor their pension savings to their personal circumstances and preferences. Accordingly, the welfare costs of "too high" and "too low" mandatory pensions are asymmetric. Whereas rational agents for

whom mandatory pension savings are "too low" can easily compensate this by additional voluntary saving, agents who are forced to save
too much cannot compensate this by additional borrowing. As the
cost of excessive pensions thus exceeds the cost of too-low pensions
from an individual perspective, mandatory pensions should always be
smaller than average pensions in the optimum. This would lead to
replacement rates for mandatory pensions of well below 100 percent,
especially since optimal consumption after retirement is typically less
than consumption earlier in the life cycle. Pension ambitions in mandatory systems may thus be considered to be too high in some mandatory systems – for example, in the Netherlands.

Four scenarios for the future pension system
By including the "heterogeneity" dimension of the pension system,
Table 11.3 extends Table 11.2, which focused on intergenerational
risk sharing only. Table 11.3 thus summarizes alternative models for
the future pension system. We will briefly discuss this second dimension for each model, in the same order as in the previous section.

Market model
The market model features low mandatory saving and leaves ample
scope for individual choice. However, a small mandatory earnings-
related pillar seems called for to address individual failures, facilitate
intergenerational risk sharing, prevent selection in insurance and avoid
moral hazard as a result of means-tested benefits (since most benefits
are means tested in this model). Defaults at the employer level may be
an attractive solution here to guide individual choice and fight adverse
selection while still allowing individuals to tailor individual arrangements to individual circumstances. By issuing tradable wage-indexed
bonds rather than large non-tradable, mandatory wage-indexed public
pensions, the government allows individuals to select their own portfolios and tailor them to individual circumstances. Individuals may
want to keep a substantial part of their life-cycle savings in liquid form
because precautionary saving is important in the face of limited public
insurance of human-capital risk during the accumulation phase and
health risk during the decumulation phase. Financial innovation may
also allow housing wealth to play an important role in insuring old-
age risks. Flexible retirement and labor markets may help individuals
to absorb risks.

Table 11.3 Multi-pillar pension systems

State	Market	Corporatist	Liberal
Pillar 0: social pension			
Public	public	public	public
Pillar 1: earnings-related pension			
Comprehensive public system, integrated with social and health insurance			
Pillar 2: supplementary private earnings-related pensions			
		earnings-related pension organized by pension funds, mandatory and employer-related[b,c]	flexible earnings-related occupational pensions[a] free choice of provider, under regulation
Pillar 3: voluntary individual savings			
Limited: for bequests and for supplementary savings	precautionary savings through voluntary pension plans supported by education and information (ICT), and light regulation	[b]	[d]
Pillar 4: non-financial assets			
[c]	basic public provision of health care, life-cycle products (e.g. reverse mortgages), informal care		tailored public provision of health care and housing, informal care

[a] Closed accounts supported by indexed bonds.

[b] Optional: supplementary individual savings, guided by strong regulation on internalities (defaults, etc.) and market failure (e.g., standards, public procurement).

[c] Health care, training, housing and social security together with pensions integrated in encompassing welfare system; cradle to grave: limited role for informal old-age care.

[d] Optional: health insurance, training and home ownership (mortgages) into pensions, but at some cost (loss of competition) limited role for informal old-age care.

Liberal model

Compared to the market model, the liberal model allows the government to set more defaults and even a mandatory level of earnings-related pension insurance. Thus, many defaults in pension insurance are set by the government rather than the employers. Moreover, the government may want to provide a higher level of non-tradable earnings-related pension claims, for example up to the modal wage. The government also is active in regulating the market for personal pension plans. It provides wage-linked and longevity bonds to help private insurance companies offer DB-type pensions that tailor to the specific preferences of retirees during the decumulation stage. The government similarly regulates health care.

State model

Better tailoring of pension contracts under mandatory public systems requires the state to gather more information about specific relevant features of its participants: not only the individual's earnings history and family status, but also information on the individual's health, financial portfolio, housing status (homeowner or renter) and preferences with regard to risk and time. The state model may thus develop into an integrated life-cycle system closely monitoring all individuals. The state thus provides not only pension insurance but also health insurance and other insurances of human capital, such as disability and unemployment insurance. If ICT reveals more specific risk features of individuals, insurance possibilities shrink as insurance becomes redistribution. The state model is well positioned to replace insurance by redistribution. This requires, however, more restrictions on individual choice.

Corporatist model

Similar to the state model, the corporatist model may develop into a comprehensive mandatory life-cycle system for workers employed in a particular sector or firm. During the accumulation phase, pension contributions may be complemented by training and other types of insurances of human capital such as disability and unemployment insurance. During the pay-out phase, health insurance and housing provisions may complement annuities.

Alternatively, the corporatist model may limit its ambition to create more scope for choice in individual pension plans (third pillar). In the latter case, use of individual information by pension funds and insurers may be forbidden, for example to prevent risk selection by insurers or for reasons of creating a level playing field between market (insurers) and non-market parties (pension funds).

11.5 Conclusions

Although each prototype model discussed in Section 11.3 can in principle perform all functions of the pension system, there are important differences. The two mandatory systems – state and corporatist – are better geared toward solving problems of adverse selection, while the systems relying more on consumer sovereignty – liberal and market – are better able to deal with unverifiable heterogeneity across individuals. As regards the function of intergenerational risk sharing, the state systems – thanks to their power to tax – are better able to commit young generations to intergenerational risk sharing. This makes it also possible to redistribute human-capital risks from the young to the old by indexing pensions to wages, which is not possible in the market model. Also other macroeconomic risks such as longevity risk and risks concerning future production can be more easily shared between multiple generations in the state model.

State-based systems tend to have problems in sharing financial risks. Redistributing these risks from the old to the young requires that the state takes substantial financial risks on its balance sheet. Active financial risk management by the state on the basis of a large portfolio of financial claims is rare, however, except for countries with large positive government wealth (e.g., Norway). In order to contain political risks, governments typically hold only a very restricted portfolio, consisting of nominal and sometimes real bonds only. Privately oriented pension systems, such as the corporatist and the market model, are better equipped for sharing financial risks. The same holds true for the liberal model because it relies on saving through private pension funds.

References

Beshears, J., J. Choi, D. Laibson, B. Madrian and B. Weller, 2008, Public Policy and Saving for Retirement: The "Autosave" Features of the Pension Protection Act of 2006, Mimeo, Harvard University.

Bohn, H., 2009, Intergenerational risk sharing and fiscal policy, *Journal of Monetary Economics*, vol. 56(6): 805–16.

Bonenkamp, J., and E. Westerhout, 2010, Intergenerational risk sharing and labour supply in collective funded pension schemes with defined benefits, CPB Discussion Paper 151, Den Haag and Netspar Discussion Paper 06/2010-019, 2010, Tilburg.

Esping-Andersen, G., 1990, *The Three Worlds of Welfare Capitalism*, Cambridge: Polity Press; and Princeton University Press.

Holzmann, R., and R. Hinz, 2005, *Old Age Income Support in the 21st Century: An International Perspective on Pension Systems and Reform*, Washington DC, World Bank.

Horst, A. van der, L., Bettendorf, N. Draper, C. van Ewijk, R. de Mooij and H. ter Rele, 2010, Vergrijzing verdeeld, CPB special publication 86, The Hague.

Mehlkopf, R., 2011, Risk sharing with the unborn, PhD thesis 2011–017.

Molenaar, R. and E.H.M. Ponds, 2009, Differentiatie naar leeftijd in de financiering van collectieve pensioenen, NEA-Paper, Netspar, Tilburg.

Sinn, H.W., 2000, Why a funded pension system is useful and why it is not useful, *International Tax and Public Finance*, vol. 7(4): 389–410.

Stiglitz, J.E., and J. Yun, 2005, Integration of unemployment insurance with retirement insurance, *Journal of Public Economics*, vol. 89(11–12): 2037–67.

Thaler, R.H., and C.R. Sunstein, 2008, *Nudge: Improving Decisions About Health, Wealth, and Happiness*, Yale University Press.

Ter Weel, B., A. van der Horst and G. Gelauff, 2010, *The Netherlands of 2040*, CPB Netherlands Bureau for Economic Policy Analysis, The Hague.

Index

Printed in the United States
By Bookmasters